The Book Your Church Doesn't Want You To Read

Editor
Tim C. Leedom

TS BOOKS TRUTH SEEKER
SAN DIEGO, CALIFORNIA

Editor: Tim C. Leedom
Technical Editor: Willam B. Lindley
Product Development: Bonnie Lange
Cover Design: Marita Bonazza
Laser Typesetting: Sam Warren
Graphics Coodinator: Nancy Melton
Publisher: Truth Seeker Company, Inc.

Those interested in contacting authors and contributors to this book may contact:

The Truth Seeker Company
P. O. Box 28550
San Diego, CA 92198
800-551-5328

Distributed by:
A & B Distributing Inc.
Brooklyn, New York
718-783-7808

Copyright ©2003 by The Truth Seeker Company, Inc.
ISBN: 0-939040-15-8
First printing August 1993
Second printing June 1995
Third printing September 2001
Fourth printing February 2003

Library of Congress Catalog No. 93-78087

Printed in Canada   10 9 8 7 6 5

Go forth, my book, and take whatever
   pounding

The heavy-fisted destinies prepare.

I know you are not anything
   astounding,

And, to be quite sincere, I don't much
   care.

Get off your overcoat. The gong is
   sounding.

The enemy has risen from his chair.

He doesn't look so overwhelming, but

His arm is long. Watch for an
   uppercut.

— Leonard Bacon

Acknowledgements

My sincere thanks to the James Hervey Johnson Charitable Educational Trust for financial assistance and the Truth Seeker Company, Bonnie Lange, William B. Lindley and Nancy Melton for their full support; to my friend Joseph Margulies for his help along the way; to Dr. Rocco Errico for his weekly input; to Jordan Maxwell for his research; and to all the other supporters who suggested, inspired, challenged and evaluated material along the way.

And a special appreciation to our authors who have put forth a tremendous effort to make this anthology a reality. These pieces are just a peek at their talents and knowledge.

For valuable assistance I want to thank Sam Warren of Warren Communications and Marita Bonazza of Coastline Printers. I also wish to thank the members of my family who have been important and loving partners. Finally, I wish to thank author Gary Gard for his humor, encouragement and tenacity; and the countless researchers, vendors, secretaries, couriers, and the many who have gone the extra mile to meet a million deadlines.

— Mahalo

Preface

*T*he Book you are holding in your hands is delivered to you with the hope that some fires will be ignited in your mind. The editor and authors who have spent years of study, research and investigation share in a general point of view – the view that the religious beliefs held by many people in the United States and other countries are totally unfounded. *The Book* has incorporated a hard look at beliefs, evidence, stories, churches and acts of omission and commission.

The foundation of *The Book* is the spirit of free inquiry, from the ancient Greeks – Protagoras, Socrates and others – through the Renaissance humanism of Erasmus and Spinoza, followed by the Enlightenment – Voltaire, John Locke, Thomas Paine, Thomas Jefferson – to the present secular culture of great scientific achievements. All through these times, those who thought for themselves, who explored new questions and found new answers, had to contend with the repressions of religious orthodoxy. This was inevitable, since their work was a mortal challenge to old ways of thinking. We who stand on their shoulders thank them.

None of the scholars or theologians who have contributed to *The Book* is naive to the point of believing that this anthology will create a "Rapture" in reverse. Knowing the reaction of established religion in the past to critique and examination, we anticipate a strong response by those who won't even read *The Book*. These leaders and followers continually take the attitude "don't bother me with facts; I've already made up my mind."

The Book is an inquiry into crucial issues of today. These issues need examination, for we are now all villagers in the global electronic village of the world of which social commentator Marshall McLuhan spoke 30 years ago. As McLuhan pointed out, the "potential is tremendous for the advancement of knowledge and understanding through television and electronics." However, he went on to warn, "the reverse of this is chilling." The reverse of "the advancement of knowledge and understanding" is "the retreat of knowledge and the diminution of understanding," also known as brainwashing, dumbing down and bubble gum for the mind. Both the advance and the retreat are happening, in fulfillment of McLuhan's prophecy.

The Book sets its tone with Robert Ingersoll and Thomas Paine. It does not back off from the challenge and exposure of the Bible and religion. The mere mention of pagan origins, astrotheology and mythology always brings howls of protest and denial from the church. *The Book* makes more than mere mention: it shows religion for what it is.

You will not find the uniformity of belief that you find in a religious tract. There are some lively disagreements among our authors. This is fitting in a book meant to challenge.

Discovering the truth of the evidence of other Saviors and of stories identical to many in the Old and New Testaments, which appeared one thousand years before Jesus, will be unsettling, as will the exposure of modern-day abuses and policies in the name of God.

To be sure, just as many will be shocked by these facts, many will be surprised by the number of intelligent, patriotic, sincere and kind men and women who do not embrace the God of the Bible. Despite the pronouncements of U.S. Presidents, like Teddy Roosevelt's calling Thomas Paine "that filthy little atheist," or Ronald Reagan's claim, "the atheists expelled God from school," the truth will prevail even against the tele-evangelists who have made the marketing of religion a fine art.

A final word. This is not an anti-religious book. The search for the meaning of life started long before Moses, Jesus, Mohammed or organized religion. *The Book* is a reference book that is meant to be challenging and informative.

Many religious people are kind, peace-loving and good. Many are not. Whether it is the belief system that molds them or their nature, it is hard to say. Most are woefully misinformed and underexposed to material that could change them for the better. But literacy takes reading, change takes effort and enlightenment takes courage. In the end, "Ye shall know the truth, and the truth shall make you free." (John 8:32)

— Tim C. Leedom, Editor

ABOUT THE EDITOR: Tim C. Leedom was educated at the University of Kansas, and completed his studies at the University of Hawaii, was the recipient of several fellowships in journalism and political science. He served as an aide to both the Governor and Lt. Governor of Hawaii, and was an administrative aide in the Hawaii State Legislature in the 1960's and 70's. He has been involved in religious research for the past decade.

Introduction

There seem to be three subjects which are among the most important things in life... politics, sex and religion. However, along the way, some wise sage coached the general population that these three subjects should never be discussed. I suggest to you that those sages – the politician and those who wanted to put someone (generally a spouse or sexual partner) in some kind of sexual bondage, and the religious leader – were the very ones who would profit most from a lack of discussion on any of those subjects.

I do not want to address the subject of politics or sex here, but rather what is commonly referred to as religion. I grew up in central Texas in one of the most fundamentalist Christian regions in America. One positive thing it provided was a respect for forces greater than man, a respect for history, and certainly a respect for some very basic concepts of interpersonal behavior. But it did little more, other than to demonstrate vividly that there is no connection between the evolution of the spirit of man and his adherence to ritual, ceremony and rote memory as dictated by some religious organization's edict.

The relationship between you, your spirit and the Creator of the Universe is a deeply personal matter. There can be no middle-man in this relationship. Not your parents, not your minister, not a bishop, nor any other self-appointed representative of God, such as the Pope and his phalanx of underlings. How absurd to think that another human being could be the representative of the Creator of the Universe, for us humans living on this planet!

Let us look at some vital facts:

Because of religion, more human beings have been murdered, tortured, maimed, denigrated, discriminated against, humiliated, hated and scorned than for any other reason in the totality of the history of man.

Today the only wars under way are religious wars. Arabs are killing Jews and vice versa. Ethnically religious groups are killing ethnically religious groups in the aftermath of the demise of the

Soviet Union. Arabs of one religion are killing Arabs of another. Catholics and Protestants are killing each other in Ireland and the British Isles. There is an endless list of clashes in Africa and the emerging nations of Southeast Asia.

Religion, more than politics and economics, kills and cripples humankind. There has never in all known history been a genocide of any kind which was not fueled by religion. Every religious organization on Earth is designed to gain economic and political power for those in the religion. Look at it closely and you will see for yourself.

I look at my family and friends in those fundamentalist religious organizations in central Texas. They are bound by ideas which are not true. They believe in myths as if they were fact. They grow old early in life. The wonderful personal resources available to them are stifled and lost. Their lives become boring and non-productive unless they free themselves from the concepts imposed upon them by their religions.

In this book, you will find that the story of Jesus and the "crucifiction" has been played out sixteen times over the last ten thousand years. You are also going to find ideas about religion that the Pope and other religious leaders don't want you to read or understand. Because if you do read and understand, you will no longer be a part of their group. What this means is that you will no longer provide them with funds, and you will no longer be a number which will give them political clout.

There are three major changes under way now in the affairs of all mankind. First is politics. We have seen the demise of Communism, and other such non-humane political concepts will fall as well. We are beginning to see the end of a long-established economic tyranny, which for centuries has gripped the affairs of nations, including ours. To these we add religion, the most crippling detriment of them all to the evolution of humankind. All of these changes are coming as we enter the "new age", now upon us. This work addresses itself most admirably to this vital effort.

— *Bill Jenkins, former ABC talk show host.*

Is There An Ultimate Source of Knowledge?

Karl R. Popper

I believe that it would be worth trying to learn something about the world even if we merely learnt that we do not know much. This state of learned ignorance might be a help in many of our troubles. It might be well to remember that, while differing widely in the various little bits we know, in our infinite ignorance we are all equal.

If only we look for it we can often find a true idea, worthy of being preserved, in a philosophical theory which we must reject as false. Can we find an idea like this in one of the theories of the ultimate sources of our knowledge?

I believe we can; and I suggest that it is one of the two main ideas which underlie the doctrine that the source of all our knowledge is super-natural. The first of these ideas is false, I believe, while the second is true.

The first, the false idea, is that we must justify our knowledge, or our theories, by *positive* reasons, that is, by reasons capable of establishing them, or at least of making them highly probable; at any rate, by better reasons than that they have withstood criticism. This idea implies, as I suggested, that we must appeal to some ultimate or authoritative source of true knowledge; which still leaves open the character of that authority – whether it is human, like observation or reason, or super-human (and therefore super-natural).

The second idea – whose vital importance has been stressed by Russell – is that no man's authority can establish truth by decree; that we should submit to truth; that *truth is above human authority*.

Taken together these two ideas almost immediately yield the conclusion that the sources from which our knowledge derives must be super-human; a conclusion which tends to encourage self-righteousness and the use of force against those who refuse to see the divine truth.

Some who rightly reject this conclusion do not reject the first idea – the belief in the existence of ultimate sources of knowledge. Instead they reject the second idea – the thesis that truth is above human authority. They thereby endanger the idea of the objectivity of knowledge, and of common standards of criticism or rationality.

What we should do, I suggest, is to give up the idea of ultimate sources of knowledge, and admit that all knowledge is human; that it is mixed with our errors, our prejudices, our dreams, and our hopes; that all we can do is to grope for truth even though it be beyond our reach. We may admit that our groping is often inspired, but we must be on our guard against the belief, however deeply felt, that our inspiration carries any authority, divine or otherwise. If we thus admit that there is no authority beyond the reach of criticism to be found within the whole province of our knowledge, however far it may have penetrated into the unknown, then we can retain, without danger, the idea that truth is beyond human authority. And we must retain it; for without this idea there can be no objective standards of inquiry; no criticism of our conjectures; no groping for the unknown; no quest for knowledge.

Excerpt from Karl R. Popper, Fellow of the Academy, On The Sources of Knowledge and of Ignorance, *a philosophical lecture from the proceedings of the British Academy, Vol. XLVI, London: Oxford University Press.*

I think that in the discussion of natural problems we ought to begin not with the Scriptures, but with experiments, and demonstrations.

— Galileo Galilei

Most intellectual progress and comprehension of complex phenomena cease once the mind deludes itself into believing it has uncovered a Holy Grail or an eternal truth. *Any meaningful analysis of reality must consider all such so-called truths as merely tentative expedients.*

— Wilson Bryan Key, *Subliminal Seduction*

Contents

Origins of Religion

Other Religions

Dead Sea Scrolls

The Bible

Jesus

Consequences

Fundamentalism Now

Church & Society

Think For Yourself

Appendix

Origins of Religion

William Lewis Edelen

Bill, with your keen intellectual awareness and your background in the biological sciences, you are obviously an unusual asset. I do want to tell you that I have come to have an increasing sense of gratitutde to men such as you who uphold the spiritual values, without which the life of man is nothing. I salute you.

— Loren Eiseley, distinguished anthropologist and
Chairman of the Department of the Philosophy of Science,
University of Pennsylvania

Religious Illiteracy

William Edelen

Fourteen organizations in this country, ranging from People for the American Way to the National Education Association, have issued a document that informs parents and teachers that public schools can be a proper place to teach Comparative Religions as an academic discipline. Such a course of study could make a major contribution toward erasing much of the religious illiteracy in this nation. It could also make a major dent in the bigotry, prejudice and religious superstitions that exist everywhere. But now, when this issue is proposed locally, some will say, "Oh, but we do not need or want our young people to be exposed to the other great religious traditions. All they need is Jesus Christ. That's where truth is, for it was Jesus who said, 'I am the Way, the Truth and the Light.' That's all our young people need."

What people taking this position do not know – and this is a mark of their own religious illiteracy – is that practically every religious leader or hero has said exactly the same thing. Zoroaster used exactly the same words, saying, "I am the Way, the Truth and the Light." The Buddha used the same language, as did Lao Tzu of Taoism. The vast majority of the mythological formulas attached to Jesus were borrowed from Mithraism, Zoroastrianism, Egypt, Babylon and the Greek Mystery religions.

A perfect example is Mithraism (6th century B.C., Persia and India). Mithras was born of a virgin, with only a number of shepherds present. Mithras was known as "the Way," "the Truth," "the Light," "the Life," "the Word," "the Son of God" and "the Good Shepherd." He was pictured carrying a lamb on his shoulders. Sunday was sacred and known as "the Lord's Day" centuries before Jesus. On December 25th, there were magnificent celebrations with bells, candles, gifts, hymns; and "communion" was observed by the followers. From December 25th until the spring equinox (Estra or Easter) were the "40 days" which later became Christian Lent. Mithras was finally placed in a rock tomb called "Petra." After three days he was removed with giant celebrations, festival and great joy.

3

Petra, the sacred rock, centuries later would become Peter, the mythological foundations of the Christian church. (Matthew 16:18: "Thou art Peter, and upon this rock I will build my church.") Christian mythology is quite obviously saturated with Mithraism.

The followers of Mithras believed that there would be a "day of judgment" when non-believers would perish and believers would live in a heaven or "paradise" (a Persian word) forever and ever. All of these mythological formulas were absorbed centuries later by the Christian cult into their rituals. Paul, who never even knew Jesus, took all of these mythological themes and attached them to Jesus, building his Christ mythology. He took Jesus out of Judaism and borrowed the Mithraic Sun-day instead of the Hebrew Sabbath. All of the Mithraic holy days were used to fill in this mythological construct: Christmas, Easter, Lent, and the spring resurrection festival. The Christian "Mass" was, and is, basically the old sacrament of the Mithraic "taurobolia" (a symbol of a divine sacrifice and of the saving effect of blood).

Well, enough of an illustrating example. My thesis stands: the study of Comparative Religions in high school could make an enormous contribution toward erasing religious illiteracy, which in turn would be a giant step forward in reducing religious bigotry, prejudice and the superstitions that so cripple the human spirit.

Excerpt from The Edelen Letter, *Vol. 2, Issue 9, September 1992, published monthly, a publication promoting religious literacy.*

To those searching for truth – not the truth of dogma and darkness but the truth brought by reason, search, examination, and inquiry, discipline is required. For faith, as well intentioned as it may be, must be built on facts, not fiction – faith in fiction is a damnable false hope.

— Thomas A. Edison

What We Must Do

By Bertrand Russell

We want to stand upon our own feet and look fair and square at the world – its good facts, its bad facts, its beauties, and its ugliness; see the world as it is and be not afraid of it. Conquer the world by intelligence and not merely by being slavishly subdued by the terror that comes from it.

The whole conception of God is a conception derived from the ancient Oriental despotisms. It is a conception quite unworthy of free men. When you hear people in church debasing themselves and saying that they are miserable sinners, and all the rest of it, it seems contemptible and not worthy of self-respecting human beings.

We ought to stand up and look the world frankly in the face. We ought to make the best we can of the world, and if it is not so good as we wish, after all it will still be better than what these others have made of it in all these ages.

A good world needs knowledge, kindliness, and courage; it does not need a regretful hankering after the past or a fettering of the free intelligence by the words uttered long ago by ignorant men. It needs a fearless outlook and a free intelligence. It needs hope for the future, not looking back all the time toward a past that is dead, which we trust will be far surpassed by the future that our intelligence can create.

I'm mad as hell and I'm not going to take it any more!

— Howard Beal, fictional character of teh movie *Network*,
railing against the abuse and absurdities of
religious and corporate tyranny.

You gain strength, courage and confidence by every experience in which you really stop to look fear in the face.

— Eleanor Roosevelt

Zoroaster

Zarathustra is the old Iranian word for "Zoroaster" (c. 628-551 BC), who founded a religion in ancient Persia.

Zoroastrianism: Blueprint For Christianity And Judaism

Zarathushtra is the Iranian word for Zoroaster, who founded a religion in ancient Persia. It was he who roused in mankind the *need* for the hatred of unworthy things – thereby discovering the devil and, incidentally, paradise, the last judgment, and the resurrection of the dead. Mithraism is an off-shoot, and Christianity stole some of the popular Zoroastrian beliefs.

Ahura Mazda was the lord of light and wisdom in ancient Iranian mythology. Originally an equal of Mithra, god of light and justice, he was later elevated to the supreme being by the prophet Zoroaster. His name was shortened to Ormazd.

Perhaps the stark contrasts found on the Iranian plateau – steep-sided mountains and flat valleys, bitterly cold winters and boiling hot summers – encouraged this singular rethinking of myth. Certainly, it had an effect on the attitudes of the peoples who came under Iranian domination. It may even be seen to linger on in the outlook of certain Christians and Muslims today.

The Religion Which Might Have Been Ours

In 480 BC, on a marble throne high above the narrow strait which stretched between the island of Salamis and the southern coast of Attica, the great Xerxes sat waiting to watch his navy defeat the Greek fleet. At his back burned the city of Athens, fired by the torches of his soldiers. At the pass of Thermopylae lay the bodies of 300 Spartans with that of their leader, Leonidas, slain by the Asiatic hosts of the Persian Empire. There remained only the task of destroying the Greek fleet, to wipe out the bitter shame of the Persian failure at Marathon ten years before, and to establish the Persian Empire in Greece, from whence it could sweep throughout Europe.

The Persian ships outnumbered the Greek fleet three to one, and were of heavier construction. But the Greeks, using the same superior strategy at sea that Miltiades had used on land at Marathon, sank

200 of the Persian vessels, captured others, and drove the rest from the strait.

The flight of the terror-stricken Xerxes signalled not only the end of his dream of conquest in Europe, but also a vastly changed religious prospect for the Western World. For, according to no less an authority than the late Max Müller, had it not been for the Persian defeats at the decisive battles of Marathon and Salamis, if, in other words, the western march of the Persian Empire had not been stopped there, Zoroastrianism rather than Judeo-Christianity might have been the prevailing religion of Europe and the Americas.

Yet in spite of these crushing military and naval defeats, with the resulting decline of the Persian Empire, and the eventual near-extinction of Zoroastrianism, so great was this religion's vitality and so appealing to the human heart were many of its conceptions and precepts that much of Zarathushtra's creed lives on in the religions of Christianity and Judaism.

What if this religion, instead of Judeo-Christianity, had become our faith? Would we have a vastly different theology and code of ethical conduct? We would believe in a loving Father-God who is omniscient and concerned with the welfare of his children. We would have, instead of Jesus, Zarathushtra who, while not peculiarly the son of God, was sent to earth by God to spread his doctrine and do his work.

We would look forward to "the Kingdom of God." We would have the ancient statement of a region of darkness and a region of light, of heaven and hell, of the good power in conflict with the evil. We would have Angra Mainyu, instead of Satan – a mere difference in name. We would have angels and archangels. We would have a statement of the final resurrection of the dead very similar to that in the Judeo-Christian Bible.

These things we have now. Did they come to us from the pious and vigorous mind of Zarathushtra by way of the later prophets of Israel and Christ, or were they original conceptions of Judeo-Christianity? How well acquainted the chroniclers of the Jewish Old Testament were with the Persian branch of the Indo-European wanderers is evidenced by their frequent reference to the Medes and the Persians. But there is also definite evidence of borrowing from Zoroastrianism in the religious creeds which Christianity absorbed from later Judaism.

Up to the time of the exile, the source of both good and evil in the religion of the Israelites was thought to be the God Jehovah. But after the exile, which is to say after the influence of Zarathushtra's monotheistic doctrine began to be felt, the Old Testament writers recorded the doctrine that Jehovah was the one God of the universe and a God of pure righteousness, while Satan was charged with all evil creations. It is probable that Satan – or the devil of later Judaism and Christianity – is none other than Angra Mainyu, the arch daeva of Zoroastrianism.

The elaborate angelology and demonology of later Judaism, the idea of a divine judgment and a final resurrection, and a future life in a region which may be definitely described – all seem to have come from the doctrines of Zarathushtra, though there is no definite proof of this. Indeed there are Christian and Hebrew commentators who believe that Zoroastrianism borrowed these conceptions from later Judaism, but they speak with less conviction than do those who hold the opposite view. Almost certainly the Magi who are said to have visited Jesus in the manger were Zoroastrian priests, and Christ's word "paradise" was taken from the Persian *pairidaeza.*

In the field of human ethics and social behavior we would have in Zoroastrianism a code which, if followed, would produce a state of human welfare that would be difficult to surpass. The chief differences would be in matters of emphasis. While Zoroastrianism and Christianity both state the necessity of faith and works, the emphasis in Christianity is on faith, in Zoroastrianism on works.

When Alexander the Great conquered Persia, and Greek cities were established there, the decline of Zoroastrianism began. Under the Mohammedans the decline continued until today there are scarcely ten thousand followers of Zarathushtra in the land of his birth.

— *From the "World Bible" edited by Robert O. Ballou*

The Power of the Sun

Many peoples have worshipped the powers of the natural world. Resplendent among these is the Sun. To a philosopher such as Plato, the Sun symbolized the ultimate. It gave the power of sight, which symbolized the power of insight. The Sun is light and fire, and many mystics all the world over have spoken of their highest experience in terms of light.

But if the Sun brings light and warmth, it also brings scorching heat and destruction. Its rays are often called arrows. Light and darkness are at war with one another. So religions focusing on the Sun have often tended to militarism. Two examples will suffice.

Zoroastrianism, whose origins are now thought to go back to the second millennium BCE, became the creed of the militant Achaemenid dynasty in Persia in the sixth century. It centered on the struggle between the forces of Order and Chaos, Light and Darkness, and the Sun was one of the powers fighting on the side of Order and Light.

A second example comes from the period when, after a century of largely untroubled peace, the Roman Empire experienced a century of wars and disasters. In their distress, they looked for a new divine champion, and went to the Sun, the Unconquered Sun, *Sol Invictus*.

In 274 CE, the emperor Aurelian actually adopted the Sun as the Supreme God of the Roman Empire. Moreover, Constantine's family were worshippers of the Unconquered Sun. When he was marching on Rome, he had his famous vision of a Cross superimposed on the Sun. It came from his family god. In the form of a chi-rho in a circle (or, as often, an iota-chi) it presented the initial letters of the name of Christ (or of Jesus Christ) in the form of a sun wheel. Constantine was in fact a syncretist. His statue in Constantinople bore the rayed crown of the Sun god, made, as he believed, from the nails of Christ's Cross. His god was a god of war, not peace.

Yet, the Sun, in its all-embracing power, could speak of peace as well as war. The rulers of Persia were drawn in the direction of universalism and toleration. What is more, the all-seeing eye of the Sun made for justice. The Persians were particularly strong about keeping one's word, about the value and importance of truth, honesty, uprightness. So although peace does not stand high among the values of traditional Zoroastrianism, the religion has much in it which gives positive content to peace. This is why the Parsis, retaining the strong monotheism of Zarathustra, have been a force for peace. They influenced the Moghul Akbar to use good counsel, not the sword, in spreading religion. Ever since they have been in the forefront in developing philanthropy and social responsibility.

From The Portable World Bible, *Viking Press, 1939*

R. I. P.
Religious Illiteracy

*"Those of us who refuse to read material that we think we might NOT
agree with are no better off than those who can't read at all."*
— T. K. Kennett

Four Americans in five believe the Bible is the inspired word of God, and many of those who do not, still regard it as the basis for moral values and the rule of law.

Four in ten Americans say they would turn to the Bible first to test their own religious beliefs, while a solid one-third believe that "holding the Bible to be God's truth is absolutely essential for someone to truly know God."

Despite the large percentage of Americans who believe the Bible is the word of God, only one-third of Americans read it at least once a week. Another 12 percent read the Bible less than weekly, but at least once a month. More than half of all Americans read the Bible less than once a month, including 24 percent who say they never read it and 6 percent who can't recall the last time they read the Bible.

This lack of Bible-reading explains why Americans know so little about the Bible that is the basis of the faith of most of them. For example, eight in ten Americans say they are Christians, but only four in ten know that Jesus, according to the Bible, delivered the Sermon on the Mount.

Fewer than half of all adults can name Matthew, Mark, Luke and John as the four Gospels of the New Testament, while many do not know that Jesus had twelve disciples or that he was born in Bethlehem. A large majority of Americans believe that the Ten Commandments are still valid rules for living today, but they have a tough time recalling exactly what those rules are.

The cycle of biblical illiteracy seems likely to continue—today's teenagers know even less about the Bible than do adults. The celebration of Easter, which Christians believe marks the resurrection of Christ, is central to the faith, yet three in ten teenagers—and 20 percent of those teenagers who attend religious services regularly — do not know why Easter is celebrated.

The decline in Bible-reading is due to many factors: the feeling that the Bible is inaccessible; the belief that it has little to say to today's world; a decline in reading in general and less emphasis on religious training.

Despite the publicity given to fundamentalist ministers and televangelists in recent years, the proportion of Americans who are fundamentalists — that is, who believe that every word in the Bible is literally true — continues to decline. Only 31 percent of Americans believe the Bible is "the actual word of God and is taken literally, word for word," down from 34 percent in 1985. Americans revere the Bible but they don't read it. Because they don't read it, they have become a nation of biblical illiterates.

Source: The People's Religion: George Gallup & Jem Castelli, Macmillan Publishing Co. 1989.

"The Bible must be seen in a cultural context. It didn't just happen. These stories are retreads from stories before. But, tell a Christian that — No, No! What makes it doubly sad is that they hardly know the book, much less its origins."
— Isaac Asimov

Horus
A Major Egyptian God

Horus: The Way, The Truth, The Life

Albert Churchward

It is a Christian belief that life and immortality were brought to light, and death, the last enemy, was destroyed by a personal Jesus only 2,000 years ago. The very same revelation had been accredited to Horus, the anointed, at least 3,000 years before. Horus, as the impersonal and ideal revealer, was the Messiah in the astronomical mythology and the Son of God in the eschatology. The doctrine of immortality is so ancient in Egypt that the "Book of Vivifying the Soul Forever" was not only extant in the time of the First Dynasty but was then so old that the true tradition of interpretation was at that time already lost.

The Egyptian Horus, as revealer of immortality, was the ideal figure of the ancient spiritualists that the soul of man, or the Manes, persisted beyond death and the dissolution of the present body.

The origin and evolution

We find, depicted on stones in many countries where the Stellar Cult people migrated, remains of this old Astronomical religion which proves their perfect knowledge of the revolutions of the Starry Vast and the Laws governing these revolutions, all of which they imaged iconographically or by Signs and Symbols. And where they have not built Pyramids they have recorded the truth in the so-called "Cups and Rings" and "curious carvings" found on boulders, cist-covers, on living rock, and on standing stones throughout the British Isles, Europe, Asia, Africa, and other parts of the world – which hitherto have been deemed to involve insoluble problems and have been to all our learned professors an outstanding puzzle in pre-historic research. But they are easily read, and the secrets are unfolded in the Sign Language of the Astronomical, or Stellar Cult Religion of the Ancient Egyptians.

The mutilation of Osiris in his coffin, the stripping of his corpse and tearing it asunder by Set, who scattered it piecemeal, has its equivalent by the stripping of the dead body of Jesus whilst it still hung upon the Cross, and parting the garments amongst the spoilers.

In St. John's account the crucifixion takes place at the time of the Passover, and the victim of sacrifice in human form is substituted for, and identified with, the Paschal Lamb. But, as this version further shows, the death assigned is in keeping with that of the non-human victim. Not a bone of the sufferer to be broken. This is supposed to be in fulfilment of prophecy. It is said by the Psalmist (34:20): "He keepeth all His bones; not one of them is broken." But this was in strict accordance with the original law of Tabu. No matter what the type, from bear to lamb, no bone of the sacrificial victim was ever permitted to be broken; and the only change was in the substitution of the human type for the animal, which had been made already when human Horus became the type of sacrifice instead of the calf or lamb.

When the Australian natives sacrificed their little bear, not a bone of it was ever broken. When the Iroquois sacrificed the white dog, not a bone was broken. This was a common custom, on account of the resurrection as conceived by the primitive races, and the same is applied to Osiris-Horus. Every bone of the skeleton was to remain intact as a basis for the future building.

It is an utterance of the Truth that is eternal to say that Horus as the Son of God had previously been all the Gospel Jesus is made to say he is, or is to become:

Horus and the Father are one.

- Jesus says, "I and My Father are one. He that seeth Me, seeth Him that sent Me."
- Horus is the Father seen in the Son.
- Jesus claims to be the Son in whom the Father is revealed.
- Horus was the light of the world, the light that is represented by the symbolical eye, the sign of salvation.
- Jesus is made to declare that He is the light of the world.
- Horus was the way, the truth, the life by name and in person.
- Jesus is made to assert that he is the way, the truth, and the life.
- Horus was the plant, the shoot, the natzar.
- Jesus is made to say: "I am the true vine."
- Horus says:

It is I who traverse the heaven; I go round the Sekhet-Arru (the Elysian Fields); Eternity has been assigned to me without end. Lo! I am heir of endless time and my attribute is eternity.

Jesus says: "I am come down from Heaven. For this is the will of the Father that everyone who beholdeth the Son and believeth in Him should have eternal life, and I will raise him up at the last day." He, too, claims to be the lord of eternity.

- Horus says: "I open the Tuat that I may drive away the darkness."
- Jesus says: "I am come a light unto the world."
- Horus says:

  I am equipped with thy words O Ra (the father in heaven) (ch.32) and repeat them to those who are deprived of breath. (ch.38). These were the words of the father in heaven.

Jesus says: "The Father which sent me, he hath given me a commandment, what I should say and what I should speak. Whatsoever I speak, therefore, even as the Father said unto me, so I speak. The word which ye hear is not mine, but the Father's which sent me."

- A comparative list of some pre-existing types to Christianity shows further how these types were brought on in the canonical Gospels and the Book of Revelation:
- Horus baptized with water by Anup = Jesus baptized with water by John.
- Anup, the Baptizer = John the Baptist.
- Aan, a name of the divine scribe = John the divine scribe.
- Horus born in Annu, the place of bread = Jesus born in Bethlehem, the house of bread.
- Horus the Good Shepherd with the crook upon his shoulders = Jesus the Good Shepherd with the lamb or kid upon his shoulder.
- The Seven on board the boat with Horus = The seven fishers on board the boat with Jesus.
- Horus as the Lamb = Jesus as the Lamb.
- Horus as the Lion = Jesus as the Lion.
- Horus identified with the Tat or Cross = Jesus identified with the Cross.
- Horus of twelve years = Jesus of twelve years.

15

- Horus made a man of thirty years in his baptism = Jesus made a man of thirty years in his baptism.
- Horus the Krst = Jesus the Christ.
- Horus the manifesting Son of God = Jesus the manifesting Son of God.
- The trinity of Atum the Father, Horus the Son, and Ra the Holy Spirit = The trinity of the Father, Son, and Holy Spirit.
- The first Horus as child of the Virgin, the second as Son of Ra = Jesus as the Virgin's child, the Christ as Son of the Father.
- Horus the sower and Set the destroyer in the harvestfield = Jesus the sower of the good seed and Satan the sower of tares.
- Horus carried off by Set to the summit of Mount Hetep = Jesus spirited away by Satan into an exceedingly high mountain.
- Set and Horus contending on the Mount = Jesus and Satan contending on the Mount.
- The Star, as announcer of the child Horus = The Star in the East that indicated the birthplace of Jesus.
- Horus the avenger = Jesus who brings the sword.
- Horus as Iu-em-Hetep, who comes with peace = Jesus the bringer of peace.
- Horus the afflicted one = Jesus the afflicted one.
- Horus as the type of life eternal=Jesus the type of eternal life.
- Horus as Iu-em-Hetep, the child teacher in the temple = The child Jesus as teacher in the Temple.
- The mummy bandage that was woven without seam = The vesture of the Christ without a seam.
- Twelve followers of Horus as Har-Khutti = Twelve followers of Jesus as the twelve disciples.
- The revelation written down by Aan (Tehuti) the scribe of divine words = The revelation by John the divine.
- The saluter Aani, who bears witness to the word of Ra and to the testimony of Horus = John who bears witness to the Word of God and the testimony of Jesus Christ.
- The secret of the Mysteries revealed by Taht-Aan = The secret of the Mysteries made known by John.
- Horus the Morning Star =Jesus the Morning Star.

- Horus who gives the Morning Star to his followers = Jesus who gives the Morning Star to his followers.
- The name of Ra on the head of the deceased = The name of the Father written on the forehead.
- The Paradise of the Pole Star-Am-Khemen = The Holy City lighted by one luminary, that is neither the Sun nor the Moon = the Pole Star.
- The Har-Seshu, or servants of Horus = The servants of Jesus Christ.

Excerpt from Churchward's book Of Religion, *first published 1924. Reprints are available from Health Research, Mokelumne Hills, CA 95245. Churchward was a student of the British poet and Egyptologist Gerald Massey.*

Mythology is what grown-ups believe, folk-lore is what they tell their children, and religion is both.

— Cedric Whitman, letter to Edward Tripp, 1969

Ancient Pagan Cross Showing the Round Orb of God's Sun on the Cross resting on top of a Christian Church in Costa Mesa, California!

Astro-Theology

Jordan Maxwell

The Christian religion is a parody on the worship of the Sun, in which they put a man whom they call Christ, in the place of the Sun, and pay him the same adoration which was originally paid to the Sun.

— Thomas Paine

In the New Testament, a provocative and most serious challenge is laid on the whole of Christianity. Since it bears directly on our subject, we will quote it: "... if Christ be not risen, then our preaching is in vain, and your faith is also in vain. Yea, and we are found false witnesses of God . . . And if Christ be not raised, your faith is vain; ye are yet in your sins." (I Cor. 15:13-17)

Let's closely examine the original, conceptual foundations of the faith, and *then* decide. But in order to do that, we must go back not 2000 years to the birth of Christ, but 10 to 15,000 years to the birth of modern man. For when one seeks to establish foundations, one must begin at the beginning.

Many thousands of years ago, in what we refer to as the "primordial world" of the ancients, human life was a far different experience from that which we enjoy today. While it is true that we have less documentation on that prehistoric world than we have on our own age, enough is known from the ancient writings to paint a rather clear picture of our remote ancestry. If we have learned anything at all, it is this: "That the more we change, the more we stay the same." And nowhere is this more clearly demonstrated than in the history of man's quest for "God", and the ancient religion we still keep holy.

According to the best understanding we have gleaned from the available records, life for our ancient forefathers was a mixture of wonder and fear. Each day, just finding food for one's family without becoming a meal oneself was a life-and-death struggle. It was from these meager, distressful conditions of the human race that our long history of the search for God and meaning of life has come.

Any evolution, at its most accelerated rate, is always agonizingly slow. But from the beginning, man's profound questions demanded answers. When no clear answers were forthcoming from the universe, man turned inward and developed his own. The study of this subject is termed *"Astro-Theology"* or the worship of the heavens.

It did not take ancient man very long to decide that in this world the single greatest enemy to be feared was the darkness of night. Simply stated,

man's first enemy was darkness.

With this one fact alone, one can readily understand why the greatest and most trustworthy friend the human race would ever have was heaven's greatest gift to the world . . . the Glorious Rising Orb of Day . . . THE SUN. With this simple truth understood, we can now begin to unravel an ancient and wonderful story.

Today, as in all of mankind's history, it has once again been told anew. This is the story of Christianity: "The Greatest Story Ever Told." We shall see that the parallels between Christian metaphors and the natural reality of sun and sky are so striking that they constitute – the whole story.

Modern-day Christianity has often belittled our ancient ancestors who are not here to defend themselves. They accuse them of being nothing more than ignorant worshippers of miscellaneous gods. Therefore we can, with assurance, summarily dismiss 14,000 years of human spirituality as ignominious myth believed by well-meaning but gullible primitives. Too much of this kind of spiritual arrogance and religious pride has continued without challenge . . . until now! The time has come to set matters straight.

The "Greatest Story" went something like this . . .

- The ancient peoples reasoned that no one on Earth could ever lay claim of ownership to the Great Orb of Day. It must belong to the unseen Creator of the universe. It became, figuratively speaking, not man's, but "God's Sun." Truly, "God's Sun" was . . . "The Light Of The World."

- As stated before, in the dark cold of night man realized his utter vulnerability to the elements. Each night, mankind was forced to wait for the "Rising of The Sun" to chase away the physical and mental insecurity brought on by the darkness. Therefore, the morning Sun focused man's attention on heavenly dependence for his frail, short existence on Earth. Doing so, it became an appropriate symbol of divine benevolence from heaven.

- So just as a small fire brought limited light into man's own little world of darkness, likewise, the "Great Fire of Day" served the whole Earth with its heavenly presence. For this reason, it was said at Deut. 4:24 and Heb. 12:29 that the God of the Bible was a "Consuming Fire" in heaven. And so He was!

- It was accepted by all that man was bound to a life on Earth, but the sky was the abode of God's Sun. He resides "up there" in . . . "Heaven."

- Ancient man saw in his male offspring his own image and likeness, and his own existence as a father was proved by the person of his son. It was assumed that "God's Sun" was but a visible representative of the unseen Creator in heaven. So it was said, "When you have seen the Son, you have seen the Father." Said another way, "The Father is glorified in His Son."

- Ancient man had no problem understanding that all life on Earth depended directly on life-giving energy from the Sun. Consequently, all life was lost without the Sun. It followed that "God's Sun" was nothing less than "Our very Savior."

- Logically, even if man himself dies, as long as the Sun comes up each day, life on Earth will continue forever. Therefore, it was said in the ancient texts that everlasting life was "the gift" that the Father gives through his Sun. Not for you personally – but for the Earth . . . everlasting life!

- Since evil and harm lurked at every turn in the fearful dark of night, all evil or harmful deeds were naturally the . . ."Works of Darkness."

- And of course the evil of night was ruled over by none other than . . . "The Prince of Darkness." Hence, evil is of the Dark or: Devil.

- We now have before us two cosmic brothers – one very good, and one very bad. One brings the "truth to light" with the "light of truth." The other is the opposite, or in opposition to the light – "The Opposer" . . . Prince of the World of Darkness.

- At this point we come to Egypt. More than three thousand years before Christianity began, the early morning "Sun/Savior" was pictured in Egypt as the "New Born Babe." The infant savior's name was "Horus."

- At daybreak, this wonderful, newborn child is of course "Born Again" (hallelujah). Horus is risen on the Horizon.

*God's Sun, The Light of the World,
with Crown of Thorns*

If people simply realized that most major religions (including Christianity) are based on astrology and sun worship – mankind would be a lot better off . . .

— the editor

- And of course "God's Sun" goes to His death wearing a "crown of thorns" or "corona." Remember the Statue of Liberty? To this day, kings still wear a round crown of spikes, symbolizing the rays of the Sun!

- The Egyptians knew that the Sun was at its highest point in the sky (or high noon) when no shadow was cast by the pyramid. At that point, all Egypt offered prayers to the "Most High" God! As stated before, to the ancients, the sky was the abode, or heavenly temple, of the "Most High." Therefore, "God's Sun" was doing His heavenly Father's work in the temple at 12 noon!

- The world of ancient man kept track of times and seasons by the movement of the Sun – daily, monthly, yearly. For this, the sundial was devised. Not only the daily movement of the Sun was tracked on the round dial, but the whole year was charted on a round calendar dial. Examples: Ancient Mexican, Mayan, Inca, Aztec, Sumerian, Babylonian, Assyrian, Egyptian, Celtic, Aryan, etc. With this method, certain new concepts emerged in the mind of ancient man.

- Since the Earth experiences four different seasons, all the same and equal (in time) each year, the round calendar was divided into four equal parts. This represented the complete story of the life of "God's Sun." The famous painting of *The Last Supper* pictures the 12 followers of the Son in four groups (of 3) . . . the four seasons of the year!

- On the round surface of the yearly calendar, you draw a vertical line directly across the middle, cutting the circle in half – one end being the point of the winter solstice; the other end being the point of the summer solstice. Then draw another straight line (crossing the first one). One end of the new line is the spring equinox; the other end is the autumn equinox.

You now have the starting points for each of the four seasons. This is referred to by all major encyclopedias and reference works, both ancient and modern, as "The Cross of the Zodiac." Thus, the life of God's "Sun" is on "the Cross." This is why we see the round circle of the Sun on the crosses of Christian churches. The next time you pass a Christian church, look for the circle (Sun) on the cross.

On December 21 or 22, the Sun, going south, reaches its lowest point in the sky (our winter solstice). By December 25th, it is clear that the Sun is returning northward. Therefore, on

Pictured here is the original concept of the Heavenly Sun hanging on the Zodiacal Cross, later to become for Christianity "God's Son Hanging on the Cross!"

Dec. 25th the sun is "Born Again." Christians stole Dec. 25 from the Roman celebration of Sol Invictus – the Sun Unconquered. And to this day, His worshippers still celebrate His birthday – Merry Christmas, and Happy New Year.

- As noted before, the year was divided into 12 equal parts, or months. And to each month was appointed a heavenly symbol or astrological "Sign." Each of the 12 monthly signs was called a "House" of the Heavenly Zodiac.

- We are told in Matthew 14:17 & 19 that God's Son tends to His people's needs with "Two Fishes." The two fishes represent the astrological sign all astrologers know as "Pisces." Thus, we have had for almost 2000 years God's Sun ruling in His "Kingdom" in the sign of Pisces/Two Fishes. As stated before, these signs are called houses. Therefore, Pisces is the "Lord's House" at this time. Truly, The Greatest "Fish" Story Ever Told!

- According to astrology, sometime after the year 2000, the Sun will enter His new Sign, or His new Kingdom, as it was called by the ancients. This next coming Sign/Kingdom, soon to be upon us, will be, according to the Zodiac, the House or Sign of Aquarius. So when we read in Luke 22:10, we now understand why God's Son states that He and His followers, at the last Passover, are to go into "the house of the man with the water pitcher." So we see that in the coming millennium, God's Sun will bring us into His new Kingdom or House of Aquarius (the man with the water pitcher).

- Once we realize that in Astrology, each month is assigned one of the so-called "Houses" of the Zodiac and in heaven are 12 houses (12 monthly signs), then the words we read of God's Son saying "In my Father's House are many mansions," makes sense (when translated correctly). The proper translation is as follows:

Father's House = Heavenly Abode

Mansions = Houses

So, correctly read in the original text, we read: "In my Father's heavenly abode are many houses." Yes, 12 to be exact.

Anyone familiar with modern-day Christianity must surely know we are said to be living in the "Last Days." This teaching is, in part, based on the idea expressed in Matthew 28:20 of the

The Pisces of the Zodiac is still prominent on church windows of all denominations

King James Bible, where God's Son says, "I am with you alway, even unto the end of the world." End of the World??!! Yet another simple mistranslation to clarify with a proper understanding of the actual words used. This "end of the world" is translated differently in various Bibles. Some say "End of Time," "End of the Days," and still others say "Conclusion of this system of things." So what does all this talk of the "End Times/Last Days" really mean?

Here is the simple answer. When the scriptures speak of "the end of the world," the actual word used is not, I repeat, <u>not</u> end of the world. The actual word in Greek is "Aeon," which, when correctly translated, means "Age," that's spelled "A G E"! Any library will have Bible Concordances. *Strong's Bible Concordance* is a good reference work to use here. Look up the word "age" in any secular dictionary or Bible Concordance. There you will find the word for "age" is from the Greek "Aeon." Remembering that in astrology each of the 12 houses (or signs) of the Zodiac corresponds to a 2000-year period of time, called an "age," we now know we are nearly 2000 years into the House or Age of Pisces. Now, correctly understood, it can rightly be said that we today, in fact, are living in the "Last Days."

- Yes, we are in the last days of the old "Age of Pisces." Soon, God's Sun will come again into His New Kingdom or "New Age" of Aquarius (man with the water pitcher). That's right, "The New Aeon" . . . "The New Age." This is the theme in the New Testament – God's Sun and his coming Kingdom/Age. "The New Age of Aquarius."

- It was well understood by ancient man that our weather was caused and controlled by the Sun. It was a simple fact that God's Sun had the power to control storms at will. The ancient Egyptians taught that He did this as He rested in His heavenly boat while crossing the sky. The story of Jesus calming the storm (Matt. 8:23-27) echoes this.

- The next point to be made requires first a little background. Christians have always referred to God as "The Father." But viewing God as a father didn't start here – it goes back far into the ancient world. The reason is: Our planet was always viewed as our "Mother Earth or Mother Nature." And since rain (the life-bringing fluid), falling from heaven, impregnated and

Aquarius

LUKE 22:10 – Jesus tells his followers that they are to enter the house of the man with a water pitcher. This is the house of Aquarius, marking the beginning of a new age. It is one of the 12 ages or houses of the zodiac in the "heavens."

brought life to Mother Earth, it was therefore believed that our Father was in Heaven.

All this life-bringing intercourse between God the Father and Mother Earth would be after a proper marriage ceremony at a spring wedding. In the area today called Israel, called by the ancients "The Land of Canaan," the (sexual/fertility) rites of spring were celebrated each year in what was called "The Marriage Feast of Canaan."

And so the New Testament story was . . . Mother Earth asked God's Sun to draw water (from the sea) for the grapes to make fine wine for the wedding feast. This marriage feast story is over 5000 years old – 3000 years before the New Testament story.

- It is at this point we need to go back to the ancient Egyptians to further understand "The Greatest Story Ever Told." Though all of the essential pieces of the Christian story were long in existence before Egypt, it was with the coming of the Pharaohs that the story was finally codified and became religious dogma. Though the story varied in some details from place to place in Egypt, the essence was always the same: God's Sun was the "Light of the World," who give His life for us.

- In ancient Egypt it was said that if you wanted to follow the life of God's Sun and thereby "live in the light of God's Word," one would first have to leave his old ways of life to "Follow the Sun." But before beginning this new life in "The Word," one must die to the old way of life and be "Born Again." Your first birth was "out of the water" your mother formed you in. Because her water broke and your new life began, rebirth is symbolized by coming out of total immersion in water – baptism – or being born again.

These points here mentioned are a few of hundreds, if not thousands, of direct connections that can be made between the Judaeo-Christian Bible Story and the far more ancient, original Story. My purpose for drawing your attention to this literary plagiarism is best stated by Alfred North Whitehead who said, "No lie can live forever," and Egyptologist Gerald Massey, "They must find it difficult, those who have taken authority as the truth, rather than truth as the authority."

Pharaoh with His Rod + Staff

First Pharaoh holds the shepherd's crook as the Good Shepherd; again later, Jesus also carries the same crook.

. . . though I walk through the valley of the shadow of death, I will fear no evil: for thou art with me – thy <u>rod</u> and thy <u>staff</u> they comfort me.

— Ps. 23:4

Now for a few thoughts on the "Old Testament" Word of God

In Mal 4:2, the God of Heaven is described as the "Sun of Righteousness with healing in His wings." The Sun with healing in His wings?? Then in the New Testament in Matt. 23:37 and Luke 13:34, we see God's Son wanting to gather all under "His wings." This is most appropriate for, in Egypt, the Sun was always pictured with His wings.

- In the ancient Egyptian understanding of things, mankind was called "the sheep of God." And the great Orb of Day, God's Sun, was the overseer or, in the exact words from the ancient Egyptian manuscript, "The Good Shepherd" – and we are His flock.

  All ancient kings thought of their people as sheep to be pastured, with themselves as "the shepherd." Sheep are ideal followers, for they do not think for themselves but will blindly follow anyone without question. Truly admirable behavior for animals, but unwise for humans.

- With the foregoing in mind, we read again from the Old Testament Book of Psalms. At Psalms 23:4 we read that old, dog-eared, tired, exhausted and equally misunderstood chestnut, used by every "man of the cloth" to put the sheep to sleep, we quote it here: "Yea, though I walk through the valley of the shadow of death, I will fear no evil, for thou art with me. Thy Rod and thy Staff, they comfort me." Thy Rod and thy Staff!!

  Here in the Book of Psalms, the Old Testament God is pictured with His Rod and Staff.

  The rod here mentioned is the king's "Rod of Discipline" and the staff is the "Shepherd's Staff," or crook. Now for the correct understanding of this old verse. Any good library book on the Egyptian religion will tell you that the ancient Pharaohs were said to be ruling for God's Sun on Earth. The Pharoah was called "King of the Kingdom" and "The Great Shepherd of His Sheep." In the hands of the Pharaoh/God (whose arms form the "Sign of the cross" on his chest), were placed the royal symbols of heavenly power, the Rod and Staff.

  Incidentally, Jesus is pictured not only with His shepherd's staff but, in Rev. 12:5 & Rev 19:15, is also said to "rule with a rod of iron."

✳ ———————————————————— ✳

Jordan Maxwell is an author, teacher and lecturer on ancient religions and Astromytholgy.

Reason and free inquiry are the only effectual agents against error.

— Thomas Jefferson
1743 - 1826

Reason And Religion

Thomas Jefferson

Letter to nephew Peter Carr, 1787

Religion. Your reason is now mature enough to examine this object. In the first place, divest yourself of all bias in favor of novelty and singularity of opinion. Indulge them in any other subject rather than that of religion. It is too important and the consequences of error may be too serious. On the other hand, shake off all the fears and servile prejudices, under which weak minds are servilely crouched. Fix reason firmly in her seat, and call to her tribunal every fact, every opinion. Question with boldness even the existence of God; because, if there be one, he must more approve of the homage of reason, than that of blindfolded fear.

You will naturally examine first, the religion of your own country. Read the Bible, then, as you would read Livy or Tacitus. The facts which are within the ordinary course of nature, you will believe on the authority of the writer, as you do those of the same kind in Livy and Tacitus. The testimony of the writer weighs in their favor in one scale; and their not being against the laws of nature, does not weigh against them. But those facts in the Bible which contradict the laws of nature, must be examined with more care, and under a variety of faces. Here you must recur to the pretensions of the writer to inspiration from God.

Examine upon what evidence his pretensions are founded, and whether that evidence is so strong, as that its falsehood would be more improbable than a change in the laws of nature, in the case he relates. For example, in the book of Joshua, we are told, the sun stood still several hours. Were we to read that fact in Livy or Tacitus, we should class it with their showers of blood, speaking of statues, beasts, etc. But it is said, that the writer of that book was inspired. Examine, therefore, candidly, what evidence there is of his having been inspired. The pretension is entitled to your enquiry, because millions believe it. On the other hand, you are astronomer enough to know how contrary it is to the law of nature that a body revolving on its axis, as the earth does, should have stopped, should not, by that sudden stoppage, have prostrated animals, trees, buildings, and should after a certain time have resumed its revolution, and that without a second general prostration. Is this arrest of the earth's motion, or the evidence which affirms it, most within the law of probabilities?

You will read next the New Testament. It is the history of a personage called Jesus. Keep in your eye the opposite pretensions: 1, of those who say he was begotten by God, born of a virgin, suspended and reversed the laws of nature at will, and ascended bodily into heaven; and 2, of those who say he was a man of illegitimate birth, of a benevolent heart, enthusiastic mind, who set out without pretensions to divinity, ended in believing them, and was punished capitally for sedition, by being gibbeted, according to Roman law . . . .

These questions are examined in the books I have mentioned, under the head of Religion. They will assist you in your enquiries; but keep your reason firmly on the watch in reading them all. Do not be frightened from this inquiry by any fear of its consequences. If it ends in a belief that there is no God, you will find incitements to virtue in the comfort and pleasantness you feel in its exercise, and the love of others which it will procure you. If you find reason to believe there is a God, a consciousness that you are acting under his eyes, and that he approves you, will be a vast additional incitement; if that there be a future state, the hope of a happy existence in that increases the appetite to deserve it; if that Jesus was also a God, you will be comforted by a belief of his aid and love.

In fine, I repeat, you must lay aside all prejudice on both sides, and neither believe nor reject anything, because any other persons, or descriptions of persons, have rejected or believed it. Your own reason is the only oracle given you by heaven, and you are answerable, not for the rightness, but the uprightness of the decision. I forgot to observe, when speaking of the New Testament, that you should read all the histories of Christ [including] those which a council of ecclesiastics have decided for us, to be pseudo-evangelists . . . . because those pseudo-evangelists pretended to inspiration, as much as the others, you are to judge their pretensions by your own reason, and not by the reason of those ecclesiastics.

Other
Religions

Ayatollah Khomeini

The late leader of the Shiite sect of the Moslem religion who was both spiritual and state leader of Iran.

Islam

Islam, the youngest of the world's major religions, originated in the seventh century with the life and mission of Mohammed, but it was not a totally new creed invented out of the blue. Its conceptual roots are in Judaism and Christianity. Moslems see their religion as a continuation and rectification of the Judeo-Christian tradition. The Jewish scriptures and the prophetic mission of Jesus are incorporated by reference in the Koran. The Koran teaches that God, the same God known to the Arabians as Allah, favored Jews and Christians by revealing His truth to them in holy books, but they deviated from what was revealed and fell into error and corruption. The people of the Arabian peninsula trace their origins to the patriarch Abraham, who, according to the Koran, was neither Jew nor Christian but a kind of universal ancestor of monotheists. Hagar, the Egyptian slave-girl, and Ishmael, the son she bore to Abraham, are believed to have reached Mecca in their exile. Abraham himself is believed to have constructed the Kaaba, the sacred shrine of Mecca, which is the object of the annual pilgrimage. Moslems believe there is and has always been since Abraham only one true religion, a consistent faith in the one omnipotent God, who from time to time has sent various messengers and prophets to reveal Himself to men and tell men what He expects of them.

These revelations were recorded in a hundred and four books, of which only four are extant: the Pentateuch, the Psalms, the Gospels, and the Koran, given successively to Moses, David, Jesus, and Mohammed. No more are to be expected, as Mohammed was the last prophet and in the Koran, "all things are revealed."

— Excerpt from Understanding Islam.

Mohammed

Mohammed was born circa 570 A.D. At age 25 he married a wealthy widow, and worked as a tradesman in her business for the next fifteen years. At age 40, Mohammed suddenly emerged as a religious prophet and the leader of a powerful new religious movement. According to his statements, his religious mission was triggered by an apparition. The vision occurred outside a secluded cave to which he would frequently retire for prayer and contemplation. The apparition was an "angel" bearing a message for Mohammed to spread. This was not just any angel, however. It called itself Gabriel – one of the most important of the Christian angels.

Mohammed was either semiconscious or in a trance when the angel Gabriel ordered him to "Recite!" and record the message that the angel was about to give him. The angel's command to him was much like the commands given earlier in history to Ezekiel of the Old Testament and to "John" of the Book of Revelation by similar Custodial personnel. When Mohammed awoke, it seemed to him that the angel's words were "inscribed upon his heart." The message given to Mohammed was a new religion called "Islam," which means "Surrender." Followers must "surrender" to God. Members of Mohammed's faith are therefore called "Moslems," which comes from the word "muslim" ("one who submits"). Islam was one more Custodial religion designed to instill abject obedience in humans. The Supreme Being of the Islam faith is named "Allah," who was said by Mohammed to be the same God as the Jewish and Christian Jehovah. Mohammed honored Moses and Jesus as Allah's two previous messengers and proclaimed Islam to be the third and final revelation from God. It was therefore the duty of all Jews and Christians to convert to Islam. Hebrews and Christians tended to be less than cooperative with Mohammed's demand. After all, they had been warned in their own apocalyptic writings about the dangers of "false prophets." The result has been some of the bloodiest fighting in world history.

— *Excerpt from The Gods of Eden.*

Politico-Religious Effects

Mohammed enjoyed absolute rule over his people as a divinely inspired and guided prophet. He led the public prayers; he acted as judge; he ruled . . . He was the state. On his death a leader was put in his place of similar authority, though without the divine prophetic guidance. He was called the "successor." The Sunni Moslems elect their ruler, but the Shi'ites . . . hold that the appointment lies with God.

The duties of this autocrat are, in theory, generally stated as follows. He shall enforce legal decisions and maintain the divinely revealed restrictive ordinances; guard the frontiers and equip armies; receive the alms; put down robberies, thieving, highwaymen; maintain the Friday services and the festivals... He must be a free, male, adult Moslem; must have administrative ability; must be an effective governor and do justice to the wronged. So long as he fulfils these conditions he is to be absolutely obeyed; private immorality or even tyranny are not grounds for deposing him . . .

Jihad is used to designate the religious duty inculcated in the Koran on the followers of Mohammed to wage war upon those who do not accept the doctrines of Islam. This duty is laid down in five suras – all of these suras belonging to the period after Mohammed had established his power. Conquered peoples who will neither embrace Islam nor pay a poll-tax are to be put to the sword, their families are liable to slavery, and all their goods to seizure.

By Mohammedan commentators the commands in the Koran are not interpreted as a general injunction on all Moslems constantly to make war on the infidels. It is generally supposed that the order for a general war can only be given by the imam.

— *Excerpt from Encyclopedia Brittanica,*
Eleventh Edition (1911)

Salman Rushdie

"To be born again," sang Gibreel Farishta tumbling from the heavens, "first you have to die. Ho ji! Ho ji! To land upon the bosomy earth, first one needs to fly. Tat-taa! Takathun! How to ever smile again, if first you won't cry? How to win the darling's love, mister, without a sigh? Baba, if you want to get born again . . ." Just before dawn one winter's morning, New Year's Day or thereabouts, two real, full-grown, living men fell from a great height, twenty-nine thousand and two feet, towards the English Channel, without benefit of parachutes or wings, out of a clear sky. "I tell you, you must die, I tell you, I tell you," and thusly and so beneath a moon of alabaster until a loud cry crossed the night, "To the devil with your tunes," the words hanging crystalline in the iced white night, "in the movies you only mimed to playback singers, so spare me these infernal noises now." Gibreel, the tuneless soloist, had been cavorting in moonlight as he sang his impromptu gazal, swimming in air, butterfly-stroke, breast-stroke, bunching himself into a ball, spread-eagling himself against the almost-infinity of the almost-dawn, adopting heraldic postures, rampant, couchant, pitting levity against gravity. Now he rolled happily towards the sardonic voice. "Ohé, Salad baba, it's you, too good. What-ho, old Chumch." At which the other, a fastidious shadow falling headfirst in a grey suit with all the jacket buttons done up, arms by his sides, taking for granted the improbability of the bowler hat on his head, pulled a nickname-hater's face. "Hey, Spoono," Gibreel yelled, eliciting a second inverted wince, "Proper London, bhai! Here we come! Those bastards down there won't know what hit them. Meteor or lightning or vengeance of God. Out of thin air, baby. Dharrraaammm! Wham, na? What an entrance, yaar. I swear: splat."

Out of thin air: a big bang, followed by falling stars. A universal beginning, a miniature echo of the birth of time . . . the jumbo jet Bostan, Flight AI-420, blew apart without any warning . . . . Who am I? Who else is there?

— *Excerpt from The Satanic Verses.*

WANTED DEAD OR ALIVE

☆ ☆ ☆ ☆ ☆ ☆ ☆ ☆ ☆ ☆

SALMAN RUSHDIE

☆ ☆ ☆ ☆ ☆ ☆ ☆ ☆ ☆ ☆

$3 MILLION DOLLAR

$ REWARD $

☞ CONTACT

THE IRANIAN

GOVERNMENT

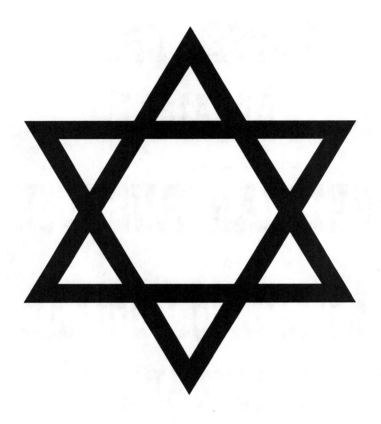

The Star of David originally appeared approximately, 6,000 B.C. in the most ancient history of India as the symbol for the Sun. Much later it was borrowed by the Semitic cult of Saturn of ancient Jerusalem, evolving later to become the Jewish Star of David.

Jewish Humanism

Sherwin T. Wine

Jewish history is the saga of a vulnerable international family. It is the tale of its struggle to survive. What is worst in Jewish history is the surrender to faith and humility. What is best in Jewish experience is the discovery of reason and dignity.

So many historians of the Jewish people have devoted their attention to what Jews theoretically believe that they have been unable to focus on what they actually do. Monotheism can produce placid peasants just as easily as it can produce nervous intellectuals. Torah study can create rote memorizers just as easily as it can produce analytic thinkers.

What is most interesting about the Jews is not a devotion to an invisible deity, who has his rivals in other traditions, and to moral platitudes, which are present in all cultures, but a personality style that deeply distrusts destiny and finds itself more comfortable with change than with eternity.

Only when we discard the conventional approach to the Jewish past can we understand the humanistic dimension of the Jewish experience. Human ingenuity and the absence of God are not the themes of Talmudic commentaries.

A *new* approach to Jewish history is necessary. But it is also difficult. Most popular presentations of the Jewish experience insist on the primacy of religious ideas. God and Torah (even when they are viewed as human creations) are regarded as the basic Jewish glue and the motivating powers of Jewish behavior. The implication is quite clear. If God and Torah are illusions, they are positive illusions. If they fade away, so will the Jewish personality – and the Jewish identity.

The religious emphasis distorts the way we approach the past. Since the most important religious figures lived a long time ago, the distant past becomes primary. The age of the prophets, priests, and rabbinic fathers outshines any other time. Moses becomes more significant than Einstein. Amos becomes more definitive than

Nathan Rothschild. The epic period of rabbinic Judaism stands out as the crucial time of Jewish achievement.

The consequences of this approach are harmful. They prevent us from seeing what we ought to see. Literature replaces events. We become more interested in the description of events than in the events themselves. If the author of the Torah tells us that Abraham was a real person and that he was very important, we tend to accept the statement – not because we have any reason to believe it, but because we are persuaded that trusting the Torah is essential to the preservation of Jewish identity.

Despite all the evidence that much of what the Torah says happened is different from what really happened, no one has boldly written a popular alternative to this priestly epic. The real history stays hidden in scholarly journals. No matter what deficiencies critical research discovers in the narrative of the Torah, the Torah never loses its status. The study of the Bible becomes a substitute for the study of Jewish history.

Since the rabbinic elite had a monopoly on published literature, personalities and events that did not fit into the rabbinic scheme were never mentioned. If you were a rabbi and had an opinion about whether chickens should be eaten with milk, you got a handsome citation in the Talmud. If you were a poet and sang the praises of Yahweh, the prayerbook acknowledged your contribution. But if you were the first Jewish banker or the best Jewish humorist, history has forgotten your name. The rabbis, like most religious elites, were not interested in preserving your memory. Only in the last two centuries would you have a chance for recognition.

Naturalistic Perspective

A humanistic approach to Jewish history needs a naturalistic perspective. The supernaturalist approach of the priestly and rabbinic theologians who edited the Bible and the Talmud is unacceptable. The semi-supernaturalist approach of contemporary historians who describe Jewish survival as a unique "mystery" is equally unacceptable. The causes of Jewish behavior and Jewish endurance are open to public investigation. If they are now unknown, they are not permanently unknowable. "Mystery" and "enigma" are contemporary coverups for supernatural direction. They suggest that the causes are beyond rational inquiry.

The laws of the Bible and the Talmud, the stories of sacred scriptures, the petitions of the prayerbook are of human creation. They are the products of human insight, human desire, and human vested interests. They are reflections of particular times and particular places. They are passionate propaganda in religious and political arguments. The stories of King Saul were written by the priestly employees of his enemy King David. The tale of Jezebel was composed by her prophetic opponents. The sacrificial ritual of Leviticus was designed by the priests who would benefit from it.

Human need — not divine aloofness — is responsible for what Jews did and said. It is also responsible for distorting what Jews did and said. The motivation for recording events and happenings was no dispassionate desire to keep a diary. It was the obvious need to use history to push political programs and religious ideologies. Is the story of the covenant between Abraham and Yahweh a journalistic observation of an actual event? Or is it a justification for the Jewish claim to all of ancient Canaan?

Holidays are not the children of supernatural decrees. They have their beginnings in the human response to natural events. Passover is not the spontaneous invention of a heavenly king. It is an evolving festival that served the nationalist fervor of patriotic rulers. Nor is Yom Kippur the creation of a judgmental god. It is a priestly device to increase the dread of Yahweh. The supernatural did not use the natural to promote its agenda. The human used the supernatural to advance its vested interests.

Seeing God behind all events is not necessary to explain what happens; human desire and natural laws do quite well. It is also potentially embarrassing. If Yahweh arranged for the Exodus, he also arranged for the Holocaust. The theological mileage that one can get from Jewish history is limited. Theology is always more interesting when it is relegated to its appropriate niche in the department of anthropology, a study of human fear and imagination.

Beyond Literature

A humanistic approach to Jewish history needs a determination to look beyond literature to *real* events. The Jewish experience is not the same as the description of that experience. The Bible is not the same as ancient Jewish history. It may be a key to what happened, but it is not a mirror of what happened. Nor are pious legends the same as Jewish history. A tradition may ascribe Davidic ancestry to

Hillel, but there is very little evidence to indicate that either Hillel or Jesus was descended from King David. Their respective protagonists simply wished to give them divine authority.

The history of a people is distinct from the value of its literature. The Torah may have a literary and religious importance above and beyond any narrative truth it may convey, but that religious importance is irrelevant to its accuracy when that accuracy counts. There is a difference between the Torah as an event in Jewish history and as a description of events. That people believed that Moses wrote the Torah is one issue. That Moses actually wrote it is another.

Jews are the products of their *real* experience – not the products of what the rabbis said their experience was. The struggle for power between kings and priests, priests and rabbis was an important political dimension in Jewish development. The Bible and the Talmud were the result of these political controversies, and the editors of these documents do not deal kindly with their opponents – who were equally as Jewish. The enemies of Jeremiah were just as Jewish and just as patriotic as Jeremiah when they refused to surrender Jerusalem to the Chaldeans. The Sadducee enemies of the rabbis were just as committed to Jewish survival as their competitors when they refused to accept the authority of the Oral Law (Talmud).

It is dangerous to pick your heroes and villains when you are able to read only one side of a religious controversy. The rabbis made sure that their view of Jewish history would prevail when they suppressed or destroyed all opposing points of view. As the victims of religious censorship, we should be aware of our victimization. The enemies of the rabbis might have given us a more balanced view of early Jewish history if their writings had survived.

Popular Religion

A humanistic approach to Jewish history needs to make a distinction between official religion and popular religion. The obsession with God is part of the official documents of the religious establishment, but it may not have been an obsession of the masses of the people. In fact, we know from all the denunciations in the Bible that polytheism was common in ancient Israel and that female deities (whom the prophets abhorred) were very popular.

The source of monotheistic ideas is no great spiritual ingenuity. It is a political structure called imperialism. World gods are the reflection of world government. Just as tribal government features tribal gods and national government features national gods, so do empires sponsor the birth of supergods. Monotheism was no Jewish invention. The Egyptians, the Persians, and the Greeks all had their fling at it. Aton, Mazda, and Zeus became divine superstars just like Yahweh – and with more reason. Yahweh, the world ruler, coincides with the advent of Assyrian, Chaldean, and Persian empires. He is a political explanation, not a spiritual revolution.

From the very beginning, monotheism was an ill-fitting shoe. It could never adequately explain the defeats and humiliations that pious Jews experienced. Only the addition of future rewards and punishment made it fit better. Popular religion still kept its demons and evil spirits, reflections of the disorder and disharmony of things. The masses experienced the terror of the world. No serene orderly deity was enough to handle the difficulties of daily living. In the end, the groom broke the glass at the end of the wedding ceremony to frighten away the evil spirits (whom Yahweh was obviously incapable of disciplining). Folk religion and the official religion very often did not coincide.

One of the reasons why the Bible is more appealing to rural Southerners than to Westchester County Jews is the fact that the authors of the documents were writing for farmers and shepherds. Some of the current emphasis on the Biblical period in Jewish history arises from the Zionist need to identify with a period in Jewish history when the Jews were free and independent on their own land. But much of it comes from the enormous discomfort that many Jews feel with what they are. They have the same distaste for a mobile, individualistic urban milieu that most historic conservatives do. They want to identify with what Jews used to be a long time ago — even though, if this option were offered, they would reject it.

The Jewish personality, with all its verbal pushy edges, is not a product of peasant lovers of the Torah. It is an urban product, finely tuned to city life and city anxiety. If a high percentage of Jews have intellectual or "cultural" interests (or pretensions), it is not because they memorized Bible verses. If most Jews adapt easily to the demand and requirements of modern urban living (and are successful out of all proportion to their numbers), it is not because they were verbally skilled in Talmudic arguments. Quite the opposite. Polish *pilpul* (Talmudic verbal games) was the direct result of an urbanized culture that placed great emphasis on talking and verbal exhibitionism. City communities value verbal skills even more than physical prowess.

Equal Time

A humanistic approach to Jewish history gives equal time to both the immediate past and the distant past. It avoids the propaganda needs of rabbinic Judaism.

The official ideology (both in its traditional and liberal forms) does not see the last two thousand years of Jewish existence to be of equal value to the first two thousand years. In the eyes of the rabbinic establishment, Amos, Hosea, Isaiah, and Jeremiah have no modern duplicates. They were spiritual phenomena unique to olden times. The events of their time are more important because these "divine" messengers responded to them, and the people of their time are more important because the prophets used them as an audience. Later centuries are inferior because they simply did not produce the prophets or the rabbinic fathers.

But such an approach is naive. What the prophets said is less important than what later centuries did with what they said. (Just as what Madison and Hamilton intended is less significant than what the American Supreme Court did with the American Constitution.) The anonymous urbanites of later years used the Bible prophet Amos for *their* purpose. Their opinions were more powerful in the development of Jewish identity than the rejected advice of an executed prophet. You will not understand Christianity by studying the life of Jesus, and you will not understand the story of Jewish identity by focusing on the life of Amos.

What is historically important is not the Amos of the distant past – but the bourgeois reformers and Marxist radicals who used him. Dead heroes are the most useful authorities. They cannot challenge what you make their words mean. Amos may have been the defender of a stern Bedouin morality that most progressives would find appalling. But today, he is dressed up to fit neatly into either liberal charity or radical redistribution. It is this phenomenon that is far more interesting than the self-proclaimed prophet of Tekoah. Most of what Amos "said" is really a reflection of what most modern Jews think and believe – and of those more recent events that produced such opinions.

Jewish radical intellectuals are not the children of the distant Amos. They are the children of verbal, alienated urbanites who have no reason to love a hostile establishment. Understanding this alienation has far more to do with Jewish identity than quotations ripped out of their pastoral context.

Using the distant past to "kosherize" the present has two harmful effects. It prevents us from really understanding the past. We are less interested in finding out what Moses and Amos and Akiba really did and said and more interested in making sure that they are on our side. It also minimizes the importance of the present and the immediate past by pretending that recent developments are really old ones. We focus on the quotation and not on the people who use it.

Most of the people whose decisions determined the character of Jewish identity are now unknown. They lived in a time when "sacred scriptures" were rampant, when nothing labeled original was deemed to have any value, and when new opinions were always disguised as interpretations of old ones. "Distant pastitis" is an old religious disease. It corrupts our judgment and prevents it from being fair to either the past or the present.

Human Motivation

A humanistic approach to Jewish history looks for human motives. If the author of the opinions in the Bible, the Talmud, and the Siddur were God, then we would be searching for divine motivations (if God can have any) that have nothing at all to do with jealousy, hatred, and the struggle for power. But if the authors of these opinions are people, then it is appropriate for us to investigate the human desires that motivated them to write what they did — which, indeed, may have a lot to do with jealousy, hatred, and the struggle for power.

Personal fulfillment and fame – important modern motivations – were not the reasons why the documents of the religious establishment were written. They were written as persuasive literature, or what we call propaganda. They were intended to persuade Jews to defend certain ideas, to adopt certain practices, and to obey certain authorities. They were also intended to persuade Jews to reject certain ideas, to discard certain practices, and to ignore certain authorities.

Jewish history is the tale of intense rivalries. Different groups vie for power, and their literature is their propaganda. The dead David and the dead Moses become the symbols of competing elites, who tell their stories to serve their interests. What happened to the Jews is no different from what happened to other nations. New groups tried to overthrow old groups. Having succeeded and feeling vulnerable, they felt the need to justify their rule.

The Secular Revolution upset this game. Emancipation liberated Jews from the control of Jewish authorities. History might be used to push passionate points of view (like this book), but competing views were no longer destroyed. The emergence of the social sciences made judgments more open to public scrutiny and challenge.

There has been more diversity of opinion and belief in Jewish history than the rabbinic establishment ever wanted to reveal. There is no unbroken chain of tradition from Moses to the present. The propaganda of the early tribal *shofetim* was replaced by the propaganda of the Davidic kings, and the royal tradition was in turn replaced by the priestly tradition. The rabbinic triumph was a radical break with the priestly authority that came before. Jewish elites were quite human in their ambitions. We make them less interesting when we turn them into noble parrots of supernatural perfection. Love, kindness, generosity, and dignity would not be commendable achievements if they did not arise out of a more sordid context. Saints are boring, and supernatural advice is always patronizing.

Sherwin T. Wine is a rabbi and honorary doctorate, founder and spokesperson for numerous organizations, including the Society for Humanistic Judaism and Americans For Religious Liberty.

Vision

Less than 4,000 years ago

there were no Jews

Less than 2,000 years ago

there were no Christians

Less than 1,400 years ago

there were no Muslims

What were they then?

Were they not what they

always had been?

— Adolph Levy

False Messiahs, Saints and Saviors

For false Christs and false prophets will rise, and show great signs and wonders, so as to lead astray, if possible, even the elect.

— Matthew 24:24

Abraham Ben Samuel Abulafia (1240-1291?) Born in Spain, Abulafia left his native land in 1260 to search for a mythical ruler in Israel. Through his boldness and charisma, he gained a large following eager to believe that redemption was at hand.

Jan Bockelson, (John of Leiden) 1590-1536. The son of a Leiden merchant, Bockelson was a tailor by trade before joining the radical Dutch Anabaptist movement. Bockelson was taken into captivity and, like Christ on the cross, was ridiculed by his captors for not saving himself if he was really the messiah. Sentenced to death, in 1535 he was shackled to a stake, scorched with heated pincers and detongued.

Sabbatai Zebi (1626-1676). The central figure in the largest messianic movement in Jewish history, Sabbatai Zebi was born in Smyrna Turkey. He was waiting for god to send him a bride. That bride was Sarah, a Polish prostitute who had long maintained that she was destined to marry the messiah. Word of Sabbatai's mission quickly spread from Jerusalem throughout Palestine and eventually across Europe. His wanton sexual activity and erratic behavior eventually drew fire from Muslim authorities, who exiled him to the remote Albanian seaport of Dulcigno (now Ulcinj, Yugoslavia) where he died on September 17, the day of Atonement in 1676.

Jemima Wilkenson (1752-1829). According to Wilkenson, the daughter of a Quaker farmer in Rhode Island, she "died" when she was 20. Before her family could bury her, however, she rose as a reincarnation of Christ, sent on a divine mission to found the Church and prepare the Chosen Few for the second Coming, scheduled to occur, she said, in her lifetime.

Jemima Wilkenson died the second time. In keeping with her instructions, members did not bury her but instead waited anxiously for her to rise once again. As her body decomposed the faith of many of the Universal Friends declined. Their numbers dwindled rapidly, and in 1874 the last believer died.

Hung Sin-tsuan. Born in Fuyuanshui village, Kwantung Province, China, Hung repeatedly failed the national civil service examination. His cousin gave him a Christian pamphlet entitled, "Good Words for Exhorting the Age." Hung believed he finally understood the meaning of the hallucinations he had suffered during his breakdown six years earlier. He proclaimed himself as sent by heaven to drive out the Tatars, and to restore in his own person the succession to China.

Together with his disciple Feng Yun-shan, he engineered the Tai Ping Rebellion (1850-1865), a revolt against the ruling Ching (or the Manchu) dynasty. The extreme poverty, crowded conditions, widespread xenophobia, and general discontent under the alien Manchus attracted legions of followers to Hung. His armies captured hundreds of cities, most notably Nanking in 1853.

Hung swallowed poison in June, 1864, six years before the fall of Nanking to Manchu forces. Hung's Tai Ping Rebellion cost millions of lives.

Orix Bovar (1917-1977). A quiet charismatic figure who drifted from astrology to mysticism, Boyar by the mid-1970s had attracted some 200 followers in New York and California. He appealed to such people as Carol Burnett and Bernadette Peters. However, he alienated many when he announced that he was Jesus Christ and began celebrating Christmas with the faithful on August 29, his own birthday.

Arrested for failing to report a death, Bovar told police (who, responding to a tip, raided the apartment where the vigil was being held) that he was trying to raise his disciple from the dead. On April 14, 1977, shortly before he was scheduled to appear in court to respond to the charges, he jumped from his 10th-floor apartment.

Joan of Arc: "Joan of the Bow" – Joan the Huntress. Joan herself stated that she received her mission "at the tree of the Fairy-ladies," a center of the Dianic cult at Domremy. In 1429, ecclesiastical judges examined her and announced that the holy angels had appointed her to save France. Later, the Bishop of Beauvais reversed this decision. In 1431, aged only 19, she was burned as a witch at Rouen, wearing a placard that said, "Relapsed, Heretic, Apostate, Idolater."

For 500 years, Joan remained a popular national heroine until she was finally canonized by Pope Benedict XV in 1920. Ironically, the same church that pronounced Joan a witch and had her killed, now claims her as a saint.

Christopher Columbus: Columbus discovered America, the most significant event for the human race after the birth, death, and resurrection of the Savior of the world. Faith liberated Columbus from the chains of human myopia, launching him on a divine mission and propelling him to a providential destination initiating the histories of the United States, Canada, and the numerous American Republics.

In 1501, Christopher Columbus, navigator and admiral, announced that he was the Messiah prophesied by Joachim, the Calabrian Abbot. His geographical discovery of a direct route for missionaries to the Orient – he died without ever learning that he hadn't reached the East Indies – was the climax of the fifteen centuries since Christ. The next climax in history would be a successful last crusade. His calling was to lead the Christian armies.

Guiseppe Desa was born in Copertino, in the heel of Italy, in 1603. Later, as St. Joseph of Copertino, he became famous as the "Flying Monk" because of his remarkable levitations during ecstatic states.

His early life was very similar to that of Jesus Christ. Joseph's father was a poor carpenter who, after considerable harassment from creditors, was forced to move his pregnant wife away from town. It is said that Joseph was born in a stable. At school he was called "Open Mouth" because of his tendency to sit motionless with mouth agape, staring at the heavens. Just over 100 years after Joseph's death, on July 16, 1767, it was formally announced that the Flying Friar had been made a saint.

Maitreya – the current "Savior" – lives in and out of London. Supposedly he descended in July of 1977 from his ancient retreat in the Himalayas. He now appears "out of the blue" and is recognized by his followers as "The Christ." His followers keep the world apprised of his appearance via a newsletter, *The Emergence*.

Messiah

Lubavitcher 'Messiah' Schneerson dies

JUNE 13, 1994 — Rabbi Menachem Schneerson, the charismatic leader of hundreds of thousands of Orthodox Jews who believe he was the Messiah, died at the age of 92. His followers danced, sang and drank cases of beer, insisting that his resurrection is near.

The Rabbi did not resurrect in three days. Many followers immediately concocted a new story in line with the 40 days fable. The Rabbi would now come back in conjunction with the comets hitting Jupiter.

The comets were seen by Jews and fundamentalists as a sign of the immediate end times. (Well, maybe next time.)

How to Recognize the Messiah

- He must be of the seed of Abraham.
  (Genesis 22:18)
- He must be of the tribe of Judah.
  (Genesis 49:10)
- He must be of the house of David.
  (Isaiah 9:7)
- He must be born of a virgin.
  (Isaiah 7:14; but see pg. 178-180, 188)
- He must be born in Bethlehem.
  (Micah 5:2; but see pg. 158-9)
- He must be God.
  (Isaiah 9:6; but see pg. 122 and Matt. 19:17)

Good News Publishers claim Jesus fits the above qualifications and is therefore the MESSIAH. Some of these claims are challenged elsewhere in *The Book*.

★ —————————————————————— ★

Many Supreme Gods

Akditi: Mother of gods, India

Ahriman: Son of Zuruam, the all-powerful evil one – Persia

Ajbit+Alom-Bhol: One of the creators of humans – Maya

Amon (aka Amon Re): Became king of gods – Egypt

Aten: God of Sun – Egypt

Bochica: Supreme creator and law giver – Chibcha Indian

Brahma: Creator and Absolute – India

Coyote: God of creation – Crow Indian

Dohit: God who created first mortal from clay – Mosetene

Gamab: Supreme god living in heavens – Damarus, Africa

Inti: Supreme god, god of sun – Inca

Jar-Sub: God of Universe – Turkey

Juck-Shilluck: Creator of the world – Africa

Kumani: Virgin goddess –India

Mahaskti: Divine mother, supreme creator of universe –
India

Num: Supreme first god, creator, home is 7th Heaven –
Samoyed

Manibozho: God who created earth and mortals out of clay –
Algonquin Indians

Marduk: Supreme god, sun god – Babylon

Maui: Sons of the sun – Polynesia

Pachacamac: Supreme god, creator of all – Yuncas

Parica: God who flooded the earth (not at the time of the Old
Testament flood) – Peru

Radogast: God of sun – Slav

Tengri: God of sky – Mongol

— *Ye Gods*, Anne Baumgartner

Kanati

The Great Hunter, First Cherokee Man, and First Conservationist. The Cherokee Artist is John Guthrie, and this painting is from the permanent collection of the Cherokee Heritage Museum and Gallery, Saunooke Village, Cherokee, North Carolina.

Chief Seattle Speaks

Chief Seattle

How can you buy or sell the sky, the warmth of the land? The idea is strange to us. If we do not own the freshness of the air and the sparkle of the water, how can you buy them?

Every part of the earth is sacred to my people. Every shining pine needle, every sandy shore, every mist in the dark woods, every clearing and humming insect is holy in the memory and experiences of my people. The sap which courses through the trees carries the memories of the red man.

The white man's dead forget the country of their birth when they go to walk among the stars. Our dead never forget this beautiful earth, for it is the mother of the red man. We are a part of the earth, and it is a part of us. The perfumed flowers are our sisters; the deer, the horse, the great eagle, these are our brothers. The rocky crests, the juices in the meadows, the body heat of the pony, and man – all belong to the same family. So, when the Great Chief in Washington sends word that he wishes to buy our land, he asks much of us. The Great Chief sends word he will reserve us a place so that we can live comfortably to ourselves.

He will be our father, and we will be his children. So we will consider your offer to buy our land. But it will not be easy. For this land is sacred to us. This shining water that moves in the streams and the rivers is not just water but the blood of our ancestors. If we sell you land, you must remember that it is sacred, and you must teach your children that it is sacred and that each reflection in the clear water of the lakes tells of events and memories in the life of my people. The water's murmur is the voice of my father's father.

The rivers are our brothers, they quench our thirst. The rivers carry our canoes and feed our children. If we sell you our land, you must remember, and teach your children, that the rivers are our brothers, and yours, and you must henceforth give the rivers the kindness you would give any brother.

We know that the white man does not understand our ways. One portion of land is the same to him as the next, for he is a stranger who comes in the night and takes from the land whatever he needs.

The earth is not his brother, but his enemy, and when he has conquered it, he moves on. He leaves his fathers' graves, and his children's birthright is forgotten. He treats his mother, the earth, and his brother, the sky, as things to be bought, plundered, sold like sheep or bright beads. His appetite will devour the earth and leave behind only a desert.

I do not know. Our ways are different from your ways. The sight of your cities pains the eyes of the red man. But perhaps it is because I am a savage and do not understand.

There is no quiet place in the white man's cities. No place to hear the unfurling of leaves in spring, or the rustle of an insect's wings. The clatter only seems to insult the ears. And what is there to life if a man cannot hear the lonely cry of the whippoorwill or the arguments of the frogs around a pond at night? I am a red man and do not understand. The Indian prefers the soft sound of the wind darting over the face of a pond, and the smell of the wind itself, cleansed by rain or scented with the pine cone.

The air is precious to the red man, for all things share the same breath: the beast, the tree, the man, they all share the same breath. The white man does not seem to notice the air he breathes. Like a man dying for many days, he is numb to the stench. But if we sell you our land, you must remember that the air is precious to us, that the air shares its spirit with all the life it supports. The wind that gave our grandfather his first breath also received his last sigh. And if we sell you our land, you must keep it apart and sacred, as a place where even the white man can go to taste the wind that is sweetened by the meadow's flowers.

So we will consider your offer to buy our land. If we decide to accept, I will make one condition. The white man must treat the beasts of this land as his brothers.

I am savage, and I do not understand any other way. I have seen a thousand rotting buffalos on the prairie, left by the white man who shot them from a passing train. I am a savage, and I do not understand how the smoking iron horse can be more important than the buffalo that we kill only to stay alive.

What is man without the beasts? If all the beasts were gone, man would die from a great loneliness of spirit. For whatever happens to the beasts soon happens to man. All things are connected.

You must teach your children that the ground beneath their feet is the ashes of our grandfathers. So that they will respect the land, tell your children that the earth is rich with the lives of our kin. Teach your children what we have taught our children, that the earth is our mother. Whatever befalls the earth, befalls the sons of the earth. Man did not weave the web of life, he is merely a strand in it. Whatever he does to the web, he does to himself.

Even the white man, whose God walks and talks with him as friend to friend, cannot be exempt from the common destiny. We may be brothers after all. We shall see. One thing we know, which the white man may one day discover – our God is the same God. You may think now that you own him as you wish to own our land: but you cannot. He is the God of man, and his compassion is equal for the red man and the white. This earth is precious to him, and to harm the earth is to heap contempt upon its Creator.

The whites, too, shall pass; perhaps sooner than all the other tribes. Contaminate your bed, and you will one night suffocate in your own waste. But in your perishing, you will shine brightly, fired by the strength of the God who brought you to this land and for some special purpose gave you dominion over this land and over the red man. That destiny is a mystery to us, for we do not understand when the buffalo are all slaughtered, the wild horses are tamed, the secret corners of the forest heavy with the scent of many men, and the view of the ripe hills blotted out by talking wires. Where is the thicket? Gone. Where is the eagle? Gone.

Reprinted from Global Outlook News, *which says that Chief Seattle was a native American "born in the last years of the 18th century. This speech was given in the early part of the 19th century. It is particularly poignant to us now."*

"This great continent could not have been kept as nothing but a game preserve for squalid savages," wrote Teddy Roosevelt as the guns fell silent on the plains.

— Vine Deloria, Jr. *The World of the American Indian*

Comment on Chief Seattle's Speech

It is a beautiful speech. It expresses sentiments that it is well worth our while to heed. It reminds us of what we have done to the Native Americans and what we are doing to our land and natural resources. It expresses a religious faith at sharp variance with the Christianity that is the subject of much in this book. It deserves inclusion in this book on its merits.

There is a second reason for including it. There are several chapters in this book devoted to how the Bible or certain parts of it came to be written. The authors have raised doubts of the divine inspiration and inerrancy of Bible text, and one has noted the "composite" nature of some of it – interwoven strands from two or more sources. The speech by Chief Seattle published here is a 20th-century example of *the same process.*

A careful reader might entertain doubts about iron horses in the plains and mass destruction of buffaloes, as told by one who lived in the Pacific Northwest and died in the 1860's, especially in a speech alleged to have been "given in the early part of the 19th century." The doubts are justified. A brilliant piece of detective work by Dr. Rudolf Kaiser, a professor in a German "hochschule", gives us a good idea of the provenance of the speech in its present form. (Much of the ecological material in the speech dates from the early 1970's.)

The religion of Mother Earth is both ancient and new. It is a reaction to both Judaeo-Christianity and the technocratic faiths. It may well become the religion of the Age of Aquarius. Chief Seattle's Speech is part of the Holy Scripture of this new religion.

By William B. Lindley, associate editor, Truth Seeker, *Freethought publication, founded in 1873.*

Dead Sea Scrolls

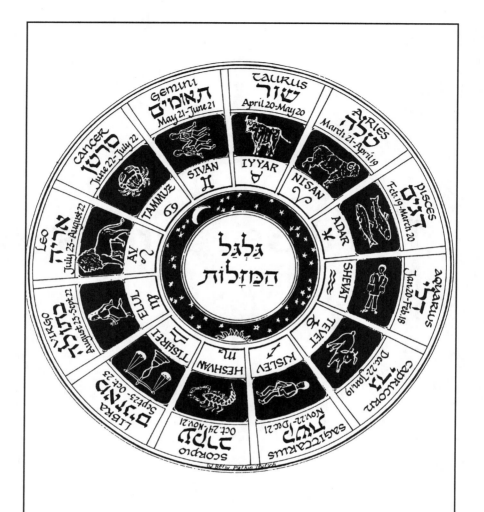

Calendar of The Zodiac

The basis for most religions in world history

Astrology In The Dead Sea Scrolls

Alan Albert Snow

It is truly amazing that any of the Dead Sea Scrolls have survived into the Twentieth century. There is now proof that there is a link between these ancient scrolls, first-century Judaism, the early Christian church, and the ancient practice of astrology. Scholars and churchmen alike are astonished to know of this connection and are still having a problem with reconciling a discredited occult practice like astrology with the edited, revised, and sanitized version of religion that is presented to the public in our modern churches.

The Dead Sea Scrolls were discovered in the Judean desert in 1947 by a Bedouin Arab in the caves near an archaeology site near Kirbet Qumran in what is now the State of Israel. Today's readers will be surprised to learn that some of the Bedouin Arabs used some of these priceless scrolls as fuel for their campfires. The clay containers that protected the scrolls for the last two thousand years were reused as water jugs on the Bedouin donkeys. Some of the leather scrolls were recycled by local cobblers by sewing them to the bottom of their sandals. Several of the scrolls found their way into the marketplace where merchants of antiquities would sell them to private collectors and tourists.

The scrolls of the astrological horoscopes were found in Cave 4 near the ruins of the Essene community in Qumran, where the community hid their religious library. At this time the Romans were invading the land of Judea and were destroying everything in their path. Some modern Biblical scholars and archaeologists believe that these scrolls could have been hidden in the caves as late as the Jewish revolt of 132 - 135 A.D.

The inclusion of *horoscopes* with the other sectarian writings and the commonly accepted Hebrew scriptures has three significant implications:

- These horoscopes were chosen to be ca[...]
  generations;
- This "science" of astrology was practi[...]
  the devotees of the Essene sect; and . . .
- It was also practiced by the early church[...]
  the Jewish and Roman rulers of first-cen[...]
  of the Gentile nations that surrounded J[...]

Many modern Biblical scholars believe tha[...]
that was so popular during the time of Jesus[...]
three magi of the Christian nativity legend in the New Testament are
now believed to have been astrologers and not the fabled "three
kings" of an alternative nativity narrative. The Hellenized Jewish
historian Josephus mentioned the "star prophecy," as did the Roman
historians Suetonius and Tacitus. Even the militant Jewish revolutionary Simon bar Kochba (Simon the "son of a star") used the star
reference in his name to show his followers that he was one of the
men whom God had destined "to go forth and rule the world."

The authors of the Dead Sea Scrolls were Zealots and believed in
the God-ordained destiny of the people of Israel. The Essenes believed
that their community was the true and righteous Israel and did not
recognize neutrality. They considered as enemies all who did not
join them. These would be the followers of the Herodians – the
Sudducees in the Temple of Jerusalem and the puppet kings appointed by the Emperor of Rome. Many different shades of Jews Zealous
for the Law (of Moses) are associated with the devotees of Qumran.

Modern Biblical scholars and archaeologists are just now learning
much that is new and enlightening about the traditional Bible
through the Dead Sea Scrolls. These first-century documents are
shedding new light on lost meanings of ancient Aramaic and
Hebrew terms that have been so clouded and mystified by sectarian
misunderstandings of ancient Biblical readings.

The connection between the Early Church and Judaism is now
believed by many modern scholars to be the Essene Qumran community. The spectacular similarities in ritual practices, teachings,
and literary terms are so obvious that only the most stubborn and
fundamentalist Christian will continue in believing in the special
uniqueness of the so-called Christian message. Christianity is now
being seen as a kind of religio-cultural mutation, over the first
hundred years of the Christian Era, of the Essene community in

Jerusalem. It is now believed that Jesus' brother, James the Righteous, is the same Teacher of Righteousness who plays such a central role in the texts of the Dead Sea Scrolls.

The Essenes called themselves the Nozrei ha-Brit, known also as the Nozrim, Nasoreans, Nazarenes, the *Keepers Of The Covenant*. The early Christians called themselves *Nazarenes* before they were called Christians in paganized Antioch. By the time that so many Gentiles were coming into the Nazarene religious community, the Nazarenes were moving farther and farther away from their Jewish roots. The Qumran community's ritual of washing in a ritual bath for the washing away of sins became the Christian baptism. The Essene common meal of bread and wine became the Christian Mass. The observant Jewish rabbi Jesus the Nazarene became the effeminate Serapis-style Gentile god.

The Hebrew scriptures were demoted to the Old Testament, as opposed to the Hellenized and paganized New Testament for the Greek world. The separation of Judaism and the new Gentile Christianity was complete.

The literal accuracy of the Bible has had to be reconsidered in the last one hundred years. The new sciences of archaeology and literary criticism have voided many of our presuppositions about the historicity of many of the events in Judea at the time of Jesus. Many modern Biblical archaeologists now believe that the village of Nazareth did not exist at the time of the birth and early life of Jesus. There is simply no evidence for it. There is a village of Nazareth that appears on the Roman Judean maps after the death of Jesus. This new archaeological discovery would agree with the way that the Essenes referred to themselves in the Dead Sea Scrolls.

As noted above, they called themselves the Keepers of the Covenant, the Nazarenes ha-Brit (the community of the Nazarenes). Jesus was referred to as Jesus the Nazarene (ha-Brit); in other words, there are now many reasons to believe that Jesus was simply an observant Essene Jew of his time, not the Greco-Roman god of the later Roman Empire State Church under Emperor Constantine!

It is now speculated that the Hellenic Greek writers of the Greek New Testament had lost this fine distinction between the late town of Nazareth and the meaning of the term Nazarenes. This could easily have happened after the destruction of the Jewish state in either 70 A.D. or 135 A.D. Much of the New Testament was written as late as seventy years after the death of Jesus the Nazarene.

Another misunderstanding in the traditional teachings of religious orthodoxy is that both the first-century Jews and early church used the same lunar calendar that is used by modern Jews all over the world for determining the true Jewish holidays. The writers of the Dead Sea Scrolls and, very likely, the early observant Hebrew Christians (the early church), carefully placed their solar calendars in the same caves where they stored their scriptures and sectarian writings.

These two sets of calendars that were in use in Judea at the time of Jesus explain the differences in the gospel stories and the conflicts in the timing of the final days of Jesus. These two calendars also explain why the followers of the Herodian High Priest in Jerusalem could work on days that were forbidden to the Essenes in the Judean desert. Their same holidays and holy days were falling on different days of the week! More of the details of the uses of the solar calendar will be brought to light as soon as these particular scrolls are studied in greater detail by modern Biblical scholars.

Scholars and other interested individuals are fortunate to be living in the late twentieth century when religious authorities and other "special interest" experts can no longer edit out the astrological references and other historically hidden information in the Dead Sea Scrolls. This rediscovered way of viewing the first-century world must be accepted and recognized by the entire modern academic community.

The intellectual elitists of the traditional orthodox religions who kept this information from fellow scholars and the general public had their monopoly broken by the (American) Biblical Archaeology Society in 1991. All of the "unpublished" Dead Sea Scrolls were finally given to the whole world in the unedited, uncensored, and unrevised two-volume set titled: *A Facsimile Edition of the Dead Sea Scrolls*, (Biblical Archaeology Society, November 19, 1991).

Alan Albert Snow is a member of the Board of Directors of the Institute for Judeo-Christian Origins Studies, California State University, Long Beach. He is also a charter member of the Institute for Dead Sea Scrolls Studies, Biblical Archaeology Society, and earned his M.A. at the School of Theology, Claremont, California.

Robert Eisenman And The "Last Revelation"

The last two or three years have been exciting times for those interested in the Dead Sea Scrolls and how they might bear on religion, especially Christianity. Dr. Robert Eisenman, professor at Cal State U, Long Beach, and chairman of the Department of Religious Studies, has been part of the action.

The various scrolls were discovered, starting in 1947 and continuing into the 1950's. Some of the material remained under study *but unpublished* for over 40 years. John N. Wilford reports in the New York Times: "All of the full-length scrolls have been published, including most of the biblical material. At issue have been hundreds of thousands of fragments from some 600 previously unpublished documents, mainly prayers, commentaries, prophecies and rules of conduct and worship." (Another source gives "more than 75,000 fragments.")

Dr. Eisenman has figured prominently in recent activity in two senses:

1) He has been instrumental in getting the fragmentary material into the public domain.

2) He has offered an interpretation of one of the fragments that bears strongly on the Christian story of Jesus as Redeemer.

Robert Eisenman found a fragment in the unpublished corpus about a Messianic leader who will either "put" or "be put to death." Another fragment, which he and Professor Michael Wise, who shares some of his views, found relates to "healing the sick," "resurrecting the dead" and "announcing glad tidings to the poor." Professor Wise claims this relates to a "suffering Messiah" very close to what is said about Jesus in Luke 4. Professor Eisenman feels it is descriptive of "God's saving acts." In these passages, Eisenman and Wise may be looking at the "missing link" between Judaism and Christianity.

In the spring of 1986 at the end of his stay in Jerusalem, Professor Eisenman went with the British scholar, Philip Davies of the University of Sheffield, to see one of the Israeli officials responsible for the long delay – an intermediary on behalf of the Antiquities Department (now "Authority") and the International Team and the Scrolls Curator at the Israel Museum. They were told in no uncertain terms, "You will not see the Scrolls in your lifetimes."

But this was not to be. The Scroll fragments did become available. Here's how it happened: first, in the late 1950's, a card index was made for each word that appeared in the fragments, with its context and reference. Next, in 1988, a "Preliminary Concordance" was published, which was effectively this card index. (The publishers apparently thought this wasn't letting the cat out of the bag, but it was.)

Thirdly, Martin Abegg, a graduate student, together with his professor, Dr. Ben Zion Wacholder, with computer assistance, reconstructed the text from the concordance and published this text. Fourthly, the Huntington Library, which had a microfilm copy of the Scroll fragments, decided to make it openly available to scholars. Dr. Eisenman was instrumental in this decision. He and others had long been urging open access.

"So what in effect do we have in these manuscripts?" asks Eisenman. Probably nothing less than a picture of the movement from which Christianity sprang in Palestine. But there is more – if we take into consideration the Messianic nature of the text, and allied concepts such as "Righteousness," "Piety," "justification," "works," "the Poor," "Mysteries," what we have is a picture of what Christianity actually *was* in Palestine. The reader, however, probably will not be able to recognize it because it will seem virtually the opposite of the Christianity with which he or she is familiar. This is particularly the case in documents such as the two Letters on Works Righteousness.

Both movements used the same vocabulary, the same scriptural passages as proof texts, similar conceptual contexts; but the one can be characterized as the mirror reversal of the other. While the Palestinian one was zealot, nationalistic, xenophobic, and apocalyptic, the overseas one was cosmopolitan, antinomian, pacifistic – in a word "Paulinized." Equally we can refer to the first as Jamesian, at least if we judge by the letter ascribed to James' name in the New Testament, which both Eusebius and Martin Luther felt should not be included in the New Testament. Of course in their eyes it should not have been, as its general thrust parallels that of many documents from Qumran and it is full of Qumranisms.

These were not people who loved their enemies. They were a militant, violent, aggressive group preparing for the last apocalyptic war against all evil.

Other interesting scroll fragments, Eisenman says, include:

- A revision of the Noah flood story that changes the chronology of events as reported in the bible;

- Mystical material similar to that contained in the Kaballah – an early book of Jewish mysticism – which attests to the rapturous excitement of these early religionists;

- "It gives a lot of ammunition to people into the liberation theology of Latin America," Eisenman said, referring to Christians who advocate religious-based social activism.

Dr. Eisenman's book, *The Dead Sea Scrolls Uncovered*, is now available, published by Element Press.

Think not that I am come to send peace on earth: I came not to send peace, but a sword.

— Jesus Christ, *Matt. 10:34*

Judge rules professor had copyright on Scrolls work

JERUSALEM — In a verdict that could have significant implications for research on the Dead Sea Scrolls, a Jerusalem court ruled Tuesday that an Israeli professor had a copyright on his reconstruction of one of the most important of the ancient Jewish manuscripts.

BACKGROUND

The case was the first court test in a controversy over publication of the Dead Sea Scrolls since tight limits on access to the documents were lifted more than a year ago. The verdict appeared to bolster the status of authorized scroll editors. About 800 scrolls, considered one of the century's great archaeological finds, were found more than 40 years ago near the Dead Sea. Written between the second century BC and AD 70, they contain the oldest known copies of the Old Testament and are believed to provide insights into Judaic history and Christianity's origins.

— The New York Times

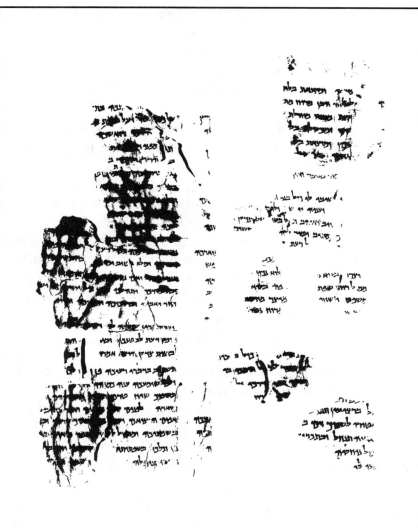

Unpublished Dead Sea Scroll

— Source: Unknown

A Jamesian-like admonition from the Dead Sea
Scrolls proves to be an interesting parallel to the
letters of James.

The Dead Sea Scrolls And The Essenes

The Dead Sea Scrolls, newly liberated from the frightened grip of Christian researchers, have shown the Essenes to have been the direct forerunners of the Christian communities.

The Essenes were the prototype Christians. We find many well-known expressions in the Dead Sea Scrolls such as . . . pierced . . . crucified Messiah, etc. . .

Christianity as "progressive revelation" turns out to be a hoax. The so-called "prophecies" referring to Jesus were mistranslated, with some verses or words omitted or added. The majority of the "prophecies" were statements after the facts. The Essenes and Zealots were never mentioned, because they *were* the Christians, or their close associates.

By Joseph Margulies, honorary president of the Jerusalem Institute of Biblical Polemics, Jerusalem, Israel. Published in the Biblical Polemics *magazine, Issue No. 48, April 1992.*

QUMRAN AND THE DEAD SEA

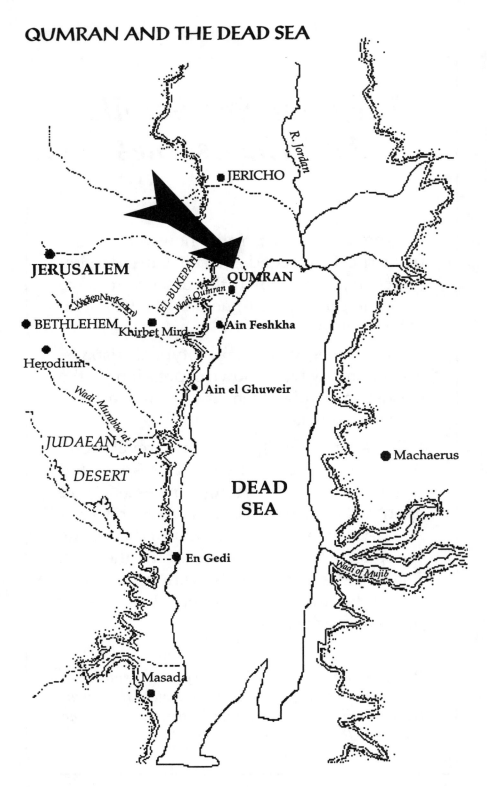

Dead Sea Scrolls Coverup

Biblical manuscripts dating back to at least 200 BC are for sale. This would be an ideal gift to an educational or religious institution by an individual or group. Box F 206.

Such was the advertisement that appeared in the *Wall Street Journal* on 1 June 1954. Were an advertisement of this sort to appear today, it would no doubt be thought some species of practical joke, not entirely in the best of taste.

Today, of course, the Dead Sea Scrolls are well enough known, if only by name. Most people, while having an extremely nebulous idea of what they are, will at least have heard of them. If nothing else, there exists an awareness that the scrolls are in some way genuinely precious items, archaeological evidence of immense importance.

The discovery of the Dead Sea Scrolls in 1947 generated a flurry of excitement both in scholarly circles and among the general public. But by 1954 that excitement had been skillfully defused. The scrolls, it was assumed, had revealed everything they were going to reveal, and this was made to seem less dramatic than had been expected.

In tracing the progress of the Dead Sea Scrolls from their discovery in the Judaean desert to the various institutions that hold them today, we found ourselves confronting a contradiction we had faced before, the contradiction between the Jesus of history and the Christ of faith. Our investigation began in Israel. It was to extend to the corridors of the Vatican, and even more ominously, into the offices of the Inquisition. We also encountered a rigidly maintained "consensus" of interpretation towards the content and dating of the scrolls, and came to understand how explosive a non-partisan examination might be for the whole of Christ tradition. And we discovered how fiercely the world of orthodox biblical scholarship was prepared to fight to retain its monopoly of available information.

Excerpt from The Dead Sea Scrolls Deception *by Michael Baigent and Richard Leigh (authors of* Holy Blood, Holy Grail).

Horoscopes

Two documents of the Dead Sea Scrolls, from cave 4, one in Hebrew, the other in Aramaic, both dating probably to the end of the first century B.C., contain fragments of 'horoscopes', or more precisely, astrological physiognomies claiming a correspondence between a person's features and destiny and the configuration of the stars at the time of his birth.

The Hebrew text, published by J. M. Allegro, is written in a childish cipher. The text runs from left to right instead of the normal right to left and uses, in addition to the current Hebrew 'square' alphabet, letters borrowed from the archaic Hebrew (or Phoenician) and Greek scripts.

The spiritual qualities of three individuals described there are reflected in their share of Light and Darkness. The first man is very wicked: eight parts of Darkness to a single part of Light. The second man is largely good: six parts of Light against three parts of Darkness. The last is almost perfect: eight portions of Light and only one of Darkness.

As far as physical characteristics are concerned, shortness, fatness, and irregularity of the features are associated with wickedness, and their opposites reflect virtue.

In the astrological terminology of the document, the "second Column" doubtless means the "second House;" and a birthday "in the foot of the Bull" should probably be interpreted as the presence at that time of the sun in the lower part of the constellation Taurus. The Aramaic "horoscope" is, according to its editor J. Starcky, that of the final Prince of the Congregation, or Royal Messiah. It is just as likely, however, that the text alludes to the miraculous birth of Noah.

Whether the sectaries forecast the future by means of astrology, or merely used horoscope-like compositions as literary devices, it is impossible to decide at present, though I am inclined towards the latter alternative. That such texts are found among the Scrolls should not, however, surprise anyone. For if many Jews frowned on astrology, others, such as the Hellenistic Jewish writer Eupolemus, credited its invention to Abraham!

By G. Vermes from The Dead Sea Scrolls in English, published by Penguin Books.

The Bible

Gideon Exposed!

The Gideon Society places Bibles in hotel rooms for your edification. Just who was Gideon? One would assume that he was a person of exemplary character and great worth to have a worldwide society named after him. Here are some of Gideon's accomplishments:

- Gideon slaughtered thousands in battle by plotting with the "Lord" to use treachery.
- Gideon murdered thousands more for worshipping "false Gods."
- Gideon tortured and killed still more for daring to taunt him.
- Gideon plundered the bodies of his victims (to fashion a jeweled priestly vestment).
- Gideon fathered an offspring who killed 69 of his stepbrothers.

Read the Bible for yourself. You will find the story of Gideon in Judges, chapters 6-9. The tale of Gideon is just one of many horror stories in the Bible, a book that glorifies behavior you abhor. Millions of people have been hoodwinked by what their clergy and leaders have told them of the Bible. Make up your own mind about the Bible — read it for yourself.

Freethought Today • P.O. Box 750 • Madison, WI 53701

Must We Bash The Bible?

William B. Lindley

The first widely-published Bible-bashing was Thomas Paine's *Age of Reason*, a book most freethinkers have found dear to their hearts since it came out in 1796. However, most of us also find the Bible to be a tiresome book, and bashing it gets to be just as tiresome. Furthermore, most of us have friends who are very nice people and who still respect the Bible and try to live by it (or so they think).

We want to enjoy our friends. We don't want to become tiresome ourselves, so most of us just drop the subject. (For clarity, "Bible-bashing" means challenging, attacking, laying waste the doctrine of Biblical inerrancy, the idea that the Bible is literally the Word of God and therefore absolute authority.)

The President of the United States declared 1983 to be the Year of the Bible, telling us that the Bible contains the solutions to all the world's problems. His successor designated 1990 as the year for reading the Bible. These bald attempts to establish religion must be countered. Church-State separationists deplore what the presidents did, but don't go on to bash the Bible. Some are Bible Christians themselves, while others find the subject tiresome, as I have said.

But gee, *somebody's* gotta do it. TV preachers, with millions of dollars behind them, are pushing the doctrine of Bible inerrancy. As Skipp Porteous of *Freedom Writer* has told us, the goal is nothing less than a "theocracy" and the destruction of our Constitutional government. We need somebody to hit them head-on, not just sit on the sidelines and call them bad names.

Now for the good news. Somebody's doing it. There are two magazines dedicated to challenging the doctrine of Biblical inerrancy, just as Thomas Paine did in his landmark book. The editors of both debate Biblical inerrantist preachers frequently, and pass the word on to their readers.

The senior publication, begun in 1983, is *Biblical Errancy*, published by Dennis McKinsey. Address: 3158 Sherwood Park Drive,

Springfield, Ohio 45505. Monthly; subscription $12 per year. Loaded with valuable information. Here is a tiny sample of his observations:

> Why are we being punished for Adam's sin? After all, he ate the forbidden fruit, we didn't; it's his problem, not ours, especially in light of Deut. 24:16, which says the children shall not be punished for the sins of their fathers.
>
> How can Num. 23:19, which says God doesn't repent, be reconciled with Ex. 32:14, which clearly says he does?
>
> We are told the Bible has no scientific errors, yet it says the bat is a bird (Lev. 11:13,19), hares chew the cud (Lev. 11:5-6), and some fowl (Lev. 11:20-21) and insects (Lev. 11:22-23) have four legs.
>
> A prophecy by Jesus in John 13:38 "The cock shall not crow, till thou [Peter] hast denied me 3 times" is false because Mark 14:66-68 shows the cock actually crowed after the first denial, not the third.
>
> Jesus told us to "honor thy father and mother" (Matt. 15:4) but contradicted his own teaching in Luke 14:26 "If any man come to me and hate not his father and mother . . . he cannot be my disciple."

The "new kid on the block," started in 1990, is *The Skeptical Review*, edited by Farrell Till, who contributes a chapter in this book, *Nonexistent Prophecies*. Address: P. O. Box 617, Canton, Illinois 61520-0617. Quarterly; subscription $4 per year (first year free!). It explores issues in more depth than does *Biblical Errancy*, and the typeset quality is higher; but *BE* covers more ground per year. But why haggle? Subscribe to both.

If you are being badgered by Bible-pushers, or if your school is, here at last is excellent information ready to use.

William B. Lindley is associate editor, Truth Seeker *magazine, a Freethought publication founded in 1873. Reprinted with revisions from* Truth Seeker, *Vol. 119, No. 3.*

Nonbelievers

According to *The World Christian Encyclopedia*, more than a billion of the world's people consider themselves nonreligious (agnostic about religious claims) or atheistic (actively opposed to religion). Nearly three-quarters of these people live in East Asia, where they are a majority of the population of China.

If the estimates of non- and anti-religious peoples are correct, nonreligious persons and atheists also make up the largest religious bloc in the world after Christianity.

Germany: 30% Nonreligious

Almost 30 percent of people polled in the Federal Republic of Germany do not believe in a god, with nearly 13 percent explicitly calling themselves atheists.

Nonbelievers: Second Largest Sector in the World

The Catholic News Service and Encyclopedia Britannica Book of the Year, 1989, shows this breakdown of world religions and nonreligions:

Christianity	(1.7 billion)	32.9%
Nonbelievers	**(1.1 billion)**	**21.6%**
Islam	(880.6 million)	17.4%
Hinduism	(663.5 million)	13.1%
Buddhism	(311.8 million)	6.1%
Chinese religions	(172.3 nmillion)	3.4%
Other:	(167.5 million)	3.4%
Tribal religions	(92 milion)	1.8%
Judaism	(18.2 million)	0.3%

Of all the tyrannies that affect mankind, tyranny in religion is the worst; every other species of tyranny is limited to the world we live in; but this attempts to stride beyond the grave, and seeks to pursue us into eternity.

— Thomas Paine
1737 – 1809

The Age of Reason

Thomas Paine

It has been my intention, for several years past, to publish my thoughts upon Religion. I am well aware of the difficulties that attend the subject; and from that consideration, had reserved it to a more advanced period of life. I intended it to be the last offering I should make to my fellow-citizens of all nations; and that at a time when the purity of the motive that induced me to it could not admit of a question, even by those who might disapprove the work.

The circumstance that has now taken place in France of the total abolition of the whole national order of priesthood, and of everything appertaining to compulsive systems of religion, and compulsive articles of faith, has not only precipitated my intention, but rendered a work of this kind exceedingly necessary; lest, in the general wreck of superstition, of false systems of government and false theology, we lose sight of morality, of humanity and of the theology that is true.

As several of my colleagues, and others of my fellow-citizens of France, have given me the example of making their voluntary and individual profession of faith, I also will make mine; and I do this with all that sincerity and frankness with which the mind of man communicates with itself.

I believe in one God, and no more; and I hope for happiness beyond this life.

I believe in the equality of man, and I believe that religious duties consist in doing justice, loving mercy, and endeavoring to make our fellow creatures happy.

But, lest it should be supposed that I believe many other things in addition to these, I shall, in the progress of this work, declare the things I do not believe, and my reasons for not believing them.

I do not believe in the creed professed by the Jewish Church, by the Roman Church, by the Greek Church, by the Turkish Church, by the Protestant Church, nor by any church that I know of. My own mind is my own church.

All national institutions of churches – whether Jewish, Christian or Turkish – appear to me no other than human inventions, set up to terrify and enslave mankind, and monopolize power and profit.

I do not mean to condemn those who believe otherwise. They have the same right to their belief as I have to mine. But it is necessary to the happiness of man that he be mentally faithful to himself. Infidelity does not consist in believing, or in disbelieving; it consists in professing to believe what he does not believe.

It is impossible to calculate the moral mischief, if I may so express it, that mental lying has produced in society. When a man has so far corrupted and prostituted the chastity of his mind as to subscribe his professional belief to things he does not believe, he has prepared himself for the commission of every other crime. He takes up the trade of a priest for the sake of gain, and in order to qualify himself for that trade, he begins with a perjury. Can we conceive any thing more destructive to morality than this?

Soon after I had published the pamphlet "Common Sense," in America, I saw the exceeding probability that a revolution in the system of government would be followed by a revolution in the system of religion. The adulterous connection of church and state, wherever it has taken place – whether Jewish, Christian or Turkish – has so effectually prohibited by pains and penalties every discussion upon established creeds, and upon first principles of religion, that until the system of government should be changed, those subjects could not be brought fairly and openly before the world, but that whenever this should be done, a revolution in the system of religion would follow. Human inventions and priestcraft would be detected, and man would return to the pure, unmixed and unadulterated belief of one God, and no more.

Every national church or religion has established itself by pretending some special mission from God, communicated to certain individuals. The Jews have their Moses; the Christians their Jesus Christ, their apostles and saints; and the Turks their Mahomet – as if the way to God was not open to every man alike.

Each of those churches show certain books, which they call revelation, or the word of God. The Jews say that their word of God was given by God to Moses, face to face; the Christians say that their word of God came by divine inspiration; and the Turks say that their Word of God (the Koran) was brought by an angel from heaven. Each of those churches accuses the other of unbelief; and for my own part, I disbelieve them all.

As it is necessary to affix right ideas to words, I will, before I proceed further into the subject, offer some observations on the word revelation. Revelation, when applied to religion, means something communicated immediately from God to man.

No one will deny or dispute the power of the Almighty to make such a communication, if He pleases. But admitting, for the sake of a case, that something has been revealed to a certain person, and not revealed to any other person, it is revelation to that person only. When he tells it to a second person, a second to a third, a third to a fourth, and so on, it ceases to be a revelation to all those persons. It is revelation to the first person only, and hearsay to every other, and consequently they are not obliged to believe it.

It is a contradiction in terms and ideas, to call anything a revelation that comes to us at second-hand, either verbally or in writing. Revelation is necessarily limited to the first communication – after this it is only an account of something which that person says was a revelation made to him; and though he may find himself obliged to believe it, it cannot be incumbent on me to believe it in the same manner, for it was not a revelation made to me, and I have only his word for it that it was made to him.

When Moses told the children of Israel that he received the two tablets of the commandments from the hand of God, they were not obliged to believe him, because they had no other authority for it than his telling them so; and I have no other authority for it than some historian telling me so. The commandments carry no internal evidence of divinity with them; they contain some good moral precepts, such as any man qualified to be a lawgiver, or a legislator, could produce himself, without having recourse to supernatural intervention.

When I am told that the Koran was written in heaven and brought to Mahomet by an angel, this comes too near the same kind of hearsay evidence and second-hand authority as the former. I did not see the angel myself and, therefore, I have a right not to believe it.

When also I am told that a woman called the Virgin Mary, said, or gave out, that she was with child without any cohabitation with a man, and that her betrothed husband, Joseph, said that an angel told him so, I have a right to believe them or not; such a circumstance required a much stronger evidence than their bare word for it; but we have not even this – for neither Joseph nor Mary wrote any such matter themselves; it is only reported by others that they said so. It is hearsay upon hearsay, and I do not choose to rest my belief upon such evidence.

It is curious to observe how the theory of what is called the Christian Church sprung out of the tail of the heathen mythology. A direct incorporation took place in the first instance, by making the reputed founder to be celestially begotten. The trinity of gods that then followed was no other than a reduction of the former plurality, which was about twenty or thirty thousand – the statue of Mary succeeded the statue of Diana of Ephesus. The deification of heroes changed into the canonization of saints. The mythologists had gods for everything; the Christian mythologists had saints for everything; the Church became as crowded with the one as the Pantheon had been with the other, and Rome was the place of both. The Christian theory is little else than the idolatry of the ancient mythologists, accommodated to the purposes of power and revenue; and it yet remains to reason and philosophy to abolish the amphibious fraud.

Nothing that is here said can apply, even with the most distant disrespect, to the real character of Jesus Christ. He was a virtuous and an amiable man. The morality that he preached and practised was of the most benevolent kind; and though similar systems of morality had been preached by Confucius, and by some of the Greek philosophers, many years before; by the Quakers since; and by many good men in all ages, it has not been exceeded by any.

Jesus Christ wrote no account of himself, of his birth, parentage, or anything else. Not a line of what is called the New Testament is of his writing. The history of him is altogether the work of other people; and as to the account given of his resurrection and ascension, it was the necessary counterpart to the story of his birth. His historians, having brought him into the world in a supernatural manner, were obliged to take him out again in the same manner, or the first part of the story must have fallen to the ground.

The resurrection and ascension, supposing them to have taken place, admitted of public and ocular demonstration, like that of the ascension of a balloon, or the sun at noon-day, to all Jerusalem at least. A thing which everybody is required to believe, requires that the proof and evidence of it should be equal to all, and universal; and as the public visibility of this last related act was the only evidence that could give sanction to the former part, the whole of it falls to the ground, because that evidence never was given. Instead of this, a small number of persons, not more than eight or nine, are introduced as proxies for the whole world to say they saw it, and all the rest of the world are called upon to believe it. But it appears that Thomas did not believe the resurrection, and, as they say, would not believe without having ocular and manual demonstration himself. *So neither will I,* and the reason is equally as good for me, and for every other person, as for Thomas.

The best surviving evidence we now have respecting this affair is the Jews. They are regularly descended from the people who lived in the times this resurrection and ascension is said to have happened, and they say, it is not true. It has long appeared to me a strange inconsistency to cite the Jews as a proof of the truth of the story. It is just the same as if a man were to say, I will prove the truth of what I have told you by producing the people who say it is false.

That such a person as Jesus Christ existed, and that he was crucified – which was the mode of execution at that day – are historical relations strictly within the limits of probability. He preached most excellent morality, and the equality of man; but he preached also against the corruptions and avarice of the Jewish priests, and this brought upon him the hatred and vengeance of the whole order of priesthood. The accusation which those priests brought against him was that of sedition and conspiracy against the Roman government, to which the Jews were then subject and tributary; and it is not improbable that the Roman government might have some secret apprehensions of the effects of his doctrine, as well as the Jewish priests. Between the two, this virtuous reformer and revolutionist lost his life.

But if objects for gratitude and admiration are our desire, do they not present themselves every hour to our eyes? Do we not see a fair creation prepared to receive us the instant we are born – a world furnished to our hands, that cost us nothing? Is it we that light up the sun, that pour down the rain, and fill the earth with abundance? Whether we sleep or wake, the vast machinery of the universe still goes on.

I know that this bold investigation will alarm many, but it would be paying too great a compliment to their credulity to forbear it upon that account; the times and the subject demand it to be done. The suspicion that the theory of what is called the Christian Church is fabulous is becoming very extensive in all countries; and it will be a consolation to men staggering under that suspicion, and doubting what to believe and what to disbelieve, to see the object freely investigated.

When the Church mythologists established their system, they collected all the writings they could find and managed them as they pleased. It is a matter altogether of uncertainty to us whether such of the writings as now appear under the name of the Old and New Testaments are in the same state in which those collectors say they found them, or whether they added, altered, abridged or dressed them up.

Be this as it may, they decided by vote which of the books out of the collection they had made should be the *Word Of God*, and which should not. They rejected several; they voted others to be doubtful, such as the books called the Apocrypha; and those books which had a majority of votes were voted to be the Word of God. Had they voted otherwise, all the people, since calling themselves Christians, had believed otherwise – for the belief of the one comes from the vote of the other. Who the people were that did all this, we know nothing of; they called themselves by the general name of the Church, and this is all we know of the matter.

When Samson ran off with the gate-posts of Gaza, if he ever did so (and whether he did or not is nothing to us), or when he visited his Delilah, or caught his foxes, or did anything else, what has revelation to do with these things? If they were facts, he could tell them himself, or his secretary, if he kept one, could write them, if they were worth either telling or writing; and if they were fictions, revelation could not make them true; and whether true or not, we are neither the better nor the wiser for knowing them. When we contemplate the immensity of that Being who directs and governs the incomprehensible *whole*, of which the utmost ken of human sight can discover but a part, we ought to feel shame at calling such paltry stories the Word of God.

Thomas Paine, political writer, statesman and author of Common Sense, *the* Declaration of Independence, Rights of Man *and* The Age of Reason.

TO MY

FELLOW-CITIZENS

OF THE

UNITED STATES OF AMERICA:

I PUT the following work under your protection. It contains my opinions upon Religion. You will do me the justice to remember, that I have always strenuously supported the Right of every Man to his own opinion, however different that opinion might be to mine. He who denies to another this right, makes a slave of himself to his present opinion, because he precludes himself the right of changing it.

The most formidable weapon against errors of every kind is Reason. I have never used any other, and I trust I never shall.

Your affectionate friend and fellow-citizen,

THOMAS PAINE.

Luxembourg, 8th Pluviose,
Second Year of the French Republic, one and indivisible.
January 27, O. S. 1794.

English Version

A Brief History Of The English Bible

Rocco A. Errico

The "Englishing" of Scripture has a long and fascinating history involving both religious and governmental politics. The term "Englishing" was coined when so many different English versions of the Bible were appearing in the British Isles culminating with the Authorized Version of Scripture better known in America as the King James Version of 1611. This article is a condensed accounting of the origin of our English Bible versions. It was originally written in response to and based upon questions I was asked about our English Bible versions during my lectures throughout the United States and Canada.

Christianity and Great Britain

The greatest obstacle to an early English translation of the Bible was the mixing and blending of languages on the isles of Britain. Christianity entered Great Britain sometime in the latter half of the second century. However, it did not take root until three or four centuries later. Ireland became the rich, fertile ground for the growth and expansion of the Christian church. Its progress in the Emerald Isle was so steady that by the sixth century Christianity had spread into Scotland and northern England. During this period of history few could read or write. It was the intense preaching of the gospel by the educated monks and their students that brought about the extension of Christianity throughout Britain.

At that particular time the language of the church's worship was Latin and its version of the Scriptures was also in Latin – the Old Latin MSS. (Old Latin was a translation from the Septuagint Greek Scriptures of the Old Testament and not from Hebrew. The New Testament was based on various Greek versions.) Jerome (342 - 420) had been commissioned by Pope Damasus in 382 to revise the Old Latin version of the gospels. He used a Greek MS as the basis of his revision but did not complete the rest of the New Testament. When Jerome revised the Old Testament he began with the Psalms. Further work on the other books of the Old Testament was based on Hebrew texts and was a direct translation. The work was completed around the latter part of the 4th century. This version, known as the Vulgate, was widely used in the West, and its original intent was to end the great differences of text in the Old Latin MSS. As the Vulgate superseded the Old Latin version, the latter lost its authority in the church. Remember, it was the educated monks who interpreted the Latin Bible in the tongues and dialects of their listeners.

Early English Manuscripts

In the middle of the seventh century the earliest beginning of an English Bible (if one could call it such) made its appearance. Bede, (673 - 735), the great Anglo-Saxon biblical scholar and "Father of English History," was the first known individual to render certain biblical subjects into the Anglo-Saxon tongue beginning with the creation story.

In South England there was a zealous monk by the name of Aldhelm, Abbot of Malmesbury who was also an outstanding musician. According to English historians, Aldhelm became the first bishop of Sherborne and the first known translator of the Psalms into Anglo-Saxon English. We are told that the people of South England received their

> religious instruction through popular poetry attuned to the harp of Aldhelm. This shrewd official observed that the usual sermon had little attraction for the ordinary run of Englishmen. Being a skillful musician, he put on the garb of a minstrel and took up a position on a bridge over which many people were obliged to pass. His artistic playing soon attracted a group of listeners. As soon as he had thus collected an audience he gave his music and words a religious turn, and by the strains of his splendid instrument and the persuasive form of his attractive language won many to Christianity." (*The Ancestry Of Our English Bible*, Price, p. 226.)

Then there appeared Richard Rolle of Hampole (1300 - 1349) who translated the Psalms into Middle English and wrote commentaries on the same. He was known as a hermit and mystic. About that same time the biblical works of William of Shoreham became popular. *"The spread of the Shoreham-Rolle versions of the Psalter was the beginning of the triumph of the English language proper."* It was these two trans-

90

lations of the Psalms that initiated a strong craving throughout Great Britain for more translations of the Bible.

Vernacular Translations Forbidden

It should be noted that Pope Innocent III, in 1199, had declared the following,

> The secret mysteries of the faith ought not to be explained to all men in all places, since they cannot be everywhere understood by all men.

Also Pope Gregory VII stated,

> Not without reason has it pleased Almighty God that Holy Scripture should be a secret in certain places, lest, it were plainly apparent to all men, perchance it would be little esteemed and be subject to disrespect; or it might be falsely understood by those of mediocre learning and lead to error.

But despite these declarations of Ecclesiastical powers, translation of Scripture could not be stopped. Men desired to drink of the fountains of knowledge that had been hidden from them by those in authority.

The Wycliffe Version

In the fourteenth century, a period of great political and sociological transition and ecclesiastical controversies, John Wycliffe, scholar and lecturer at Oxford, translated the Bible from Latin into English. The New Testament was translated about 1380; and in 1382 the entire Bible was finished. Other scholars under the direction of Wycliffe worked on the translation of the Old Testament. In fact most of the work of the Old Testament was translated by his devoted disciples and co-workers. Wycliffe died two years after the completion of the Bible in 1382. His translation was stilted and mechanical. The language of his work, a Midland dialect, did not represent the central strand of development in English. Wycliffe's version needed revision, and it was undertaken not long after his death.

The Response

What was the reaction of the religious world? What did church authorities have to say? Archbishop Arundel in 1412, when writing the Pope concerning Wycliffe said,

> . . . that wretched and pestilent fellow of damnable memory, the very herald and child of anti-Christ, who crowned his wickedness by translating the Scriptures into the mother tongue.

A provincial council at Oxford early in the 15th century stated,

> No one shall in the future translate on his own authority any text of Holy Scriptures into the English tongue—nor shall any man read this kind of book, booklet or treatise, now recently composed in the time of the said John Wycliffe or later, or any that shall be composed in the future, in whole or part, publicly or secretly under penalty of the greater Excommunication.

Did this decree put out the flaming desire to see the light of Scripture translated into the common tongue of English? No!

The Renaissance

The fifteenth century, the great epoch of awakening, witnessed the Renaissance. Its first powerful stirrings occurred in Italy under the guidance of certain freethinkers and writers of that country. No one was able to hold back the tide of change and the profound forces at work in the culture of Europe. The church also was impacted by these powerful forces. There was another translator by the name of William Tyndale (1494? - 1536) who, because of persecution in England, had to cross over to the Continent to translate the Bible into English.

Tyndale was a Greek scholar and had access to the Greek text of Erasmus and other biblical writings which Wycliffe did not possess. He was martyred before he completed the Old Testament, and there was much blood shed by religious powers in the ensuing days. But, because of the "new birth movement" of that age the Ecclesiastical walls of ignorance and fear could not hold back the rising flood of translations of the Bible into English.

Next came Miles Coverdale (1488 - 1568), a friend of Tyndale. This version was based on Tyndale's translation of Scripture with some help from the Latin text and other versions. Then the Matthew's Bible made its appearance. This version was based on the work of Tyndale and Coverdale, that is, it was a revision of the work of Tyndale, pieced out with Tyndale's unpublished MSS and portions of the Coverdale's Old Testament. The editor of this version was John Rogers (1500 - 1555). He was the first British Protestant Martyr under Queen Mary. In 1537 under the name of Thomas Matthew, he published the first complete version of the Bible in English.

In 1539, the *Great Bible* made its showing and was based upon the Matthew, Coverdale and Tyndale translations. This Bible won out among all the other translations and was *"appointed to the use of the Churches."* For nearly 30 years (except in the reign of Queen Mary) it was the only version that could lawfully be used in England. It is very important to remember the name of this Bible because the *King James Version* derived its "translation" not only from the *Great Bible* but, as you will see, from the *Bishops' Bible* as well.

The Counter Reformation

The Counter Reformation began to take hold in England under Queen Mary, and many Protestant scholars took refuge in Geneva. Thus, in 1560, the Geneva version of the Bible came into existence. This translation was a revision of the *Great Bible* and was based on other English reworked versions of Scripture. It is interesting to know that the *Geneva Bible* was the English translation which the Puritans brought with them to America.

The notes and annotations in the Geneva Bible were strongly Protestant and leaned heavily toward Calvinism. (John Calvin, 1509-1564, French reformer and theologian, was also thought of, by certain individuals, as a "theocratic tyrant." Calvinism: the theological system formulated by John Calvin. He strongly advocated the absolute authority of the Bible, that the State must be subject to the Church, and many other biblical doctrinal beliefs.)

Shakespeare quoted the *Geneva Bible* in his works. It was after meditation on the Geneva translation that John Bunyan wrote his famous *Pilgrims' Progress*. The Geneva version of the Bible became very popular. The Archbishop of Canterbury, along with other bishops during the reign of Queen Elizabeth, decided to make a revision of the *Great Bible of 1539*. The decision was prompted by the popularity of the *Geneva Bible*. This "new" translation or revision was called the *Bishops' Bible of 1568*.

The Authorized Version

James Stuart of Scotland, since 1603 King of England, ordered that a new "revision" be made of the Bishops' Bible. Remember, the Bishops' Bible is a revision of the *Great Bible* which was based on other English translations and revisions. This work was immediately begun by 47 scholars under the authorization of King James.

In 1611 the new version was published. Although the title page described it as *"newly translated out of the original tongues"*, the statement is not entirely in accord with the facts. The work was actually a revision of the Bishops' Bible on the basis of the Hebrew and Greek. It did not win immediate universal acceptance, taking almost fifty years to displace the Geneva Bible in popular favor. In other words, the KJV was a revision of the Bible based on the Bishops' Bible which was a revision of the Great Bible, the Great Bible being based on the Matthew, Coverdale and Tyndale Bibles.

The Deluge of English Versions

The nineteenth and twentieth centuries have brought many more translations of Scriptures such as the *Revised Standard* version, the *American Standard* version, the New English Bible, TANAKH-The Holy Scriptures - The New JPS translation according to the traditional Hebrew Text, *The New American Bible*, the Amplified, Weymouth, Moffatt, the Wuest expanded version and many others too numerous to mention.

Most of the English versions of Scripture of the 20th century are translated works from Greek and Hebrew. Old Testament translations into English are usually based on the Hebrew 10th-century Massoretic text. This text was named after the Massoretes, Jewish grammarians who worked on the Hebrew text between the 6th and 10th centuries. (There is a Greek rendering of the Hebrew text known as the Septuagint and it has been translated into English from the Greek text of the 5th century C.E.)

New Testament English translations are usually based on various Greek texts and versions. However, in 1957 there appeared for the first time a translation of Old and New Testaments into English from the Aramaic, Semitic Peshitta Texts (fifth and sixth centuries), also known as the Lamsa translation. The translator, Dr. George M. Lamsa, claimed there are about ten to twelve thousand outstanding differences between these Aramaic Peshitta manuscripts and those of the Hebrew and Greek texts of the Bible.

Our Modern World

In the last sixty years, and especially in the last three decades, significant changes have taken place in the field of biblical scholarship. New methodologies for interpreting and translating Scripture are being employed. These modern and current sociological and historical methods provide us with the necessary tools to carefully analyze the social and historical contexts of biblical narratives. The present research and scholarship draws on biblical and extra-biblical evidence to help us understand the people of the Bible, their world and their faith. There is an ongoing explosion of pertinent information in the fields of religion, philology, sociology, archaeology and ancient history which has uncovered the early world of Mesopotamia and the basic social and religious structure of first-century Palestine.

Our present knowledge of Aramaic and Hebrew usage of words, idioms and special religious and philosophical terminology has clarified many obscure passages of Scripture. Discovery and work on the Dead Sea Scrolls has aided biblical scholarship in its perception and presentation of the overall Jewish background of the times and will continue to yield more information. (The Dead Sea Scrolls were hidden in desert caves by Jews as they fled Roman soldiers in 68 C.E.)

Today, in the Western world, there is a greater comprehensive knowledge of Eastern people culturally and psychologically than in the past. Many native-born Near Eastern authors have helped us realize the unique thought patterns of their people, their customs and mannerisms which are so distinct from ours. As our understanding of the Near Eastern world increases, especially of biblical days, so will our English translations of the Bible reflect our new comprehension.

Rocco A. Errico, PhD, is a lecturer, author, ordained minister, and Bible scholar whose approach emphasizes Eastern sources and customs, especially the Aramaic language.

The Bible was written and put together by human beings doing the best they knew how.

— A Humanist

Inspired Words of God

Question: Can a document, tampered with by kings, tyrants, fools and scholars be the "true" inspired words of God?

The *Revised Standard Version* of the Bible, published in 1952, is an authorized revision of the *American Standard Version*, published in 1901, which was a revision of the *King James Version*, published in 1611.

The following are all *inspired* versions of the New Testament, many with glaring contradictions. These do not include the many versions of the Bible itself.

- The New Testament of Our Lord and Savior Jesus Christ, American Bible Union Version (John A. Broadus et al)
- The New Testament (Henry Alford)
- Good News for Modern Man
- The New Testament in Basic English
- The New Testament in the Language of Today (Wm. F. Beck)
- The Berkeley Version of the New Testament (Gerrit Verkuyl)
- The New Testament: An American Translation (Edgar J. Goodspeed)
- The New Testament in the Translation of Monsignor Ronald Knox
- The New Testament According to the Eastern Texts (George M. Lamsa)
- The New Testament: A New Translation (James Moffatt)
- The Centenary Translation: The New Testament in Modern English (Helen Barrett Montgomery)
- The New American Standard Bible: New Testament
- The New English Bible: New Testament
- The New Testament: A New Translation (Olaf M. Norlie)
- The New Testament in Modern English (J.B. Phillips)
- The Emphasized New Testament: A New Translation (J.B. Rotherham)
- The Twentieth Century New Testament
- The New Testament in Modern Speech (Richard F. Weymouth)
- The New Testament: A Translation in the Language of the People (Charles B. Williams)

— Editor

Nonexistent Prophecies: A Problem For Bible Inerrancy

Farrell Till

Any challenge to the integrity of the Bible will very likely draw the familiar prophecy-fulfillment response. "If the Bible is not inspired of God," Christian fundamentalists will ask, "how do you explain all of the prophecies that Jesus fulfilled?" The answer to this question is quite simple. The so-called prophecy fulfillments that the New Testament writers claimed in the person and deeds of Jesus of Nazareth were prophecy fulfillments only in the fertile imagination of the writers. The famous virgin-birth prophecy (Isaiah 7:14 and Matt. 1:23), the prophecy of the messiah's birth in Bethlehem (Micah 5:2 and Matt. 2:6), the prophecy of King Herod's slaughter of the children of Bethlehem (Jere. 31:15 and Matt. 2:18) – these and many like them became prophecy fulfillments only through the distortions and misapplications of the original Old Testament statements.

To discuss these in depth would require an entire book, so instead I will concentrate on another aspect of the prophecy-fulfillment argument: New Testament claims of prophecy fulfillment for which no Old Testament sources can be found. An example would be John 7:37-38, where Jesus allegedly said, "If anyone thirsts, let him come to me and drink. He who believes in me, as the Scripture has said, Out of his heart will flow rivers of living water." At that time, the only scriptures were the Old Testament, yet try as they have, Bible inerrantists have never found this statement that Jesus said was in the scriptures of his day. The prophecy was nonexistent.

Similar to this is a "prophecy fulfillment" that was referred to in Matthew 2:23. Here it was claimed that when Joseph took his family to Nazareth, he fulfilled that "which was spoken by the prophets, 'He [Jesus] shall be called a Nazarene.' " In all of the Old Testament, however, neither the word Nazareth nor Nazarene is even mentioned, so how could it be true that the prophets (plural) had predicted that the messiah would be called a Nazarene? To avoid admitting that a mistake was made, inerrantists point out that Matthew did not say that this prophecy had been written; he said only that it had been "spoken" by the prophets.

A weakness in this "explanation" is the fact that Matthew routinely introduced alleged prophecy fulfillments by saying that thus-and-so had been "spoken" by the prophets. He claimed, for example, that the preaching of John the Baptist fulfilled what had been "spoken" by Isaiah the prophet: "The voice of one crying in the wilderness, Make ye ready the way of the Lord, Make his paths straight" (2:3). However, this statement that Matthew said Isaiah had spoken is a quotation of what had been written in Isaiah 40:3.

Other written "prophecies" that Matthew introduced by saying that they had been "spoken" can be found in 4:14-16 (Isaiah 9:1-2), 12:17-21 (Isaiah 42: 1-4), 13:35 (Psalm 78:2), and 21:4-5 (Zechariah 9:9). Since all of these alleged prophecy statements can be found written in the Old Testament, we can only assume that Matthew's style was to use the word spoken to introduce statements that had in fact been written. Undoubtedly, he intended the expression to mean the same thing in 2:23 as it did elsewhere when he referred to things that had been "spoken" by the prophets. Hence, he made a mistake in 2:23, because no prophet (much less prophets) had ever written anything about Nazareth or Nazarenes.

In telling the story of Judas's suicide, Matthew erred again in claiming that Jeremiah had prophesied about the purchase of the field where Judas was buried. After casting down in the sanctuary the thirty pieces of silver that he had been paid for betraying Jesus, Judas went away and hanged himself.

The priests then took the money and bought the potter's field to bury Judas in. Matthew claimed that this was a prophecy fulfillment: "Then was fulfilled that which was spoken through Jeremiah the prophet, saying, And they took the thirty pieces of silver, the price of him that was priced, whom certain of the children of Israel did price; and they gave them for the potter's field, as the Lord appointed me" (27:9-10). In reality, however, no statement like this can be found in the book of Jeremiah. Inerrantists will sometimes defend Matthew by referring to Zechariah 11:12-13, which makes mention of thirty pieces of silver but in a context entirely different from the statement that Matthew "quoted." Besides, even if Zechariah had obviously written the statement that Matthew quoted, this would hardly acquit Matthew of error, because he said that Jeremiah, not Zechariah, had made the prophecy.

A more serious nonexistent prophecy concerns the very foundation of Christianity. On the night of his alleged resurrection, Jesus said to his disciples, "Thus it is written, that the Christ should suffer, and rise again from the dead the third day" (Luke 24:46). The Apostle Paul agreed with this claim that the scriptures had referred to a third-day resurrection of the messiah: "For I delivered unto you first of all that which also I received: that Christ died for our sins according to the scriptures; and that he was buried; and that he hath been raised on the third day according to the scriptures" (1 Cor. 15:4-5).

Two New Testament writers, then, claimed that the scriptures had spoken of a resurrection of the messiah on the third day. The problem that this claim poses for the prophecy-fulfillment argument is that no one can cite a single Old Testament scripture that mentions a third-day resurrection. As a matter of fact, no one can even cite an Old Testament scripture that clearly and undeniably refers to a resurrection of the messiah, period, but that is another article for another time.

There are other major weaknesses in the prophecy-fulfillment argument, but the fact that New Testament writers so often referred to prophetic utterances that can't even be found in the Old Testament is enough to cast serious doubt on their many claims of prophecy fulfillment. If they were wrong when they referred to prophetic statements that cannot be found anywhere in the Old Testament, how can we know they were right when they claimed fulfillment of statements that can be found? The truth is that we can't.

Farrell Till is the editor of The Skeptical Review, *a journal of Bible criticism, and is engaged in formal, organized debates, both written and verbal, with Biblical inerrantists.*

NOTE: A more detailed refutation of the prophecy-fulfillment argument is available in the author's booklet *Prophecies: Imaginary and Unfulfilled,* published by Skepticism, Inc., P. O. Box 617, Canton, IL 61520-0617.

O ye of little faith . . .

— Jesus of Nazareth

Prayer

We will pray that God take the lives of these Hitler-like men from the face of the earth.

> — Rev. R.L. Hymers, Pastor, Fundamentalist Baptist
> Tabernacle of Los Angeles, praying for the deaths of
> Justice William Brennan and four other Justices, 1986.

We all pray to god . . . we asked him to tell us who our enemies are . . . He said the atheists, secular humanists and sinners.

> — Dr. Robert Schuller,
> relating results of Joint Prayer Session of
> Churches Uniting for Global Mission
> Trinity Broadcasting Network,
> Spring 1992

Prayer is only another form of meditation or auto-suggestion. It matters not if there is a god listening, as long as you believe there is. I once attended a class on hypnosis and found that about a fourth of my fellow students were "men of the cloth." Of course they were there only to learn how to counsel members of flocks better. Oral Roberts must have been a graduate student.

> — Sam Warren, Humanist Fellowship

Hands that help are better far than lips that pray.

> — Robert Green Ingersoll

And when thou prayest, thou shalt not be as the hypocrites are: for they love to pray standing in the synagogues and in the corners of the streets, that they may be seen of men. Verily I say unto you, they have their reward. But thou, when thou prayest, enter into thy closet, and when thou hast shut thy door, pray to thy Father which is in secret; and thy Father which is in secret shall reward thee openly.

> — Jesus Christ (Matt. 6:5,6)

(and Jesse Helms wants it in school classrooms??)

Noah's Flood As Composite Literature

Howard M. Teeple

Before we examine the Noah's ark story, we should locate the real problem and bring it out into the open. The basic problem is not the interpretation of archaeological, geological, or literary evidence, but rather, the interpretation of the Bible. It is the *fundamentalist* approach to the Bible that is the *fundamental* problem. As we use the term "fundamentalist," we are not referring to particular sects, but to an ultraconservative point of view in respect to the Bible. What is the fundamentalist approach?

Attitude Toward The Bible

The fundamentalist approach begins with the supposition that God inspired the whole Bible verbatim, so that every word of it is literally "God's word." Therefore, the fundamentalists are obsessed with the faith that "the Bible is true." This belief seems so important that they regard it as a fundamental doctrine that every person should accept. A story that the Bible plainly presents as a story, for example, is the parable of the Prodigal Son, recognized as fiction. But any story in a historical framework is stoutly defended by them as literal history. This includes the story of the Flood.

The attitude that the whole Bible must be true leads to the opinion that there can be no factual errors and no contradictions. They who hold this opinion either ignore or oppose the suggestion that the biblical Flood story contains contradictions. Needless to say, they do not like the idea that two Flood stories are interwoven in Genesis.

Method Of Interpretation

The fundamentalists' attitude toward the Bible determines their method of interpreting it. One feature of their method is the screening out of evidence they dislike. When contradictions are encountered in the bible, one statement may be accepted and the conflicting statement ignored. An example is the question of how many animals of a kind were taken aboard the ark in the Flood story.

God's instruction to Noah to take two of each kind (Gen. 6:19) is readily accepted, while the contradictory instruction to take seven pairs of birds and seven pairs of clean animals (Gen. 7:2-3) is usually ignored. If someone does call attention to such details, he is liable to be denounced for "picking the Bible to pieces." Actually, the failure to consider all the evidence is a violation of another basic principle of scholarship. The only way really to understand the Bible is to consider all the evidence, both inside and outside it.

Another feature of the fundamentalists' method is the reinterpretation of biblical passages to make the Bible agree with their beliefs. A related feature is the effort to twist evidence outside the Bible to support their beliefs. A popular form of twisting outside evidence is the misuse of archaeology to force it to support the historical accuracy of the Bible. This practice is engaged in not only by fundamentalists, but also by various writers and occasionally even by archaeologists themselves for the sake of producing something sensational.

Sir Charles Marston, Werner Keller, and others wrote books to defend the traditional view of the Bible, using archaeology as evidence. Even the famous Jewish archaeologist, Nelson Glueck, was too eager to find archaeological support for the Old Testament. On the other hand, books by Frederic Kenyon, Millar Burrows, André Parrot, and others represent honest, accurate use of archaeology in the interpretation of the Bible. The truth is that some archaeological evidence supports the Bible, but other archaeological discoveries disagree with it.

Effects Of Fundamentalism

When belief in the literal truth of the whole Bible becomes essential in a religion, that religion is placed on a very shaky foundation. It is easily demonstrated that the Bible is a human product of its time, containing some history, some fiction, some borrowing from neighboring religions, some truth, some errors, and some contradictions. Many undesirable effects result from making the truth of religion dependent upon the truth of such notions:

- A low standard for religion is set. Religion is forced to continue to contain some of the superstitions and ignorance of the ancient past. A distorted sense of values in religion results when unimportant or erroneous beliefs are regarded as of equal value with religious principles and ethics.

- Much modern knowledge and many ideals are shut out of religion because they are not in the Bible. Intelligent development of religion is blocked.

- Misunderstanding of the Bible itself is a consequence. The nature of the Bible, the religious development within it, and the relation of the Bible to the total history of religion are hidden from view by the fundamentalist approach. For example, within the Old Testament there is a shift from the narrow racism in Ezra and Nehemiah to the broad universalism in Second Isaiah (Isa. 40-55) and Jonah. Treating the whole Bible as literally the word of God prevents its readers from understanding the variety and development within it.

- Often the noblest passages of the Bible are not given a fair chance to speak to us today because they are equated with inferior passages. Belief in the unity of the Bible obscures the fact that sometimes a biblical writer was trying to elevate religion to a higher plane than the level in some other biblical books. Second Isaiah's effort to promote universalism is an example.

- The unreasonable claims and conjectures made to protect the belief in the literal truth of the whole Bible tend to bring religion into disrepute in the sight of the general public. Religion is ill-served by this. The wild claims include those made to support the belief in the Flood and the Ark.

The Story In The Bible

The Flood story in Genesis is more complex than the other Flood accounts. Unlike them, it contains significant contradictions and inconsistencies. One is the number of birds and clean animals taken aboard; another is the term for deity: "the Lord" vs. "God."

Another contradiction is the duration of the Flood. In Gen. 7:12; 8:6, 10a, 12a, the total of 54 days (40 plus 7 plus 7) passed from the time that the Flood began until Noah left the ark. In Gen. 7:11; 8:13a, 14-16a, however, the period was the equivalent of a solar year.

Biblical fundamentalists invariably either ignore these differences or try to interpret the verses to eliminate the difference and to harmonize the passages. Such procedure fails because it distorts the evidence. Either device – ignoring parts of the text or reinterpreting parts of the text — usually leads to misinterpretation of the text.

The Discovery Of Sources – Composite Literature

The only way to understand the cause of the inconsistencies is to recognize that we have before us an example of ancient composite literature. Two separate written sources have been interwoven into one account, without rewriting them to make their vocabulary, style, and ideas agree with each other. This produces contradictions and inconsistencies, and sometimes duplications.

Composite literature was very prevalent in the ancient world, and a major contribution of modern biblical scholarship is the recognition that much of both the Old Testament and the New Testament is composite. The same two sources that are used in the Genesis Flood story run through the Pentateuch, where they are combined with other source material.

The presence of several sources for the Creation story in the Bible was first observed when J.B. Witter in 1711 recognized the significance of the different terms for God. Gradually biblical scholars discovered more and more evidence of earlier sources and later editing in the Pentateuch. The famous Graf-Wellhausen Hypothesis assigned letters to the four main sources: J, E, P, and D. The two sources for the Flood story are J and P.

Although the hypothesis has been revised and refined, it is basically sound. Orthodox Jews and Christians attack it because it upsets the traditional view that Moses wrote the Pentateuch, but the evidence for written sources is quite decisive. The contradictions, duplications, and linguistic inconsistencies cannot be sensibly explained as the composition of a single writer.

Parallels With Other Flood Stories

The Flood accounts in both J and P contain these essential features of the Mesopotamian versions:
- A god becomes displeased with mankind.
- Therefore the god decides to destroy all mankind, except one man and his wife or family, by means of a Flood.
- A deity – either the same or a different god – warns the man that the Flood is coming; the god tells him to build a boat, and to put aboard himself, his wife, and some animals.

- Storm or heavy rain is a major – and sometimes only – cause of the Flood.

The other Flood stories generally have these same features in common. Thus these elements were characteristic of the basic story.

The Mesopotamian Versions

J has additional parallels with one or more of the Sumerian and Babylonian versions of the story. The exact day that the Flood will begin was predetermined; a special period of seven days preceded the Flood; one or more intervals of seven days occurred at the end of the Flood; the hero opened a window or hatch at the end of the voyage; a covering for the ark is mentioned; a dove and a raven were sent out from the Ark as the Flood neared its end, and the raven did not return. In J, as in the Sumerian and Babylonian accounts, the hero offered a sacrifice after emerging from the Ark. The Lord liked the smell of burnt offering, as did gods in general in the *Gilgamesh Epic*.

P, too, has parallels with one or more of the Mesopotamian accounts. The size of the Ark is given; the deity specifies its size, shape, and number of decks; pitch is used in its construction; the ark's door is mentioned; the ship lands on a mountain or mountains. After the Flood was over, the god Enlil blessed the hero and his wife in the *Gilgamesh Epic*, as God blessed Noah and his sons in P.

The large number of parallels demonstrates that both the J and P Flood accounts are derived ultimately from the Mesopotamian versions that preceded them. An interesting discovery is that J's parallels are generally not in P. This fact indicates that J's source was not identical with P's source, which is not surprising, considering that many forms of the story were in circulation, and that P was incorporated in Genesis four or five centuries later than J.

Greek, Roman, And Syrian Versions

The Greek and Roman versions of the Flood story have been changed yet further from the Mesopotamian accounts. This is in harmony with the fact that they were written later than the two Hebrew stories adapted to other cultures. Lucian probably used a Hellenistic source which combined elements from the Hebrew and non-Hebrew accounts.

Story Or History?

When the Genesis Flood is traced back to its ultimate sources, which are the Sumerian story and the Babylonian versions of it, those sources very clearly are fictional. The sources are poetry, composed and transmitted for entertainment and to promote various ideas.

The differences between the Hebrew versions and the Mesopotamian versions are not at all an indication that the Hebrew accounts are independent in origin. Josephus, writing in the first century of the Christian era, clearly illustrates for us the ease with which Jews (and others) readily appropriated and reinterpreted foreign material. In his treatise *Against Apion* he comments on Berossus' account:

> This author, following the most ancient records, has, like Moses, described the Flood and the destruction of mankind thereby, and told of the ark in which Noah, the founder of our race, was saved when it landed on the heights of the mountains of Armenia (I. 128-30).

In Berossus' account the name of the man who was saved by a boat he built is Xisuthros; Josephus conveniently ignores this fact and claims that Berossus was writing about Noah.

The prominence of the mythological features demonstrates that the story is indeed a myth, not a report or even a faint "memory" of a historical event. If we are to be fair to it, we must accept it on its own terms, as a story.

This chapter is an extract from the book: The Noah's Ark Nonsense, *written by Howard M. Teeple and published by the Religion and Ethics Institute, Inc., Evanston, Illinois, 1978. Dr. Teeple, a Bible scholar and former fundamentalist, has written numerous books and articles, including* The Literary Origin of the Gospel of John.

CBS airs fraudulent arkaeology special in 1993. The "Ark" wood turned out to be contemporary pine soaked in juices and baked in an oven.

— *Time Magazine,* July 5, 1993

God

God, to me, it seems is a verb
not a noun, proper or improper . . .
Yes, God is a verb, the most active . . .

— Buckminster Fuller

God is the Pronoun whose antecedents differ with
each individual and society.

Weston La Barre, *The American Rationalist*

"If God did not exist, it would be necessary to invent
him," suggested Voltaire as if to say God was an
invention of man. Even a three-year-old child, when
told God created man, the earth, the sea, and all
creatures great and small, will ask: "Who created
God?"

— "Is God dead?" Cover of *Time Magazine,* 1966

I cannot imagine a God who rewards and punishes
the objects of his creation, whose purposes are
modeled after our own – a God, in short, who is but a
reflection of human frailty. Neither can I believe that
the individual survives the death of his body, although
feeble souls harbor such thoughts through fear or
ridiculous egotism.

— Einstein

It may be that our role on this planet is not to worship
God . . . but to create him.

— Arthur C. "2001" Clarke

If we affirm that God does not exist, perhaps only then can we begin to recognize fully that human beings are autonomous and that we are responsible for our own destinies and those of our fellow human beings. Perhaps only then can we summon the courage and wisdom to develop a rational ethics based on a realistic appraisal of nature and an awareness of the common moral decencies.

— Paul Kurtz, *Forbidden Fruit*

There are many gods which Christians reject. I just believe in one less god than they do. The reasons that you might give for your atheism toward the Roman gods are likely the same reasons I would give for not believing in Jesus.

— Dan Barker

A questioner declared that few churches allow black Africans to pray with the white because the Bible says that is the way it should be, because God created Negroes to serve.

"But suppose God is black. What if we go to Heaven and we all our lives have treated the Negro as an inferior and we look up and he is not white? What then is our response?"

There was no answer, only silence.

— Sen. Robert F. Kennedy,
Suppose God Is Black, Look Magazine

. . . And the people bowed and prayed, to the neon god they'd made . . .

— Simon and Garfunkel

Bible Morality

John E. Remsburg

The Ten Commandments in the Old Testament and the Sermon on the Mount, including the Golden Rule, in the New, are supposed to comprise the best moral teachings of the Bible. They are declared to be so far superior to all other moral codes as to preclude the idea of human origin.

The Decalogue is a very imperfect moral code; not at all superior to the religious and legislative codes of other ancient peoples. The last six of these commandments, while not above criticism, are in the main just, and were recognized alike by Jew and Gentile. They are a crude attempt to formulate the crystallized experiences of mankind. The first four (first three according to Catholic and Lutheran versions) possess no moral value whatever. They are simply religious emanations from the corrupt and disordered brain of priestcraft. They only serve to obscure the principles of true morality and produce an artificial system which bears the same relation to natural morality that a measure of chaff and grain does to a measure of winnowed grain.

As a literary composition and as a partial exposition of the peculiar tenets of a heretical Jewish sect, the Sermon on the Mount is interesting; but as a moral code, it is of little value. Along with some admirable precepts, it contains others, like the following, which are false and pernicious:

- Blessed are the poor in spirit;
- Blessed are the meek, for they shall inherit the earth;
- If thy right eye offend thee, pluck it out;
- If thy right hand offend thee, cut it off;
- Whosoever shall marry her that is divorced, committeth adultery;
- Resist not evil;
- Whosoever shall smite thee on the right cheek, turn to him the other also;

- If any man will sue thee at the law, and take away thy coat, let him have thy cloak also;
- Love your enemies;
- Lay not up for yourselves treasures upon earth;
- Take no thought for your life, what ye shall eat, or what ye shall drink, nor yet for your body, what ye shall put on;
- Take therefore no thought for the morrow.

Christians claim that unbelievers have no moral standard, that they alone have such a standard – an infallible standard – the Bible. If we ask them to name the best precept in this standard they cite the Golden Rule. And yet the Golden Rule is purely a human rule of conduct. "Whatsoever ye (men, not God) would that men should do to you, do ye even so to them." This rule enjoins what Christians profess to condemn, that every person shall form his own moral standard. In this rule, the so-called divine laws are totally ignored.

The Golden Rule, so far as the Bible is concerned, is a borrowed gem. Chinese, Greek, and Roman sages had preached and practiced it centuries before the Sermon on the Mount was delivered. This rule, one of the best formulated by the ancients, is not, however, a perfect rule of human conduct. It does not demand that our desires shall always be just. But it does recognize and enjoin the principle of reciprocity, and is immeasurably superior to the rule usually practiced by the professed followers of Jesus: Whatsoever we would that you should do unto us, do it; and whatsoever we wish to do unto you, that will we do.

The three Christian virtues, faith, hope, and charity, fairly represent this whole system of so-called Bible morals – two false or useless precepts to one good precept. Charity is a true virtue, but "faith and hope," to quote Volney, "may be called the virtues of dupes for the benefit of knaves." And if the knaves have admitted charity to be the greatest of these virtues, it is because they are the recipients and not the dispensers of it.

Bible Models

The noblest types of manhood, like Bruno, Spinoza, Paine, and Ingersoll, have been slandered, anathematized, and slain by Christians, while the gods, the heroes, the patriarchs, the prophets, and the priests of the Bible have been presented as the highest models of moral excellence. Of these, Jehovah, Abraham, Jacob, Moses, David, Paul, and Christ are represented as the greatest and the best.

Who was Jehovah? "A being of terrific character – cruel, vindictive, capricious, and unjust." – Jefferson.

Who was Abraham? An insane barbarian patriarch who married his sister, denied his wife, and seduced her handmaid; who drove one child into the desert to starve, and made preparations to butcher the other.

Who was Jacob? Another patriarch, who won God's love by deceiving his father, cheating his uncle, robbing his brother, practicing bigamy with two of his cousins, and committing fornication with two of his housemaids.

Who was Moses? A model of meekness; a man who boasted of his own humility; a man who murdered an Egyptian and hid his body in the sand; a man who exterminated whole nations to secure the spoils of war, a man who butchered in cold blood thousands of captive widows, a man who tore dimpled babes from the breasts of dying mothers and put them to a cruel death; a man who made orphans of thirty-two thousand innocent girls, and turned sixteen thousand of them over to the brutal lusts of a savage soldiery.

Who was David? "A man after God's own heart." A vulgar braggadocio, using language to a woman the mere quoting of which would send me to prison; a traitor, desiring to lead an enemy's troops against his own countrymen; a thief and robber, plundering the country on every side; a liar, uttering wholesale falsehoods to screen himself from justice; a red-handed butcher, torturing and slaughtering thousands of men, women, and children, making them pass through burning brick-kilns, carving them up with saws and axes, and tearing them in pieces under harrows of iron; a polygamist, with a harem of wives and concubines; a drunken debauchee, dancing half-naked before the maids of his household; a lecherous old libertine, abducting and ravishing the wife of a faithful soldier; a murderer, having this faithful soldier put to death after desolating his home; a hoary-headed fiend, foaming with vengeance on his dying bed, demanding with his latest breath the deaths of two aged men, one of whom had most contributed to make his kingdom what it was, the other a man to whom he had promised protection.

Who was Paul? A religious fanatic; a Jew and a Christian. As a Jew, in the name of Jehovah, he persecuted Christians; as a Christian, in the name of Christ, he persecuted Jews; and both as a Jew and a Christian, and in the name of both Jehovah and Christ, he practiced dissimulation and hallowed falsehood.

Who was Christ? He is called the "divine teacher." Yes, –

He led
The crowd, he taught them justice, truth, and peace,
In semblance; but he lit within their souls
The quenchless flames of zeal, and blessed the sword
He brought on earth to satiate with the blood
Of truth and freedom his malignant soul.

— Shelley

Immoral Teachings Of The Bible

In the modern and stricter sense of the term, morality is scarcely taught in the Bible. Neither *moral, morals,* and *morality,* nor their equivalents, *ethical* and *ethics,* are to be found in the book. T. B. Wakeman, president of the Liberal University of Oregon, a life-long student of sociology and ethics, says:

> The word 'moral' does not occur in the Bible, nor even the idea. Hunting for morals in the Bible is like trying to find human remains in the oldest geologic strata – in the eozoon, for instance. Morals had not then been born.

I refuse to accept the Bible as a moral guide because it sanctions nearly every vice and crime. Here is the long list of wrongs which it authorizes and defends:

- Lying and deception
- Theft and robbery
- Wars of conquest
- Cannibalism
- Slavery
- Adultery and prostitution
- Intemperance
- Ignorance
- Unkindness to children
- Tyranny
- Cheating
- Murder
- Human sacrifices
- Witchcraft
- Polygamy
- Obscenity
- Vagrance
- Injustice to woman
- Cruelty to animals
- Intolerance and persecution

The Bible is, for the most part, the crude literature of a people who lived 2,000 years, and more, ago. Certain principles of right and wrong they recognized, but the finer principles of morality were unknown to them. They were an ignorant people. An ignorant people is generally a religious people, and a religious people nearly always an immoral people. They believed that they were God's chosen people – God's peculiar favorites – and that because of this they had the right to rob and cheat, to murder and enslave the rest of mankind. From these two causes, chiefly, ignorance and religion, i.e., superstition, emanated the immoral deeds and opinions which found expression in the writings of their priests and prophets.

The passages in the Bible which deal with vice and crime may be divided into three classes:

1. There are passages which condemn vice and crime. These I endorse.

2. There are many passages in which the crimes and vices of the people are narrated merely as historical facts without either sanctioning or condemning them. The book merits no censure because of these.

3. There are numerous passages which sanction vice and crime. These, and these alone, suffice to prove the charges that I make against the Bible as a moral guide.

✮ _____ ✮

John E. Remsburg was one of the ablest and best-known freethought writers and speakers of the last quarter of the nineteenth-century and president of the American Secular Union. This article is from one of his books, The Bible, *Truth Seeker Company, New York, 1905.*

The Bible teaches that woman brought sin and death into the world. She was to play the role of a dependent on man's bounty for all her material wants, and for all the information she might desire . . . Here is the Bible position of woman briefly summed up.

— Elizabeth Cady Stanton

Inerrancy

(I)nspiration was completely adequate to accomplish the task of giving God's will to man in written form in all its parts... divine superintendence extended to the verbal expression of the thoughts of the writers. . . the Scriptures never deceive nor mislead. . . the Bible is binding on all people and. . . all people will give an account for how they lived in light of its teaching. . . "Inerrant" means "wholly true" or "without mistake" and refers to the fact that the biblical writers were absolutely errorless, truthful, and trustworthy in all of their affirmations. The doctrine of inerrancy does not confine itself to moral and religious truth alone. Inerrancy extends to statements of fact, whether scientific, historical, or geographical. The biblical writers were preserved from the errors that appear in all other books.

— Dave Miller, 1992
(Dave Miller teaches at the Brown Trail School of Preaching in Bedford, Texas.)

I write as a Christian who loves the church. I am not a hostile critic who stands outside religion desiring to make fun of it... I look at the authority of the Scriptures as one who has been both nurtured by and then disillusioned with the literal Bible. My devotion to the Bible was so intense that it led me into a study that finally obliterated any possibility that the Bible could be related to on a literal basis...The Bible is not a scientific textbook... A literal Bible presents me with far more problems than assets. It offers me a God I cannot respect, much less worship... Those who insist on biblical literalism thus become unwitting accomplices in bringing about the death of the Christianity they so deeply love.

— John Shelby Spong

Ralph Nielsen, 334 Lauder, Moscow, ID 83843-2514, offers a $1,000 reward to anyone who can take all accounts of the resurrection in the four gospels, Acts, and 1 Corinthians 15, and write a single narrative in which he includes every event and detail mentioned in the separate accounts and do so without omitting anything or injecting inconsistency, contradiction, or purely speculative materials into the narrative. To sweeten the pot a little, *The Skeptical Review* (Farrell Till, ed.) will add another $1,000 to Mr. Nielsen's offer. (See also *No Stone Unturned* by Dan Barker, elsewhere in this book.)

In the first year of King Cyrus of Persia, in fulfillment of the word of the LORD spoken by Jeremiah, the LORD stirred up the spirit of King Cyrus of Persia so that he sent a herald throughout all his kingdom and also declared in a written edict: "Thus says King Cyrus of Persia: The LORD, the God of heaven, has given me all the kingdoms of the earth, and he has charged me to build him a house at Jerusalem, which is in Judah. Whoever is among you of all his people, may the LORD his God be with him! Let him go up."

Thus ends Second Chronicles.

In the first year of King Cyrus of Persia, in order that the word of the LORD by the mouth of Jeremiah might be accomplished, the LORD stirred up the spirit of King Cyrus of Persia so that he sent a herald throughout all his kingdom, and also in a written edict declared: "Thus says King Cyrus of Persia: The LORD, the God of heaven, has given me all the kingdoms of the earth, and he has charged me to build him a house at Jerusalem in Judah. Any of those among you who are of his people — may their God be with them! — are now permitted to go up to Jerusalem in Judah, and rebuild the house of the LORD, the God of Israel — he is the God who is in Jerusalem;

Thus begins Ezra.

The Bible is kinda like a high school band on the first day of school — tain't easy to harmonize.

— California Cracker

Rescuing The Bible From Fundamentalism

John Shelby Spong, Bishop of the Episcopal Church
Reviewed by William B. Lindley

The Bible is indeed a prisoner of fundamentalism – of the literalist mind-set, of the doctrine of Biblical inerrancy. Bishop Spong seeks to rescue it by "entering" the experience that underlies what was written. He believes "that we can discern the hand of a transcendent deity underneath these literal words." Does he succeed?

Most of the book is a review in plain language of the prevailing opinion among Bible scholars on how, when and why the various books of the Bible came to be written, what points of doctrine were being made. (The New Testament predominates, about two-to-one.) These opinions are at variance with literalism, as Spong points out repeatedly, and a good portion of his book notes the Bible's many contradictions and atrocities.

Starting 200 years ago with Thomas Paine's *Age of Reason*, and continuing with G. W. Foote, Robert Green Ingersoll, Bertrand Russell, and others, up to the present-day *Biblical Errancy* and *Skeptical Review*, freethinkers have been trying to get this word out, and now Bishop Spong joins us. He does this to shock liberal Christians out of their profound ignorance of the Bible, out of their tendency to sweep literalism under the rug, to look the other way. He shares with Thomas Paine an outrage at Chapter 31 of the Book of Numbers, total incredulity at the wildly incoherent accounts of the crucifixion and resurrection, and many other points. I only wish he had properly acknowledged Thomas Paine and the other pioneers. Whether his failure here is a moral one or a matter of ignorance, I cannot tell.

I think Spong oversimplifies the contrast between first-century "superstition" and 20th-century scientific "enlightenment". Some Bible doctrine was irrational by first-century standards, as shown by Paul's experience on the Areopagus (Acts 17). Spong seems not to understand the concept of reference frames in science. He faults the weatherman for being geocentric in talking about sunrise and sunset. There's nothing unscientific about adopting a geocentric frame for convenience. Similarly, when he rejects demons as an ancient superstition, he overlooks the charming story of the witch doctor who, viewing germs in the microscope, said, "So that's what evil spirits look like!"

In his thorough repudiation of literalism, he does away with major portions of traditional Christian doctrine: original sin, the Incarnation (God made flesh in Jesus), the Trinity, the physical resurrection, Christ as Savior. He even expresses doubt about the afterlife. The orthodox might think there's nothing left, but Spong would disagree. To him, unbelievers "live in a world of dreadful transcendent emptiness", and some Christians are in a "sterile camp" of "empty postmodern secularity". He says: " ... the yearning to be restored to (union with God is) in the depths of every human psyche." He cannot yet acknowledge that people at home in this natural universe are far from feeling or being empty.

In wanting the Bible to be in some nonliteral sense the Word of God, he wants to have his cake and eat it too. He wants universalism, but is tied to Jesus Christ, a first-century figure. He wants to toss the miracles out, but to keep an ineffable divinity. However, the book is valuable for unbelievers in two ways:

(1) it is evidence that *Christians* are trying to shake loose of the nonsense of Biblical inerrancy, and

(2) it offers a platform for friendly, constructive debate. And his challenge to his fellow Christians to acquire Biblical literacy cannot be faulted. It is a good-faith effort.

Reprinted from Truth Seeker Vol. 119, No. 3, 1992.

As the historical world of Christendom sinks ever more deeply into the darkness of an irrecoverable past, theology is faced with the choice either of relapsing into a dead and archaic language or of evolving a whole new form of speech.

— Thomas J. J. Altizer

Evangelist Billy Sunday

Evangelist Billy Sunday preached a fundamentalist brand of Christianity. "Soaking it into Satan," as he said, he smashed pulpit furniture to attract attention, advertised with calliopes, and once when he claimed to have seen so much sin in one community, he prayed at a meeting, "O Lord, the next time you come here, bring along plenty of antiseptic and rubber gloves." Sunday persuaded thousands to "hit the sawdust trail," but he also helped bring discredit on the revivalist movement.

The rivers of America will run with blood before they take our holy, god-inspired Bible from our schools.
— Billy Sunday
early 20th-century
American preacher

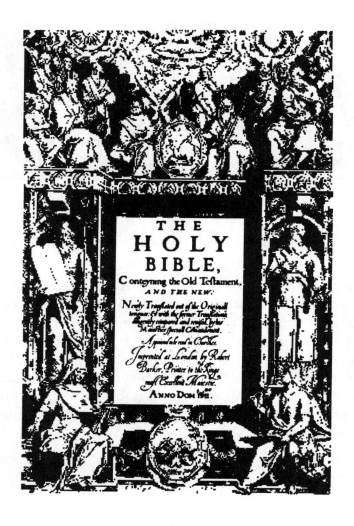

King James I (King of England) was a known
homosexual who murdered his young lovers
and victimized countless heretics and women.
His cruelty was justified by his "divine right" of
kings.

— *James the First* by Otto J. Scott

Destructive Divines

A. J. Mattill, Jr.

Some Reflections on C.S. Lewis' "Modern Theology
and Biblical Criticism"

In this address to priests of the Church of England, C.S. Lewis charges that "the undermining of the old orthodoxy has been mainly the work of divines engaged in New Testament criticism." On this point Lewis is absolutely correct. New Testament scholars do deserve the major blame (or credit?) for this work of demolition. As we reflect on Lewis's remarks, we shall see precisely how the destructive divines undermine "the old orthodoxy."

Jonah, John, and Jesus

To defend orthodoxy, Lewis challenges the authority of New Testament experts, "the authority in deference to whom we are asked to give up a huge mass" of age-old beliefs. He is "skeptical about this authority" because specialists in New Testament lack "literary judgment." They fail to reconstruct convincingly the genesis of biblical texts: "what vanished documents each author used, when and where he wrote, with what purposes, under what influences."

An example of their poor judgment is their classification of the Fourth Gospel as a "spiritual romance," as "a poem not a history."

Lewis may well be correct in claiming that most, if not all, New Testament scholars are more or less incompetent as literary critics, since they spend their time in detailed study of the New Testament and lack "a wide and deep and genial experience of literature in general." Lewis, however, in criticizing the literary acumen of Johannine students, ensnares himself. He accuses them of "crass insensitivity" in judging the Fourth Gospel by the same canons as the book of Jonah, for any competent literary critic could recognize that the former is a history whereas the latter is "a tale with as few even pretended historical attachments as Job, grotesque in incident."

Lewis here is repeating his earlier assessment of Jonah, when he placed Jonah at the opposite end of a scale of historical writings from the memoirs of David's court (2 Samuel 9-20; 1 Kings 1-2), Mark, or Acts. What Lewis fails to note is that Jesus himself regarded Jonah as a historical book, factual and authentic. Jonah was a sign to Jesus' generation. The men of Nineveh repented at his preaching, and "as Jonah was three days and three nights in the belly of the big fish, so will the Son of Man be three days and three nights in the heart of the earth" (Matthew 12:38-42; 16:1-4; Luke 11:29-32).

If Lewis is correct about the non-historical nature of the book of Jonah, then Jesus lacked literary judgment. And if Jesus cannot be trusted even as a literary critic, how can he be trusted in spiritual matters as Lord and Savior? Lewis can hardly shore up Christian orthodoxy by undercutting Jesus' authority.

It is, of course, possible that Matthew and Luke err in their reporting of Jesus' attitude toward Jonah. If so, Matthew and Luke are not the dependable historians Lewis would like them to be. Or it may be that Jonah is a historical book and Jesus, Matthew, and Luke are reliable literary authorities after all. But that would call into question Lewis's competence as a critic and his distrust of New Testament scholarship.

Messiah and Megalomania

Furthermore, Lewis seems unaware of the fact that the more trust one puts in the Fourth Gospel's portrait of Jesus the more difficult it is to defend the sanity of Jesus. Thus psychologists have found that the megalomania of John's Jesus mounts ceaselessly, for he is continually occupied with his ego, openly proclaiming his messianic dignity (John 6:29, 35, 38, 40, 47-58; 7:38; 8:12; 11:25-26; 14:6, 13-14). By way of contrast, the Jesus of the Synoptics keeps his messiahship a secret (Mark 9:9, etc.). Thus the combined Jesus of all four gospels sometimes proclaims himself as Messiah and sometimes refrains from doing so, which is conduct like that of paranoids.

The Spiritual Gospel and the Synoptics

Even if Lewis is correct in classifying the Fourth Gospel as something other than a "spiritual romance," it is hardly the "reportage ... pretty close up to the facts" that he thinks it is, for it is too different from the Synoptics in style, chronology, theology, and omissions and additions to be straight history. Thus already about A.D. 230 Clement of Alexandria labeled John, probably more truly than anyone before or since, "a spiritual gospel," to suggest that John is more interested in the spiritual or mystical or theological meaning of Jesus' words and the events of his life than in Lewis's close-up reportage. John concentrates more on religious truths than on historical facts.

But so far as the defense of Christian faith is concerned, the crucial matter is not that of correctly identifying the genre of the Fourth Gospel but that of whether John can be reconciled with the Synoptics. Critical investigators find this reconciliation difficult in the extreme, if not impossible.

Lewis fails to notice that "the spiritual gospel" contradicts the Synoptics in numerous ways. Here are just a few:

- Mark 1:4,9; 10:18 vs. John 1:29-34; 3:26
- Matt. 4:12,17; Mark 1:14; Luke 3:19,20 vs. John 3:22-24
- Matt. 17:11-13 vs. John 1: 19-21
- Matt. 21:12,13 vs. John 2:11-16 (timing)
- Matt. 26:17; Mark 14:12; Luke 22:7 vs. John 13:1,2,29; 18:28; 19:14,31,42

Whether or not New Testament scholars lack "literary judgment," the fact remains that they have succeeded brilliantly in delineating the differences and contradictions between John and the Synoptics. We can readily see how devastating this criticism is to "Christian orthodoxy" when we recall that orthodoxy's picture of Christ is based largely on the Fourth Gospel.

Church and Canon

There is an important part of literary criticism which Lewis neglects, perhaps because he does not really distrust the divines at this point, namely the question of authorship: Who wrote the books of the Bible?

As Lewis must have known, critical scholarship rejects the traditional authorship of many of the twenty-seven books in the New Testament canon, and has been even more successful in setting aside the traditional authorship of numerous Old Testament books. Whereas the church has claimed that the Bible was written by some forty amanuenses of God, with one viewpoint, we can now quip that the Bible was written by some four hundred authors and redactors with four hundred different points of view. The church, on the other hand, has claimed inspired prudence in choosing aright the books of the canon as books really written by the authoritative persons whose names they bear.

The church's claim to special inspiration in forming the canon is obviously endangered if it erred in even one instance. If it made as many mistakes as scholarship indicates, then its claim to inspired prudence in selecting the books of the canon is thoroughly shattered.

And what becomes of the "old orthodoxy" or of any form of Christianity without an infallible canon and without an infallible church which determined the canon in the first place?

Straining at Gnats

Lewis distrusts the destructive divines not only because they are incompetent literary critics but also because they constantly operate on the principle that "the miraculous does not occur" and therefore they reject as unhistorical all passages which narrate miracles. Even "more strangely, after swallowing the camel of the Resurrection," they strain "at such gnats as the feeding of the multitudes."

This latter charge is certainly true of John Knox. Knox affirms the resurrection of Jesus as a "special act of God," but places it in "an altogether different category" from the miracles recorded of Jesus' earthly career. "Speaking broadly," Knox would say "that they did not" happen. For one thing, "the element of the miraculous grows in bulk and importance as one moves from our earlier sources to our later. Paul's letters, our earliest literary sources, say nothing of any miracles in the earthly life." But in the Synoptics we find an abundance of miracles: healing powers, calming the sea, walking on water, multiplying loaves and fishes, raising the dead, and supernatural portents attending Jesus' birth and death. But the miracles of the Fourth Gospel "are greater and vastly more impressive."

Lewis's logic is superior to that of Knox. If there is a God of miracles who is committed to Jesus' mission and acted mightily to raise him from the dead when Jesus was really graveyard dead, why should we strain at the lesser miracles recorded in the Gospels?

Yet we should note that this inconsistency among liberal biblical scholars arises not only from a skepticism about, or even denial of, lesser miracles, but it also grows out of the nature of our sources, which do display a suspicious growth of the miraculous from early to later sources. But when liberals discard the smaller miracles they reject large portions of the gospel records and thus make the gospels unreliable as sources for the ministry of Jesus. And if the accounts of lesser miracles cannot be trusted, then there is no sufficient reason to trust the accounts of the super-miracle of Jesus' resurrection.

Supernatural Short Circuits

When we behold Lewis's labored defense of Jesus' miracles, we can better understand why liberal theologians deny even Jesus' miracles. According to Lewis, the account in John 2:1-11 of Jesus' turning the water into wine is, contrary to liberal criticism, no parable but a miracle "meant perfectly literally, for this refers to something which, if it happened, was well within the reach of our senses and our language."

Lewis reasons as follows: This miracle is not isolated from other divine acts. God does what he has always been doing, making wine. God is always turning water into wine, "by creating a vegetable organism that can turn water, soil, and sunlight into a juice which will, under proper conditions, become wine." At Cana, "God, now incarnate, short circuits the process: makes wine in a moment: uses earthenware jars instead of vegetable fibers to hold the water. But he uses them to do what He is always doing. The miracle consists in the short cut."

In this way Lewis believes he has established the credibility of this and other miracles of Jesus by showing their "fitness" to nature – they are "invasions" of a supernatural Power, but they are not arbitrary invasions by an alien god. Rather they are appropriate invasions by the sovereign God of nature.

For many modern people, it is precisely these outside "invasions," "interruptions," and "short circuiting" of the usual course of nature that are so difficult to accept, no matter how appropriate Lewis may find them to be, for nature appears to do "all things spontaneously of herself without the meddling of the gods" (Lucretius).

And it is not too clear just what Lewis's argument from "fitness" proves. When has nature of herself made wine? Nature of course produces grapes, but without Lewis's "proper conditions" (human intervention) she makes no wine, much less the highest quality wine, as at Cana.

This story is really the Christian counterpart to the pagan legends of Dionysus, the Greek god of wine, who at his annual festival in his temple of Elis filled three empty kettles with wine – no water needed! And on the fifth of January wine instead of water gushed from a spring in his temple at Andros. If we believe Jesus' miracle, why should we not believe Dionysus's? Both are "within the reach of our senses and our language," and both are appropriate to nature, to use Lewis's criteria of credibility.

Eschatological Errors

If literary criticism and the denial of miracles are devastating to Christianity, how much more so is the study of the New Testament's teaching on "last things." Here more clearly than anywhere else we see the truth of Lewis's charge that New Testament scholarship is largely responsible for destroying Christian faith.

A large segment of New Testament specialists is convinced that the people of the New Testament believed they were living in the last century, not the first. Jesus' title, "Messiah," means "inaugurator of the end." Thus Jesus came preaching, "The time is fulfilled, and the kingdom of God is at hand" (Mark 1:15; similarly Mark 9:1; 13:30; Matthew 10:23; 23:29-36; Luke 12:49-50).

If Jesus did not make such statements about the nearness of the end of the world, then the gospels are not trustworthy accounts of this crucial message at the heart of Jesus' life and ministry. How, then, can we know whether the rest of the gospel records is true?

But if Jesus did make such promises, as Lewis himself admits that he did, then he was mistaken on the all-important matter of last things. Moreover, he made solemn promises he failed to keep. We can be as certain that Jesus taught the speedy coming of the kingdom as we can be of any matter in biblical studies. If Jesus had had his way, and his ministry to usher in the kingdom had not failed, we and this world would not be here today. The first century would have been the last.

The following passages indicate how pervasive this imminent expectation is in the New Testament:

- Matt. 3:2, 7, 10; 4:17; 6:11, 24-34; 7:13-14; 10:23; 12:32; 16:27-28; 21:18-19; 23:39; 24:6, 33-36; 26:29, 64.
- Mark 1:15; 9:1; 11:12-14; 12:34; 13:4, 29-32; 14:25, 62; 15:43.
- Luke 3:17-18; 9:27; 10:9, 11; 11:30; 12:22-48; 14:31-33; 18:7-8; 19:11; 21:7-9, 28, 31-32, 36; 22:18; 23:51; 24:21.
- John 14:19; 16:16-17; 21:22-23.
- Acts 1:5-8, 10-11; 2:17, 44-47; 3:19-21, 24; 4:34-37; 6:10; 7:55-56; 10:42; 13:41; 14:22; 17:31; 24:15, 25; 26:6-7, 22-23; 28:31 (Western text in Latin).
- Romans 8:18, 38; 10:4; 13:11-12; 16:20.
- 1 Corinthians 3:22, 7:26, 29-31; 10:11; 15:51-52.
- 2 Corinthians 5:1.

- Galatians 6:10.
- Ephesians 1:21.
- Philippians 4:5.
- Colossians 1:24.
- 1 Thessalonians 3:4; 4:15-18; 5:10.
- 2 Thessalonians 2:1-12.
- 1 Timothy 4:1, 8; 6:14, 19.
- 2 Timothy 3:1; 4:1.
- Titus 2:13.
- Hebrews 1:2, 14; 2:5; 6:5; 8:13; 9:11; 10:25, 27; 12:22; 13:14.
- James 2:12; 5:8-9.
- 1 Peter 1:20; 4:5, 7, 17; 5:1.
- 2 Peter 3:3-13.
- 1 John 2:18; 4:3.
- Jude 17-23.
- Revelation 1:1, 3, 19; 2:10; 3:10, 11, 16; 6:11; 8:13; 10:6, 7; 12:5; 14:7; 17:8; 22:7, 10, 12, 20.

In short, "destructive divines" have discovered that New Testament writers looked forward to the personal return of Christ in their own generation and that the nearness of Jesus' return was the regulative idea in their lives.

The implications of this miscalculation are enormous. If the apostles and others were mistaken as to the immediacy of the end, then they may have been mistaken about Jesus' messiahship, on which that expectation was founded, and also mistaken about his resurrection, on which their belief in his messiahship was strengthened, if not founded.

Adam and Jesus

But we cannot lay all the blame (or credit?) upon Lewis's destructive divines. Their work has been reinforced by experts in other fields, especially in the sciences and comparative religion, who have shown that Adam and Eve were not historical persons and that the Fall of Genesis 3 was not a historical event.

In this connection we are reminded of Augustine (354-430), who shrewdly observed that the whole Christian religion may be summed up in the actions of two men, Adam and Jesus, the one to ruin us, the other to save us.

But now we know, if we know anything, that evolution demolishes the historical Adam and apocalyptic discredits the historical Jesus. Hence, the entire Christian system collapses, for there was none to ruin us, none to save us.

And since the fall and curse of Genesis 3 are not events which actually happened, we cannot explain why people and animals suffer so much in a divinely created world. As a result, the Christian belief in an omnipotent, omnibenevolent god suffers shipwreck. And that means it is all over for Christianity and other theistic religions. Hence the divines, with assistance from other researchers, have been even more destructive than Lewis feared.

Hoping against Hope

Lewis concludes his address with the hope that "the whole thing will blow over." But, as we have seen by probes into several areas, modern theology and biblical criticism have done their work of demolition too well to "blow over." Contrary to Lewis, we can never "stick to mere textual criticism of the old sort, Lachmann's sort."

In fact, Lewis himself is too badly infected with skeptical higher criticism to turn back the hands of time to the days of Karl Lachmann (1793-1851). Lewis declares he is no fundamentalist; he admits that the Bible "may no doubt contain errors;" he regards Jonah and Job as unhistorical; he doubts, denies, or overlooks many biblical miracles, and he finds Jesus mistaken about the nearness of the end.

Lewis, in other words, is on the slippery slope sliding toward the very apostasy he warns priests against.

Unringing the Bell

To sum up: we have granted that there is much truth in Lewis's critique of "modern theology and biblical criticism." Biblical scholars, especially New Testament critics, have indeed undermined Christianity. They may, as a whole, not be fully competent in every department of literary criticism. They often do strain at the gnats of Jesus' own miracles and yet swallow the camel of Jesus' resurrection. And many biblical theologians do assume that miracles do not occur.

But the fact that Lewis often speaks truth does not mean that he has succeeded in undoing the destructive work of the divines, for that destruction lies in areas not effectively touched by Lewis's arguments: John and the Synoptics, authorship, the credibility of miracles, eschatology, and evolution.

If Lewis's successors want to save Christianity, they will have to reconcile John and the Synoptics, restore the traditional authorship of the biblical books, make credible the divine "short circuits," explain away the eschatological errors of the New Testament, resurrect Adam as a historical figure, and restore Jesus as a credible end-time prophet. Then we can have a Christian orthodoxy based upon the actions of Adam and Jesus.

And beyond all that, if Lewis's disciples have slid as far down the slippery slope as Lewis had, they will need to show us how to put on the brakes to avoid sliding to the bottom of complete apostasy.

In my estimate, however, the destructive divines, with assistance from discerning thinkers in other fields, have done their work so convincingly that the chances of the needed restoration of Christianity are as small as the chances of unringing the bell or of reconstructing the pig out of the sausage.

A. J. Mattill, Jr. is an author, lecturer, and professor of Biblical studies at several southern colleges.

C.S. Lewis (1898-1963) was an English Christian apologist and writer, author of The Screwtape Letters, Mere Christianity, *and much more.*

"How are you ever goin' to keep 'em down on the farm after they've seen Pa-ree?" Apparently, a lot of preachers are at long last beginning to see the Pa-ree of responsible Bible criticism, and no one is ever going to get them back down on the inerrancy farm

— Farrell Till

Zeus and Jesus

Zeus: Greek form of Sanskrit *Dyhaus pitar,* "Father Heaven," probably linked with Babylonian myths of *Zu the Storm-Bird*, a thrower of thunderbolts. The Romans called him *Jupiter,* or *Jove*; the European Christians substituted Jesus for Zeus.

Jesus

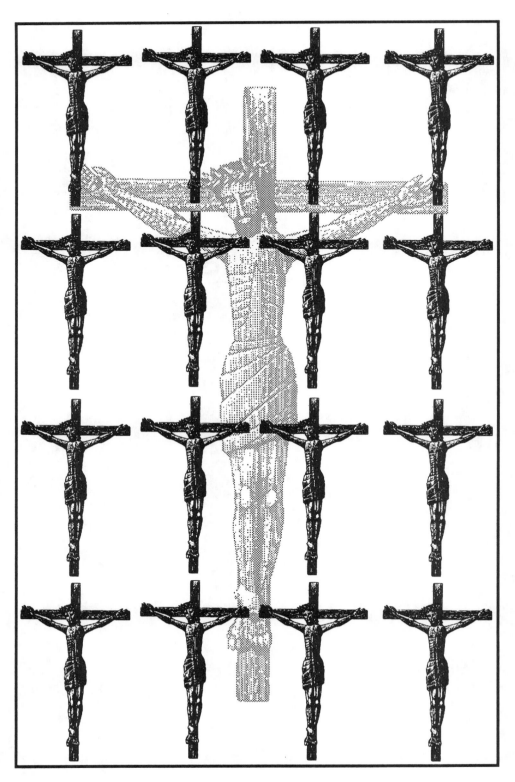

132

The World's Sixteen Crucified Saviors

Kersey Graves

Rival Claims Of The Saviors

It is claimed by the disciples of Jesus Christ that he was of supernatural and divine origin; that he had a human being for a mother, and a God for his father; that, although he was woman-conceived, he was Deity begotten, and molded in the human form, but comprehending in essence a full measure of the infinite Godhead, thus making him half human and half divine in his sublunary origin.

It is claimed that he was full and perfect God, and perfect man; and while he was God, he was also the son of God, and as such was sent down by his father to save a fallen and guilty world; and that thus his mission pertained to the whole human race; and his inspired seers are made to declare that ultimately every nation, tongue, kindred, and people under heaven will acknowledge allegiance to his government, and concede his right to reign and rule the world; that "every knee must bow, and every tongue confess that Jesus is Lord, to the glory of God the Father."

But we do not find that this prophecy has ever been or is likely to be fulfilled. We do not observe that this claim to the infinite deityship of Jesus Christ has been or is likely to be universally conceded. On the contrary, it is found that by a portion, and a large portion of the people of even those nations now called Christian, this claim has been steadily and unswervingly controverted, through the whole line of history, stretching through the nearly two thousand years which have elapsed since his advent to earth.

Even some of those who are represented to have been personally acquainted with him – aye! some of his own brethren in the flesh, children in the same household, children of the same mother – had the temerity to question the tenableness of his claim to a divine emanation. And when we extend our researches to other countries, we find this claim, so far from being conceded, is denied and contested by whole nations upon other grounds. It is met and confronted by rival claims.

Upon this ground hundreds of millions of the established believers in divine revelation – hundreds of millions of believers in the divine character and origin of religion – reject the pretensions set up for Jesus Christ. They admit both a God and a Savior, but do not accept Jesus of Nazareth as being either. They admit a Messiah, but not the Messiah; these nations contend that the title is misplaced which makes "the man Christ Jesus" the Savior of the world. They claim to have been honored with the birth of the true Savior among them, and defend this claim upon the ground of priority of date. They aver that the advents of their Messiahs were long prior to that of the Christians, and that this circumstance adjudicates for them a superiority of claim as to having had the true Messiah born upon their soil.

It is argued that, as the story of the incarnation of the Christians' Savior is of more recent date than those of these oriental and ancient religions (as is conceded by Christians themselves), the origin of the former is thus indicated and foreshadowed as being an outgrowth from, if not a plagiarism upon the latter – a borrowed copy, of which the pagan stories furnish the original. Here, then, we observe a rivalship of claims, as to which of the remarkable personages who have figured in the world as Saviors, Messiahs, and Sons of God, in different ages and different countries, can be considered the true Savior and "sent of God;" or whether all should be, or the claims of all rejected.

For researches into oriental history reveal the remarkable fact that stories of incarnate Gods answering to and resembling the miraculous character of Jesus Christ have been prevalent in most if not all the principal religious heathen nations of antiquity; and the accounts and narrations of some of these deific incarnations bear such a striking resemblance to that of the Christian Savior – not only in their general features, but in some cases in the most minute details, from the legend of the immaculate conception to that of the crucifixion, and subsequent ascension into heaven – that one might almost be mistaken for the other.

More than twenty claims of this kind – claims of beings invested with divine honor (deified) – have come forward and presented themselves at the bar of the world, with their credentials, to contest the verdict of Christendom, in having proclaimed Jesus Christ, "the only son, and sent of God:" twenty Messiahs, Saviors, and Sons of God, according to history or tradition, have, in past times, descended from heaven, and taken upon themselves the form of men, clothing themselves with human flesh, and furnishing incontestable evidence of a divine origin, by various miracles, marvelous works, and superlative virtues; and finally these twenty Jesus Christs (accepting their character for the name) laid the foundation for the salvation of the world, and ascended back to heaven.

1. Chrishna of Hindostan.
2. Budha Sakia of India.
3. Salivahana of Bermuda.
4. Zulis, or Zhule, also Osiris and Orus, of Egypt.
5. Odin of the Scandinavians.
6. Crite of Chaldea.
7. Zoroaster and Mithra of Persia.
8. Baal and Taut, " the only Begotten of God," of Phoenecia.
9. Indra of Tibet.
10. Bali of Afghanistan.
11. Jao of Nepal.
12. Wittoba of the Bilingonese.
13. Thammuz of Syria.
14. Atys of Phrygia.
15. Xamolxis of Thrace.
16. Zoar of the Bonzes.
17. Adad of Assyria.
18. Deva Tat, and Sammonocadam of Siam.
19. Alcides of Thebes.
20. Mikado of the Sintoos.
21. Beddru of Japan.
22 Hesus or Eros, and Bremrillah, of the Druids.
23. Thor, son of Odin, of the Gauls.
24. Cadmus of Greece.
25. Hil and Feta of the Mandaites.
26. Gentaut and Quexalcote of Mexico.
27. Universal Monarch of the Sibyls.
28. Ischy of the island of Formosa.
29. Divine Teacher of Plato.
30. Holy One of Xaca.
31. Fohi and Tien of China.
32. Adonis, son of the virgin Io of Greece.
33. Ixion and Quirinus of Rome.
34. Prometheus of Caucasus.
35. Mohamud, or Mahomet, of Arabia.

These have all received divine honors, have nearly all been worshipped as Gods, or sons of God; were mostly incarnated as Christs, Saviors, Messiahs, or Mediators; not a few of them were reputedly born of virgins; some of them filling a character almost identical with that ascribed by the Christians' bible to Jesus Christ; many of them, like him, are reported to have been crucified; and all of them, taken together, furnish a prototype and parallel for nearly every important incident and wonder-inciting miracle, doctrine and precept recorded in the New Testament, of the Christians' Savior. Surely, with so many Saviors the world cannot, or should not, be lost.

And now, upon the heel of this question, we find another formidable query to be met and answered, viz.: was he (Christ) the only Savior, seeing that a multitude of similar claims are now upon our council-board to be disposed of ?

We shall, however, leave the theologians of the various religious schools to adjust and settle this difficulty among themselves. We shall leave them to settle the question as best they can as to whether Jesus Christ was the only son and sent of God – "the only begotten of the Father," as John declares him to be (John 1:14) – in view of the fact that long prior to his time various personages, in different nations, were invested with the title "Son of God," and have left behind them similar proofs and credentials of the justness of their claims to such a title, if being essentially alike – as we shall prove and demonstrate them to be – can make their claims similar.

We shall present an array of facts and historical proofs, drawn from numerous histories and the Holy Scriptures and bibles appertaining to these various Saviors, which include a history of their lives and doctrines, that will go to show that in nearly all their leading features, and mostly even in their details, they are strikingly similar.

A comparison, or parallel view, extended through their sacred histories, so as to include an exhibition presented in parallels of the teachings of their respective bibles, would make it clearly manifest that, with respect to nearly every important thought, deed, word, action, doctrine, principle, precept, tenet, ritual, ordinance or ceremony, and even the various important characters or personages, who figure in their religious dramas as Saviors, prophets, apostles, angels, devils, demons, exalted or fallen genii – in a word, nearly every miraculous or marvelous story, moral precept, or tenet of religious faith, noticed in either the Old or New Testament Scriptures of Christendom – from the Jewish cosmogony, or story of creation in Genesis, to the last legendary tale in St. John's "Arabian Nights" (alias the Apocalypse) – there is to be found an antitype for, or outline of, somewhere in the sacred records or bibles of the oriental heathen nations, making equal if not higher pretention to a divine emanation and divine inspiration.

This is admitted by all historians, even the most orthodox, to be of much more ancient date; for while Christians only claim, for the earthly advent of their Savior and the birth of their religion, a period less than nineteen hundred years in the past, on the contrary, most of the deific or divine incarnations of the heathen and their respective religions are, by the concurrent and united verdict of all history, assigned a date several hundred or several thousand years earlier, thus leaving the inference patent that so far as there has been any borrowing or transfer of materials from one system to another, Christianity has been the borrower.

And as nearly the whole outline and constituent parts of the Christian system are found scattered through these older systems, the query is at once sprung as to whether Christianity did not derive its materials from these sources – that is, from heathenism, instead of from high heaven – as it claims.

As far back as 1200 B. C., sacred records were extant and traditions were current, in the East, which taught that the heathen Savior (Virishna) was:

- Immaculately conceived and born of a spotless virgin, "who had never known man."
- That the author of, or agent in, the conception, was a spirit or ghost (of course a Holy Ghost).
- That he was threatened in early infancy with death by the ruling tyrant, Cansa.
- That his parents had, consequently, to flee with him to Gokul for safety.
- That all the young male children under two years of age were slain by an order issued by Cansa, similar to that of Herod in Judea.
- That angels and shepherds attended his birth.
- That it occurred in accordance with previous prophecy.
- That he was presented at birth with frankincense, myrrh, &c.
- That he was saluted and worshipped as "the Savior of men," according to the report of the late Christian Missionary Huc.
- That he led a life of humility and practical moral usefulness.
- That he wrought various astounding miracles, such as healing the sick, restoring sight to the blind, casting out devils, raising the dead to life, &c.
- That he was finally put to death upon the cross (i. e., crucified) between two thieves.
- After which he descended to hell, rose from the dead, and ascended back to heaven "in the sight of all men," as his biblical history declares.

The *New York Correspondent*, published in 1828, furnishes us the following brief history of an ancient Chinese God, known as Beddou:

> All the Eastern writers agree in placing the birth of Beddou 1027 B. C. The doctrines of this Deity prevailed over Japan, China, and Ceylon. According to the sacred tenets of his

religion, 'God is incessantly rendering himself incarnate,' but his greatest and most solemn incarnation was three thousand years ago, in the province of Cashmere, under the name of Fot, or Beddou. He was believed to have sprung from the right inter-costal of a virgin of the royal blood, who, when she became a mother, did not the less continue to be a virgin; that the king of the country, uneasy at his birth, was desirous to put him to death, and hence caused all the males that were born at the same period to be put to death, and also that, being saved by shepherds, he lived in the desert to the age of thirty years, at which time he opened his commission, preaching the doctrines of truth, and casting out devils; that he performed a multitude of the most astonishing miracles, spent his life fasting, and in the severest mortifications, and at his death bequeathed to his dis-ciples the volume in which the principles of his religion are contained.

Here, it will be observed, are some very striking counterparts to the miraculous incidents found related in the Gospel history of Jesus Christ. And no less analogous is the no less well-authenticated story of Quexalcote of Mexico, which the Rev. Mr. Maurice concedes to be, and Lord Kingsborough and Niebuhr (in his history of Rome) prove to be much older than the Gospel account of Jesus Christ. According to Maurice's "Ind. Ant.," Humboldt's "Researches in Mexico," Lord Kingsborough's "Mexican Ant.," and other works, the incarnate God Quexalcote was born (about 300 B. C.) of a spotless virgin, by the name Chimalman, and led a life of the deepest humility and piety; retired to a wilderness, fasted forty days, was worshipped as a God, and was finally crucified between two thieves; after which he was buried and descended into hell, but rose again the third day.

The following is a part of Lord Kingsborough's testimony in the case: "The temptation of Quexalcote, the fast of forty days ordained by the Mexican ritual, the cup with which he was presented to drink (on the cross), the reed which was his sign, the 'Morning Star,' which he is designated, the 'Teoteepall, or Divine Stone,' which was laid on his altar, and which was likewise an object of adoration, – all these circumstances, connected with many others relating to Quexalcote of Mexico, but which are here omitted, are very curious and mysterious."

Again "Quexalcote is represented, in the painting of Codex Bor-gianus, as nailed to the cross." One plate in this work represents him as being crucified in the heavens, one as being crucified between two thieves. Sometimes he is represented as being nailed to the cross, and speaks of his burial, descent into hell, and his resurrection; while the account of his immaculate conception and miraculous birth are found in a work called "Codex Vaticanus."

Other parallel incidents could be cited, if we had space for them, appertaining to the history of this Mexican God. And parallels might also be constructed upon the histories of other ancient Gods, – as that of Sakia of India, Salivahana of Bermuda, Hesus, or Eros, of the Celtic Druids, Mithra of Persia, and Hil and Feta of the Mandaites.

We will close with the testimony of a French philosopher, Bagin, on the subject of deific incarnations. He says, "The most ancient histories are those of Gods who became incarnate in order to govern mankind. All those fables are the same in spirit, and sprang up everywhere from confused ideas, which have universally prevailed among mankind, – that Gods formerly descended upon earth."

Now, we ask the Christian reader,

> What does all this mean? How are you going to sustain the declaration that Jesus Christ was the only son and sent of God, in view of these historic facts? Where are the superior credentials of his claim? How will you prove the miraculous portion of his history to be real and the others false?

We boldly say it cannot be done. Please answer these questions, or relinquish your doctrine of the divinity of Jesus Christ.

Kersey Graves, The World's Sixteen Crucified Saviors, *Truth Seeker Co., New York, 1875. This is an excerpt from his book, which is still in print. Available from Health Research, Mokelumne Hill, CA 95245.*

EDITOR'S COMMENT: This article reflects the same problems, short falls and fallacies for which the Christian crucification story is guilty. It is also another example of composite literature.

The original true believers were taking mythology and materializing it into symbols that represent their saviors.

This 6th-century representation of Jesus is the oldest known hand-painted icon in the world. It is believed to have been inspired by the Holy Shroud of Edessa.

Santa Caterina Monastery Library, Sinai

Jesus: The Aramaic-Speaking Shemite

Rocco A. Errico

In this perspective of Jesus my intent is to bring the reader into the Eastern Mediterranean setting (the Aram-Mesopotamian culture and language) from which the dramatic and impelling life of this famous Galilean Jew appears to us. This will enhance the reader's perception of Jesus in his own Aramaic-Hebrew culture, religion and social atmosphere.

Ethnically speaking, Jesus was a Shemite (in English the letter "h" is dropped and it is spelled and pronounced as "Semite"). The term "Shemite" is derived from one of the sons of Noah whose name was Shem, Gen. 5:32. The expression "Shemite" applies to many Semitic dialects. It also refers to all the descendants of Shem, such as the Akkadians, Arameans, Assyrians, Chaldeans, Hebrews and Arabs.

What kind of temperament does a son of the Near East, especially a Semite, possess? What of his manner of speech, his deep religious feelings and what would be his general outlook on life? When we discover the answers to these questions we will be able to see, at least in part, the human Jesus beginning to emerge from his own inherited Eastern psychological environment. As we begin to comprehend the rich cultural and religious philosophy of Jesus' time, in its Judaic context, a clearer sense of the man and his teachings may be grasped.

The four Gospels, Matthew, Mark, Luke and John, are the main sources available to help us uncover the Semitic Jesus. In the modern sense these Gospel writings are not biographical material about Jesus. In fact, no contemporary stylized biographies can be found anywhere in Scripture. As a general rule, ancient Easterners had no deep interest in the details of a great man's life from birth to death. Their basic interest in such a man would be in his teachings and the overall impact of those teachings upon their lives. The Gospels were written after Jesus' death. These writings began as recollections of his words and acts as a teacher and healer. The stories of his birth, death and resurrection were added later.

The texts of the Gospels should not be thought of as mythical creations just because the historians of Jesus' day did not mention him in their writings. We need to keep in mind that he was a provincial teacher from a small village in Galilee and was not widely known. The primary characteristics of Jesus' human nature were not different from those of anyone else in his community.

Since the Gospels are the source of our inquiry, how reliable are the Gospels? For the last two and a half centuries, the four Gospels have been and continue to be subjected to many scholarly (and not so scholarly) historical debates, academic research, and fiery discussions. Despite the fact that the writers and editors of the Gospels present us with a partial and theologically colored portrait of Jesus, we can still find the human, Semitic Nazarene teacher within their pages. This vital point must be considered and included in the search for the man Jesus.

For example, consider the viewpoint of the late Lebanese scholar, Dr. Abraham Rihbany, who was a dedicated minister and an adept, prolific writer/author on the Near East. In his book *The Syrian Christ*, he states his poignant view very clearly and succinctly:

> In the Gospel story of Jesus' life there is not a single incident that is not in perfect harmony with the prevailing modes of thought and the current speech of the land of its origin. [Since] I was born not far from where the Master was born, and brought up under almost the identical conditions under which he lived, I have an inside view of the Bible which by the nature of things, a Westerner cannot have. And I know that the conditions of life in Syria today are essentially as they were in the time of Christ, not from the study of the mutilated tablets of the archaeologist and the antiquarian, . . . but from the simple fact that, as a sojourner in this Western world, whenever I open my Bible it reads like a letter from home. Its unrestrained effusiveness of expression; its vivid, almost flashy and fantastic imagery; its naive narrations; the rugged unstudied simplicity of its parables; its unconventional portrayal of certain human relations; as well as its all-permeating spiritual mysticism, might all have been written in my primitive village home, on the western slopes of Mount Lebanon some thirty years ago. . . .

Let us view the Semitic Jesus in the light of his own language, people and times. We will see him from the background of the ancient Aramaic language, Hebrew Scriptures, customs, metaphors and psychology, as well as from the unencumbered Aramaic style of writing behind the teachings and narratives of the Gospels.

To this day the Galilean teacher receives on-going worldwide acclaim and worship through many forms, yet he never sought worshippers. He never attempted to inaugurate a new system of worship, nor to undermine the religion of his forefathers. He discounted honors and notoriety. He came not for humankind to sacrifice to him, but that he might serve humanity.

From a purely historical perspective, it is certain that Jesus never thought of himself as possessing any superhuman nature; nor was he conscious of any supernatural birth. These ideas which we find in the Gospels of Matthew and Luke were theological and christological additions made by church scribes when these two Gospels were compiled.

In his book *How To Understand The Gospels*, Anthony C. Deane, Canon of Windsor, says:

> Saint Mark is not afraid to attribute human limitations to our Lord; he feels grief, anger, surprise, amazement, fatigue; he asks questions for information; at times he is unable to do what he wills.

Though the humanity of Jesus appears in the Gospels, the theology which developed in and among the early communities of believers in the latter half of the first century C.E. (Common Era) began to overlay Jesus' historical sayings and to obscure his essential human nature.

Jesus never claimed that he was God's only son! He felt himself to be fully human and was motivated by his deep faith and personal relationship with God. He taught no abstruse and mysterious doctrines. He did not wait for people to come to him; he went to them. He preached in synagogues, in the marketplaces, at private homes, on hilltops, at the seashore, and anywhere else he could find listeners. Jesus originated no new terms and used only familiar ideas. His comforting and charismatic personality, his plain words and simple parables captivated the harried Galileans who eagerly listened to him.

The Aramaic Language

Before continuing our view of Jesus in his Near Eastern setting, we need to look into a brief history of the Aramaic language. It made its historical appearance toward the end of the second millennium B.C.E., in Mesopotamia – the fertile crescent of the ancient Near East. Gradually, at the onset of the first millennium B.C.E., the written and spoken forms of the Aramaic tongue began making inroads throughout Near Eastern lands. It was the language of the Arameans, Assyrians, Chaldeans, Hebrews and Syrians.

Historians inform us that the term "Aramaic" is derived from Aram. According to Hebrew Scripture, Aram was a grandson of Noah, Gen. 10:22. Aramaic is a Semitic (more precisely – Shemitic) language. The word "Aram" is formed from an Aramaic noun and adjective: "Araa" meaning earth, land, or terrain and "Ramtha" meaning high. The fertile valley, Padan-Aram (Mesopotamia or Beth Nahreen "the land between the rivers.") was the territory in which the descendants of Aram dwelt and in which Aramaic developed and remained pure. In time, because of the practicality of its alphabet and simplicity of style in writing and speaking, it attracted all classes of people, government officials, merchants, and writers.

Thus, by the 8th century B.C.E., Aramaic became the common tongue among the majority of Semitic clans and was the major language from Egypt to Asia Minor to Pakistan. It was employed by the great Semitic empires, Assyria and Chaldea (Babylon). It was also the language of the Persian (Iranian) government in its Western provinces. This Semitic tongue continues to be spoken and written in today's world by a variety of Chaldean, Assyrian and other Semitic communities in the Near and Middle East, Australia, the United States and elsewhere. These communities regularly speak the Aramaic language at home, in their social, political, domestic meetings and in their religious worship Liturgy.

Biblical as well as secular history records the various expulsions of the tribes of Israel from their homeland to Assyria and Chaldea. Historically, the two most important exiles are: In 721 B.C.E., the Assyrians took the ten Northern tribes of the House of Israel captive to Nineveh and scattered them throughout Mesopotamia (Northern Iraq, Afghanistan and Pakistan). These warring conquerors repopulated Northern Israel with some of their own people and other Semitic clans who spoke Aramaic in its Assyrian dialect. (Eastern Aramaic was divided into two dialects, the Northern vernacular spoken in Assyria and the Southern vernacular spoken in Chaldea, i.e., Babylon.) These new inhabitants of the northern sector of Palestine intermarried with the remnant of Israelites that were left behind by the invading armies of Assyria. The descendants of these mixed marriages came to be known as Samaritans. The second exile: In 587 B.C.E., Nebuchanessar, the Chaldean King, deported the remaining two tribes of the House of Judah, the southern kingdom of Israel, to Babylon.

Then in 539 B.C.E., Cyrus, the ruler of Persia (Iran) conquered the great city of Babylon and ended the Chaldean empire. The Persian King granted freedom to the exiled Jews who were living in Babylon. They could now return to Palestine under the protection of the Persian power. By this time, the Jewish people who returned to their homeland were speaking the Southern dialect of Aramaic. Therefore, during the first century in Palestine, the people of Judea spoke in the Southern dialect of Aramaic. But in Galilee, Jesus, his disciples, followers and contemporaries spoke in the Eastern, Northern dialect of Aramaic.

It is interesting to note that the manner of speech, the phraseology, the idioms and the orientation in the four Gospels: Matthew, Mark, Luke and John are vividly and distinctively Aramaic. The constant repetitions are characteristic of Eastern speech. Such phrases as "Truly, truly, I say to you," or "In those days," "And it came to pass," "And he said to them," are peculiarly Aramaic. Hebrew was spoken in some areas of the Holy Land, but there is some discussion among present-day scholars as to its widespread use during the first century C.E.

The first-century evidence clearly indicates that Aramaic was the most common language used throughout Palestine. The message of Jesus of Nazareth was proclaimed and taught all over Palestine, Lebanon, Syria, and Mesopotamia in the Eastern Aramaic language. Aramaic remained the common language of the Near East until the 7th century C.E.; then Arabic gradually began to supplant Aramaic. Nonetheless, the Christians of Mesopotamia (Iraq), Iran, Syria, Turkey and Lebanon kept the Aramaic tongue alive domestically, scholastically and liturgically. In spite of the pressure of the ruling Arabs to speak Arabic, Aramaic is still spoken today in its many dialects, especially among the Assyrians and Chaldeans. It is known as Syriac but this is a misnomer. Syriac is the Greek term for Aramaic.

Another important aspect of the Aramaic language was its use as the major tongue for the birth and spread of spiritual and intellectual ideas in and all over the Near East. According to the research and opinion of an outstanding Aramaic and Arabic scholar, Professor Franz Rosenthal, in the *Journal of Near Eastern Studies:*

> In my view, the history of Aramaic represents the purest triumph of the human spirit as embodied in language over the

crude display of material power. . . . Great empires were conquered by the Aramaic language, and when they disappeared
and were submerged in the flow of history, that language persisted and continued to live a life of its own. . . the language
continued to be powerfully active in the promulgation of
spiritual matters. It was the main instrument for the formulation
of religious ideas in the Near East, which then spread in all
directions all over the world . . The monotheistic groups continue to live on today with a religious heritage, much of which
found first expression in Aramaic.

The Eastern Temperament and the Common Language

The best way to understand the Eastern temperament and daily
language of the Semites is to receive firsthand information from an
Easterner himself. Dr. Rihbany says,

> The Oriental [Easterner] I have in mind is the Semite, the
> dweller of the Near East, who, chiefly through the Bible, has
> exerted an immense influence on the life and literature of the
> West. The son of the Near East is more emotional, more intense,
> and more communicative than his Far-Eastern neighbors. Al-
> though very old in point of time, his (the Semite) temperament
> remains somewhat juvenile and his manner of speech intimate
> and unreserved.

> From the remote past, even to this day, the Oriental's
> [Easterner's] manner of speech has been that of a worshiper, and
> not that of a business man or an industrial worker in the modern
> Western sense. . . his daily language is essentially biblical. He
> has no secular language. The only real break between his scrip-
> tures and the vocabulary of his daily life is that which exists
> between the classical and the vernacular. . .

> An Easterner's chief purpose in a conversation is to convey an
> impression by whatever suitable means, and not to deliver his
> message in scientifically accurate terms. He piles up his
> metaphors and superlatives, reinforced by a theatrical display
> of gestures and facial expressions in order to make the hearer
> feel his meaning. He speaks as it were in pictures. With him the
> spoken language goes hand in hand with the most ancient
> gesture language. His profuse gesticulation is that phase of his
> life which first challenges the attention of Western travelers in
> the East. He points to almost everything he mentions in his
> speech and would portray every feeling and emotion by means
> of some bodily movement. . .

> It is also because he loves to speak in pictures and to subor-
> dinate literal accuracy to the total impression of an utterance,

that he makes such extensive use of figurative language. Instead of saying to the Pharisees; "your pretensions to virtue" and good birth far exceed your actual practice of virtue,' John the Baptist cried: Oh generation of vipers, etc.' Just as he loves to flavor his food strongly and to dress in bright colors, so is he fond of metaphor, exaggeration, and positiveness in speech. To him mild accuracy is weakness.

The supreme choice of the Oriental [Easterner] has been religion. What has always seemed to him to be his first and almost only duty was and is to form the most direct, most intimate connection between God and the soul. It is from this Eastern psychological background, religious temperament and language that not only the Gospels' portrait of Jesus comes to us, but also the Bible in its entirety.

The following aspects of Jesus are depicted in the Semitic Aramaic setting and emphasize the purely human side of him. Many of the following Aramaic terms attributed to Jesus, or those that he may have used himself, have been misunderstood over the centuries, and some of them no longer carry their original meaning.

Yeshua – The Name of Jesus

Jesus (*Yeshu* – the northern Galilean Aramaic dialect) was a common Aramaic name in the first century C.E. Our English form of Jesus' name comes from a shortened classical Hebrew/Aramaic form of *Yeshua*. However, the name *Yeshua* is, in turn, a shortened form of the name of the great biblical hero Joshua, son of Nun. The Hebrew name in full is *Yehoshua*. "Joshua" was the name commonly used before the Babylonian exile. Among the Jews after the Chaldean (Babylonian) exile, the short form of the term was adopted – *Yeshua*.

Despite this change, the name "Joshua" did not die out entirely. "Jesus" was a common name in Palestine and remained popular among the Jews until the beginning of the second-century C.E. The Jews stopped using "Jesus" as a personal name and revived the classical term "Joshua." Thereafter, "Jesus" became a rare name among the second century Jewish people.

Bar-nasha – The Son of Man

In the three major Semitic languages – Aramaic, Hebrew and Arabic – the term "son of man" means a "human being." In everyday language, Jesus referred to himself as a human being. According to the Gospels, he used the term "son of man" approximately twenty-eight times. "Son of man" is a peculiar Aramaic expression of speech to the Western mind and it has caused a great deal of confusion when attempting to interpret the Gospels without the knowledge of the Aramaic language. The word itself in Aramaic is *bar-nasha*, a compound noun. *Bar* means "son" and *nasha* means "man." It is improper to literally translate this Aramaic term *bar-nasha* as "the son of man." Yet, many biblical translators have and still do render this term literally.

In Aramaic when the word *bar* "son" is joined to other words, those words change meaning. For example, *barabba* literally translated means the "son of the father," but properly translated it means "he resembles his father;" *bar-agara* literally translated means "son of the rooftop," but properly translated it means "a lunatic." Additional examples are *bar-zauga*, "son of the yoke" – a friend, a companion; *bar-hila*, son of power – soldier; *bar-yolpana*, son of learning – disciple. Thus, *bar-nasha*, son of man – man, human being.

Bar dalaha – The Son of God

In the Aramaic-Semitic language and culture, the term *bar dalaha*, "son of God," "God's son" or "God's child," is used many ways and may refer to an orphan, a meek young man (in contrast, a meek, mature individual is often called a "man of God"), a peacemaker, a good, kind or pious individual. The word "son," as we learned from the term "son of man," is subtly used to infer "likeness," "resemblance" and to be "in the image of." Thus, "son of God" signifies "like God" or "God-likeness." The intended meaning of "son of God" depends on the context in which it is used in the various passages of the Bible.

The few times that Jesus referred to himself as "son of God," as recorded in the Gospels, were always within the religious tenor and meaning of his day. This "special sonship" in Hebrew scripture and in the New Testament never refers to a "physical-divine" sonship, but rather to a spiritual relationship between the God of Israel and the individual designated as "son." Biblically speaking, "sonship" is a spiritual relationship between God and a human being which is based on love, respect and doing the will of God. Often when Easterners call someone "son" or "my son" it is their way of showing affection and referring to that person as a "beloved." In all forms of relationships, everyday verbal expressions remain more intimate and flowery than those of the West. To this day the religious language of Semites, all over the Middle East, bears witness to their poetic intimacy and imagery in their devotion to God.

Ehedaya – The Only Begotten Son

Jesus never claimed he was God's only son. The claim that Jesus was God's "only begotten son" was made by others. This term is found exclusively in the Gospel of John. The term "only begotten," which appears in John's Gospel as a translation of the Greek word "monogenes," cannot be justified. It is an improper English rendering of this Greek word. "Monogenes" is composed of two Greek words. "Monos" means "singular;" "genos" means "kind." When these two words are combined they literally mean "one of a kind."

However, "genos" is distantly related to the verb "gennan" which means "to beget." It is improper to translate "monogenes" as "only begotten." A better rendering would be "unique son." Jerome, in the Latin Vulgate, translated "monogenes" as "only begotten" in answer to the Arian doctrine which taught that Jesus was not begotten, but made.

The Aramaic word is "Ehedaya" and means a "sole heir," the "beloved," hence, "unique, beloved son." Once again we are dealing with Semitic figures of speech. The term "Ehedaya" in the Aramaic language is not to be taken literally. The gospel writer, by using this term, places Jesus in a precious and endearing setting which is typically an Eastern manner.

M'sheeha – The Messiah

The term "M'sheeha," "Messiah," the "Anointed," the "Appointed One" is a title and not a proper name. The Greek term "Christos," "Christ," is a Greek translation of the Aramaic word "M'sheeha" and has the same significance. Years after the death of Jesus the term "Christ" became a proper name, and Jesus of Nazareth became known as "Jesus Christ." A better rendering in English would be "Jesus the Christ," because Jesus had become known as an "Anointed One." According to Hebrew Scripture, kings, priests and sometimes prophets were anointed with consecrated oil into their respective offices.

Anointing with consecrated oil, applied to the crown of the head like an ointment, is a very ancient rite. In Hebrew the word "anoint" is *mashach*, hence the title "Messiah" (Anointed One). The act of anointing was considered a transfer of divine powers to the person who was being anointed. Hence, he became known as the "Lord's anointed," (a son by adoption). The Kings of Israel were known as "the Lord's Anointed Ones," or "the Lord's Christs." David called King Saul the "Lord's Anointed" (Messiah-Christ). The above interpretation of the word "messiah" was its original meaning.

Prior to the reign of King David the Hebrews had no thought of a Messiah. The pre-exilic prophets had hoped and worked for their nation to cleanse itself morally so that Israel could become a great beacon to guide all the nations of the earth into paths of justice. According to Isaiah's vision, Israel, having cleansed itself, would then be ruled by a king from the family of David. Under the wise and powerful leadership of this prophesied King, justice, peace, compassion and national contentment would reign and abound in Israel, so much so that other nations would also benefit from this national spiritual revival.

However, after the exile and return of the people of Israel to their homeland, known as the Second-Temple Era, the messianic concept gradually changed. From 167 B.C.E. to the time of the birth of Jesus, the messianic idea underwent many modifications. Malachi predicted that Elijah would appear and prepare the way for the Messiah – a human, earthly Messiah endowed by the God of Israel with the necessary power to lead the people in the paths of peace and justice. After this prediction more and more writings began to appear which transformed the earlier messianic concepts. It was predicted that the Messiah would be an aggressive, militant and political leader who would destroy the enemies of God's people.

It should be noted that the messianic hope was not peculiar only to the Jewish-Christian religion. In almost all ancient religions this belief was expressed, especially whenever nations fell prey to hatred, injustice, persecution and the devastation of war. The hearts of the people were filled with the hope that a Power in the form of some great leader would bring national peace and salvation.

During the first century C.E. a myriad of concepts concerning the Messiah were prevalent, such as a Prince-Messiah of the House of David, a Priest-King, a Warrior, a Mediator between God and man, a pre-existent Messiah, and a Messiah endowed with superhuman powers to destroy Satan and his kingdom. Jesus, a Mediterranean peasant from half-heathen Galilee, a simple teacher and preacher with a small discipleship of fisherman and crowds of poor peasants who followed him, could not possibly measure up to the expectations and requirements set down for a great hero – "a Prince-Messiah of the House of David." We can now understand why Jesus forbade his immediate followers to call him "Messiah-Christ."

Before concluding, one other point needs to be mentioned. The apostle Paul, a visionary who had the ability to enter altered states of consciousness (trances), cast Jesus in yet another messianic role. To Paul, Jesus was a mystical Messiah – a mystical Christ, the heavenly man who conquered principalities and powers of the air. He added his messianic revelation to the already prevailing ideas which were adopted and attributed to Jesus by the second generation of believers. No evidence has been found that the members of the Jerusalem church accepted Paul's mystical Christ who transcended all Jewish expectations. Jesus' immediate disciples who walked, talked and sailed with him on the lake of Galilee never for a moment thought they were associating with the Creator of heaven and earth. The bond of union among the Jewish believers in Jesus was more fraternal than creedal. What they had in common was their devotion to their teacher and his teachings.

Conclusion

Jesus, a Semite and a man among men, continues to speak through all the ages. His human personality, his loving nature and his simple teachings will live forever and continue to enrich and embrace the hearts of the human family everywhere. When the unpretentious teachings of Jesus are fully realized, all subtle forms of imperialism which advocate absolutism – such as an infallible church, infallible bible, infallible doctrines or infallible anything – can no longer stand. The desire for infallibility is a lust for undisputed authority, absolute power, and seeks to dominate individual freedom and free thought.

The human Jesus was a simple man. His source was God, and his spiritual insight continues to ignite the hearts and souls of men, women and children the world over.

Rocco A. Errico, PhD, is a lecturer, author, ordained minister, and Bible scholar whose approach emphasizes Eastern sources and customs, especially the Aramaic language.

The need of the Western readers of the Bible is . . . to have real intellectual, as well as spiritual, fellowship with those Easterners who sought earnestly in their own way to give tangible form to those great spiritual truths.

— Dr. Abraham Rihbany

The Last Supper

This famous painting by Leonardo da Vinci is depicted in a Western setting.

The Passover (Last Supper) symbolizes the Sun/Son image with the twelve disciples, who depict the twelve months in a year and are arranged in four groups of three, signifying the seasons.

—Jordan Maxwell

The Last Supper

Rocco A. Errico

Most readers of the Bible visualize this momentous scene of the last supper in a totally Western setting, not realizing that they are being influenced by the famous painting of Leonardo da Vinci. This renowned Italian artist gave the world a beautiful character study in his painting of the last supper. However, we must understand that da Vinci was not portraying an historical Eastern setting. His entire work – the room, the table, the attire of the apostles and Jesus, and even the seating arrangements – are of his day and time. What we have in this painting is an Italian provincial scene and not one of the Near East.

The following description, then, is based on the typical Eastern customs observed at such a supper. Jesus and his disciples sat on the floor in a circle in one of the small rooms of a "balakhana," an inn for men only. The apostles and Jesus all wore hats during the supper. Spread on the floor in the center of the room was a cloth called in Aramaic "pathora." Placed on the pathora were an earthen cup, a little jar filled with wine, and two or three large dishes. The cup was put in the center within reach of everyone in the circle. The jar was near Jesus.

According to eastern customs, on such occasions each of the few large plates contained a different kind of food. Bread is passed around. Meat is wrapped in thin loaves of bread, (this is called sop) put into pockets, and often carried home. The guests do not hesitate to reach for food on other men's dishes.

The posture of the beloved disciple, John, who was leaning on Jesus' chest, is also a common social custom. To this day, very close male friends still maintain this attitude while eating together, and it is as natural as shaking hands in the West. However, this show of affection is especially practiced when intimate friends are about to part from one another, as on the eve of a journey or when about to face a perilous assignment.

During this supper Jesus "let himself go," that is, he expressed his feelings freely and openly to his disciples. He let them know of his disappointment in one who was about to betray him, and because these men would never meet in this manner again, he also made other statements which are often spoken at a "farewell supper." The things Jesus said and did at the last supper were not isolated or uncommon events in the Semitic culture. A brotherly atmosphere and intimate, emotional expressions usually characterize a supper of this type among Eastern people, especially in the shadow of approaching danger.

It is the custom of a gracious host to ask for a joyous ending to a visit by having the whole company of men drink from one cup as a sign of their friendship. The phrase, "Do this in remembrance of me," is an affectionate request and means, "I love you; therefore I am always with you." When Jesus had made this request of his disciples they understood his loving statement to mean, "A powerful bond of love is between us, and because of this love we cannot be separated from one another." In other words, he would no longer be with them.

At Eastern feasts, and especially in the region of Galilee, sharing food with those who stand and serve wine and water to the guests is common. However, exchanges of food with friends take on a deeper meaning. Choice portions of food are handed to friends as signs of close intimacy. This is never done with an enemy. Once again, Jesus let his feelings be revealed when he handed Judas, the betrayer, his "sop." "And when he had dipped the sop, he gave it to Judas Iscariot, the son of Simon" (John 13:16). By understanding this Eastern custom, one quickly comprehends the act of love Jesus demonstrated by sharing his sop with Judas, for Jesus truly practiced his own teachings: "Love your enemies." In essence, he was telling Judas, through this sharing, that he did not in fact consider him an enemy. Jesus felt deep compassion and love for Judas, and with this symbolic gesture he was saying, "Here is my bread of friendship, and what you have to do, do it quickly." Shortly after, Jesus was betrayed and sold to his priestly adversaries by Judas.

It was at this supper that Jesus sealed his love and friendship with his disciples. Pointing to the lamb and the bread and then to the wine, he said that his body was to become like the lamb and bread, broken and eaten; his blood was like the wine, drunk by all. He gave his life to reveal a new way of living for all mankind.

Excerpt from Let There Be Light, The Seven Keys *by Rocco A. Errico, published by DeVorss & Company, Marina Del Rey, CA 90294, 1990.*

154

The theme of 12 is carried to the Rose Windows of most churches – The origins – the "heavens" with 12 signs of the Zodiac, the 12 sheep, Apostles and stations of the Cross.

THERE IS NO EVIDENCE . . .

That Jesus Was Born in 4 B.C.

That He Was Born in a Manger.

That He Was a Carpenter.

That He Was Crucified on Mt. Calvary.

— The People's Almanac #3,
David Wallechinsky and Irving Wallace
Bantam Books, 1978

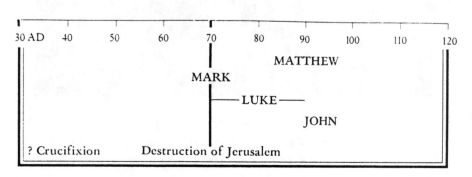

Consensus of most bibical historians on the dating of the Gospels

Locating Jesus In Time, Space And Archaeology

Gerald A. Larue

Within fifty years after Jesus' death, Christian writers began to try to anchor his life in time and space. By this time, Paul was dead and his expectations that Jesus would soon return and establish his kingdom had not been fulfilled. Roman soldiers had destroyed the Jewish temple in Jerusalem and had wiped out the Jewish Essene community at Qumran. Masada, the last Jewish holdout against the Romans, had fallen under a brilliant Roman assault. It was clear that to survive, Judaism and its offspring, Christianity, would have to redirect their thinking and their missions.

In his letters, which are the earliest New Testament writings, Paul paid scant heed to Jesus' life-story. Whether he made more of Jesus' biography in his public lectures cannot be known. Nor is it possible to ascertain what stories about Jesus' life may have circulated among Jesus' followers. Sometime after the year 70 of the Common Era (CE), the Gospel of Mark was written. This writer opened his account with an adult Jesus arriving at the Jordan river for baptism by John the Baptizer. He related nothing of Jesus' birth or childhood.

When Was Jesus Born?

The Gospels of Matthew and Luke display greater interest in an expanded life story of Jesus. These documents, which seem to have been written some ten years after Mark, used Mark as a basis for their writings, but added separate and conflicting accounts of Jesus' birth and infancy. The Gospel of Matthew claimed that Jesus was born in Bethlehem during the reign of King Herod the Great and that to protect the infant Jesus from the monarch's soldiers, the family fled to Egypt and returned to Palestine only after Herod had died. According to the Jewish historian Josephus, Herod died following a lunar eclipse.

Modern astronomers inform us that such eclipses which would be visible in Palestine occurred on March 14, in 4 Before the Common Era (BCE) and on January 10 in 1 BCE. Therefore, depending upon which eclipse is meant, Herod died in either 4 BCE or 1 BCE and Jesus would therefore be born either before 4 BCE or 1 BCE. These dates provide little or no help in fixing a time for Jesus' birth in history. On the basis of information in the Gospel of Matthew we simply cannot know when Jesus was born.

The Gospel of Luke (1:5) also noted that Jesus was born during Herod's reign. The writer linked the birth story to a world-wide census instigated by Caesar Augustus (Gaius Octavius) who ruled between 30 BCE and 14 CE, at the time when Cyrenius (P. Sulpicius Quirinius) was governor of Syria. From a number of sources, we know that Quirinius was governor between the years 6 - 7 CE. Because Luke 2:2 noted that this was the first enrollment (*apographe*), some scholars have conjectured that Quirinius may have been responsible for more than one census.

They suggest that perhaps the 6 - 7 CE census that we know of was the second census and perhaps Quirinius had been governor at an earlier time. There is a gap in the known list of governors that falls between 3 - 2 BCE, so perhaps Quirinius was the governor whose name is missing between these dates. This would harmonize the Matthean and Lukan accounts so that it could be estimated that Jesus was born between 3 and 2 BCE. The theory is forced. Whenever one must rely on a series of "maybes" and "perhapses" that rise out of lack of good evidence, it is time to become uneasy. In any event, the separate and different accounts in the Gospels do not provide any real help in establishing Jesus' birth date.

Where Was Jesus Born?

Both Matthew and Luke stated that Jesus was born in Bethlehem. Matthew's Gospel (2:3-6) sought to make Jesus' birthplace a fulfillment of a prophecy found in the book of Micah (5:2):

> But you, O Bethlehem Ephrathah, who are little to be among the clans of Judah, from you shall come forth one who is to be ruler in Israel, whose origin is from old, from ancient days.

This particular passage is one of several similar passages added to the original writings of the prophet Micah. The contributor was not someone who lived during the prophet's lifetime in the eighth century BCE, but was a sixth-century BCE editor. While the Jews were in exile in Babylon, some of them dreamed of the restoration of Judah under a monarch from the lineage of David — perhaps from the royal Hebrew family that was captive in Babylon. This addition to the work of Micah echoes that dream. Although the prophecy had nothing to do with Jesus, the writer of Matthew reinterpreted it and tried to make it apply to Jesus.

A conservative Christian colleague once said, "Isn't it wonderful that the Holy Spirit could give the passage one meaning in the sixth century and a whole new meaning in the first century!" This I call the "double-bounce" theory of biblical interpretation. The colleague admitted that the same Holy Spirit might give still another meaning to the passage in a later time (the theory would then become "triple-bounce"!). The statement in Micah had nothing to do with Jesus' birth and the use of the prophecy represents the intent of the writer of Matthew to prove that Jesus was the long-awaited Jewish messiah.

There is in Bethlehem a Church of the Nativity, built, so local guides will tell you, over the very grotto where Jesus was born. In fact, a star set in the floor of a niche is said to mark the very spot where the baby is supposed to have rested. Over the centuries, hundreds of thousands of pilgrims have worshipped in this church and at this spot in the belief that this was Jesus' birthplace. Could they all have been in error, or could this really be the place where Jesus was born? Matthew and Luke disagree on the locale of the birthplace in Bethlehem. Matthew wrote of wise men visiting the infant Jesus in a house which was, presumably, the place where he was born (2:11). By the middle of the 2nd Century CE, Jesus' birthplace was identified as a cave – a not unreasonable assumption inasmuch as caves were, and still are, used to house animals in that region.

Most modern scholars believe that Jesus was born in Nazareth, not in Bethlehem. The birth stories are pious fiction or legends composed by Christian writers to demonstrate that Jesus fulfilled Jewish expectations and Jewish prophecy concerning the coming of a messiah. Therefore, references to governmental figures are designed to locate Jesus in time, and the identification of the birth cave and the subsequent erection of a shrine over the cave constitute efforts to locate Jesus in space. The needs of worshippers are met, insofar as through visits to this sacred space they feel that they are able to come into some sort of intimate contact with the founder of their faith system. The work of archaeologists casts doubt on the tradition and the sites.

Childhood And Youth

As the Jesus story in the gospels progresses, Matthew and Luke come into conflict. According to the Matthew tradition, Joseph, Mary and Jesus fled to Egypt to avoid Herod's soldiers (2:13-15). Luke, on the other hand, wrote that Jesus was circumcised and then taken to Jerusalem for purification rites before the family returned to Nazareth (2:21-39). There was a time when the church was able to produce Jesus' foreskin as a tangible artifact of the circumcision, but I have been unable to learn what has happened to that precious bit of infant skin in more recent times.

There seems to be little doubt that Jesus grew up in Nazareth in Galilee as the son of the local carpenter, Joseph. Archaeological and historical research into the history of Nazareth indicates that although it was inhabited as early as Neanderthal times (c. 70,000 - 35,000 BCE), in Roman times it housed only a small Jewish community – a village so small and so insignificant that it was ignored in first-century CE geographical references.

Therefore, the Church of the Annunciation, which commemorates the place where the angel Gabriel informed the Virgin Mary that she was to be divinely impregnated when the Holy Spirit would "come upon" her and "overshadow" her (Luke 1:35), is an early Byzantine structure, probably built during the fifth century CE. All of the other locales (and there are several), which pilgrims to Nazareth are told are associated with Jesus' life, are late inventions and have nothing to do with Jesus. Perhaps the only authentic relic of the past that might be associated with Jesus is 'Ain Myriam, the one local spring from which water has been flowing for centuries.

Ministry

So far, excavations associated with sites listed in Christian scriptures as those visited by Jesus have produced nothing that sheds any direct light upon his life. This is particularly true when we look at the environs of Jerusalem. Of course, the Mount of Olives is still there, virtually peppered with sacred spots.

There are the ruins of the Eleona Church where Jesus is supposed to have instructed his disciples about the end of the world; there is the Church of the Lord's Prayer, where Jesus is supposed to have taught his disciples to pray; there is the Mosque of the Ascension, formerly the Church of the Ascension, marking the very spot from which Jesus made his ascension into heaven; there is the Franciscan chapel *Dominus flevit* where Jesus is said to have wept over Jerusalem; there are the Church of Mary Magdalene, the Garden of Gethsemane Church, the Grotto of the Betrayal where Judas betrayed Jesus; the Tomb of the Virgin Mary where her body rested before ascending to heaven; and finally the entrance to Jerusalem and Via Dolorosa – the way of sorrows or the way of the cross.

Each site commemorates some Gospel account concerning Jesus' life. None of the locales have any basis in fact. All are separated from Jesus' time by hundreds of years. They are nothing more than structures built to commemorate Gospel stories but without historical bases for their location.

Within the city of Jerusalem, the site of the ancient Jewish temple is covered by the magnificent mosque Harem es-Sharif – the sacred enclave – and other Muslim shrines. We can learn nothing of the Jewish temple in Jesus' time from this locale, except perhaps that the Western wall, where pious Jews still weep over the destruction of the Temple in 70 CE, remains as a testimonial to the kind of protective walls that once surrounded the structure. Excavations within and around the walled city of Jerusalem provide information about the ancient city, but not about the temple proper nor about Jesus.

The streets that Jesus may have walked are not those where today's faithful Christians carry wooden crosses, observe the stations of the cross and try to ignore souvenir merchants with their olive wood artifacts. The streets of Jesus' day are 10 to 15 or more feet below present walkways, and there is no way of determining whether the way of the pilgrims corresponds to Jesus' reputed journey with the cross.

There is a bit of exposed pavement known as the *Lithostratos* that has been exposed by excavation in the church built by the Sisters of Sion. The stones appear to have been part of the Praetorium or courtyard of the Antonia – the fortress tower named by King Herod to please Mark Antony. Portions of that same courtyard have been found in excavations under the Convent of the Flagellation and the Greek Orthodox Convent. On the basis of these finds it has been suggested that the *Lithostratos* covered an area of some 1,500 square meters. It is quite possible that Jesus stood somewhere on this pavement when he was judged by Pilate.

Crucifixion

The Via Dolorosa leads to the Church of the Holy Sepulchre which houses both the place of the crucifixion and Jesus' burial site. The site of crucifixion was called "Golgotha," the place of the skull (Matt. 27:33; Mark 15:22; Luke 23:33; John 19:17). It was located "near the city" (John 19:20) and outside the city, according to Hebrews 13:12. Certainly the burial place would be outside the city walls and probably the place of execution would be too.

It is recorded that when Hadrian visited Jerusalem, he erected a sanctuary to the Roman god Jupiter on the site of the Jewish temple which had remained a desolate ruin since its destruction in 70 CE. Many view Hadrian's act as an act of desecration, and perhaps it was. On the other hand, it is well known to historians and archaeologists that holy places tend to retain their sacredness and magical power.

However, Hadrian did bar the Jews from Jerusalem, no doubt in part as a reaction to the revolt by Jews (114-117 CE) that had shaken Rome's eastern empire just before Hadrian became emperor and also to the Bar-Cochba revolt (132 CE) which occurred after he assumed the throne. He did erect a shrine to Jupiter on the holy mountain of Gerazim which was sacred to the Samaritans and he did erect a temple to Venus on Golgotha. It is quite likely that his motivation was, in part, to humiliate the Jews, to desecrate their holy places, and to demonstrate the superiority of the Roman deities over those of the subject people.

Early Christians may have retained some memory of the place where the crucifixion occurred, although their concerns appear to have been focussed less on the past and on Jesus' personal history and more on the expected return of Jesus. Perhaps Hadrian deliberately built the Venus temple on a place sacred to Christians, but it was not until Jerusalem became a Christian city when it was conquered in 325 CE that Golgotha became a Christian shrine. By this time Venus had been worshipped at the site for nearly 200 years.

Constantine ordered the Venus shrine destroyed, and during the demolition an empty tomb that was supposed to be that of Jesus was "discovered." How it was determined that this was the tomb of Jesus is not recorded, but it should be noted that empty tombs abound in Palestine and most archaeologists have looked into dozens of them. By 335 CE, the church that now forms the foundation for the present-

day Church of the Holy Sepulchre was erected, although only fragments of that early structure remain.

Wondrous discoveries were supposed to have been made at the
tomb site. Queen Helena had a dream in which the hiding place of
the cross was disclosed. Sure enough, while the queen sat nearby,
workers probed a pit and three crosses were found. At this point, I
prefer to let the great American writer, Mark Twain, tell the story as
he learned it when he travelled to Palestine in 1867. He published it
in *The Innocents Abroad* in 1869.

> Here, also a marble slab marks the place where St. Helena, the
> mother of the Emperor Constantine, found the crosses about
> three hundred years after the Crucifixion. According to the
> legend, this great discovery elicited extravagant demonstrations
> of joy. But they were of short duration. The question intruded
> itself: "Which bore the blessed Savior, and which the thieves?"
> To be in doubt in so mighty a matter as this — to be uncertain
> which one to adore — was a grievous misfortune. It turned the
> public joy to sorrow. But when lived there a holy priest who
> could not set so simple a trouble as this to rest? One of these soon
> hit upon a plan that would be a certain test. A noble lady lay
> very ill in Jerusalem. The wise priests ordered that the three
> crosses be taken to her bedside one at a time. It was done. When
> her eyes fell upon the first one, she uttered a scream that was
> heard beyond the Damascus Gate, and even upon the Mount of
> Olives, it was said, and then fell back into a deadly swoon. They
> recovered her and brought in the second cross. Instantly she
> went into fearful convulsions, and it was with the greatest
> difficulty that six strong men could hold her. They were afraid,
> now, to bring in the third cross. They began to fear they had
> fallen upon the wrong crosses, and that the true cross was not
> with this number at all.
>
> However, as the woman seemed likely to die with the convul-
> sions that were tearing her, they concluded that the third could
> do no more than put her out of her misery with a happy
> dispatch. So they brought it, and behold, a miracle! The woman
> sprang from her bed, smiling and joyful, and perfectly restored
> to health. When we listen to evidence like this, we cannot but
> believe. We would be ashamed to doubt, and properly, too. Even
> the very part of Jerusalem where this all occurred is there yet.
> So there is really no room for doubt.

But who would have dared to chop the sacred cross into the
thousands of fragments that are enshrined in Roman Catholic churches throughout the world? If one is to believe that the fragments are

truly those from the cross on which Jesus died, then the cross must have been destroyed. More objective scholars suggest that the bits of wood may have been gathered from around the site of the Church of the Holy Sepulchre. In that case, they could just as well have been fragments from the wood of the demolished shrine sacred to Venus.

There have been challenges to the Church of the Holy Sepulchre. One is the so-called Garden Tomb which is located outside the present Turkish walls of Jerusalem. Apparently, those who prefer the Garden Tomb do so because the Church of the Holy Sepulchre lies within the present walls of the ancient city. Through archaeological research, we think we now know the course of the ancient walls, and if the tracing is correct, the Church of the Holy Sepulchre definitely lies outside the ancient city walls even though it is located within the present Turkish walls.

In other words, the location of the Church of the Holy Sepulchre is not an unlikely place for the burial. The Garden Tomb is a late selection and is accepted as authentic only by those millions who follow fundamentalist media preachers. During Passover-Easter season, we see the televangelists standing beside what they term the "true tomb," that is, the Garden Tomb. No present-day scholar attributes any validity to their claims. The so-called Garden Tomb was discovered in 1867. The tomb was probably cut into the rock during the early Byzantine period in the fourth or fifth centuries CE and has nothing to do with the time of Jesus. And, of course, there is no proof that the tomb in the Church of the Holy Sepulchre was that of Jesus.

Perhaps the most dramatic claims are those concerning an artifact known as the "Shroud of Turin" that some believe was associated with Jesus' burial. Few readers of the popular press know that during the fourteenth century there were several shrouds, each of which claimed to be the one that enveloped Jesus' body at the time of burial. Pseudo-scientific claims for the authenticity of the Turin shroud produced dramatic terms to explain the body image, including "radiation scorch" resulting from "bursts of radiant energy," whatever those terms meant. Carbon-14 dating has demonstrated that the Shroud is a 14th-century forgery and is one of many such deliberately created relics produced in the same period, all designed to attract pilgrims to specific shrines to enhance and increase the status and financial income of the local church.

Shrines And Symbols

I have no quarrel with those who visit sacred places for the renewal and deepening of their faith. I can appreciate the fact that since the establishment of the Church of the Nativity and the Church of the Holy Sepulchre in the fourth century, millions of Christians have made pilgrimages to these sites and have paid homage to their beliefs. I can also understand the ways in which those who go to these shrines today can feel a linkage to the hundreds of thousands of others who have preceded them over the centuries. But to make a pilgrimage that links one to a Christian fellowship that extends back through time and that deepens one's commitment to the highest values and ethics of the Christian faith is quite different from visiting these shrines in the belief that the spots are sacred because they have had some actual physical association with Jesus.

To hear and watch pre-Easter advertisements by fundamentalist ministers who seek to persuade the uninformed to join them in a trip to Jerusalem to visit, among other places, the Garden Tomb which they state is the authentic tomb of Jesus, insults my intelligence, promotes ignorance and discards the best results of conscientious modern historical and archaeological scholarship.

As an educator in the humanities, as one committed to seeking to help produce a culturally literate society and committed to educating students and the public in the best understanding of the past, I am frustrated by the ignorance of history and science in so many of my audiences. Many participants come from solid liberal churches and from good high schools and colleges. Unfortunately, in these institutions, the findings of the best biblical scholarship are ignored or watered down, and as a result faith tends to replace reason.

Jesus is an important figure in western thought, but the Jesus that seems to matter most is the Jesus of religious fiction, the so-called "Christ of faith." As a symbol, Jesus can be an inspirer of the finest ethical traditions that humans have developed. What must be clearly maintained is the fact that we are dealing with a faith symbol and that the historical Jesus has been lost in the mist of time. The Christ of faith is a creation of religious believers who have taken the historical figure and clothed it in mythological swaddling bands in the same way that ancient Egyptians took Osiris, who may have been a historical figure, and mythologized him. Osiris was then clothed in the garments of divinity, and sacred spots associated with his fictionalized life were sanctified and became holy.

Conclusion

Our problem, as I see it, is two-fold. The first part is associated with the greed of towns, cities, churches and parishes, that seek to bring tourists and pilgrims to their shrines. They beckon to men and women who spend time gawking at places that may have little to do with what their guides are telling them.

The second problem lies with the educated clergy and teachers in our western world. For whatever reasons, perhaps fear of parishioners, fear of being challenged, fear of controversy, they fail to educate their parishioners and their students by making available the best evidence we have of the past. Of course there are pressure groups, largely composed of fundamentalists, who constantly threaten those of us who do not teach or accept their particular interpretation of the Bible, of Jesus or of life itself. When we, who are committed to the best information and evidence that our research can produce, fail to challenge their assumptions, when we fail to set forth our best evidence, when we bow to the pressure from these special groups and remain silent, we fail in our highest calling as teachers, leaders, thinkers and rationalists and betray our personal sense of integrity.

We can locate Jesus in a general way in time during the first century CE. He may have been born in any one of the few years before the start of the Common Era. He died during the time of Pontius Pilate (26-36 CE), perhaps in the year 29 or 30. We can locate Jesus vaguely in space, but the locales now associated with him are questionable. We cannot locate him archaeologically, because so far, archaeologists have found only what at best might be termed tangential evidence. We can recreate dimensions of the world in which he lived but, outside of the Christian scriptures, we cannot locate him historically within that world.

Gerald A. Larue is emeritus professor of bibical history and archaeology, University of Southern California, and chairs the Committee for the Scientific Examination of Religion. He is the author of numerous books.

The exact contrary of what is generally believed is often the truth.

— Jean de la Bruyere

JESUS CHRIST LIBERATOR

— © 1984 Robert Lentz, Bridge Building Images

Archbishop George Augustus Stallings, Jr., said "Jesus was Afro-Semitic – a black man." Founder of the Imani Temples of African Catholic Congregation, Stallings asked his Catholic congregation on Easter to burn the white pictures and replace them with black Christs. The Archbishop says the popular notion of a white Christ a myth.

The idea of a black Jesus is not novel nor unfounded. In 1894, Bishop Henry McNeal Turner of the African Methodist Episcopal Church said god was a Negro.

Most U.S. churches have a white, sometimes blue-eyed Jesus - which is totally fictious.

"Myths are wonderful – you can do anything with them anytime you want"

— *Siegel Schuster, creators of* **Superman**

Ernest Renan

Scholar and skeptic, was subjected to persecution by the established church for evidence he presented that was contrary to church propaganda and dogma.

The Christ

John E. Remsburg

"We must get rid of that Christ, we must get rid of that Christ!" So spoke one of the wisest, one of the most lovable of men, Ralph Waldo Emerson. "If I had my way," said Thomas Carlyle, "the world would hear a pretty stern command – Exit Christ."

Since Emerson and Carlyle spoke, a revolution has taken place in the thoughts of men. The more enlightened of them are now rid of Christ. From their minds he has made his exit. Or quote the words or Prof. Goldwin Smith, "The mighty and supreme Jesus, who was to transfigure all humanity by his divine wit and grace – this Jesus has flown." The supernatural Christ of the New Testament, the god of orthodox Christianity, is dead. But priestcraft lives and conjures up the ghost of this dead god to frighten and enslave the masses of mankind. The name of Christ has caused more persecutions, wars, and miseries than any other name has caused. The darkest wrongs are still inspired by it.

Two notable works controverting the divinity of Christ appeared in the last century, the *Leben Jesu* of Strauss, and the *Vie de Jesus* of Renan. Strauss, in one of the masterpieces of Freethought literature, endeavors to prove, and proves to the satisfaction of a majority of his readers, that Jesus Christ is a historical myth. This work possesses permanent value, but it was written for the scholar and not for the general reader. In the German and Latin versions, and in the admirable English translation of Marian Evans (George Eliot), the citations from the Gospels – and they are many – are in Greek.

Renan's *Life of Jesus*, written in Palestine, has had, especially in its abridged form, an immense circulation, and has been a potent factor in the dethronement of Christ. It is a charming book and displays great learning. But it is a romance, not a biography. The Jesus of Renan, like the Satan of Milton, while suggested by the Bible, is a modern creation. The warp is to be found in the Four Gospels, but the wool was spun in the brain of the brilliant Frenchman.

Renan himself repudiated to a considerable extent his earlier views regarding Jesus. When he wrote his work he accepted as authentic the Gospel of John, and to this Gospel he was indebted largely for the more admirable traits of his hero. John he subsequently rejected. Mark he accepted as the oldest and most authentic of the Gospels. Alluding to Mark he says:

> It cannot be denied that Jesus is portrayed in this gospel not as a meek moralist worthy of our affection, but as a dreadful magician.

This chapter on *The Christ* was written by one who recognizes in the Jesus of Strauss and Renan a transitional step, but not the ultimate step, between orthodox Christianity and radical Freethought. By the Christ is understood the Jesus of the New Testament. The Jesus of the New Testament is the Christ of Christianity. The Jesus of the New Testament is a supernatural being. He is, like the Christ, a myth. He is the Christ myth. Originally the word "Christ," the Greek for the Jewish "Messiah" (the anointed), meant the office of title of a person, while Jesus was the name of the person on whom his followers had bestowed this title. Gradually the title took the place of the name, so that "Jesus," "Jesus Christ," and "Christ" became interchangeable terms – synonyms. Such they are to the Christian world, and such, by the law of common usage, they are to the secular world.

It may be conceded as possible, and even probable, that a religious enthusiast of Galilee, named Jesus, was the germ of this mythical Jesus Christ. But this is an assumption rather than a demonstrated fact. Certain it is, this person, if he existed, was not a realization of the Perfect Man, as his admirers claim.

Silence Of Contemporary Writers

Another proof that the Christ of Christianity is a fabulous and not a historical character is the silence of the writers who lived during and immediately following the time he is said to have existed.

That a man named Jesus, an obscure, religious teacher, the basis of this fabulous Christ, lived in Palestine about 2,000 years ago, may be true. But of this man we know nothing. His biography has not been written. A. Renan and others have attempted to write it, but have failed – have failed because no materials for such a work exist. Contemporary writers of his times have not one word concerning him. For generations afterward, outside of a few theological epistles, we find no mention of him.

The following is a list of writers who lived and wrote during the time, or within a century after the time, that Christ is said to have lived and performed his wonderful works:

Josephus	Persius	Lucanus
Arrian	Pompon Mela	Phaedrus
Philo-Judaeus	Plutarch	Epictetus
Petronius	Quintius Curtius	Damis
Seneca	Justus of Tiberius	Silius Italicus
Dion Pruseus	Lucian	Aulus Gellius
Pliny the Elder	Apollonius	Statius
Paterculus	Pausanias	Columella
Suetonius	Pliny the Younger	Ptolemy
Appian	Valerius Flaccus	Dio Chrysostom
Juvenal	Tacitus	Hermogones
Theon of Smyran	Florus Lucius	Lysias
Martial	Quintilian	Valerius Maximus
Phlegon	Favorinus	

Enough of the writings of the authors named in the foregoing list remains to form a library. Yet in this mass of Jewish and Pagan literature, aside from two forged passages in the works of a Jewish author, and two disputed passages in the works of Roman writers, there is to be found no mention of Jesus Christ.

Philo was born before the beginning of the Christian era, and lived until long after the reputed death of Christ. He wrote an account of the Jews covering the entire time that Christ is said to have existed on earth. He was living in or near Jerusalem when Christ's miraculous birth and the Herodian massacre occurred. He was there when Christ made his triumphal entry into Jerusalem. He was there when the crucifixion with its attendant earthquake, supernatural darkness, and resurrection of the dead took place – when Christ himself rose from the dead, and in the presence of many witnesses ascended into heaven.

These marvelous events which must have filled the world with amazement, had they really occurred, were unknown to him. It was Philo who developed the doctrine of the Logos, or Word, and although this Word incarnate dwelt in that very land and in the presence of multitudes revealed himself and demonstrated his divine powers, Philo saw it not.

Josephus, the renowned Jewish historian, was a native of Judea. He was born in 37 A.D., and was a contemporary of the Apostles. He was, for a time, Governor of Galilee, the province in which Christ lived and taught. He traversed every part of this province and visited the places where but a generation before Christ had performed his prodigies. He resided in Cana, the very city in which Christ is said to have wrought his first miracle. He mentions every important event which occurred there during the first seventy years of the Christian era. But Christ was of too little consequence and his deeds too trivial to merit a line from this historian's pen.

Justus of Tiberius was a native of Christ's own country, Galilee. He wrote a history covering the time of Christ's reputed existence. This work has perished, but Photius, a Christian scholar and critic of the ninth century, who was acquainted with it, says: He (Justus) makes not the least mention of the appearances of Christ, of what things happened to him, or of the wonderful works that he did" (Photius' Bibliotheca, code 33)

Judea, where occurred the miraculous beginning and marvelous ending of Christ's earthly career, was a Roman province, and all of Palestine is intimately associated with Roman history. But the Roman records of that age contain no mention of Christ and his works. Greek writers of Greece and Alexandria who lived not far from Palestine and who were familiar with its events, are silent also.

Josephus: Late in the first century, Josephus wrote his celebrated work, *The Antiquities of the Jews*, giving a history of his race from the earliest ages down to his own time. Modern versions of this work contain the following passage:

> Now, there was about this time, Jesus, a wise man, if it be lawful to call him a man, for he was a doer of wonderful works; a teacher of such men as receive the truth with pleasure. He drew over to him both many of the Jews, and many of the Gentiles. He was (the) Christ; and when Pilate, at the suggestion of the principal men amongst us, had condemned him to the cross, those that loved him at the first did not forsake him; for he appeared to them alive again the third day, as the divine prophets had foretold these and ten thousand other wonderful things concerning him; and the tribe of Christians, so named from him, are not extinct at this day. (Book XVIII, Chap. iii, sec. 3)

For nearly sixteen hundred years Christians have been citing this passage as a testimonial, not merely to the historical existence, but to the divine character of Jesus Christ. And yet a ranker forgery was never penned.

Its language is Christian. Every line proclaims it the work of a Christian writer. "If it be lawful to call him a man." "He was the Christ." "He appeared to them alive again the third day, as the divine prophets had foretold these and ten thousand other wonderful things concerning him."

These are the words of a Christian, a believer in the divinity of Christ. Josephus was a Jew, a devout believer in the Jewish faith – the last man in the world to acknowledge the divinity of Christ. The inconsistency of this evidence was early recognized, and Ambrose, writing in the generation succeeding its first appearance (360 A.D.), offers the following explanation, which only a theologian could frame:

> If the Jews do not believe us, let them, at least, believe their own writers. Josephus, whom they esteem a great man, hath said this, and yet hath he spoken truth after such a manner; and so far was his mind wandered from the right way, that even he was not a believer as to what he himself said; but thus he spake, in order to deliver historical truth, because he thought it not lawful for him to deceive, while yet he was no believer, because of the hardness of his heart, and his perfidious intention.

Its brevity disproves its authenticity. Josephus' work is voluminous and exhaustive. It comprises twenty books. Whole pages are devoted to petty robbers and obscure seditious leaders. Nearly forty chapters are devoted to the life of a single king. Yet this remarkable being, the greatest product of his race, a being of whom the prophets foretold ten thousand wonderful things, a being greater than any earthly king, is dismissed with a dozen lines.

The Four Gospels were unknown to the early Christian Fathers. Justin Martyr, the most eminent of the early Fathers, wrote about the middle of the second century. His writings in proof of the divinity of Christ demanded the use of these Gospels had they existed in his time. He makes more than 300 quotations from the books of the Old Testament, and nearly one hundred from the Apocryphal books of the New Testament; but none from the four Gospels. Rev. Giles says:

> The very names of the Evangelists, Matthew, Mark, Luke, and John, are never mentioned by him (Justin) – do not occur once in all his writings.

Papias, another noted Father, was a contemporary of Justin. He refers to writings of Matthew and Mark, but his allusions to them clearly indicate that they were not the *Gospels* of Matthew and Mark. Dr. Davidson, an English authority on the canon, says: "He (Papias) neither felt the want nor knew the existence of inspired Gospels."

Excerpts from John E. Remsburg's book: The Christ *reprinted by Prometheus Books, New York, 1994.*

CHRIST THE BRIDEGROOM

Christ the Bridegroom

As Christ in the Desert seems to choose the solitary life of the desert, this Christ is the friend, the beloved companion. He is open to intimate conversation, to the loving gesture. This is the Christ the mystics will seek as Bridegroom.

The Secret Gospel

Morton Smith

The Public awaketh . . .
found on the Church's editing floor

Recently, a "secret gospel" has come to light which bears interestingly on the anointing ritual discussed. It was discovered by Professor Morton Smith when reading some old manuscripts in the ancient monastery of Mar Saba in the Judean Wilderness. In his book *The Secret Gospel* (1974), he records how he recognized the transcript of a hitherto unknown letter from the second-century Church Father Clement of Alexandria. The purpose of the letter was to attack the teachings of one of the most important gnostic groups, the Carpocratians, who flourished at least as early as the second century. In the course of his writing, Clement reveals the contents of what appears to have been an original sequence concerning the young rich man mentioned in Mark's Gospel, and which must have been purged from the version that was allowed to circulate among the faithful.

Further references also make it seem that Jesus was understood to have indulged in possible homosexual practices concerned with a particular form of baptism. These missing elements in the usual form of Mark, although well known apparently in the Church's inner circles, were part of secret traditions not thought suitable for general reading. It seems that Clement's unknown correspondent had been somewhat taken aback to be confronted by "heretics" who knew of a version of Mark which appeared to be genuine, but of which he knew nothing. Clement acknowledges its authenticity and says that it was, indeed, part of an enlarged version of the Second Gospel, written by Mark, who had left it to the church in Alexandria "where it is even now most carefully guarded, being read only to those who are being initiated into the great mysteries."

It would seem that some official of the church there had "leaked" its contents to Carpocrates. Nevertheless, Clement warns his reader, "one must never give way, nor . . . should one concede that the secret

175

gospel is by Mark, but should deny it on oath. For," the bishop admits frankly, "not everything that is true needs necessarily to be divulged to all men . . ."

Putting the pieces together, Professor Smith has shown that the story of the raising of Lazarus, found only in the Fourth Gospel, really related to the rich young man whom Jesus had sent away disquieted (Mark 10: 17-23). It was he whom the Master raised from the dead:

> And Jesus, being angered, went off with her into the garden where the tomb was. And straightway, a great cry was heard from the tomb. And going near, Jesus rolled away the stone from the door of the tomb. And straightway, going in where the youth was, he stretched forth his hand. But the youth, looking upon him, loved him, and began to beseech him that he might continue with him. And going out of the tomb, they came into the youth's house, for he was rich. And after six days, Jesus told him what to do. In the evening, the youth came to him, wearing a linen robe over his naked body. And he remained with him that night, for Jesus taught him the mystery of the Kingdom of God.

Clement denies that the phrase "naked man to naked man" was in the original secret gospel, as the Carpocratians had apparently affirmed to the anxious inquirer.

Bearing in mind that only Mark has that curious story about "a young man wearing a linen cloth over his naked body" in the Garden of the Agony (14: 51-52), Smith connects the incident with the earlier nocturnal initiation story of the secret gospel and gives good reason to believe that at least one element of the Church preserved a tradition that the Master "baptized" initiates himself, always at night, and with some kind of erotic ritual. That being so, we may connect the semen-anointing of the gnostics' "Father-son/youth" ceremony with this initiatory "baptism," and suspect that the "water" used was, in fact, the seminal fluid procured during the Elect's sexual activities. As far as the Marcan story of the raising of the dead is concerned, it was used merely to illustrate in mythical terms, possibly for recitation during the ceremony, the life-giving nature of the anointing, or "baptism," likeing it to the raising of one spiritually dead into everlasting life.

Morton Smith, professor of ancient history at Columbia University, has a Ph.D. from the Hebrew University and a Th.D. from Harvard. He is published by Harper & Row.

The cross, the pagan image of Jesus and circle of heaven have been institutionalized again and again. Here the image is found on the Abbey of Mossac, Southern France.

Mary

The oldest story in the world is the virgin mother and the newborn baby

Fathers of the Christian church strongly opposed the worship of Mary because they were well aware that she was only a composite of Mariaune, the Semitic God-Mother and Queen of Heaven, Aphrodite-Mari, the Syrian version of Ishtar, Juno the Blessed Virgin, the Moerae or trinity of Fates, and many other versions of the Great Goddess.

Even Diana Lucifera, the Morning Star Goddess, was assimilated into the Christian myth as Mary's mother, Anna or Dinah. Churchmen knew the same titles were applied to Mary as to her pagan forerunners: queen of heaven, empress of hell, and lady of the world.

— Women in Mythology

Virgo.

This ancient story of the Virgin Mother of Krishna being visited by the spirits before the birth of God's Sun, later became the Virgin Mary's being visited by God's angel announcing the coming of her "Son."

Christmas Surprise

Each year, during the winter solstice, American communities are transformed into gigantic merchandising centers relating to the Christian interpretation of this period. Evergreen trees, both natural and fabricated, are sold together with decorative ornaments, tinsel, and colored lights. Gift giving in gaudy wrappings is promoted. Stores and often streets are transformed. Robust, red-suited Santa Clauses ho-ho everywhere, and wide-eyed children, led by parents, are presented to Santa to express desires for certain gifts and to assure Santa of their merits while minimizing their shortcomings. Christmas carols and hymns are piped into the shopping areas in the hoped-for effect of softening buyer resistance and encouraging the purchase of items that would never be bought under ordinary circumstances. It is a time marked by greed on the parts of merchants and gift-receivers and by pressures of duty, obligation, and guilt for gift-givers.

One can understand the attitudes of merchants who take advantage of any occasion to sell their wares. After all, they are in business, and business operates for profit. Whatever encourages shoppers to buy is to be utilized.

Threaded throughout this gigantic merchandising effort are references to the supernatural birth of Jesus of Nazareth, to a unique star that guided wise men to the birthplace, to choirs of angels who announced the birth to shepherds, and to the insistence by the Christian church that in some mystical, wondrous way the divine intruded into the realm of the human and the supernatural impinged upon the natural. And the Christian church also engages in merchandising its product. Choirs sing Christmas hymns over radio and television. Tinsel and trees, creches and stars adorn the exteriors and interiors of church buildings. Children re-enact the gospel birth stories, and, in Christian homes across the land, the effectiveness of the union of religion and business can be seen in decorated fireplaces, rooms, and trees and in mounds of gaudily wrapped gifts.

There can be no doubt that kind and generous statements and acts abound during this period. Outcasts on skid rows are fed Christmas dinners, food and clothing are distributed to the destitute, and, even in prisons, turkey with all the trimmings is served to inmates.

Humanists can only approve of gestures of goodwill and kindliness – no matter what the motivating occasion. We can understand the efforts of merchants and appreciate the wonderment of little children at the transformation of their visual world. What Humanists do not accept is the presentation of the gospel birth stories as historically real or accurate. Humanists can believe that a child Jesus was born. But, like modern biblical scholars, they can doubt that the birthplace was Bethlehem; they can interpret the ideas of virgin birth, wondrous stars, angelic choirs, the visits of the magi and shepherds, the attempted murder of the infant by Herod as two-thousand-year-old Christian folklore to be placed in the same category as hero stories and myths emanating from other ancient cultures – but not to be believed. There is absolutely no reason to accept the birth narratives as having any foundation in historical reality.

— Gerald A. Larue, *Humanism and Christmas*

Jesus Christ can be calculated only approximately. It says regarding the date attributed to Christ's birth: "The date of December 25 does not correspond to Christ's birth but to the feast of the Natalis Solis Invicti, the Roman sun festival at the solstice.

— *The Watchtower*, Dec. 15, 1990

The first Christmas manger scene was assembled 767 years ago – using live animals and people . . . Exchanging gifts was once a pagan practice associated with New Year's . . . and the earliest carols were not sung – they were danced!

St. Francis of Assisi is credited with creating the first Nativity scene. In the year 1223, the revered saint, then known as Brother Francis, was teaching the villages of Greccio in central Italy the true meaning of Christmas.

To illustrate the story of the birth of Christ, he brought together the local people and their livestock, and created a living manger scene. The idea caught on, and soon manger scenes using carved figures became popular throughout Italy at Christmas time.

Originally, giving gifts had nothing to do with Christmas. Ancient Romans used to exchange presents on the first day of the new year. Early Christian Church leaders frowned upon the pagan custom, but ordinary people refused to give it up.

As time passed, the church linked the exchange of gifts with the story of the Three Kings bringing presents to the Christ Child. And for 700 years, we've been giving each other Christmas presents.

— Larry Haley

Virgin Birth: "Holy Virgin" was the title of harlot-priestesses of Ishtar, Asherah, or Aphrodite. The title didn't mean physical virginity; it simply meant "unmarried." The function of such "holy virgins" was to dispense the Mother's grace through sexual worship; to heal; to prophesy; to perform sacred dances, to sail for the dead; and to become Brides of God . . .

— *Women's Dictionary of Myth*

Catholic writer Maria Teresa Petrozzi comments in *Bethlehem:* "Starting from the 16th century, [Bethlehem] suffered from the bitter and bloody struggles between Latins [Roman Catholics] and Greeks [Greek Orthodox believers] for the hegemony in the Nativity Church." These recurrent "bloody struggles" for control often centered on the silver star in the Grotto of the Nativity, which is located underground, beneath the Church of the Nativity. This star is said to mark the actual site of Christ's birth.

R.W. Hamilton reports in his book, *The Church of the Nativity, Bethlehem,* "It is well known that two of the questions in the dispute between France and Russia which led up to the Crimean war were concerned with the rival claims to possession of the keys of the main doors of the basilica and of the crypt (Grotto of the Nativity), and with the mysterious theft one night in 1847 of the silver star with a Latin inscription which was let into a slab of marble beneath the Altar of the Nativity.

As a result of the continuous interdenominational conflicts throughout the centuries over rights in these places, "the rights of each denomination are now carefully prescribed. Of the 53 lamps in the grotto, for example, the Franciscans are allowed 19. The Altar of the Nativity is owned by the Greeks, and the Latins are not allowed to hold services there."

— *Historical Sites in Israel*

It is also noteworthy that during the month of December, Bethlehem and its surroundings are subject to wintry cold weather, chilling rains, and sometimes snow. One does not find shepherds with their flocks outside at night during that time. This is not a recent weather phenomenon. The Scriptures report that Judean King Jehoiakim was "sitting in the winter house, in the ninth month [Chislev, corresponding to November-December], with a brazier burning before him.: (Jewremiah 36:22) He needed the extra heat to keep warm. Further, at Ezra 10:9, 13, we find clear evidence that the month of Chislev was the "season of showers of rain." All of this indicates that weather conditions in Bethlehem in December do not fit the Bible's description of the events connected with the birth of Jesus Christ. – Luke 2:8-11

In a footnote Hamilton writes: "An account of the Nativity which occurs in the apocryphal "Book of James" or "Protevangelium," written about the same period, also introduces a cave, but describes it as lying half-way to Bethlehem. So far as it has any historical value the story suggests that the tradition was not yet linked with any single spot, certainly not with the Cave of the Nativity.

Third-century religious writers Origen and Eusebius tie the tradition as then known to a particular site. Hamilton reasons: "Once the story had become attached to a particular cave it was not likely to wander; and it is safe to infer that the cave shown to visitors soon after A.D. 200 was identical with the present Cave of the Nativity."

What can we conclude from the historical evidence at hand and, more important, from the Scriptural fact that neither Jesus nor his disciples assigned any importance to his birthplace? It is evident that when Queen Helena, the mother of Constantine the Great, fixed the site of the Church of the Nativity in the year 326 C.E., it was not on the basis of history or Biblical proof.

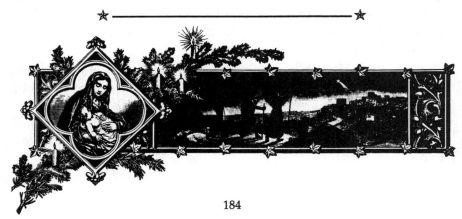

Krishna   *Christ*

- Both are held to be really god incarnate.
- Both were incarnated and born of a woman.
- The mother in each case was a holy virgin.
- The father of each was a carpenter.
- Both were of royal descent.
- Each had the divine title of "Savior."
- Both were "without sin."
- Both were crucified.
- Both were crucified between two thieves.
- Each taught of a great and final day of judgment.

Christ In Glory

Virgo the Virgin welcoming God's Sun coming on a cloud!

Probing The Mystery Of Jesus' Second Coming

Shmuel Golding

The events recorded in the New Testament following the death of Jesus would suggest that the disciples did not expect anything more from their master. He had been nailed to a cross and with him were killed all the messianic hopes. Luke makes this very clear and in Chapter 24 of his Gospel, we read the account of two of his disciples returning in disappointment to their home in Emmaus (Luke 24:13).

The reason for the disciples' feeling of disappointment was that they had believed Jesus to be the long-awaited Jewish Messiah as seen in Luke 24:21. But they could see that Jesus had died without accomplishing what a Messiah was predicted to do. In the story, Jesus enlightens them and in Luke 24:27 it says, "And beginning at Moses and all the prophets, he expounded unto them in all the scriptures the things concerning himself."

Today when we ask Christians, how is it possible for Jesus to be the Messiah when he clearly did not do the things a Messiah must do, we are given the answer that he will accomplish all things at his second coming. Jesus was given another chance. His death was only temporary. He arose from the dead and will one day return and do all the things he did not do when he was alive.

Therefore any person, who, at some future date, establishes a Messianic era will be seen to be the true Messiah, but presumably Christians will argue that such a person could only be Jesus who has returned. However, if Messianic expectations are only to be fulfilled by a second coming, what was the point of a first coming? Both John's Gospel and Paul's epistles present Jesus as a pagan deity, who as Matthew and Luke enlighten us was born of a virgin, just as were Adonis, son of the virgin Myrha, and Hermes, son of the virgin Maia. He was a member of a holy trinity as were Mithra and Osiris, Hermes Tris-Megistus (the thrice-mighty Hermes). He performed miracles like the god Dionysus, who turned water into wine, and he was put to death as were sixteen crucified pagan saviors before him. According to this, Jesus was just another sinbearer, another of the god-men of pagan mythology.

But by the Messiah of Israel, prophecies such as Isaiah 2 and Ezekiel 38 should have been fulfilled. Because such prophecies were not, and never have been fulfilled by anyone to this day, Jesus, we are told, will come back again and accomplish all things. But why does this future task only have to be fulfilled by Jesus? It is merely because he has been for so long the established Messiah in the mind of the Christian world.

Yet if we are to follow the subject of the second coming as it is written in the New Testament, we will find that the disciples understood that it would be in their own lifetime. Jesus himself spoke about his second coming, but nowhere in the Gospels did he tell his disciples about a return from heaven some thousands of years later.

Let us examine the New Testament references to the second coming. In Matt. 10:23, Jesus addressed his 12 disciples, and told them that they will "not have gone over all the cities of Israel, till the Son of man be come."

Almost two thousand years have gone by since this statement was made and whether or not the 12 disciples managed to travel to all the cities of Israel, one thing is certain, the Son of Man did not come.

Matt 16:28 explicitly states that "There are some of those who are standing here who will not taste death until they see the Son of man coming in his Kingdom." It is plain to all that none of those to whom Jesus spoke these words is still alive today. Matt. 16:24, especially, indicates that he was speaking to his disciples.

Another whole chapter, that of Matt 24:1-51, is considered to be a prophecy made by Jesus. Fundamentalists believe that this prophecy will be fulfilled in the "last days", by which they mean prior to Jesus' second coming. However, modern scholars claim that this chapter records events which had already taken place (since Matthew was written in approximately 80-90AD).

A point which has been overlooked by fundamentalists is the fact that Jesus was addressing his disciples in private (Matt. 24:3): "And they came unto him privately, saying, Tell us, when shall these things be? And what shall be the sign of thy coming, and of the end of the world?" Jesus then gave a list of happenings, adding to it, "Then shall they deliver you up to be afflicted, and shall kill you: and you shall be hated of all nations for my name's sake" (Verse 9). Thus it appears from those words that the twelve disciples would be around to witness the second coming and the end of time.

Jesus continues, "And then shall appear the sign of the Son of man in heaven: and then shall all the tribes of the earth mourn, and they shall see the Son of man coming in the clouds of heaven with power and great glory." In Verse 33 he was even more explicit: "So likewise ye, when ye shall see all these things, know that it is near, even at the doors."

And in Verse 34 he went on to elaborate, stating, "Verily I say unto you, This generation shall not pass, till all these things be fulfilled."

Yet as the whole world knows, that generation did pass away without Jesus returning. A few of those events did happen during the lifetime of the disciples. For example, the temple was destroyed, false Christs sprang up as mentioned by Paul, and some of the disciples were persecuted by the Romans. It is probable that John lived to a very old age, but he never saw any sign of the Son of man coming from heaven, and with John's death that generation passed away.

Some fundamentalists are of the opinion that "that generation" means the generation alive when this prophecy comes to pass, which they believe has yet to happen. But we need only point out that Jesus was definitely not speaking to some future generation, he was speaking to his disciples and directed this prophecy to them personally. This was not an original prophecy but was based upon Daniel and rehashed to fit the events of the day.

In Mark 14:62, Jesus told the chief priests, "Ye shall see the Son of man sitting on the right hand of power and coming in the clouds of heaven". Yet history shows this to be a false prophecy, because the chief priests have been dead for 1900 years or more. They never lived to see Jesus coming in the clouds of heaven, for, as the world knows, Jesus never returned.

There is a parable in Luke 18:1-5 about a judge who feared neither man nor God. He was described as being unjust. Yet when a certain widow woman implored him daily for his help, he avenged her lest by her continual coming she should weary him. Now we see what is stated in Luke 18:7-8, "and shall not God avenge his own elect, which cry day and night unto him, though he bear long with them? I tell you that he will avenge them speedily. Nevertheless when the Son of man cometh, shall he find faith of the earth?"

If Christians see themselves as God's elect, in this context, it would appear that Jesus was more unjust than the unjust judge of the parable. For 2000 years Christendom has prayed to Jesus day and night: He made a promise to avenge them speedily on his return to earth, but this can no longer be considered speedy by anyone with the least intelligence. The unjust judge did not keep this poor woman waiting 2000 years as Jesus kept his elect waiting, yet this, it would seem, is the whole point of the parable.

Jesus ought to have returned during the lifetime of one of his disciples, because Jesus said, "If I will that he tarry till I come, what is that to thee?" (John 21:22). It was thus believed by the disciples that John, the beloved disciple, would never die. John lived for many years after the death of Jesus, and like the high priest who was also expected to see Jesus' return, he died without it happening.

It is evident throughout the epistles that Paul was not accepted by the apostolic group. He met with opposition and contention throughout his ministry. After establishing churches in Asia Minor he found that all those in Asia had left him. He wrote an epistle to the Romans, yet on his arrival in Rome, only three believers were there to comfort him in his bonds. In Corinth also, Paul was judged by fellow believers and so he said in 1 Cor 4:3, "But with me it is a very small thing that I should be judged of you, or of man's judgment: yea, I judge not mine own self."

He then told those who were contending with him, " . . . judge nothing before the time." In other words, Paul told them to wait "until the Lord come who both will bring to light the hidden things of darkness and will manifest the counsels of the hearts: and then shall every man have praise of God". It is obvious from these words that Paul believed Jesus would return in his lifetime to vindicate him in this controversy. But Jesus didn't arrive, and the controversy continues to this day as modern scholars expose Paul as a fraud and accuse him of establishing a religion different from the one which Jesus and the apostles followed.

Again, Paul when writing to Timothy expressed, "That thou keep this commandment without spot, unrebukeable until the appearing of our Lord Jesus Christ" (1 Tim 6:14). Paul must have expected Jesus to return during Timothy's lifetime. The promise of Jesus' coming was to be soon, very quickly, in certain people's lifetime, yet they are long since dead. Almost two thousand years have passed since the promise of a soon return, and fundamentalists of today still echo this age-old promise.

The writer of Hebrews states, "Nor yet that he should offer himself often, as the high priest entereth into the holy place every year with blood of others; for then must he often have suffered since the foundation of the world: but now once in the end of the world hath he appeared to put away sin by the sacrifice of himself," (Heb 9:25-26). But what about today, 2000 years later? If the time of Jesus was considered to be the "end of the world" as the writer of Hebrews suggests, then we must be living in a new world, so this new world must by now be in need of a new sacrifice. It is obvious to any intelligent reader that Jesus did not come at the "end of the world", for the world is still going on as it has been for millions of years.

And again in Heb. 9:28, " . . . and unto them that look for him shall he appear the second time . . . " According to these words Jesus' second coming will only be seen by those who look for him. Therefore the second coming is something secret that will only be known to those who believe in it, requiring no visible appearance to the rest of mankind.

Jesus was expected to return during the lifetime of certain children to whom John addressed his epistle. (I John 2:28), "And now, little children, abide in him; that, when he shall appear, we may have confidence and not be ashamed before him at his coming." They all died without Jesus ever returning.

Shmuel Golding is contributing editor of Biblical Poblemics *in Jerusalem, Israel.*

A dead Messiah could not be victorious. The Messiah must come into the presence of God on high, there to have bestowed upon him the crown he had earned, and there to await the signal for his second advent in triumph. "Hereafter shall ye see the Son of Man sitting at the right hand of Power, and coming in the clouds of heaven."

— Hugh J. Schonfield

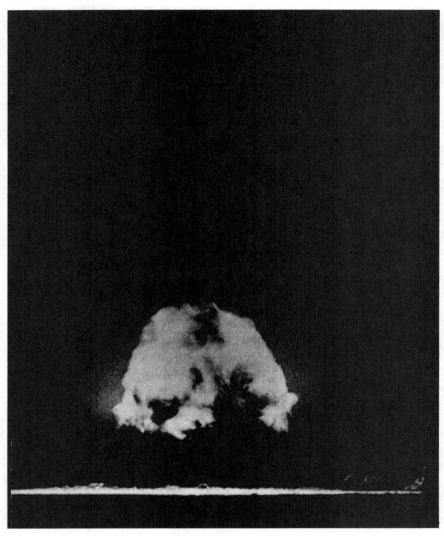

Trinity

The First Atomic Bomb, called Trinity, July 16, 1945.

The opening of the sixth seal begins what all nations fear
— nuclear war. But the Soviet leaders, in a desperate
situation, decide to launch a first strike.

— Hal Lindsey, *The Rapture*, 1983.

Editor's Note: Another in a long line of wrong prophesies.

The End(s)

Prophecies have been with us for centuries, even before Jesus and Christianity. The overall success rate of predictions is miserable, even with rewrites and redating.

In Matt. xvi. 28, for example, Jesus says; "Truly I say unto you, there are some standing here who shall not taste of death, till they see the Son of man coming in his kingdom." This implies that the time of the fulfillment of these hopes was not thought of by Jesus and his disciples as at all remote. It means that Jesus promised the fulfillment of all Messianic hopes before the end of the existing generation. Most Christians were already very surprised that Christ hadn't returned within the first decade or so after his resurrection. They decided that the End had been deferred to allow more time to baptize more people before the last judgment.

1889 — "The 'battle of the great day of God Almighty' (Rev. 16:14), WHICH WILL END IN A.D. 1914 with the complete overthrow of earth's present rulership, is already commenced." *THE TIME IS AT HAND p. 101, 1980 ed.*

1897 — "Our Lord, the appointed King, IS NOW PRESENT, SINCE OCTOBER 1874 A.D." *STUDIES IN THE SCRIPTURES Vol. 4, p. 621, 1897 ed*

1916 — "The six great 1000-year days beginning with Adam are ended, and the great 7th day, the 1000 YEARS OF CHRIST'S REIGN, BEGAN IN 1873." *THE TIME IS AT HAND p. 2 (foreword)*

1920 — "Therefore we may CONFIDENTLY EXPECT that 1925 will mark the return of Abraham, Isaac, Jacob and the faithful prophets of old." *MILLIONS NOW LIVING WILL NEVER DIE p. 89.*

1931 — "There was a measure of disappointment on the part of Jehovah's faithful ones on earth concerning the years 1914, 1918 & 1925, which disappointment lasted for a time . . . AND THEY ALSO LEARNED TO QUIT FIXING DATES." *VINDICATION p. 338, 339*

1966 — "Six thousand years from man's creation will end in 1975, and the seventh period of a thousand years of human history will begin in the fall of 1975 C.E." *LIFE EVERLASTING p. 29*

1968 — "There are only about 90 months left before 6000 years of man's existence on earth is completed. The majority of people living today will probably be alive when Armageddon breaks out." *KM 3/68*

1992   The Jehovah's Witnesses are praying that this is "their decade." Current *final* predictions give us less than eight years.

1992 — Jesus will come in the feast of trumpets October 28th (Ad in Los Angeles Newspaper, by COC Mission Seoul, Korea)

And, in a sermon at the Fundamentalist Bible Tabernacle in Los Angeles, the Rev. R.L. Hymers thundered that the Middle East crisis and the West's need for Arab oil "may very well be . . .[what] unites the West under one man that the Bible calls in First John the Antichrist."

Doomsday sentence: The leader of a doomsday sect in South Korea was sentenced Friday to two years in prison for swindling $4.4 million from his fanatical followers.

Lee Jang-rim, 44, had led the Mission for Coming Days, which had about 10,000 followers. It was one of several to predict that the end of the world would come in late October.

Some 20,000 people were caught up in the doomsday craze. Several believers killed themselves and others deserted their homes, schools and jobs.

This is prophesied for the tribulation period! And he [Antichrist] doeth great wonders, so that he maketh fire come down from heaven on the earth in the sight of men (Revelation 13:13)!

Beloved, Rexella and I have been crying out for months that the stage is now set for the Rapture, then the unveiling of Antichrist, and his three-and-a-half years of deceptive peace followed by three-and-a-half years of international terror. Finally – Armageddon begins . . . as the glorious return of Christ with His saints occurs (Revelation 19:11-19). We believe these events have never been nearer and, in fact, could happen at any time.

When you send your ministry support gift of $20 or more, we will immediately send you *Thinking the Unthinkable: Are All the Pieces in Place?* by John Wesley White. It will bless and edify you and, at the same time, challenge you to help us share the gospel worldwide.

— Jack Van Impe Ministries International.

Flash – update 1993

Cult leader, David Koresh, aka Jesus, leader of Branch Davidian, was waiting for judgment day. Cult kills 73 members, including many children, in mass suicide in addition to four federal agents, FBI reports.

The Cross

The Pagan and Christian uses of the cross are identical

Herbert Cutner, in *Jesus: God, Man, or Myth* (The Truth Seeker, 1950), says,

> A *stauros* was a mere stake, and horrible to contemplate; it was used in the cruelest fashion to execute criminals and other persons . . . It was sometimes pointed and thrust through the victim's body to pin him to earth; or he was placed on top of the stake with its point upwards so that it gradually pierced his body; or he was tied upon it and left exposed till death intervened; and there were other methods too. There is not a scrap of evidence that a *stauros* was ever in the form of a cross or even of a T shape.

If Jesus had been executed, mythically or historically, it would not have been with outstretched arms on a cruciform structure.

Cutner reports that scholars have been aware of the error but have been unable to resist the traditional mistranslation. In the 18th century some Anglican bishops recommended eliminating the cross symbol altogether, but they were ignored.

There is no cross in early Christian art before the middle of the 5th century, where it (probably) appears on a coin in a painting. The first clear crucifix appears in the late 7th century. Before then Jesus was almost always depicted as a fish or a shepherd, never on a cross.

Constantine's supposed 4th-century vision of a cross in the sky was not of the instrument of execution: it was the Greek letter "X" (chi) with a "P" (rho) through it, the well-known "monogram" of Christ, from the first two letters of Χριστόσ.

Any bible that contains the word "cross" or "crucify" is dishonest. Christians who flaunt the cross are unwittingly advertising a pagan religion.

Doctrine

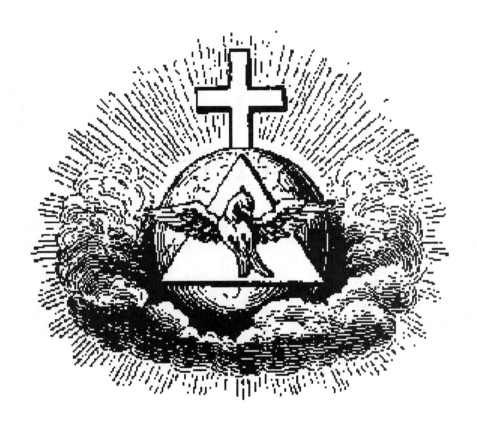

At first, Christianity did not hold to the Trinity doctrine. That doctrine developed slowly and did not become officially a creedal fact until C.E. 325.

Adrian C. Swindler
From *The Trinity: An Absurdity Borrowed From Paganism.*

The Trinity

God found out about the Trinity in 325 A.D.
— Dr. Rocco Errico

Christ, according to the faith, is the second person in the Trinity, the Father being the first and the Holy Ghost the third. Each of these three persons is God. Christ is his own father and his own son. The Holy Ghost is neither father nor son, but both. The son was begotten by the father, but existed before he was begotten – just the same before as after. Christ is just as old as his father, and the father is just as young as his son. The Holy Ghost proceeded from the Father and Son, but was equal to the Father and Son before he proceeded, that is to say, before he existed, but he is of the same age of the other two.

So, it is declared that the Father is God, and the Son God and the Holy Ghost God, and that these three Gods make one God.

According to the celestial multiplication table, once one is three, and three times one is one, and according to heavenly subtraction if we take two from three, three are left. The addition is equally peculiar, if we add two to one we have but one. Each one is equal to himself and the other two. Nothing ever was, nothing ever can be more perfectly idiotic and absurd than the dogma of the Trinity.

Is it possible for a human being, who has been born but once, to comprehend, or to imagine the existence of three beings, each of whom is equal to the three?

Think of one of these beings as the father of one, and think of that one as half human and all God, and think of the third as having proceeded from the other two, and then think of all three as one. Think that after the father begot the son, the father was still alone, and after the Holy Ghost proceeded from the father and the son, the father was still alone – because there never was and never will be but one God.

At this point, absurdity having reached its limit, nothing more can be said except: "Let us pray."

By Robert Green Ingersoll from his book, The Foundations of Faith, *1895, from the Dresden Edition of his works, vol. 4, pp. 266-8.*

As far back as we can go into the ancient world, we find that all known cultures had a "Three-In-One" *triune* god. The very first trinity was simply the three stages of life of the Sun.

1) **New Born,** at dawn;

2) **Mature,** full-grown at 12 noon; and

3) **Old and Dying,** at the end of the day (going back to The Father).

All three were of course one *divinity!* The Trinity is no mystery!

Paganism, Astrology & Christianity: The True Trinity?

Parish churches repeated in folk variations the artistry of the great cathedrals and abbeys. The twelfth-century church of Barfreston in Kent . . a tympanum "Christ in Glory" surrounded first by a band of animals playing musical instruments, then (the outermost arch) the Signs of the Zodiac.

— After Jesus The Triumph of Christianity, 1992
The Reader's Digest, Inc., Illustrator Chris Majadini

Paul recalled his vision on the Damascus road as "a light from heaven, brighter than the sun shining round me and those who had journeyed with me. And when we had all fallen to the ground, I heard a voice."

— Acts 26:13-14

A.K.A. medical signs of desert sunstroke . . . or religious fanaticism?

— Editor

Paul: First Christian Heretic

Shmuel Golding

During these first three-and-a-half centuries of the common era, the most powerful rival of Christianity was the religion known as Mithraism. It had been introduced to Rome by Cilician seamen about 70 BCE, and later spread throughout the Roman world. Prior to the triumph of Christianity, it was the most powerful pagan faith in the Empire. It was suppressed by the Christians in 376-77 C.E., but its actual collapse seems to have been due rather to the fact that by that time, many of the doctrines and ceremonies of Mithraism had been adopted by the church. Without the need of any mental somersaults, Jesus Christ had supplanted Mithra in man's worship. This fusion of one God with another is called theocrasia, and nowhere did it go on more vigorously than in the Roman Empire.

Tarsus, the chief city of the Cilicians, and the home of Paul, was one of the chief centers of Mithra worship. H.G. Wells considered it highly probable that Paul had been influenced by Mithraism, because he used phrases very much like Mithraistic ones. What becomes amply clear to anyone who reads Paul's various epistles side by side with the Gospels, is that Paul's mind was saturated by an idea which does not appear prominent in the reported sayings and teachings of Jesus: the figure of a sacrificial person who is offered as an atonement for sin. What Jesus had preached was a new birth of the human soul. What Paul preached was the ancient religion of priest, altar and bloodshed. Jesus to Paul was the Easter lamb, the traditional human victim without spot or blemish who haunts all the pagan religions.

Mithra was sometimes termed the god out of the rock, and services were conducted in caves. Jesus' origin in a cave is a clear instance of the taking over of a Mithraic idea. Paul says, "They drank from that spiritual rock and that rock was Christ" (I Cor. 10:4). These are identical words to those found in the Mithraic scriptures, except that the name Mithra is used instead of Christ. The Vatican hill in Rome that is regarded as sacred to Peter, the Christian rock, was already sacred to Mithra. Many Mithraic remains have been found there. The merging of the worship of Attis into that of Mithra, then later into that of Jesus, was effected almost without interruption.

Aided by research into the texts of the New Testament and quoting from modern scholars, the fact emerges that the beliefs set forth by Paul were altogether different from those expounded by Jesus and his disciples. What is more, we see from the New Testament itself that Paul was not accepted by the other believers and that his message was rejected by the early church.

Paul claimed to have come to Jerusalem, and to have learned his Judaism there "at the feet of rabbi Gamaliel" (Acts 22:3). He stated that at one point in his life he was a strict Pharisaic Jew (Acts 26:5). What changed him? What event turned a "reportedly" observant Jew into a heretic?

We will let Paul speak for himself. There are in fact three passages in Acts, describing Paul's "conversion." In the first account (Acts 9:7) it is stated that the men who were with him "also heard the voice of Jesus." Later, when testifying before a Jewish audience, Paul changed his story. This time he spoke of a great light and said that they "saw the light but did not hear the voice . . ." (Acts 22:9). The third time when Paul spun his yarn was to King (Herodes-) Agrippas. This time he left the man Ananias out of his story and instead Jesus himself gives him instructions for his future mission. (Acts 26:13ff) To us it is highly suspicious that Paul's story should have three versions.

He also claimed to be an apostle (I Cor. 15:9), to have been instructed by the risen Christ, to have seen Christ and to have received his authority from him (II Cor. 12:1ff). Yet, for all Paul's claims, they were doubted and disputed by the original apostles and Jewish believers. They did not accept him as a true believer, but considered him preaching falsehood.

Paul, if he knew anything of the life and teaching of Jesus as described in the Gospels, chose to ignore it. Instead he presented to the Gentile world a mystery religion in which he transformed Jesus into a divine spirit who existed before the world began and who had gone away to prepare the kingdom of God, not on this earth but in the world of the hereafter.

Shmuel Golding is contributing editor of Biblical Poblemics *in Jerusalem, Israel.*

The seven-pointed star on this man's forehead identifies him as a priest of the sun god from Roman Egypt. Sun worship, a monotheistic religion which originated in Persia, had become a chief imperial cult by the middle of the third century. It was to remain the predominant religion of the empire, until replaced by Christianity in the decades following 312.

666

Do You Believe In Satan?

	Yes	No	Don't Know
Northern Ireland	66	22	12
United States	66	28	6
Republic of Ireland	57	34	9
Spain	33	53	14
Italy	30	55	15
Great Britain	30	60	10
Norway	28	62	10
Belgium	20	59	21
Netherlands	20	66	14
West Germany	18	70	12
France	17	76	7
Denmark	12	77	11

Source: 1981 Gallup Poll

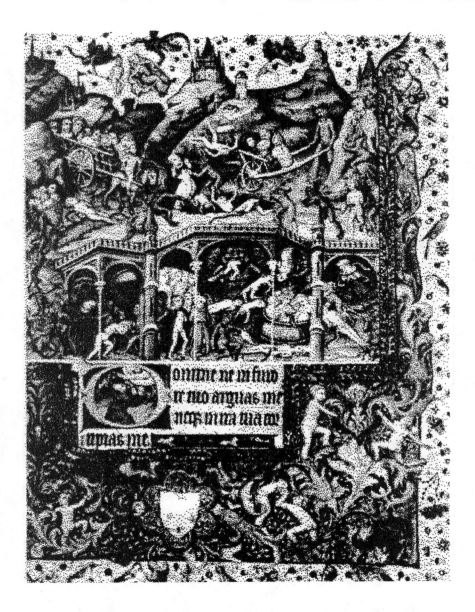

The way to hell, as pictured by the medieval church, began at the mouth of a terrifying pit where damned souls arrived by the cartload (upper left). Here fiends stripped them naked and pitched them into the two gaping tunnels at left and center. Their bloody remains were carried off for further torture by a monklike assistant (far right), after their bodies had been boiled in oil or partially devoured by a batlike monster (center).

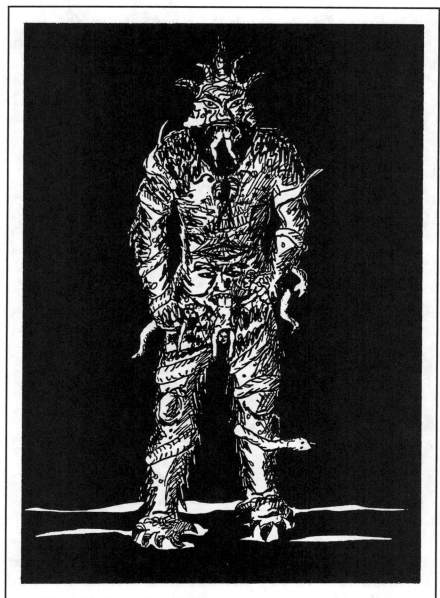

"E-V-I-L" personified became the "D-E-V-I-L"

(1) Baalzebub was a local "baal" or god – god of the Philistine city of Ekron, in II Kings.

(2) Beelzebul is mentioned in the Gospels as "prince of demons," *incorrectly* called "Beelzebub" in the King James Version, through mistaken identity with the god of II Kings.

The Supreme Spirit of Evil

Satan, A.K.A. Lucifer, Beelzebub, Devil

Christianity has created its own version of evil, with its own persona and image, while rejecting prototypes and forerunners as creatures of mythology and superstition.

But of the tree of the knowledge of good and evil, thou shalt not eat of it: for in the day that thou eatest thereof thou shalt surely die.

Genesis 2:17

Editor's Note: Tradition has favored the apple, but no one seems to know why. One wag recently commented that if God allowed the First Family to eat every fruit bearing seed, then the forbidden fruit must have been one which bore no seed in itself. This fruit may well have been the banana — a fitting symbol of our ancestors' favorite diet.

Original Sin

Austin Miles

(The Doctrine of Original Sin) declares that (man) ate the fruit of the tree of knowledge – he acquired a mind and became a rational being. It was the knowledge of good and evil – he became a moral being. He was sentenced to earn his bread by his labor – he became a productive being. He was sentenced to experience desire – he acquired the capacity of sexual enjoyment. The evils for which (the preachers) damn him are reason, morality, creativeness, joy – all the cardinal values of his existence.

— Ayn Rand

Christians believe in guilty babies; Catholics believe in guilty embryos. *(Psalm 51:5)*

— Wm. B. Lindley

During the early part of 1990, a book titled *The Agony of Deceit* was released. This work, put together by Michael Horton, an Episcopal priest, purported to lay on the table the theological, doctrinal, and scriptural errors of the televangelists. Coming from the perspective of a prominent clergyman, this book initially aroused my intellectual curiosity. That is, until I *read* it and discovered that the greatest *deceit* is the book itself.

What the Rev. Michael Horton would do to us would be far more dangerous and damaging to our mental health than the antics of the TV preachers. Passing off the preaching of the televangelists as unsound, Rev. Horton points us to the way of *true* Christianity. He first spells out the significance of "original sin."

For those who are not familiar with this story from the Bible, it started with the very first couple to walk the earth. God created Adam and Eve "in his own image," declared that what He had made "was very good," then got so enraged with them that He cursed the entire human race with an uncontrollable fury that continues to this very day. Unable to resolve the dilemma of homo sapiens using the free will that He had given them, God in exasperation came down to earth and had Himself nailed to a cross to appease his own wrath. Even this drastic action had little effect.

On page 135, Rev. Horton tackles this sacred subject and explains how original sin still applies to those of us who are struggling in the 20th Century, especially the little babies, the worst offenders of all:

> The idea meant by the expression 'original sin' is that all humans are born sinners. There is no such thing as an innocent little baby. From conception, each of us merits the wrath and judgment of God (Psalm 51:5) . . . Due to original sin, I am bent toward myself and I am charged with Adam's guilt. I can be sent to hell whether I have personally committed a sin or not . . . (Page 137) But original guilt, after all, is the whole point of this biblical teaching.

The Catholic church in particular, steeped in the theology of sinful babies, convinces the devout that any child not baptized will be plunged into hell with the rest of the damned, even if the child dies at birth.

Guilt is the cornerstone of the church and fear is its steeple. In Rev. Horton's effort to strip us down completely, he tells us on pages 139 and 140:

> He (God) does not help those who help themselves, but saves those who are entirely helpless to lift a finger.
>
> But the issue is not a matter of getting the sinner to like God, but of getting God to like the sinner. Over and over in the Bible we read that God 'maintains his wrath against his enemies,' (Nahum 1:2) and that 'God's wrath remains on' the unbeliever every day of his life (John 3:36). Paul says to unbelievers, 'You are storing up wrath' (Romans 2:5).
>
> The Bible speaks vividly of 'the fury of the wrath of God Almighty' (Rev. 19:15) and of the 'wrath of the Lamb' (Rev. 6:16) . . . God cannot accept us the way we are. He is perfect and we are wicked, self-centered to the very core of our being. In order for His wrath to be propitiated, His justice must be satisfied . . .

Rev. Horton continues with this advice for the televangelists:

> Need we burden the viewer with such theological details? Indeed we must. We must burden the viewer with his rightful sense of guilt.

This fate of eternal wrath and guilt is apparently reserved for those who are *not* necessarily evil-doers, such as the little babies. The transgressors, on the other hand, are blessed, and receive special favors and status from God. This strange sense of justice is clarified on page 142:

> . . . of course that means that even though the believer will sin many times, God has nevertheless declared that person to be a perfectly law-abiding citizen. The basis for our relationship with God is Christ's track record, not our own.

So, the actual sinner can go right on sinning, no matter whom he offends, and still be, in God's eye, a law-abiding citizen. He is freed from guilt, and God bestows His mercy and grace upon him, that is, as long as he is a 'believer' and under control of the church.

It is the *innocent* upon whom excessive guilt should be heaped. For these hapless creatures, God demands an extraordinary performance of mental and physical endurance. While bogged down under the crushing weight of preacher-inflicted guilt, these individuals are expected to "run the race for the crown" swiftly and victoriously. These spiritual olympics almost always end up with hell as a reward. The practicing sinners in the meantime are being ushered directly into heaven. As the Bible says, "God's ways are not our ways."

What is particularly astonishing about the ramblings of The Rev. Michael Horton is that what he is saying is absolutely, positively, *scripturally correct!* It is all there in the Bible that has been handed down to us generation after generation. The "Words of God" that Rev. Horton quoted are not taken out of context; and this is exactly what the Christians are preaching and using to hold people in obedience to them.

The Bible, which was written by *man* (I have discovered 17 versions of the original King James Bible) is the ultimate tool for the orchestrated, professional manipulation of the human race by playing upon man's deepest fears and superstitions.

A contributing writer to *The Agony of Deceit*, Dr. W. Robert Godfrey, explains another mind-deluder springing from "original sin" that will assist the Christian in his own entrapment. His views are significant, since Dr. Godfrey is Professor of Church History at Westminster Theological Seminary, Escondido, California. This means that the following doctrine is drilled into seminary students:

> Elders are appointed for our sakes, and we need to submit ourselves to their authority in the local church if we are to be obedient to the Lord and His vision of the Christian life . . . Elders are necessary to teach and admonish and discipline us. But how can elders carry out that work unless we submit to them? What is church membership but joining our local congregation and submitting to the authority of the elders? To be sure, elders are not infallible. Sometimes they can deviate; indeed, they have, from time to time, been known to leave the faith entirely. But the fact that some elders are unreliable does not eliminate our responsibility to find godly elders and submit to them.

Perpetual submission is the goal. This keeps people in bondage to one another, which at the same time makes the pastor's quest to control his flock through guilt easier. The pastor is under submission to the hierarchy. The hierarchy is under submission to no one, and that includes God.

Dr. Godfrey preaches that even when these elders betray us through misconduct, we are given the responsibility to go and submit to another elder who may do the same thing to us.

The need to be punished is paramount in Christian theology. Dr. Godfrey advises on page 157:

> Many people do not like the idea of a disciplined church. They believe they should be able to do whatever is right in their own eyes. Such an attitude reflects the militant individualism of our society. But it does not reflect Christ's teaching about the life of His church. Proper discipline by the officers of the church is necessary for the well-being of individual Christians as well as for the church as a whole. Such discipline can take place only in the context of membership in a local church.

Dr. W. Robert Godfrey has served as chairman of the Consultation on Conversion in Hong Kong, for the Lausanne Committee on World Evangelism, and is a senior editor of *Eternity* magazine.

With a heap offering of guilt, fear, the wrath of God and sinful babies, Rev. Michael Horton says:

> I, for one, have been deeply impressed with the reverence and comfort of these truths . . . We need to rediscover for ourselves the richness of biblical, historic Christian truths, and then integrate those truths into our daily practice and share them with our neighbors.

Only a sick mind could ever take comfort in the so-called truths as described. And to suggest that Christians attempt to pollute the minds of their neighbors with this madness is enough to demand that all of them be put into strait-jackets. As chemical waste dumped into rivers fouls the water, the spiritual sludge of Christianity poisons our minds.

In his closing statements on page 150, Rev. Horton does give a tidbit of excellent advice:

> It is time we – all of us – give serious thought to what the content of the gospel really is.

I will give a big "Amen" to that.

When I Was A Christian . . .

When I was a Christian and deeply involved with the church, I read the Bible, yet I really did *not* read it. The preachers skillfully guided me over the majority of its passages, which I later found to be horrifying. Cloaked in the beauty of its poetic language, and having temporarily taken leave of my capacity to think or reason, I missed the real blood-and-guts issue of this classic literature.

One of the first things that I read in the Bible as an adult while in the state of non-thinking, was that God rested from his work on the seventh day. The All-Powerful, Omnipotent, Omnipresent, Omniscient God got tired? And He had to rest!?

This fatigue overtook the Almighty after He had created all living things "after their kind." After what kind? If this was "THE" creation of the world and its creatures, where did God get his models from which to pattern his creatures if nothing had existed before that? Moreover, how did I miss this? Perhaps I was preoccupied with my original sin of being born.

Why didn't I question how and where Cain found a wife when, according to the Bible we are supposed to believe, there were only four people in existence: his father, mother, and brother, along with himself? But then again, it was considered taboo in those days, indeed in bad taste, to challenge the Bible. Having been indoctrinated from an early age, I just blindly accepted what *inquiring minds* would have found to be absurd.

If God can do anything, if He is the master architect of the universe who can control any and all things, then why did he viciously cause to drown the entire human race, with the exception of Noah and his family, because he got irritated with a few? Then Noah, the man who found such favor with God, went out and got drunk as soon as the waters subsided.

In the meantime, countless innocents, including little babies, lived out their last moments of life in terror as the relentless, mountainous waters swelled around them and without mercy, angrily swallowed them up. This would seem to be a logical heavenly action. God's wrath is especially severe on little babies. They are filled with sin.

God once (according to the words attributed to Him), became so outraged over attempted census-taking in Israel that He killed seventy thousand men! (1 Chronicles 21:2,7,14) Now I personally rebelled over giving information to the 1990 census-takers, but I wouldn't even think of carrying my displeasure to that extreme.

The God that the *born-again* Christians demand that we love, instructed Moses to order three million people to stone to death one man who had upset Him. (Numbers 15:35,36) Talk about overkill! In a strange case of holy retribution, a ranting God struck an entire city of men down with hemorrhoids! (1 Samuel 5:8,9)

With His short-fused temper, why doesn't God justifiably strike down these preachers who use His name to steal, instead of allowing them to continue swindling people? This would make more sense than the repeated wholesale slaughter at the hand of God over something trivial.

To reassure us, the Bible proclaims that "God is not the author of confusion." Yet, we read in that same Bible that God Himself purposely caused the greatest confusion known to man, when He confounded their language at the construction site of the Tower of Babel so that the people He had created could not communicate with one another and complete the project.

These self-contradictions, found throughout the Bible, are so numerous, that not only can they often be found on the same pages, but in at least one case, within a few lines of each other. Galatians 6:2 instructs us to "Bear ye one another's burdens," and then down eight lines to Galatians 6:5 we are informed: "For every man shall bear his own burden." Small wonder the Christians walk around in a daze.

I first became suspicious of the authenticity of the Bible by observing the conduct of those who practice its precepts. When I finally broke free of the church and Christianity, I switched the button of my brain back to "on," and then re-read the Bible. It is an overwhelming experience to actually *read* that book in its entirety while in a thinking, analytical state, and to concentrate on what the words unquestionably say. Anyone who does this could never again say that they want to "live according to the Bible."

The Bible, as we know it, is not the authentic word of God. It cannot stand up under examination. I will now offer you shocking proof that man not only tampered with the Bible in order to control his fellow man through guilt and fear, but also made king-size blunders in the process.

One day while randomly reading my Bible, I made a startling discovery. After reading 2 Kings 19, I flipped a number of pages and read some more. To my astonishment, I found myself reading the same words. Now, class, open your Bibles to 2 Kings 19 — and also to Isaiah 37. *These books are word for word identical!* No Bible scholar has been able to give me a satisfactory explanation for this.

Perhaps there is an "original sin," man's innate determination and ability to pervert everything, even the concept of God. To attribute the deeds and thoughts described in the Bible to a benevolent, Almighty God would indeed be blasphemy.

Austin Miles is an minster, author of many articles, and books. He is the Author of Don't Call Me Brother *and* Setting The Captives Free, *Prometheus Books, Buffalo, New York.*

EDITOR'S NOTE: It is encouraging to see that Episcopalian clergy are not of one mind on original sin. Bishop John Shelby Spong, whose book *Rescuing the Bible from Fundamentalism* is reviewed elsewhere in this book, writes on p. 234 of that book:

> To view human life as depraved or as victimized by original sin is to literalize a premodern anthropology and a premodern psychology . . . To traffic in guilt as the church has done . . . is simply no longer defensible, if it ever was.

The "Impaled" Savior

Facts, fiction, history, plagiarism and myth are interchangeable in the Crucifixion and Resurrection story – "The Greatest Story Ever Told." Several glaring inconsistencies are the "Christian eyewitness" accounts of what was said on the cross, what Jesus' final words were and whether Jesus was crucified as in the religious story or more probably impaled, not on a cross, but a stake.

The Resurrection: What Is The Evidence?

Tovia Singer

Since the claim of the resurrection is the foundation of the Christian faith, we should certainly examine the credibility of this story. What is the evidence for the belief that Jesus rose from the grave? The entire claim hangs exclusively on the New Testament texts. Is this testimony reliable? As a seeker of truth, you are the judge.

Obviously, a judge must be impartial, and weigh all of the evidence. Realize this is not a routine case; your relationship with God is at stake. As an individual examining the case for the resurrection should not be swayed by conjecture or hearsay, but demand clear proof.

If you were the judge presiding over a murder case, you would want to be absolutely certain before convicting the defendant. If the prosecutor calls his key witnesses, but each tells a different story, his case would be very shaky. The defense attorney will argue for the acquittal of his client by demonstrating the weakness of the prosecutor's case. He will impeach the state's witnesses by showing how their accounts are contradictory.

Tovia Singer is a rabbi/exit counselor and director of Jews For Judaism — a national organization dedicated to countering the efforts of Christian groups and cults that specifically target Jews for conversion. He is the author of numerous articles, and is a frequent guest on television and radio shows.

	Matthew/Paul	Mark	Luke	John
Does Mary wish to tell the disciples what had happened?	YES--"They departed quickly...and ran to tell the disciples." (28:8)	NO--"...they said nothing to anyone; for they were afraid." (16:8)	YES--"Returning from the tomb, they told all this to the eleven..." (24:9)	YES--Mary Magdalene tells the disciples, "I have seen the Lord." (20:18)
After seeing the angels, whom does Mary meet first, Jesus or the disciples?	Jesus* (28:9)	Jesus* (16:9)	THE DISCIPLES* (24:4-9)	Jesus* (20:14)
	*Entirely contradicting Luke's post-resurrection story, Matthew, Mark and John all insist that Mary met Jesus before she was able to tell any of the disciples what had happened (Matthew 28:8; Mark 16:9; John 20:14), whereas Luke asserts that Mary revealed all to the disciples before ever encountering Jesus! -Luke 24:4-10			
A) To whom does Jesus make his first appearance? *B) Where does this appearance take place?*	A) The two Marys B) On the way to Jerusalem, after leaving the tomb (28:9) *Paul - 1 Corinthians* A) Cephas (Peter) 15:5 B) ?	A) Only Mary Magdalene B) Mark's story does not indicate where this appearance takes place. It is quite clear, however, that it occurs sometime after Mary fled the tomb. (16:8-9)	A) Cleopas and another** B) Emmaus** (24:13, 18) ***Contradicting Mark's resurrection tale, Luke asserts (24:34) that when the two followers who met Jesus on the road to Emmaus returned to Jerusalem and told the eleven about their encounter, the disciples declared "It is true!," whereas Mark insists that when the two reported their encounter, the disciples did not believe! -Mark 16:13*	A) Only Mary Magdalene B) At the tomb (20:1, 11-14)
Is Mary permitted to touch Jesus after the resurrection?	YES--"...they came and held him by his feet, and worshiped him." (28:9)	*Not mentioned in Mark*	YES--"Behold my hands and my feet...handle me and see..." (24:39; 1 John 1:1)	NO--Jesus said to her, "Touch me not; for I am not yet ascended to my Father..." (20:17)
How many times does Jesus appear after the resurrection?	Two Times 1st) 28:9-10 2nd) 28:17-20 *Paul - 1 Corinthians* Six Times 1st and 2nd) 1 Cor. 15:5 3rd) 1 Cor. 15:6 4th and 5th) 1 Cor. 15:7 6th) 1 Cor. 15:8	Three Times 1st) 16:9 2nd) 16:12** (See** above, right) 3rd) 16:14-18	Two Times 1st) 24:13-31 2nd) 24:36-51 ****Contradicting Luke's post-resurrection story entirely, John has the apostles receive the Holy Spirit on the first Easter Sunday (John 20:22), whereas Luke insists that the Holy Spirit was bestowed on the Pentecost, fifty days latter! -Acts 1:5, 8; 2:1-4*	Four Times 1st) 20:14-17 3rd) 20:26-29 2nd) 20:19-23*** 4th) 21:1-23
Before whom, and in what chronological order, do these appearances take place?	1st) Mary Magdalene and the other Mary. (28:9) 2nd) 11 disciples**** (28:16) *Paul* *1 Corinthians* 1st) Cephas (Peter) 15:5 2nd) All 12 apostles**** 15:5 3rd) 500 people 15:6 4th) James 15:7 5th) All 12 apostles 15:7 6th) Paul 15:8	1st) Mary Magdalene (16:9) 2nd) Two strolling followers** (16:12) (See** above, right) 3rd) 11 disciples**** (16:14)	1st) Cloepas and another unknown follower. (24:13) 2nd) Eleven disciples**** "...and them that were with them." (24:33) *****According to Matthew, Mark and Luke, Jesus made this appearance to all the eleven surviving disciples. Paul has this event take place in the presence of all twelve apostles (1 Corinthians 15:5), although Judas had long since died (Matthew 27:5; Acts 1:18). Contrary to all this, John's story places only ten disciples at the scene, Thomas being absent! -John 20:24*	1st) Mary Magdalene (20:14) 2nd) Ten disciples**** (Thomas was not there) (20:24) 3rd) Eleven disciples (20:26) 4th) Peter, Thomas, the two sons of Zebedee (James and John), Nathanael and two other disciples. (21:2)
Where do these appearances take place?	1st) Leaving the tomb, going to the disciples. (28:8) 2nd) On a mountain in the Galilee. (28:16) *(But some doubted it! -28:17)*	1st) After fleeing the tomb (16:8-9) 2nd) As they walked to the country (16:12) 3rd) At a meal (16:14)	1st) Emmaus (24:13) 2nd) Jerusalem (24:33, 49), NOT in the Galilee, as Matthew would have us believe (Mt. 28:6-7, 16).	1st) At the tomb (20:14) 2nd & 3rd) In Jerusalem, behind closed doors. (20:18-29) 4th) The Sea of Tiberias (21:1)

       'For error is manifold, truth but one'

	Matthew	Mark	Luke	John
Who carried the cross?	Simon of Cyrene (27:32)	Simon of Cyrene (15:21)	Simon of Cyrene (23:26)	Only Jesus himself carried the cross (19:17)
A) At what time was Jesus crucified? *B) On which day was Jesus crucified?*	A) Not mentioned in Matthew B) The first day of Passover, 15th day of Nissan.* (26:20-30) (See* below, left)	A) 9:00 am - "It was the THIRD hour when they crucified him." (15:25) B) The first day of Passover, 15th day of Nissan.* (14:17-25) (See* below, left)	A) Not mentioned in Luke B) The first day of Passover, 15th day of Nissan.* (22:14-23) (See* below, left)	A) 12:00 pm noon - Jesus was not crucified until after the SIXTH hour! (19:14-15) B) The day before Passover, 14th day of Nissan.* (13:1, 29, 18:28, 19:14) (See* below, left)
A) Did Jesus drink? *B) What was in the drink?*	A) YES B) Wine mixed with gall. (27:34)	A) NO B) Jesus was offered wine mixed with myrrh (15:23)	A) Not mentioned in Luke B) Vinegar (sour wine) (23:36)	A) YES B) Vinegar (sour wine) (19:29-30)
Did either one of the two thieves believe in Jesus?	Neither one of the thieves believed in Jesus. (27:44)	Neither one of the thieves believed in Jesus. (15:32)	In Luke's story, only one thief does not believe, but ONE DOES! (23:39-41)	Not mentioned in John
What were Jesus' last dying words on the cross?	"Eli, Eli, lama sabachthani?" That is, "My God, my God, why hast thou forsaken me?" (27:46)	"Eloi, Eloi, lama sabachth-ani?" Meaning, "My God, my God, why hast thou forsaken me?" (15:34)	"Father, into thy hands I commend my spirit." (23:46)	"It is finished" (19:30)
When did Mary pre-pare the spices?	Not mentioned in Matthew	Mary prepared the spices after the Sabbath was over. (16:1)	Mary prepared the spices before the Sabbath started. (23:56)	Nicodemus, not Mary, pre-pared the spices before the Sabbath. (19:39)
Had the sun yet risen when the women came to the tomb?	It was toward dawn of the first day of the week. (28:1)	YES--They came to the tomb when the sun had risen. (16:2)	At early dawn they went to the tomb (24:1)	NO--Mary came early to the tomb, while it was STILL DARK. (20:1)
How many days, and how many nights, was Jesus in the tomb?	3 days and 2 nights** (28:1)	3 days & 2 nights** (16:2)	3 days and 2 nights** (24:1)	2 days and 2 nights** (20:1)
	**Although Jesus had prophesied that he would be in the tomb for three days and three nights! -Matthew 12:40			
A) How many people came to the tomb? *B) Who were they?*	A) TWO B) Mary Magdalene and the other Mary (28:1)	A) THREE B) Mary Magdalene, Mary the mother of James and Salome (16:1)	A) FOUR+ B) Mary Magdalene, Mary mother of James, Joanna and other women (24:10)	A) ONE B) Only Mary Magdalene came to the tomb. (20:1)
Was the stone removed when the women ar-rived at the tomb?	NO--After the women arrive at the tomb, an angel rolls back the stone. (28:1-2)	YES--When they arrived, the stone had already been rolled away. (16:4)	YES--When they arrived, the stone had already been taken away. (24:2)	YES--When Mary arrived, the stone had already been taken away. (20:1)
A) How many angels were at the tomb? *B) What were they (was he) doing?* *C) Where were they (was he)?*	A) One angel B) Sitting (28:2) C) On the stone, which he rolled away from the tomb	A) One young man B) Sitting (16:5) C) On the right side, in-side the tomb	A) Two men B) Standing (24:4) C) By them, inside the tomb	The angeles are completely absent when Mary comes to the tomb. When Mary arrives a second time, she finds two angels sitting; one at the head and one at the feet. (20:1-2,12)
*What are the angels' instructions to Mary and the others*** at the tomb?* ****No others in John*	"He is not here; for he has risen...go quickly and tell his disciples he is going before you to the Galilee!"**** (28:6-7)	"Do not be amazed...he has risen...But go tell his disciples and Peter he is going before you to Gali-lee!"**** (16:6-7)	In Luke's story (24:5-7), the women are specifically not instructed to go to the Gali-lee, but to "Stay in Jerusa-lem!"**** (24:49) See also - "He commanded them that they should not leave Jerusa-lem!" (Acts 1:4) Luke's post-resurrection tale does not permit any of his followers to leave Jerusalem because Luke must have the apostles stay in Jerusalem for the Pentecost (Acts 2:1).	The angels only ask "Why are you weeping woman?" As Mary responds, she turns around and sees Jesus standing there. Completely contradicting all three synoptics, John's story (20:2) has Mary clueless as to what happened to Jesus' body when she returns to the tomb. There are no angels giving instructions to the women in Jo-hn's story. On the contrary, in the fourth Gospel, it is Jesus, not the two angels, who instructs Mary about the resurrection! (20:13-17)

*Because all three synop-tics insist that the Last Supper was a Passover Seder, they must there-fore hold that the cruci-fixion occurred on the first day of Passover, rather than the eve of Passover, as John would have us believe (19:14).

****Luke contradicts Matthew (28:16) and Mark (16:7), whose post-resurrection tale has the apostles depart Jerusalem, and go to the Galilee, which is about an 80-90 mile journey, whereas Luke insists that the apostles were never told to, and never did, leave Jerusalem and go to the Galilee! -Luke 24:5-7, 49; Acts 1:4

Angels and the Tomb

So-called eyewitness accounts of the four Gospels are inconsistent at best. Further adding to the questionability of originality or fact of the Jesus story is the sameness of other mythical saviors predating Jesus — including Krishna and Horus.

No Stone Unturned

Dan Barker

I have an Easter challenge for Christians.

My challenge is simply this: tell me what happened on Easter.

I am not asking for proof. My straightforward request is merely that Christians tell me exactly *what* happened on the day that their most important doctrine was born.

Believers should eagerly take up this challenge, since without the resurrection, there is no Christianity. Paul wrote, "And if Christ be not risen, then is our preaching vain, and your faith is also vain. Yea, and we are found false witnesses of God; because we have testified of God that he raised up Christ: whom he raised not up, if so be that the dead rise not." (I Cor. 15:14-15)

The conditions of the challenge are simple and reasonable. In each of the four gospels, begin at Easter morning and read to the end of the book: Matt. 28, Mark 16, Luke 24, and John 20-21. Also read Acts 1:3-12 and Paul's tiny version of the story in I Corinthians 15:3-8.

These 165 verses can be read in a few moments. Then, without omitting a single detail from these separate accounts, write a simple, chronological narrative of the events between the resurrection and the ascension: what happened first, second, and so on; who said what, when; and where these things happened.

Since the gospels do not always give precise times of day, it is permissible to make educated guesses. The narrative does not have to pretend to present a perfect picture – it only needs to give at least one plausible account of all of the facts. Additional explanation of the narrative may be set apart in parentheses. *The important condition to the challenge, however, is that not one single biblical detail be omitted.* Fair enough?

I should admit that I have tried this challenge myself. I failed. An Assembly of God minister whom I was debating a couple of years ago on a Florida radio show loudly proclaimed over the air that he would send me the narrative in a few days. I am still waiting. After my debate at the University of Wisconsin, "Jesus of Nazareth: Messiah or Myth," a Lutheran graduate student told me he accepted the challenge and would be contacting me in about a week. I have never heard from him. Both of these people, and others, agreed that the request was reasonable and crucial. Maybe they are slow readers.

Many bible stories are given only once or twice, and are therefore hard to confirm. The author of Matthew, for example, was the only one to mention that at the crucifixion dead people emerged from the graves of Jerusalem, walking around showing themselves to everyone — an amazing event that could hardly escape the notice of the other gospel writers, or any other historians of the period. But though the silence of others might weaken the likelihood of a story, it does not disprove it. Disconfirmation arises with contradictions.

Thomas Paine tackled this matter 200 years ago in *The Age of Reason*, stumbling across dozens of New Testament discrepancies:

> I lay it down as a position which cannot be controverted, first, that the *agreement* of all the parts of a story does not prove that story to be true, because the parts may agree and the whole may be false; secondly, that the *disagreement* of the parts of a story proves *the whole cannot be true.*

Since Easter is told by five different writers, it gives us one of the best chances to confirm or disconfirm the account. Christians should welcome the opportunity.

One of the first problems I found is in Matt. 28:2, after two women arrived at the tomb: "And, behold, there was a great earthquake: for the angel of the Lord descended from heaven, and came and rolled back the stone from the door, and sat upon it." (Let's ignore the fact that no other writer mentioned this "great earthquake.") This story says that the stone was rolled away after the women arrived.

Yet Mark's gospel says it happened *before* the (three) women arrived: "And they said among themselves, Who shall roll away the stone from the door of the sepulchre? And when they looked, they saw that the stone was rolled away: for it was very great."

Luke writes: "And they found the stone rolled away from the sepulchre." John agrees. No earthquake, no rolling stone. It is a three-to-one vote: Matthew loses. (Or else the other three are wrong.) The event cannot have happened both before and after they arrived.

Some bible defenders assert that Matthew 28:2 was intended to be understood in the past perfect, showing what had happened before the women arrived. But the entire passage is in the aorist (past) tense, and it reads, in context, like a simple chronological account. Matt. 28:2 begins, "And behold," not "For, behold." If this verse can be so easily shuffled around, then what is to keep us from putting the flood before the ark, or the crucifixion before the nativity?

Another glaring problem is the fact that in Matthew the first post-resurrection appearance of Jesus to the disciples happened on a mountain in Galilee, as predicted by the angel sitting on the rock; "And go quickly, and tell his disciples that he is risen from the dead; and behold, he goeth before you into Galilee; there shall ye see him." (This must have been of supreme importance, since this was *the* message of God via the angel(s) at the tomb. Jesus had even predicted this himself during the Last Supper, Matt. 26:32.) Matt. 28:16-17 says, "Then the eleven disciples went away into Galilee, into a mountain where Jesus had appointed them. And when they saw him, they worshipped him: but some doubted."

Reading this at face value, and in context, it is clear that Matthew intends this to be the *first* appearance. Otherwise, if Jesus had been seen before this time, why did some doubt? Mark agrees with Matthew's account of the angel's Galilee message, but gives a different story about the first appearance.

Luke and John give different angel messages and then radically contradict Matthew. Luke shows the first appearance on the road to Emmaus and then in a room in Jerusalem. John says it happened later that evening in a room, minus Thomas. These angel messages, locations, and travels during the day are difficult to reconcile.

Believers sometimes use the analogy of the five blind men examining an elephant, all coming away with a different definition: tree trunk (leg), rope (tail), hose (trunk), wall (side), and fabric (ear). People who use this argument forget that each of the blind men was *wrong*. An elephant is not a rope or a tree. And you can put the five parts together to arrive at a noncontradictory aggregate of the entire animal. This hasn't been done with the resurrection.

Another analogy sometimes used by apologists is comparing the resurrection contradictions to differing accounts given by witnesses of an auto accident. If one witness said the vehicle was green and the other said it was blue, that could be accounted for by different angles, lighting, perception, or definitions of words.

I am not a fundamentalist inerrantist: I'm not demanding that the evangelists must have been expert, infallible witnesses. (None of them claimed to have been at the tomb itself, anyway.) But what if one witness said the auto accident happened in Chicago and the other said it happened in Milwaukee? At least one of these witnesses has serious problems with the truth. Luke says the post-resurrection appearance happened in Jerusalem, but Matthew says it happened in Galilee, *60 to 100 miles away!* Something is very wrong here.

This is just the tip of the iceberg. Of course, none of these contradictions prove that the resurrection did *not* happen, but they do throw considerable doubt on the reliability of the supposed witnesses. Some of them were wrong. Maybe they were all wrong.

Protestants and Catholics seem to have no trouble applying healthy skepticism to the miracles of Islam, or to the "historical" visit between Joseph Smith and the angel Moroni. Why should Christians treat their own outrageous claims any differently? Why should someone who was not there be any more eager to believe than doubting Thomas, who lived during that time, or the other disciples who said that the women's news "seemed to them as idle tales, and they believed them not" (Luke 24:11)?

Thomas Paine points out that everything in the bible is *hearsay.* For example, the message at the tomb (if it happened at all) took this path, at minimum, before it got to our eyes: God, angel(s), Mary, disciples, gospel writers, copyists, translators. (The gospels are all anonymous and we have no original versions.)

But first things first: Christians, either tell me exactly what happened on Easter Sunday, or let's leave the Jesus myth buried next to Eastre (Ishtar, Astarte), the pagan Goddess of Spring after whom your holiday was named.

This article was copied and distributed around the country in many different forms. A lot of readers sent it to their area ministers and priests. Only two attempts at accepting the challenge were made and neither one of them kept to the terms, preferring to pick and choose particular contradictions to explain. Dan Barker is the public relations director for the Freedom From Religion Foundation, Madison, Wisconsin.

Rejoice! He is risen!

Our Risen Savior
The Light of the World

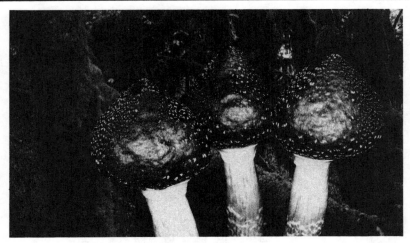

Mushroom

The early "Psilocybe Cubensis" mushroom was referred to in the Bible (see Exodus 16; 14, 15) manna literally meant "what is this?" Later it was interepted as "food from God." The High Priest and his soon to be "high" followers would gather to celebrate the rising of the sun each morning.

Jewish High-Priest

Full sacerdotal robes and mushroom cap. – Garb, (Robes + Cap), cremonies (greeeting of rising sun), sacraments + rituals (gathering of God's manna) are all practiced today. The worship of the Sun dates back to Shemitic/Hebrew cults. Out of ignorance the current religious will not recognize any paralels to the early cults.

The High Priest

John Allegro

No one religion in the ancient Near East can be studied in isolation. All stem from man's first questioning about the origin of life and how to ensure his own survival. Out of this sense of dependency and frustration, religion was born.

Our present concern is to show that Judaism and Christianity are such cultic expressions of this endless pursuit by man to discover instant power and knowledge. Granted the first proposition that the vital forces of nature are controlled by an extra-terrestrial intelligence, these religions are logical developments from the older, cruder fertility cults. With the advance of technical proficiency the aims of religious ritual became less to influence the weather and the crops than to attain wisdom and the knowledge of the future. The Word that seeped through the labia of the earth's womb became to the mystic of less importance than the Logos which he believed his religion enabled him to apprehend and enthuse him with divine omniscience. But the source was the same vital power of the universe and the cultic practice differed little.

To raise the crops the farmer copulated with his wife in the fields. To seek the drug that would send his soul winging to the seventh heaven and back, the initiates into the religious mysteries had their priestesses seduce the god and draw him into their grasp as a woman fascinates her partner's penis to erection.

For the way to god and the fleeting view of heaven was through plants more plentifully endured with the sperm of God than any other. These were the drug-herbs, the science of whose cultivation and use had been accumulated over centuries of observation and dangerous experiment. Those who had this secret wisdom of the plants were the chosen of their god; to them alone had he vouchsafed the privilege of access to the heavenly throne. And if he was jealous of his power, no less were those who served him in the cultic mysteries. Theirs was no gospel to be shouted from the rooftops: ;Paradise was for none but the favored few. The incantations and rites by which they conjured forth their drug plants, and the details of the bodily and mental preparations undergone before they could ingest their god, were the secrets of the cult to which none but the initiate bound by fearful oaths, had access.

Very rarely, and then only for urgent practical purposes, were those secrets ever committed to writing. Normally they would be passed from the priest to the initiate by word of mouth; dependent for their accurate transmission on the trained memories of men dedicated to the learning and recitation of their "scriptures." But if, for some drastic reason like the disruption of their cultic centres by war or persecution, it became necessary to write down the precious names of the herbs and the manner of their use and accompanying incantations, it would be in some esoteric form comprehensibly only to those within their dispersed communities.

Such an occasion, we believe, was the Jewish Revolt of AD 66. Instigated probably by members of the cult, swayed by their drug-induced madness to believe God had called them to master the world in his name, they provoked the mighty power of Rome to swift and terrible action. Jerusalem was ravaged, her temple destroyed. Judaism was disrupted,m and her people driven to seek refuge with communities already established around the Mediterranean coastlands. They mystery cults found themselves without their central fount of authority, with many of their priests killed in the abortive rebellion or driven into the desert. The secrets, if they were not to be lost for ever, had to be committed to Writing, and yet, if found, the documents must give nothing away or betray those who still dared defy the Roman authorities and continue their religious practices.

The means of conveying the information were at hand, and had been for thousands of years. The folk-tales of the ancients had from the earliest times contained myths based upon the personification of plants and trees. They were invested with human faculties and qualities and their names and physical characteristics were applied to the heroes and heroines of the stories. Some of these were just tales spun for entertainment, others were political parables like Jotham's fable about the trees in the Old Testament, while others were means of remembering and transmitting therapeutic folk-lore. The names of the plants were spun out to make the basis of the stories, whereby the creatures of fantasy were identified, dressed, and made to enact their parts. Here, then, was the literary device to spread occult knowledge to the faithful.

To tell the story of a rabbi called Jesus, and invest him with the power and names of the magic drug. To have him live before the terrible events that had disrupted their lives, to preach a love between men, extending even to the hated Romans. Thus, reading such a tale, should it fall into Roman hands, even their mortal enemies might be deceived and not probe farther into the activities of the cells of the mystery cults within their territories.

The ruse failed. Christians, hated and despised, were hauled forth and slain in their thousands. The cult well night perished. What eventually took its place was a travesty of the real thing, a mockery of the power that could raise men to heaven and give them the glimpse of God for which they gladly died. The story of the rabbi crucified at the instigation of the Jews became an historical peg upon which the new cult's authority was founded. What began as a hoax, became a trap even to those who believed themselves to the spiritual heirs of the mystery religion and took to themselves the name of "Christian." Above all, they forgot, or purged from the cult and their memories, the one supreme secret on which their whole religious and ecstatic experience depended: the names and identity of the source of the drug, the key to heaven – the sacred mushroom.

The fungus recognized today as the *Amanita muscaria*, or Fly-Agaric, had been known from the beginning of history. Beneath the skin of its characteristic red-and-white-spotted cap, there is concealed a powerful hallucinatory poison. Its religious use among certain Siberian peoples and others has been the subject of study in recent years, and its exhilarating and depressive effects have been clinically examined. Theses include the stimulation of the perceptive faculties so that the subject sees objects much greater or much smaller than they really are, colors and sounds are much enhanced, and there is a general sense of power, both physical and mental quite outside the normal range of human experience.

The mushroom has always been a thing of mystery. The ancients were puzzled by its manner of growth without seed, the speed with which it made its appearance after rain, and its as rapid disappearance. Born from a volva or "egg" it appears like a small penis, raising itself like the human organ sexually aroused, and when it spread wide its canopy the old botanists saw it as a phallus bearing the "burden" of a woman's groin. Every aspect of the mushroom's existence was fraught with sexual allusions, and in its phallic form the ancients saw a replica of the fertility god himself. It was the "son of God," its drug was a purer form of the god's own spermatozoa than that discoverable in any other form of living matter. It was, in fact, God himself, manifest on earth. To the mystic it was the divinely given means of entering heaven; God had come down in the flesh to show the way to himself, by himself.

To pluck such a precious herb was attended at every point with peril. The time – before sunrise, the words to be uttered – the name of the guardian angel, were vital to the operation, but more was needed. Some form of substitution was necessary, to make an atonement to the earth robbed of her offspring. Yet such was the divine nature of the Holy Plant, as it was called, only the god could make the necessary sacrifice. To redeem the Son, the Father had to supply even the "price of redemption." These are all phrases used of the sacred mushroom, as they are of the Jesus of Christian theology.

Our present study has much to do with names and titles. Only when we can discover the nomenclature of the sacred fungus within and without the cult, can we begin to understand its function and theology. The main factor that has made these new discoveries possible has been the realization that many of the most secret names of the mushroom go back to ancient Sumerian, the oldest written language known to us, witnessed by cuneiform text dating form the fourth millennium BC. Furthermore, it now appears that this ancient tongue provides a bridge between the Indo-European languages (which include Greek, Latin, and our own tongue) and the Semitic group, which includes the languages of the Old Testament, Hebrew and Aramaic. For the first time, it becomes possible to decipher the names of gods, mythological characters, classical and biblical, and plant names. Thus their place in the cultic systems and their functions in the old fertility religions can be determined.

The great barriers that have hitherto seemed to divide the ancient world, classical and biblical, have at last been crossed and at a more significant level than has previously been possible by merely comparing their respective mythologies. Stories and characters which seem quite different in the way they are presented in various locations and at widely separated points in history can now be shown often to have the same central theme. Even gods as different as Zeus and Yahweh embody the same fundamental conception of the fertility deity, for their names in origin are precisely the same. A common tongue overrides physical and racial boundaries. Even languages so apparently different as Greek and Hebrew, when they

can be shown to derive from a common fount, point to a communal-
ity of culture at some early stage. Comparisons can therefore be
made on a scientific, philological level which might have appeared
unthinkable before now.1 Suddenly, almost overnight, the ancient
world has shrunk. All roads in the Near East lead back to the
Mesopotamian basin, to ancient Sumer. Similarly, the most important of the religions and mythologies of that area, and probably far
beyond, are reaching back to the mushroom cult of Sumer and her
successors.

*John Allegro worked originally on the Dead Sea Scrolls and is a renown
and well respected author. This excerpt comes from the S*acred Mushrooms
and the Cross.

And when the dew that lay was gone up, behold, hpon the
face of the wilderness *there lay* a small round thing, as
small as the hoar frost on the ground

And when the children of Israel saw *it*, they said one to
anotherm, It *is* manna: for they wist not what it was. And
Moses said unto them, This *is* the bread which the Lord
hath given you to eat.

— Exodus 16; 14 & 15

Baptism

In 418 AD, a Catholic church council decided that every human child is born demonic as a result of its sexual conception, thus automatically damned unless baptized.

During a Catholic baptismal ceremony, the priest still addresses the baby,

> I exorcise thee, thou unclean spirit . . . Hear thy doom, O Devil accursed, Satan accursed.

This exorcism is euphemistically described as "a means to remove impediments to grace resulting from the effects of original sin and the power of Satan over nature . . ."

Thus, paganism was kinder to infants and their mothers than Christianity, so that theologians often felt called upon to explain God's apparent cruelty in allowing infants to die unbaptized, so condemning them before they had a chance for salvation.

In the 16th and 17th centuries, churchmen insisted that God's cruelty was perfectly just. Said Martin Del Rio, S.J.,

> If, as is not uncommon, God permits children to be killed before they have been baptized, it is to prevent their committing in later life those sins which would make their damnation more severe. In this, God is neither cruel nor unjust, since, by the mere fact of original sin, the children have already merited death . . .

> *— Women's Encyclopedia of Myth,*
> Barbara G. Walker, Editor

Consequences

The Constantine Cross

In this sign you will conquer.

Blood On The Ground, Churches All Around

Frank Mortyn

It's 1992. Rioters are taking control of the streets of Los Angeles. The street gangs are the Blues and the Reds, known as Crips and Bloods. The gangs unite their efforts to defy the armed forces of Police Chief Daryl Gates.

And where is Chief Gates? He is sipping cocktails at a fund-raising party while Los Angeles begins to burn.

Now let us suppose, with about 50 dead in Los Angeles, that a national political leader feels called upon to comment. Hear Dan Quayle, Vice-President of the United States, addressing the Commonwealth Club, San Francisco, May 19 1992:

"So I think the time has come to renew our public commitment to our Judeo-Christian values . . . "

A journalist has a similar urge. William A. Rusher says in his comments on the Los Angeles riots in the *Las Vegas Review-Journal*, May 5 1992:

> Simply put, the secular humanists have been gnawing away at the foundations of Western Civilization . . . and have finally succeeded in producing, especially in our inner cities, an almost totally amoral kind of human being . . .

Well, now! What if secular humanism were swept away and Christianity put in charge? What would happen? What would be different? History can tell us. That's what history is for. Let's go back to the year 532 C.E. (Common Era).

Twelve Thousand Bodies

They lie scattered across the benches. Sprawled on the stone floors of the stadium.

The sun beats down on the silence. The bodies have not yet rotted much. There is still no noticeable stench. But rats have already discovered the carnage.

Close to the exits, panic-stricken thousands had clawed at one another. They were trying to escape the advancing soldiers of the Imperial Guard. Few succeeded. Many people were crushed, their bodies mangled underfoot. The hum and buzz of flies was the only sound now over this spectacle of death.

From all around, the air is suddenly alive with the joyous sound of bells. Hundreds of bells, from hundreds of churches. No sound of any call to Allah or indication of any other religion besides Christianity. This is *Christian City*. In the broad boulevards and narrow alleys around the Hippodrome, thousands and thousands of corpses lie on the paving stones. They lie where they fell. They had fallen, screaming in terror, pursued by the Guards.

Who were these dead? They were the youth of Christian City. They had formed rival gangs. The Blues and the Greens. The two rival gangs had united to riot together in their contempt for the Emperor. The Emperor Justinian was overcome with fear. Get ready to flee, said the Emperor.

But Justinian was saved! His wife, the Empress Theodora, was stronger than he. She gave courage to the Emperor and his followers. They decided to stay and fight. This was the woman who had been on the stage, no princess but merely a showgirl. The people of Constantinople called her "whore."

The Emperor's swordsmen were highly trained. They were proud professionals, carrying on the traditions of the Roman Empire. They were unflinchingly loyal to Emperor Justinian and his wife Theodora. They killed rioters without mercy. The Guards did not take prisoners. They pursued the youth of Christian City and killed them. In five days of disorder, thirty thousand died. Their corpses tell us of life in Christian City, called Constantinople.

This was Christianity's showplace. Separation of Church and State? Not here. This was Christianity's chance. A chance to show history what Christianity can do when it achieves power over civil life. How did Christian City get started?

A Roman Emperor, Constantine the Great, claimed he had seen a cross in the sky. He went on to win in battle. For his own political ends, Constantine blessed Christianity. Henceforth, he said, Christianity would be an appropriate religion for the Empire. Christianity gained momentum which, to our day, it has never lost.

Emperor Constantine became a master planner of the Christian faith. Even in our own time you find him honored in sects of the Episcopal tradition. The Nicene Creed is recited; it was compiled in Constantine's reign. The mystical doctrine of the Trinity – Father, Son and Holy Ghost, three gods in one – is a product of the Ecumenical Council convened by Constantine. And he gave us Constantinople. From the beginning, it was Christian City. The showplace of the Faith. Church and State not separated but united. Christianity was triumphant.

Constantinople was far more Christian than Rome. Rome was just a Christian excrescence layered upon the foundations of hundreds of years of paganism. No – Constantinople was utterly Christian, in conception as well as design. It smothered the remains of smaller towns which had preceded it – such as Byzantium. And who remembers the Greek settlement of Thrace? The great new metropolis of Constantinople had conquered its forebears. Constantinople was the jewel in the crown of our Lord Jesus Christ. Constantinople was Christianity in full flower. It deserves the title: Christian City.

See the blood, running across the paving stones. Hear the wailings, the mourning of countless bereaved citizens. Make yourself at home, visitor. You are in Christian City.

See the Hippodrome now. Only a few Guards remain. The flies are buzzing more loudly now, clouds of them hovering over every mound of corpses. Let us stroll the streets of Christian City. Hear the mourners wailing in just about every house. See those people! Some weep, mourning their dead. Searchers pick their way among the dead, seeking their kin. The pavements are still wet with blood.

But – wait! Lift up your eyes to the horizon. See the churches! Oh, just look at that marvelous church! What a masterpiece! The whole world will wonder. The Emperor Justinian, he who presided over the massacre of thirty thousand in five days of urban disorders, will be remembered in 1992 as the builder of Hagia Sophia. Still standing, after 1400 years? Yes. For Justinian built it to last. He succeeded. And visitors from all the world still come to to see it.

The glories of Constantinople's architecture are stunning. Historians will write appreciatively of the "Byzantine" style. It has the flavor of the East, in the service of Christian faith. The result is dazzling. Decorated with marvelous mosaics, each church models the cosmos with its portrayals of celestial beings.

Just look at Christian City's mighty walls! There are two walls, one inside the other. And atop the walls are ninety-six towers! How can an enemy ever take such a city? In Rome — the barbarians will rule. But Constantinople? Never! So they thought. For Constantinople shows the world what a society is like when Christianity governs every aspect of its operation. A thoroughly Christianized civilization! A Christian Reconstructionist dream.

The thirty thousand corpses are beginning to stink.

Did It Work?

Let it be clear to us all! The worst, the bloodiest urban riots of all time took place in the most Christian of cities, Constantinople in the year 532 CE.

Meanwhile, where were the humanists? Not much in evidence, unfortunately. The Dark Ages were upon Europe.

But across the sea in Athens, we can suppose that there were still a few philosophers, clad in white, walking quietly amid the trees. If their pavements were slippery, it was because of fruit from olive branches, not blood from tormented bodies, shed by Christian swords.

Today's freethinkers can look with sorrow on the spectacle of death which occurred when Christianity took charge of civil life. The more you know about it, the more likely you are to say to the Christians: "Thank you but NO to your vision of a Christian society." It had its chance. Did Christian City work? Thirty thousand deaths say "No."

Frank Mortyn, editor of Contact, *published by the Humanist Fellowship of San Diego, is a physicist who enjoys writing and lecturing on freethought topics. Reprinted from Truth Seeker, Vol. 119, No. 3.*

During World War II, while I was serving with the Third Army in Germany, I removed a belt buckle from the uniform of a dead German soldier. The lettering on the buckle read: *Gott Mit Uns* (God Is With Us).

— From *Slaughterhouse Five*, Kurt Vonnegut

Onward Christian Soldiers, marching as to war, with the Cross of Jesus, going on before . . .

— Sabine Baring-Gould

There was a time when religion ruled the world. It is known as The Dark Ages.

— Ruth Hurmence Green, author,
The Born Again Skeptic's Guide to the Bible

WAR

It was Pope Urban II who inaugurated the crusades at the Council of Clermont in 1095, and by this act formally instituted wars organized and administered by religion.

Almost all Europe, for many centuries, was inundated with blood, which was shed at the direct instigation or with the full approval of the ecclesiastical authorities.
— *History of the Rise and Influence of the Spirit of Rationalism in Europe* (Appleton, 1866) Volume II, p. 32

Both (the northern and southern Christians) read the same Bible and pray to the same God, and each invokes his aid against the other.
— Abraham Lincoln

God is on our side, and Satan is on the side of the United States.
— Saddam Hussein

God has revealed to me that those doing battle for Allah and our country and meet death will immediately go to Heaven. . . .
— The Ayatollah Khomeini, Spring 1984

As one chaplain explained his concern, "it may not be the church's function and duty to teach and to encourage men to kill; but it is the church's function and duty to undergird a man with such a faith and with such an understanding of the issues involved that he will be able to accomplish what is expected of him by his God and by his country."

As a means of guarding against the likelihood of pacifist chaplains, known pacifist ministers were rejected unless they agreed to sign a statement testifying that they no longer held the pacifist view.

The state sets the context for patriotic obedience, and in the case of military obedience, the chaplaincy gives religious sanction to it.

The peace testimony arises from the same understanding of the nature of God and of human beings. How can one kill another child of God, a potential channel of Truth, no matter how misguided he or she may seem at the moment?
— Gordon Brown, *Introducing Quakers*

— Jeff MacNelly, reprint by permission:
Tribune Media Services

We are all prisoners of war . . .

. . . while war has been used by religious leaders and followers alike as a way of justifying their own greed, power and stupidity – stupidity of God and humanity.

— U.S. Senator Wayne Morse

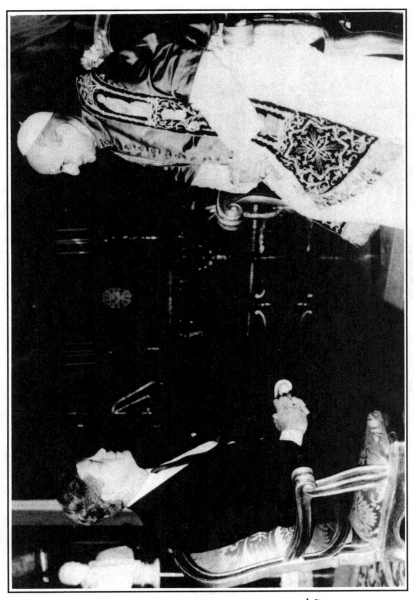

Pope Paul VI pressured President John F. Kennedy in 1963 to recognize the Vatican. Kennedy, an avowed Catholic and State/Church Separationist, resisted. In 1984, President Ronald Reagan recognized the Vatican and appointed William Wilson as ambassador.
— *Associated Press Photo*

Europe Decays And
The Popes Thrive

Joseph McCabe

During the fourth century, along with the lowering of character in the Roman Church there was a singular transformation of its originally simple offices. The Pagans were accustomed to highly-colored and picturesque ceremonies, and the new Church indulgently met their wishes. Hymns, altars, and statues; incense, holy water, and burning candles; silk vestments and bits of ritual – these things were borrowed freely from the suppressed temples.

There must have been a remarkable resemblance between the services in the suppressed temple of Mithra on the Vatican Hill and the services in the new temple dedicated to St. Peter on, or near, the same spot. Other religions contributed their share. The Pagans had been accustomed to variety, and so the worship of the saints and the Virgin Mother, which was unknown in the Church for three centuries, was encouraged.

Then relics had to be invented for the saints, just as saints were sometimes invented for relics. We hear every few years of bishops being directed "in a vision" to discover the body of some martyr or saint. Palestine also began to do a magnificent trade in relics with Italy; beginning with the "discovery of the true cross," at which no historian even glances to-day.

The events I have described bring us to the close of the fourth century, when Pope Innocent I, a strong man, undertook to enforce the Papal claim in the West. In the Eastern Church there was still nothing but contempt for that claim. In the year 381, the Greek bishops met at Constantinople, and in the third canon of the Council they expressly laid it down that the Bishop of "new Rome" (Constantinople) was equal in rank to the Bishop of "old Rome."

The great figure of the African Church – indeed, of the whole Church – at the time was St. Augustine. Catholic Truth is very concerned to show that this great leader recognized the Papal claim, and it repeatedly puts into his mouth the famous phrase: "Rome has spoken; the case is settled." The heretic Pelagius was then active, and the implication is that St. Augustine recognized the condemnation of this man by Rome as the authoritative settlement of the dispute.

Now, not only did neither Augustine nor any other bishop use those words, but they are an entirely false summary of what he did say. His words, in his 131st sermon, are: "Already the decisions of two (African) councils have been sent to the Apostolic See, and a rescript has reached us. The case is settled." The settlement lies plainly in the *joint* condemnation of Pelagius by Africa and Rome. Nor did the matter end here. Pope Zosimus at first pronounced in favor of Pelagius, and the African bishops forced him to recant. In order to justify his further interference, the Pope then quoted two canons of the Council of Nicæa which astonished the Africans.

After inquiry in the East, it was proven that *these canons were Roman forgeries,* and the African bishops, maliciously informing the Pope of their discovery, trusted that they would hear "no more of his pompousness." They did hear more of it, and a few years later they sent the Pope a letter (happily preserved) in which they scornfully reject his claim to interfere, and advise him not to "introduce the empty pride of the world into the Church of Christ, which offers the light of simplicity and lowliness to those who seek God." And Catholic Truth has the audacity to tell the faithful that these African bishops admitted the supremacy of the Pope!

Rome fell in the year 410, but the charm of the great city laid its thrall upon the barbarians, and the Roman See suffered comparatively little. The Spanish Church was next overrun, and the Vandals, crossing the Straits of Gibraltar, trod underfoot the African colony and, as they were Aryans, ruined its Church.

The provincial bishoprics no longer produced prelates of any strength or learning, and the weak new men, quarrelling incessantly amid the ruins of the Empire, began to appeal more frequently to Rome. Dense ignorance succeeded the culture of the great Empire. The Popes did not rise, but the other bishops fell. "In a land of blind men," says an old French proverb, "the one-eyed man is king."

That the Roman bishopric did not change for the better in that age of general corruption is shown by its official records. At the death of Zosimus, it became again the bloody prize of contending factions. Two Popes, Eulalius and Boniface, were elected, and on Easter morn, when each strove desperately for the prestige of conducting the great ceremony, a mighty struggle reddened once more the streets and squares of the city.

A few years later, however, Rome again obtained a strong and zealous Pope, Leo I, and the claim of supremacy advanced a few steps farther. The Church still resisted the Papal claim. When Leo attempted to overrule Bishop Hilary of Gaul, one of the few strong men remaining in the provinces, Hilary used "language which no layman even should dare to use."

In the East, Leo was not innocent of trickery. His Legates attempted to impose upon the Greeks the spurious canons which Pope Zosimus had attempted to use in Africa, and they were mercilessly exposed. In the fifteenth session of the Council of Chalcedon, the Greek bishops renewed the famous canon which declared the Bishop of Constantinople equal to the Bishop of Rome. In an ironical letter, they informed Leo of this, yet we find the Papal clerks sending to Gaul, in Leo's name, shortly afterwards, an alleged (and spurious) copy of the proceedings at Chalcedon, in which the Greek bishops are represented as calling Leo "head of the universal Church"! We shall see that there is hardly one of even the "great" Popes who did not resort to trickery of this kind.

The Greek Church has retained to this day its defiance of Rome. Western Christendom, on the other hand, has submitted to the Papacy, and we have next to see how this submission was secured. This is explained in part by the enfeeblement of the provincial bishoprics, but especially by the dense ignorance which now settled upon Europe. The products of the church's pious forgery industry included documents less innocent than the pretty stories about St. Agnes and St. Cecilia. Some of these – certain spurious or falsified canons of Greek council – we have already met. The forgers grew bolder as the shades of the medieval night fell upon Europe, and some romances of very practical value to the Papacy were fabricated.

The chief of these, *The Acts of St. Silvester,* is believed by many scholars to have been composed in the East, about the year 430. However that may be, it soon passed to Europe, and it became one of the main foundations of the Papal claim of temporal supremacy. After giving a gloriously fantastic account of the conversion and baptism of the Emperor Constantine, it makes that monarch, when he leaves Rome for the East (after murdering his wife and son), hand over to the Papacy the secular rule of all Europe to the west of Greece! It is a notorious and extravagant forgery, but it was generally accepted, and was used by the Popes.

A similar document, *The Constitution of St. Silvester,* is believed by modern historians to have been fabricated in Rome itself, in the year 498. Two Popes were elected once more, and on this occasion the customary deadly feud existed for three years. The document is supposed to have been invented, in the course of this struggle, by the supporters of the anti-Pope.

Rome and Italy were now so densely ignorant that forgers – of relics, legends, canons, pills, or anything else – enjoyed a golden age. The one force on the side of enlightenment was the heretical and anti-clerical King of Italy, Theodoric the Ostrogoth; and the Roman clergy intrigued so busily against his rule that he had to imprison Pope John I.

Rome split into Roman and Gothic factions, and terrible fights and bribery assisted "the light of the Holy Ghost" in deciding the Papal elections. Early in the sixth century there were six Popes in fifteen years, and there is grave suspicion that some were murdered.

At last Pope Silverius opened the gates of Rome to the troops of the Greek Emperor, but the change of sovereign only led the Papacy to a deeper depth of ignominy. The Greek Empress Theodora, the unscrupulous and very pious lady who had begun life in a brothel and ended it on the Byzantine throne, had a little heresy of her own; and a very courtly Roman deacon, named Vigilius, had promised to favor it if she made him Pope. "Trump up a charge against Silverius (the Pope), and send him here," she wrote to the Greek commander at Rome; and the Pope was promptly deposed for treason and replaced by Vigilius. But Pope Vigilius found it too dangerous to fulfill his bargain; and, amid the jeers and stones of the Romans, he was shipped to Constantinople to incur the fiendish vengeance of the pious Theodora. The Romans, who openly accused him of murder, heard with joy of his adventures and death, and they vented their wrath upon his friend and successor, Pope Pelagius.

Such had already become the Papacy which Catholic historians describe as distinguished for holiness and orthodoxy, under special protection of the Holy Spirit, from its foundation. But this is merely a mild foretaste of its medieval qualities. For a time Gregory the Great (590-604) raised its prestige once more; but even the pontificate of that deeply religious man has grave defects. His fulsome praise of the vicious and murderous Queen Brunichildis and of the brutal Eastern Emperor Phocas, and his wild rejoicing at the murder of the Emperor Maurice (who had called him "a fool") are revolting.

His ignorance and credulity were unlimited. His largest works, *The Magna Moralia* and *The Dialogues,* are incredible hotch-potches of stories about devils and miracles. He sternly rebuked bishops who tried to educate their people, and he did not perceive that the appalling vices and crimes which he deplores almost in every letter – the general drunkenness and simony and immorality of the priests, and the horrible prevalence of violence – were mainly due to ignorance. He was one of the makers of the Middle Ages.

After Gregory, the Papacy sinks slowly into the fetid morass of the Middle Ages. The picture of the morals of the Roman Church by Jerome in the fourth century, of the whole Western Church by the priest Salvianus in the fifth century, and by Bishop Gregory of Tours in the sixth century, are almost without parallel in literature.

It would, however, be dreary work to follow the fortunes of the Papacy, as well as we can trace them in the barbarous writings of the time, through that age of steady degeneration. Contested elections, bloody riots, bribes, brawls with the Eastern bishops punctuate the calendar. Twenty obscure Popes cross the darkening stage in the course of a hundred years. I resume the story at the point where the Popes begin to win temporal power.

In the eighth century, the Greek emperors were again in the toils of heresy, and the ruling people in the north of Italy, the Lombards, were still Aryans. The Popes began to look beyond the Alps for an orthodox protector, and their gaze was attracted to the Franks. Rome found it convenient to regard the Franks as an enlightened and pious race, though we know from the reports of St. Boniface to the Popes that the Frank clergy and princes were among the worst in Europe.

Clerics, we read, had four or five concubines in their beds. Drunkenness, brawling, simony, and corruption tainted nearly the whole of the clergy and the monks. These things were overlooked; nor did the Lateran (at that time the palace of the Popes) rebuke Charles Martel for his own corruption in despoiling the Church.

Charles Martel paid no attention to the flattering offer of the Popes, but his son Pippin found occasion to use it. He was "Mayor of the Palace," and he desired to oust the king and occupy his throne. He sent envoys to Pope Zachary to ask if he might conscientiously do so. Not only *might* he, Zachary replied, but he *must;* and from that time onward, Rome was able to claim that Pippin and his famous son, Charlemagne, owed their throne to the Papacy.

It was not long before Pope Stephen II, being hard pressed by the Lombards, appealed to the gratitude of the ignorant Frank, and a very remarkable bargain was struck. Pippin accepted the title of "Patricius" (vaguely, Prince) of Rome, and in return he promised to wrest from the Lombard heretics the whole territory which belonged to the Popes.

It is true that very considerable estates had previously been given to the Papacy. Gregory the Great, who believed that the end of the world was at hand, had induced large numbers of nobles to leave their estates to the Church, since their sons would have no use for them, and he farmed and ruled immense territories. He became the richest man and largest slave-holder in Europe. Gregory had been as shrewd in material matters as he had been credulous in religion. But historians suspect, with good reason, that the Papal envoys showed Pippin *The Acts of St. Silvester,* and in virtue of it, claimed nearly the whole of Italy.

The gruff and superstitious Pippin swore a mighty oath that he would win back for "the Blessed Peter" the lands which these hoggish heretics had appropriated, and he went to Italy and secured them. What precise amount of Italy he handed over to the Papacy we do not know. The Papacy has not preserved the authentic text of a single one of these "donations" on which it bases its claims of temporal power.

There is a document, known as the "Fantuzzian Fragment," which professes to give the terms of "the Donation of Pippin," but scholars are agreed that this is a shameless Roman forgery. It is, however, certain that Pippin gave the Papacy, probably on the strength of the older forgery, a very considerable part of north and central Italy, including the entire Governorship of Ravenna, and returned to France.

To this territory, the Papacy had no just title whatever, and the King of the Lombards at once reoccupied it. Pope Stephen stormed the French monarch with passionate and piteous appeals to recover it for him, but Pippin refused to move again. Then the Pope took a remarkable step. Among his surviving letters there is one addressed to Pippin which is written *in the name of St. Peter.* The Pope had forged it in the name of Peter, and passed it off on the ignorant Frank as a miraculous appeal from the Apostle himself. By that pious stratagem and the earlier forgery, the Papacy obtained twenty-three Italian cities with the surrounding country.

Those who affect to doubt whether the Pope really intended to deceive the King seem to forget that the Papacy of the time was deeply stained with crime and forgery. In 768, a noble of the Roman district named "Toto" got together a rabble of priests and laity, and elected his own brother. "Pope" Constantine was a layman, but he was hastily put through the various degrees of ordination and consecration by obliging bishops.

No doubt these bishops then claimed their reward and disturbed the older officials. At all events, we read that the chief official of the Papal court, Christopher, and his son Sergius fled to the Lombards, borrowed an army, and marched back upon Rome. A fierce and deadly battle, in which the Lombards won, was followed by the first of a series of horrible acts of vengeance, which will henceforward, from time to time, disgrace the Papacy.

The wretched Constantine, duly consecrated by three bishops, was put upon a horse, in a woman's saddle, with heavy weights to his feet, and conducted ignominiously through the streets of Rome. He was then confined in a monastery, to await trial; but Christopher and Sergius broke into the monastery and cut out the man's eyes. In this condition, his blind face still ghastly from the mutilation, Constantine was brought before a synod in the Pope's palace and tried. The infuriated priests thrashed the wretch with their own hands, and "threw him out."

The end of Constantine is, in the chronicles, left to the imagination. His brother also lost his eyes. One of the consecrating bishops lost his eyes and his tongue. In short, the supporters of the premature Pope were punished with a savagery that tells us plainly enough the character of the Papacy at that time.

Catholic Truth – which, however, generously admits that there were "some bad Popes," though this does not affect its claim of the special interest of the Holy Ghost in the Papacy – imagines the Pope serenely aloof from these horrors. Listen to the sequel. Christopher and Sergius presumed too much upon their services to Pope Stephen, and he grew tired of them and plotted with the Lombard King. They discovered or suspected the plot, and sought to kill the Pope; and it is enough to say that before many days they themselves had their eyes cut from the sockets.

Christopher was mutilated so brutally that he died. There are some Catholic writers who make a show of liberality, and admit that the Pope was "implicated" in this. But the sordid truth is known to us and to these writers on the most absolute authority of the time. In the *Liber Pontificalis* itself, we have the explicit testimony of Pope Hadrian I, the greatest Pope of the time, that *Pope Stephen ordered the eyes of Christopher and Sergius to be cut out, and for the sordid reason that King Didier promised to restore the disputed lands if he did so.* Stephen, Hadrian says, admitted this to him.

To such depths had "the Vicars of Christ" sunk now, that the greed of temporal sovereignty and wealth was added to the ambition for religious supremacy. And they had, naturally, allowed all Europe to sink to the same level. As the letters of St. Boniface and other contemporary documents affirm, the moral condition of England, France, and Germany – Spain had now passed to the Arabs – was unspeakable. Monasteries and nunneries were houses of open debauch – Boniface describes the English nuns as murdering their babies – and the clergy very corrupt. But here I must confine myself to the Vicars of Christ.

Joseph McCabe (1867-1955), was an ex-priest and author of many books. This article is from Popes and Their Church *and is available at most public libraries. Published in London, by Watts 1953.*

The Church of Rome has made it an article of fact that no man can be saved out of their church, and other religious sects approach this dreadful opinion in proportion to their ignorance, and the influence of ignorant or wicked priests.

— John Adams, Second President of the United States

If all records told the same tale – then the lie passed into history and became truth. "Who controls the past," rants the Party slogan, "controls the future. Who controls the present controls the past."

— George Orwell, *1984*

God, The Devil And The Fifty-Yard Line

Steven H. Homel

If the courts are the arena of our worldly problems, then, according to most religions, our soul is the battlefield of the spirit. We are the objects of a celestial tennis match between God and the devil. Men of the cloth may not have a competitive image, but what they preach as the gospel certainly does: it always portrays our existence as a struggle between the forces of good and evil.

Competition isn't foreign to religious leaders. The history of religion-based wars is a 6,000-year-old testimony to this fact – true believers of one faith battling with the true believers of another faith. Usually, the wars of ancient times were supposed to be governed by whose god was the most powerful. The advent of a single god presented a competitive problem: who's the adversary when both sides have the same god, such as Moslems and Christians?

This problem was easily resolved by establishing assistant gods for each sub-sect who represented the "true path" to God. I don't think that war was the purpose for creating such intermediaries, but these figures did serve as rallying points to form competitive sides with opposing views. Human response has been so molded to accept competition as a primary law of existence that God wasn't allowed to stand alone. He had to have another god to compete with – so the devil sprang into being.

It is clear that even in the spiritual world, we are led to believe that an arena of battle exists. Into the bargain, it is a participating sport. We are not only part of the game – we're the ball. It's our souls that get booted back and forth between heaven and hell. It wouldn't surprise me in the least to find out that heaven and hell are separated by a fifty-yard line.

Excerpt from The Competition Obsession: a philosophy of non-competitive living *by Steven H. Homel, published by ACS Publishing Company, San Diego, California, April 1981.*

The Puritan Theocracy: In the New England Primer the lesson for the letter "A" began in typical fashion: "In Adam's Fall/ We Sinned all." It also included "Samuel anoints/ Whom God appoints" and "Job feels the rod/ Yet blessed God."

Hermes Vs. Puritans

Stephan A. Hoeller

The contemporary social arena of the United States is characterized by a cacophony of competing voices, all claiming to be the authentic, the true voice of this country. On the left of the socio-political spectrum, we hear many voices heavily colored by late nineteenth and early twentieth century European thoughts. I am referring here primarily to the dialectical materialism of Marx and Engels in its several variants, some amplified by Lenin. Marxist thought has become well-nigh normative for the American left.

On the opposite end of the spectrum we find a frequently confused melange of nineteenth century Protestant fundamentalist Christianity, liberally mixed with the economic outlook of the Industrial Revolution. As the Left talks of concern for the disadvantaged and other human values, so the Right dwells on tradition and family values, by which it means anything from the work ethic of the last century to sexual repression and the bashing of almost anyone who disagrees with these positions.

Who or what, then, is the true American? Who speaks for America? Does the land of the free and home of the brave, the land of opportunity, the nation of the Statue of Liberty, have an authentic voice? Or, is the cacophony of voices we hear the only voice of this land and this culture?

In my view there are three Americas. The first is ancient, or "Shamanic America," (discussed in another chapter in my book). The second is "Hermetic America," and the third is "Puritan America," which in most respects has acted as the opposing force to Hermetic America.

To gain an understanding of Hermetic America, we need to go back a considerable distance in history, to the Alexandrian period of late antiquity. At this time, the Greek god Hermes, son of Zeus, messenger of the gods and patron of communications and commerce, became fused archetypally with the god-form of the Egyptian god Thoth, lord of mind, scribe of the gods and patron of transformation. The result was the splendid mystery system of gnosis, closely related in spirit to the schools of Christian gnosticism. A large and deeply inspiring body of mystical literature came into existence, all attributed poetically to Hermes-Thoth and designed to facilitate the spiritual insight, transformation, and ultimate liberation of the human soul.

The hermetic renaissance was in full swing when Columbus came to America. It flourished in England at the time of Elizabeth I, and thus the immediate ethnic and cultural parent-country of North America became thoroughly "hermeticized" at the very time when England was beginning her colonial expansion in the world.

Thus hermetic and neo-hermetic currents were rapidly transplanted from England to America and were frequently reinforced by the emigration to the New World of European esotericists of a hermetic orientation, such as German Rosicrucians from Central Europe. From Lord Francis Bacon, the Elizabethan scholar and hermetic wise man, to Johannes Kepler, the German astronomer and wizard, and beyond, esoteric influences, largely of hermetic origin, were brought to bear on the newly founded colonies of North America.

By the time of the American Revolution, the hermetic renaissance was fused to a considerable extent with the originally French movement of the enlightenment. Thus the normative leadership of the American Revolution, particularly its intellectual wing led and exemplified by Benjamin Franklin, was thoroughly imbued with the spirit of the hermetic enlightenment.

The founders of the American republic proceeded to create a model government, hitherto unheard of in history, a republic founded on the philosophy of the hermetic enlightenment and expressing, with certain modifications made necessary by the different historical era, the wisdom of the Corpus Hermeticum and other hermetic books.

This is how Hermes came to America, and this is how we can state today, perhaps to the discomfort of some, that the chief inspirer of the American republic was not Moses or Jesus, and even less Saint Augustine or Saint Thomas Aquinas, but rather Hermes Trismegistus of old. Hermes, who survived among the alchemists, magicians, Rosicrucians, esoteric Freemasons and the French enlightenment philosophers, crossed the Atlantic on his winged sandals and stood with his caduceus in the first assemblies of the Continental Congress.

There is no doubt that mystical, hermeticized freemasonry played a great role in the eighteenth century establishment of a hermetic republic on the far side of the Atlantic. The emissary of the revolutionary colonists to France, Benjamin Franklin, was an ardent Freemason who established close links with leading members of that fraternity at the Lodge of the Nine Sisters in France.

Hermetic America

The question now arises: What was the content of this hermetic teaching that was transmitted to the early leadership of the American republic by various circles of the hermetic-Rosicrucian-Masonic enlightenment? To answer this question, I begin with a shorthand account, or abbreviated summary, of those points of the hermetic transmission that have a direct bearing on the founding of the American republic.

The first of the important principles brought into the fabric of the new commonwealth from the hermetic enlightenment was the separation of church and state. This principle was unheard of in any part of the world or in any government at the time of the founding of the United States. Under the Constitution, no longer was there an established faith. By law the government completely disengaged itself from the business of religion. The most that religious minorities could expect from other governments up to this time was "tolerance." This meant that, while maintaining an officially established state religion, the authorities would nevertheless patiently endure (tolerate means "to endure" in Latin) the exercise of a different religion on the part of some.

The prototype of tolerant monarchs was no doubt Frederick the Great, who uttered the famous words, "Let everyone be saved after his own fashion," but who still maintained the established Lutheran Church of Prussia. The founders of the American republic clearly went beyond that.

The popularly advanced theory accounting for the separation of church and state in America is that, since there were several religions present and flourishing in the colonies, it was best to make religion a private matter and thus diffuse potential sectarian dissension. However, in view of the hermetic influences that were brought to bear on the founders, it might be assumed that this was not the only reason for their attitude. The hermetic enlightenment as a whole was not interested merely in the absence of religious strife; rather, it felt that there was something profoundly *wrong* with the theologies of all existing religious denominations in the culture, and that for this reason, none of them ought to be supported. The issue was not that one did not know which of the religions was right, but rather that one knew, or at least suspected, that all of them were wrong.

One of the major disagreements between the hermetic enlightenment on the one hand and the various denominations of Christianity and Judaism on the other concerned the God concept. All denominations of Christendom at that time, as well as followers of Judaism, were adherents of theism, a belief in a personal God, creator, maintainer, and judge of the world, who is personally involved in the management of creation at every moment of time. In the eyes of the hermetic thinkers of the enlightenment, this concept had shown itself to have not only theoretical flaws, but also to be responsible for certain practical ills, such as the divine right of rulers, the presence of religious law within the fabric of society, and many more.

If God was actively involved in all the affairs of the world and of humans, it was easy to envision that this same God instituted the existing governmental and social structure and that the state ought to enforce God's ordinances in order to please Him. By their separation of church and state, we can infer that the founders of the United States were not in favor of such a God.

The men and women of the enlightenment were usually not theists, but deists. Deists accepted a Supreme Being as the ultimate origin and the final destiny of all beings and of the universe, but they were convinced that this Godhead did not actively manage the universe or interfere in the affairs of humankind. Theirs was the "Alien God" of the hermeticists and Gnostics, also known at times as Deus Absconditus, "the God who has gone away."

(Esotericists of various schools and historical periods shared in this conviction. The aforementioned late nineteenth century figure of the esoteric revival, H. P. Blavatsky, was extremely emphatic in her denial of a theistic concept of God. The heterodox religious views of many of the founding fathers were not only a matter of privately held conviction: Benjamin Franklin even wrote a liturgy for a new religion based on deistic, hermetic principles, and sent a copy of it to Jean Jacques Rousseau, who accepted it with pleasure and presumably with approval.)

The second distinctively hermetic feature of the American republic was the three-branch theory of government. Although it is not very well known, the United States became and remained in effect a constitutional, elective monarchy, wherein the monarch (named, or misnamed, "president") has far broader powers than the present constitutional monarchs of Europe. At the time the Constitution was framed there was even serious debate that the president ought to have the title "Serene Highness," indicating the monarchial character of the office.

Another important consideration is the source of the legitimacy of government. In the prevailing arrangement in Europe at the time, it was understood that the source of legitimacy was the will or grace of God. However, the founders of American government decided that the will of the people, or "the just consent of the governed," made a government legitimate. Here we find the hermetic principles powerfully at work again. Ever since Alexandrian Egypt, hermetic teachings have always given prominence to the god-like power and dignity of the human soul. The human soul is not a mere creation of God, but rather is divine in origin and in its essential nature, and as such cannot be forever subjected to external authority.

The human was constituted as someone who causes events to occur and not as someone who is the passive recipient of the effects of an external divine will. As free agents, citizens may contract with each other to form associations such as state and nation and are not destined to remain subjects of rulers who are foisted on them. The social contract theory of Montesquieu also served as one of the inspirations for this feature of American government.

Finally, one must consider the hermetic principle, more than any other, came to permeate not only American government but the entire history of the United States. The hermetic vision of existence declares that life is a process, not a fixed condition. Because of this, life cannot be managed, but rather must be permitted to function. In this vision, government is like a master of the alchemical art, who guards and oversees the process, but does not interfere with it. The less governmental interference with the life process of the body politic, the better.

If citizens are free to move about, to keep their earnings, to take up trades and professions and engage in business as they choose, the process works. Thus, politically, religiously, socially, and economically, the existing forces, rather like the alchemical salt, sulphur, and mercury, freely interact with each other. The result is growth, transformation, and the unfolding of countless, latent potentials of a beneficent nature. The guiding principle of this process is not the petty, obsessive, and tyrannical Old Testament God, but rather Hermes, shepherd of the forces of being, the facilitator and wise alchemical transformer of all things.

Puritan America

In contrast to the hermetic spirit, however, is another element in American life, which from the very beginning was different from and indeed antagonistic toward the hermetic enlightenment. This opposing idea was puritanism, or the Calvinist Protestant form of Christianity. In many ways puritanism became an entire lifestyle, a powerful force, influencing public life throughout American history.

The puritans were transplanted from England, following in the footsteps of John Calvin, the theocratic tyrant of Geneva, who was known to put people into prison for such "crimes" as dancing. Inspired by Calvin's disciple, John Knox, the ranting scourge of Scotland, English puritans had become the cause of much anguish in their home country. Some of them came to America in 1630, close on the heels of the Pilgrims, who were not puritans and who had arrived in 1620.

Oliver Cromwell, whose associates cruelly executed King Charles I, instituted a pious dictatorship in which Christmas was outlawed and merry old England was stripped of virtually all color and beauty. This cruel and boring regime was eventually replaced by the restored monarchy of the House of Stuart, and Cromwell's puritan friends were increasingly subjected to the ire of just about everybody. Many of them decided to sail over the Atlantic, to join their fellows in Massachusetts.

The puritans are remembered in sentimentalized literature and art as a harmless sort of immigrant folk, and are confused with the Pilgrims, who sought religious freedom denied to them in their homeland. However, the truth is that the puritans had denied similar freedom to so many for so long that they were driven out of their homeland as a punishment for very real misdeeds. They soon distinguished themselves in the New World by hanging not a few alleged witches, and this at a time when that curious practice was already nonexistent elsewhere. Looking to more recent times, we note that the Dutch puritans who settled South Africa became the inventors and perpetuators of apartheid. An altogether unpleasant record, one might say.

Unfortunately, matters did not rest there. Puritan ideology exercised an uncanny influence on practically all of American Protestantism (and, one must admit, on much of Irish-dominated, Jansenist American Catholicism also). Not only the direst extensions of the Calvinist tradition, such as the Presbyterian and Reformed churches, but innumerable other ecclesiastical bodies have become saturated with Calvinist ideas and with puritan values and life-style.

In innumerable ways, the United States became a very Calvinist country, more so than Switzerland, Scotland, and Holland, the original strongholds of this faith. Deism and the hermetic world view appealed to the cultural elite, while puritanism, originally ensconced in New England, spread its principles (modified at times) to the broad masses and to every state. Whether Jacksonian Democrat or Lincolnian Republican, the "Common Man" of American history always had at least a partially Calvinist element in his character.

Four features of Calvinism (or puritanism) need to be emphasized here. The first is that the God-image of Calvinism is Old Testament in the extreme. Luther was the reformer representing Christ, Calvin the one representing Yehovah. It has been wisely noted by C. G. Jung and others that the God whom people worship places his signature on their psyches. The God-image of the Calvinists is radically at odds with the deism of the founders of the republic, and its influence has been characterized by harshness, vengefulness, and cold-hearted cruelty. (It must be remembered that Calvin and his associates did not avail themselves of the refined and softened theology of later rabbinical Judaism, in which this God-image underwent salutary modifications. Calvin's God came straight out of the Old Testament and out of his projections placed upon the same).

The second point is that Calvinism is by nature and history theocratic in orientation. Pious dictatorship had been very much a part of the history of this religion. The petty, intolerant, and obsessive image of its God was mirrored in the public conduct and policy of its members. Early American history bears abundant testimony to the Calvinist desire to control public as well as private life. Witches were hanged, and sinners were placed in the pillory or branded with a scarlet letter as part of this syndrome. A fairly direct line runs from Cotton Mather and his clerical judges to such modern movements as the Moral Majority. Clearly, the hermetic principle of the separation of church and state was never seriously endorsed by the Calvinist mentality.

A prominent feature of Calvinist belief is the doctrine of predestination. While originating in abstract theology, this doctrine came to be universally interpreted to mean that those following the Calvinist ethic were the new "chosen people." Material wealth and success were regarded as the signal hallmarks of divine favor accorded to those predestined for salvation. From this it followed that Calvinists, and those influenced by them, became ambitious, success-oriented, and often ruthless.

Euphemistically, this attitude was submerged under the innocuous term "the work ethic," ostensibly a wholesome, decent, and virile creed, which at the same time carried an enormous shadow. This feature of Calvinism soon joined in an unholy alliance with the capitalism born of the industrial revolution. The robber baron, the unscrupulous business person of our culture, is not a hermetic but a Calvinistic figure. Thus, from early times onward, the Calvinist or puritan spirit countermanded and minimized many of the great advantages the hermetic spirit had bestowed on America. This tendency has not ceased even today.

Finally, puritanism is in fact what we colloquially mean by the term. It is characterized by extreme moralizing in respect to personal life and conduct, conjoined with considerable laxity when moral principles are applied to politics or business. It implies a joyless, dour attitude toward the pleasurable side of human life on the surface, compensated by fierce greed and a lust for power underneath. (A poignant jest has it that a Calvinist preacher declared ice cream must have been invented by the devil because it tastes so good. Along the same line, H.L. Mencken defined Puritanism as "the haunting fear that someone somewhere may be happy.") Depth psychology reveals that this kind of obsessive, repressed life-style holds great dangers for the psyches of those who adopt it. At the time of his first visit to the United States, Jung spoke of this matter in an interview printed in The New York Times of September 29, 1912:

> When I see so much refinement and so much sentiment as I
> see in America, I look for an equal amount of brutality. The pair
> of opposites – you find them everywhere. I find the greatest
> self-control in the world among the Americans – and I search
> for its cause . . . I find a great deal of prudery. I ask, what is the
> cause and I discover brutality. Prudery is always the cover for
> brutality. It is necessary – it makes life possible until you dis-
> cover the brute and take real control of it. When you do that in
> America, then you will be the most feeling, the most
> temperamental, the most fully developed people in the world.

The natural result of a lack of self-knowledge is the exercise of a repressive and judgmental will. Those who do not know themselves must ever try to control themselves, without knowing whom or what they are attempting to control. The Calvinistic moral attitude is the direct antithesis of the gnosis represented by Jung. Prudery, repression, and artificial rules for moral behavior serve only to hide (at times to fortify) dangerous instinctual forces and psychological complexes in the unconscious. Thus Jung foresaw many of the future dilemmas of American culture.

Defending Our Hermetic Heritage

From this vantage point it is clear that the principal features of hermetic America and puritan America have differences which are portentous and still very much with us. A profound and seemingly irreconcilable conflict rends the soul of America in two. While in some subtle way, this conflict may also be envisioned as an alchemical process, it is still incumbent upon those who perceive the hermetic heritage of this country to try to defend it and save it from being engulfed by its opposite. Only by recalling and supporting the hermetic qualities of the American vision will the beneficent alchemical operation envisioned by the founders be permitted to do its work.

What then should be the course of action? First, let us recognize the existence of the conflict and consciously understand and articulate its nature and significance. In the legend of the grail-hero Parsifal, the hero encounters the wounded fisher king Amfortas, and asks a simple question: "What ails thee, uncle?" If, like Parsifal, we ask the right question, we too may become the healers of the kingdom. What ails our culture more than any other illness is the continuing, insidious, and perilous conflict between the original hermetic archetypal matrix of the republic on the one hand, and the puritan complex on the other. Crime, economic woes, blunders in foreign policy, the human failings of statesmen: all of these are symptoms of the greater, underlying conflict. Will the hermetic vision prevail? Or will the encroachments of an archaic, unconscious religiosity, and of a gravely flawed world view and life-style based on them, drive the American people and culture farther and farther away from the goals envisioned by the founders of this nation?

Finally, we need to take our stand and begin vigilantly to sift the hermetic wheat from the puritan chaff in contemporary public life.

Conservatives ought not to allow themselves to be taken in by slogans and ideas that are not truly conservative at all. What sane individual could envision Dr. Franklin storming clinics where abortions might be performed? Could Thomas Jefferson sanction the government interfering with the most private activities of citizens in their homes? These men, like other sensible persons everywhere, knew freedom to be one and undivided; they knew that people are either free privately as well as in public, or they are not free at all.

Liberals ought to cease seeking remedy for all ills in more government, manipulation, and interference. The passing of large numbers of laws, as Lao Tse recognized, leads to greater lawlessness; the increase of regulations increases confusion and unruliness. Governments do not exist to manage and regulate the lives of citizens but to ensure a setting in which the inherent powers and talents of persons can develop and flourish. Every good government in history has been small in size, restrained in the exercise of power, and kept at a distance when it concerned the personal, economic, and political freedoms and privacy of people. The advancement of commendable causes ought not to be used as an excuse to increase government and to dwarf the freedom and initiative of individuals.

Hermetic America contains the remedy for the ills that have befallen us in this age. The remedy is freedom. With freedom, the alchemy of the spirit corrects the flaws of culture and rectifies the excesses of civilization.

Stephan A. Hoeller, PhD., is a Gnostic and Jungian scholar whose fourth book, Freedom: The Alchemy of a Voluntary Society, *was published by Quest Books in June 1992.*

The idea that religion and politics don't mix was invented by the Devil to keep Christians from running their own country.

— Rev. Jerry Falwell

Toward no crimes have men shown themselves so cold-bloodedly cruel as in punishing differences of belief.

— James Russell Lowell

Theocracy

I hope I live to see the day when, as in the early days of our country, we won't have any public schools. The churches will have taken them over again and Christians will be running them. What a happy day that will be! — Rev. Jerry Falwell, 1979

The Supreme Court of the United States of America is an institution damned by God Almighty. — Rev. Jimmy Swaggart, 1986

I believe this notion of the separation of church and state was the figment of some infidel's imagination. — Rev. W. A. Criswell, Dallas TX, 1984

In a state where the majority of people are Catholic, the church will require that legal existence be denied to error, and that if religious minorities exist, they shall have only a *de facto* existence without opportunity to spread their unbeliefs.
 — Civilta Cattolica (Jesuit), 1948

The majority of our leaders are pro-abortion. So you don't go in there and say, "I'm an advocate against abortion." No, you say, "I'm interested in housing, or development, or sanitation." And you keep your personal views to yourself until the Christian community is ready to rise up, and then, wow! They're gonna be devastated!
 — Antonio Rivera, Christian Coalition NYC, 1992

I want to be invisible. I do guerilla warfare. I paint my face and travel at night. You don't know it's over until you're in a body bag. You don't know until election night.
 — Ralph Reed, Christian Coalition, 1991

Theocracy is the worst of all governments. If we must have a tyrant, a robber baron is better than an inquisitor. The baron's cruelty may sometimes sleep... But the inquisitor who mistakes his own cruelty and lust of power and fear for the voice of Heaven will torment us infinitely because he torments us with the approval of his own conscience...
 — C. S. Lewis, Christian writer

During almost fifteen centuries has the legal establishment of Christianity been on trial. What have been its fruits? More or less, in all places, pride and indolence in the clergy; ignorance and servility in the laity; in both, superstition, bigotry and persecution.
 — James Madison

Social realities as well as religious principles must be taken into account in judging the wisdom of any legislation. Citizens who come to different conclusions are not necessarily immoral or unChristian. The tendency to so brand one's political opponents suggests a kind of moral fascism. — *America* (Jesuit), 1980

The majority has no right to impose its religion on the rest. That's a tradition as sacred as the Constitution itself to this country. — Rev. William R. Harper (Episcopal), 1986

And of all the plagues with which mankind are cursed Ecclesiastic tyranny's the worst.
 — Daniel Defoe

From Petra, Majorca he came
to build
Our Mission San Juan de Capistrano
with faith in God
and Love for Mankind

— Fr. Junipero Serra

Father Serra And The Skeletons of Genocide

Jose Ignacio Rivera

Junipero Serra was the first Father-President of the Alta California Missions, and has been beatified, which is the next-to-last step of canonization. Born Miguel Jose Serra, November 24, 1713 of a farming family on the Spanish island of Mallorca, Father Serra was raised in the village of Petra (Fogel 1988:41). Father Serra had a distinguished career as an academic in Europe. Upon arriving in the New World, Father Serra grabbed his chance to fulfill a life-long dream of becoming a spiritual *conquistador* and leading a nation of pagans to the fold of the church. Being one of the first priests in Alta California, and Father-President of the Alta California missions, Father Serra was instrumental in the formation of the missions' policies, attitudes, and treatment toward the Native Californians. It is this mission legacy that forms one of the bases of Father Serra's candidacy for sainthood, which is still pending.

Through a selective and myopic interpretation of historical events, individuals who wish to perpetuate the popular romantic days of Spanish California myth have created a pristine picture of Father Serra. In defense of Father Serra, Bishop Thaddeus Shubsda of Monterey Diocese commissioned the Serra Report, which is a compilation of eight interviews. The mythic image created within the Serra Report is one of Father Serra possessing a totally forgiving nature for any and all transgressions committed by Native Californians, completely innocent of and separated from any association of forced residency or punishment, such as floggings.

This almost antiseptic image of Father Serra is reinforced by Dr. Nunis in the Serra Report, with statements like "There's no evidence that Serra ever instituted physical punishment or any kind of unusual punishment" (Costo 1987: 218). "Unusual punishment" by whose standards, the zealous missionaries who ordered it, or the Indios who received it? Unfortunately, the Indigenous perspective is lacking, or is superficially addressed by the supporters of canonization.

What seems to be occurring is a conflict of perspectives, definitions, and interpretations between the canonization supporters, a group some would identify as "apologists," and the "detractors" who challenge the historical accuracy of Father Serra's case. The apologists have found it necessary to degrade the Indigenous People of California to elevate Serra's reputation.

This paper will address the apologists' myths with historical documentation, especially the letters written by Father Serra connecting him to floggings and forced residency. The apologists are guilty of the same academic sins they accuse the detractors of, and should have conducted a more diligent literature search. A rigorous analysis of the anthropological data should have also been conducted before perpetuating outdated ethnocentric myths about Native Californians.

Pro-Serrans Denigrate Detractors

The ultimate question of whether Father Serra merits sainthood or not rests with the Catholic Church itself, since sainthood is an internal honored position, requiring a lengthy evaluation process based upon established criteria.

Questions have been raised to challenge the myths and the aura of quaint pastoral romanticism shrouding colonial California. The three main points used in the Serra Report to defend canonization are firstly, that Father Serra's detractors are coming from an emotional point of view, rather than using a scholarly approach, and are making historically unsound, unfounded allegations that reflect a lack of research and that neglect the facts. Secondly, Father Serra is being blamed for abuses that occurred long after his death in 1784, and thirdly, no one has yet produced any documentation that Father Serra mistreated anyone.

Most of the Serra Report interviewees exhibited an 18th-century European perspective, through a parochial interpretation of historical events, and accepted that period's highly ethnocentric assessment of the Indigenous people at face value. According to this 18th-century European perspective, Native California was comprised of wandering bands of neo-Neanderthals with limited intelligence, possessing only a rudimentary culture and technology. Dr.

Nunis in the Serra Report reinforces the ethnocentric image by stating that the padres gave the Indians

> warm blankets so you (the Indians) wouldn't freeze to death. Now the Indian didn't have to bury himself in (the) sand to keep warm . . . the California Indians had, at best, a modest level of civilization. I'm being kind . . . Life was very hard. Very hard. They simply had to really grub for a living. And that living meant just eating and staying alive . . . They had no idea of a social compact, in the strongest sense of the word . . . They had no sense of morality (Costo 1987: 219).

Significant literature was either overlooked or discounted, and the scholars who disagreed with canonization were trivialized. Dr. Engstrand in the Serra Report said the detractors are "some amateur anthropologists and archaeologists, people from the '60s who want a cause, or who want to promote general Indian welfare, (and) receiv(ing) a lot of publicity, they think it is a good one to beat the drums about" (Costo 1987: 195). Even the clergy who have published in defense of Father Serra concede several points of what the Indigenous community considers to be human rights abuses.

The apologists justified the human rights abuses because such acts were an accepted form of punishment in Europe. The Indigenous perspective was ignored, dismissed, or erroneously interpreted by the apologists. Prominent members of the Native Californian community pointed out that the contributors to the Serra Report who are attempting to interpret an Indigenous perspective are not observed in, much less participating with, the native community.

The Serra Report puts forth a blanket condemnation of all detractors, overlooking that many are Native Americans who were raised in the Catholic tradition. There are many distinguished and respected scholars who are critical of the historical interpretations used to support canonization. Dr. Gloria Miranda describes the authors of historical accounts that were critical of the mission system and contemporary detractors as those who " . . . were very blatant in their anti-Spanish and anti-Catholic attitudes . . . (with) a deep-rooted and irrational dislike for Catholicism . . . (and because of) that point it is not sound criticism, based on a valid argument. It's based on an emotional and a religious perspective" (Costo 1987: 213-214). Interestingly enough, Bancroft noted the courage of Padre Antonio de la Concepción Horra, for complaining to his collegues of the many abuses suffered by the neophytes within the California mission system. Padre Horra was beaten, declared insane, and exiled from

California for his "disloyalty" (Bancroft, 1886: 593). No doubt Hubert Bancroft was one of the historians the apologist was referring to.

Punishment Saves

The methods Father Serra instituted in the mission system, and the personal philosophy that guided his motives, should be examined. Father Serra felt that pain and penance were necessary for the purification of the flesh. The painful subject of self-flagellation is often dismissed by the apologists, but it is an important point when dealing with Father Serra's personal philosophy of conversion, punishment, and the purification of the flesh to save the soul. In Father Maynard Geiger's work, *"Palou's Life of Fray Junipero Serra"* (1955), published by the Academy of American Franciscan History, there is an interesting letter. Father Palou in his letter said:

> St. Prosper includes the virtue of penance among the effects of temperance: *Vitiosa castigat* (it punishes vices). In such a manner did Fray Junipero exercise this virtue, that for the mortification of his body he was not content with the ordinary exercises of the college in regard to acts of discipline, vigils and fasts, but he privately scourged his flesh with rough hair shirts, made either of bristles or with points of metal wire, with which he covered his body. He also took the discipline unto blood during the most silent part of the night, when he would betake himself to one of the tribunes of the choir. Although the place was so remote and the hour so quiet, there were friars who heard the cruel strokes . . . Not content to mortify his body for his own imperfection and sins, he also did penance for the sins of others. By strong censures he would move his listeners to sorrow and penance for their sins; he struck his breast with the stone, in imitation of St. Jerome; in imitation of his St. Francis Solanus, to whom he was devoted, he used (a) chain to scourge himself; he used the burning torch, applying it to his uncovered chest, burning his flesh in imitation of St. John Capistran and various other saints. All this he did with the purpose not only of punishing himself, but also of moving his hearers to penance for their own sins. (Geiger 1955: 279, 280)

The most damaging blows to the apologists come from Father Serra's own pen. Father Antoine Tibesar in his four-volume *Writings of Junipero Serra* (1956), published by the Academy of American Franciscan History as well, is a rich source that allows one an insight into Father Serra's thinking through his pen. Serra in 1752 requested the Tribunal of the Inquisition to look into local witchcraft, and was appointed Head Inquisitor of Sierra Gorda, Mexico.

In a letter written by Serra on September 1, 1752 as Inquisitor he reported on people "who are addicted to the most detestable and horrible crimes of sorcery, witchcraft, and devil worship . . . the inquiry into which appertains to your Venerable Holy Tribunal of the Inquisition. And if it is necessary to specify one of the persons guilty of such crimes, I accuse by name a certain Melchora de los Reyes Acosta, a married mulattress, an inhabitant of the said mission" (Tibesar 1956: 19-21). Father Serra brought this inquisitional mentality to California, and instituted it within the missions system, especially for "neglect in matters of faith."

Hubert H. Bancroft described Father Serra as

> kind-hearted and charitable to all, but most strict in his enforcement of religious duties. It never occurred to him to doubt his absolute right to flog his neophytes for any slight negligence in matters of the faith. His holy desires trembled within him like earthquake throbs; in his eyes there was but one object worth living for, the performance of religious duty, and but one way of accomplishing that object, a strict and literal compliance with Franciscan rule; he could never understand that there was anything beyond his narrow field of vision (Bancroft 1886: 415).

The methods Father Serra institutionalized within the mission system to convert and control the Native Californians are his legacy. Father Zephyrin Engelhardt explained how Father Serra did not have to apply the lash with his own hand, but supervised the ordered punishment at the hands of another Indian. Father Engelhardt, in his publication *The Missions and Missionaries of California,* said:

> (The Indians) needed a punishment which touched their carnal nature. As they remained children, with regard to the use of their mental faculties, they had to be treated like unruly boys if other remedies failed. The lash was accordingly applied. It was the only punishment that convinced . . . The chastisement (floggings) was not inflicted by the missionary, but at his direction by one of the chief Indians or an Indian official. This manner of correcting the guilty in Lower California originated with the Rev. Juan Maria Salvatierra, and Fr. Serra retained it for the Indians under his charge. (Engelhardt 1912: 276)

In *The Conflict Between the California Indians and White Civilization* (1976), Dr. Sherburne Cook said, "Omitting the doubtful cases, 82.5 per cent of the persons were punished for political offenses," both *during* and after Father Serra's tenure. Political offenses not only included fugitivism, apostasy, conspiracies, but religious crimes like unauthorized dances or ceremonies in particular. Father Serra gave advice to other Franciscans about their duty in administering punishment. In a letter to Father Fermin Francisco Lasuen written at Monterey on July 10, 1778, Father Serra advised him:

> You should quietly visit your old home at the presidio [military fort], and put it in readiness, in case anything might happen. You could tell everybody that you are doing this in case it should be necessary to take up your quarters there. And while doing that, and afterwards, you should continue your work in the mission, just as if you had a legion of soldiers at your side. Punishment should be given to everyone who deserves it. (Tibesar 1956: 209)

The Revolts

The San Diego revolt of November 4, 1775, is famous, in that the Kumeyaay people revolted against the strict discipline of Serra's missionary vision. Several villages were united to assert their sovereign dignity, led by two Kumeyaay neophytes Carlos and Bernardo. In a letter written at San Diego to Fernando Rivera y Moncada dated October 5, 1776, in what the apologists claim to be Father Serra's letter pleading for leniency toward the rebellious Indians, we get an insight to his concept of forgiveness.

> It seems that the best way to carry out the orders and will of His Excellency would be (to) promptly and energetically set about capturing most of all the missing murderers, and the one who was in command of all the enemy forces, or anyone else who you may know enjoyed or is now enjoying a privileged position among them. You should assemble them, together with those you now hold prisoners, and by means of an interpreter lay the case vigorously yet clearly before them. First of all you should make them reflect on the great amount of evil they have done; then point out the severe punishment they deserve, and the undisputed power which our King and lord has to wipe them out of existence, as indeed they deserve . . .

Especially from an Indigenous perspective, the clergy and the military worked hand in hand to control the Native Californians. Contrary to the apologists, Father Serra was not above calling out the soldiers to retrieve runaway neophytes, as well as setting the precedent in justifying this policy. Father Serra in fact complained about not having enough soldiers to bring back his runaway neophytes. In a letter to the Governor, Fernando Rivera y Moncada, written at Monterey, July 24, 1775, Father Serra said:

> You had not answered the note I wrote to you a week ago, in
> which I requested an escort of soldiers to go to bring back some
> of the new Christians of this mission who had fled to the pagans
> ... Now, my dearest Sir, I state to you that these wayward sheep
> are my burden, and I am responsible for them ... (Tibesar 1956:
> 285)

By Father Serra's own pen, too many neophytes were running way
from his benevolent love, and this proves he *did believe in, and
practiced forced residency.* If the missionaries were loved so much
among the Native Californians as the apologists insist, then why did
they need a military escort?

After Father Serra sent the military to bring the runaway
neophytes back, what did he expect the soldiers to do when they
encountered the fugitives? Punishments such as floggings were
expected and routinely administered for attempting to run away
from the "strict and literal compliance with Franciscan rule." The
runaway attempt would have deadly consequences if the fugitives
resisted returning to the mission. Especially in light of Serra's letters,
the clergy and the soldiers are equally guilty of human rights abuses,
which include flogging and forced residency.

Two letters come forward that give one an insight into Father
Serra's reputed quality of forgiveness, and his attitude toward the
Native Californians. Writing to Father Lasuen at Monterey, on
January 12, 1780, Serra said:

> I am grieved exceedingly at Carlos' and Bernardino's con-
> tinued bad conduct. I have a particular affection for them, and
> long for the salvation of their souls. With that end in view, I
> would not feel sorry(,) no matter what punishment they
> (receive), if they would commute to prison for life, or in the
> stocks every day(,) since then it would be easier for them to die
> well. (Tibesar 1956: 419, 421, 423)

In another letter written from Monterey to Father Lasuen on
December 8, 1781, Father Serra talks about the Colorado River Indian
revolt, and offers advice on a course of punishment should the
Kumeyaay again revolt at San Diego. Father Serra said:

> Your people at San Diego will be well acquainted with the revolt
> of the Colorado River Indians. But tell them to wait a while and
> see if (Colorado Indians) come out as easily as they did from
> their revolt. They indeed will be happy as long as they are quiet.
> If once they were to rise up again in revolt, they would certainly
> have to pay double – both for the old and for the new.

Home Rule – Under Padres

Even though the self-professed goal of the mission system was to prepare the natives for eventual independence in 10 years, the missionaries were very reluctant to grant it, and were jealous of others intruding on what they considered to be their private domain. Often the missionaries would select the candidates whom the neophytes could vote for as alcalde, if not make the appointment outright. If the appointed alcalde became too independent, especially contradicting the wishes of the mission padres, steps were taken to put him in his place. Two letters written by Father Serra shed some light on his thoughts concerning what he perceives to be the inability and irresponsibility of Indigenous leadership, and their punishment. Writing to Father Lasuen on August 16, 1779, Father Serra advised:

> If (the military's) intention is to get hold of Indians to work for them, pay close attention as to whom the orders are directed – whether it is to the Indian alcalde, or to Your Reverences. You will have plenty of opportunities, in one way or another, to upset their plans. But stand firm against them . . . because no Indian has authority to dispose of his people without the consent of the Fathers. (Tibesar 1956: 365, 367)

The second letter written to Governor Felipe de Neve, on January 7, 1780, is more revealing in stressing the missionary's absolute right to punish Indigenous leaders and commoners alike.

> I had pointed out, on a number of occasions, to Your Lordship the inability I detected in (the Indians) for managing their own affairs . . . And while the situation appears to be as I have described it, it also would seem that the best method to rid ourselves of all annoyances would be (the) arrest and punishment of the entire group of malcontents. This would be a great advantage, even if only considering that it would put a stop to the many offenses which they commit against the law of God . . . the natives of these parts will, in the course of time, develop into useful vassals for our religion and for our State . . . (Tibesar 1956: 407-415)

Devil's Advocate, Culpable Ignorance

One of the best kept secrets of the canonization debate, the report of the Devil's Advocate, has been hidden from objective scholarly review. The investigation of the Devil's Advocate is a required step in the canonization process. Why has his report been hidden so long? The report of the Devil's Advocate should be made available for scholarly review, not the *Reader's Digest,* or National Security clearance version, but the original unabridged report of the Devil's Advocate. After all, what is there to hide?

Even Father Guest admitted within the Serra Report that there were "grave cultural errors made by the Spanish Franciscans." The Serra Report tried to justify the creation of extremely filthy living conditions in which diseases ran rampant, and forced residency within them, as "inculpable ignorance" (Costo 1987: 227). The Native Californians after becoming neophytes were not extended the right of "inculpable ignorance;" instead, they were held very culpable when discovered practicing their ancient religious beliefs, or acting to preserve their dignity as a sovereign people.

From an Indigenous perspective the justification of "inculpable ignorance" is analogous to someone in a humanistic fervor, wanting to plant fruit trees to feed the hungry masses, but knowing nothing of biology. The zealot plants his seeds in good faith and leaves, but when the plants grow up they produce stinging nettle and thorns, not food. Due to "inculpable ignorance," the legacy of misery created by the nettles and thorns in the fields and homes of the Indigenous residents is not the zealot's fault.

Again the problem between the apologists and the detractors lay in their interpretation as to what is considered "moderate punishment" or "human rights abuses." Cited by Sherburne Cook, a letter from Father Serra to Soler written from Monterey, on February 10, 1784 concerns the punishment of the Gabrielenos who confessed to organizing a mission revolt. Father Serra in that letter considered a moderate punishment to be twenty-five lashes (Cook 1976: 128). Then there was the novenario, which consisted of twenty-five lashes for nine days, or longer if the crime was severe enough.

So now we end up playing a numbers game. Twenty-five lashes or less is considered saintly, twenty-five to, let's say, fifty would be a venial sin, and over fifty would be like a felony which could exempt one from canonization. Obviously from the Indigenous perspective, the floggings, imprisonment, forced residency, the constant demand for labor, and the strict discipline of the mission padres were *a violation of Indigenous human rights.* In the words of a young medicine woman, Toypurina, who was arrested for organizing a revolt at mission San Gabriel:

I hate the padres and all of you (addressing her military interrogators) for living here on my native soil – for trespassing upon the land of my forefathers and despoiling our tribal domains (Temple 1958: 148).

Conclusion

Not citing civil or canon law, but in the words of Jesus himself, where does he speak of the methods instituted by Father Serra within the mission system, such as floggings, imprisonment, and forced residency to convert their brethren to Christianity?

Going to Scripture, in Matthew 7:15-19, it says, "beware of false teachers, who come to you in sheep's clothing but inwardly are ravenous wolves. You will know them by their fruits. Are grapes gathered from thorns, or figs from thistles? So, every sound tree bears good fruit, but the bad tree bears evil fruit. A sound tree cannot bear evil fruit, nor can a bad tree bear good fruit. Every tree that does not bear good fruit is cut down and thrown into the fire." In the mission revolts Toypurina, Pacomio, Bernardo, Estanislao (Stanislaus), Francisco, Carlos, Benito, Andres, and many other neophytes have tried more than once to burn the mission tree.

To degrade an entire race of people, in order to strengthen a case for canonization, is not only degrading to the concept of sainthood, but a sinful act in itself. If the justification for Father Serra's canonization is based on his alleged elevation of the Native Californian's condition through the missions system, then it should be the Native Californian community leading this cause. Is it not strange that most of the Native community are apathetic or leading the cause to block canonization? The expropriation of Indigenous lands, forced residency, and floggings are considered by the Indigenous community to be human rights abuses, and the fruits of the "Mission Tree." Many within the Native California community, with the support of the larger Native American community, are still chopping away, to cast the "Mission Tree" into the Fire.

Jose Ignacio Rivera is a student, teacher, writer, and Native American, currently doing doctoral work in California ethno-history at University of California, Berkeley.

Native Americans were perceived as "heathens" – within one century after the "discovery" of America, 50 million non-Christian natives were killed by Catholic and Christian soldiers, explorers, and missionaries.

Missionaries

I shall give thee the heathen for thine inheritance and the uttermost parts of the earth for thy possession. Thou shalt break them with a rod of iron.

— Psalms 2:8,9

They came with a Bible and their religion – stole our land, crushed our spirit . . . and now tell us we should be thankful to the "Lord" for being saved.

— Chief Pontiac

Leading up to the overthrow of Hawaii's Queen Liliuo Kalani in 1893 by an alliance of churches, missionaries and sugar growers was the battle for the soul of its native people. Reverend Asa Thurston reminded his brethen "we missionaries need men who have their eyes fixed on the glory of God in the salvation of the heathen." While overthrowing the monarchy illegally and violently, the Congregational Board of Missions reminded the missionaries "you are to aim at nothing less . . . than raising the whole people to a state of Christian civilization."

— Theon Wright, *The Disenchanted Islands*

Missionaries are perfect nuisances and leave every place worse than they found it.

— Charles Dickens

The Catholic Church

Dial-the-Pope: 1-900-568-7722

Even though John Wycliffe died peacefully at home in bed on New Year's Eve, the Church exhumed his body 44 years later. For the crime of translating the Latin Bible into English, they burned his bones, and scattered the ashes in a nearby river. (see illustration in *Life As A Freethinker*, page 422.)

— Fact

But because I have been enjoined, by this Holy Office, altogether to abandon the false opinion which maintains that the Sun is the center and immovable, and forbidden to hold defend, or teach, the said false doctrine in any manner . . . I abjure, curse, and detest the said errors and heresies, and generally every other error and sect contrary to the said Holy Church . . .

— Galileo Galilei

No good Catholic would kneel before an image of Isis if he knew that it was a she. Yet every one of the mythic motifs now dogmatically attributed to Mary as a historic human being belongs also – and belonged in the period and place of the development of her cult – to that goddess mother of all things, of whom both Mary and Isis were local manifestations: the mother-bride of the dead and resurrected god, whose earliest known representations now must be assigned to a date as early, at least, as c. 5500 B.C.

— *Women in Mythology*

E.T. a Catholic?

Steve Yozwiak, Arizona Republic

The Catholic Church could have a new missionary frontier on its hands. That's assuming the new telescope in southeastern Arizona that is run by the church's Vatican Observatory locates planets orbiting other stars – and that those planets have intelligent inhabitants.

"The church would be obliged to address the question of whether extraterrestrials might be brought within the fold and baptized," the Rev. George Coyne, director of the Vatican Observatory, said in a story published recently in London's Daily Telegraph. "One would need to put some questions to him (an alien), such as: 'Have you ever experienced something similar to Adam and Eve, in other words, original sin? Do you also know a Jesus who has redeemed you?' "

The Rev. Chris Corbally, a staff astronomer and project scientist in Tucson, said the possibility of encountering alien life raises profound theological questions. "Surely, it would be fascinating to have a real encounter with another intelligence," Corbally said. "I think we'd have to consider whether we should baptize him."

Corbally denied that the Vatican Observatory is teaming up with the National Aeronautics and Space Administration to "spread the Gospel to extraterrestrials." But he said the Vatican's new telescope on Mount Graham, 70 miles northeast of Tucson, is expected to be capable of detecting emerging solar systems when it becomes operational in spring.

The telescope will be part of the new Mount Graham International Observatory, which is overseen by the University of Arizona. Corbally said the Vatican's telescope on Mount Graham, with a 6-foot-diameter mirror, is expected to be one of the most accurate in the world.

"We would be open to that sort of thing," Corbally said of the search for extraterrestrial life. "Certainly, some of our efforts should be directed toward that." But he added that the Vatican has no plans to convert beings from other worlds. "We're not about to rush off to every UFO sighting to try to meet an alien," he said.

In addition to the Vatican Telescope, the $200 million Mount Graham International Observatory is to include three other telescopes. The Columbus Project, the world's most powerful telescope, is a joint venture of the University of Arizona, Ohio State University and the Italian National Observatory in Arcetri, Italy.

Fundamentalism
Now

DON'T LET THEM GET AWAY WITH IT!

Well organized, well financed, and focused, the Religious Right has their eyes on school boards, the Republican Party and the White House. Their blueprint is a theocracy for all. Watch out for 1996!

The Religious Right's March Across America

Once again the Religious Right has taken upon itself to save America. The goals are the same – elimination of the separation of Church and State, establish prayer in schools, creationism and the establishment of a Christian Nation.

This time the Christian Right is more armed, more financed and more desperate.

— *Tim Leedom*

I started Christian Coalition five years ago because I saw a need for a large national grassroots citizen action organization that would speak out against the anti-Christian bigotry we see in the news coverage, on university campuses, in the schools, in the political debate, and in many other areas of American life. I saw a need for an organization that would stand up for our values and our beliefs. I wanted to make sure Christian and pro-family Americans gained a voice in our government.

- Over the last 24 months, Christian Coalition has . . .
- Sponsored 103 Citizen Action Training Schools all across America to teach Christians how to make their voices heard in government.
- Established 425 new chapters in all 50 states, bringing the total number of Christian Coalition chapters to 922
- Distributed 40 million non-partisan voter guides to inform citizens where candidates for elected office stand on key issues.
- Distributed 25 million Congressional Scorecards to ensure an informed Christian vote.
- Opened a fully-staffed governmental affairs office in Washington to ensure that people of faith are represented before Congress.

— *Pat Robertson*

1994 Religious Right Agenda Report
compiled by *People for the American Way*

ALABAMA

The *Christian Coalition* is urging its Alabama members to contact the Mobile County school superintendent to protest a directive from district officials telling principals to discontinue Bible readings over the intercom.

ARIZONA

Traditional Values Coalition of Arizona, with help from Lou Sheldon's *Traditional Values Coalition,* has begun to collect signatures for a petition drive to place a Colorado-style anti-gay measure on the ballot. Lou Sheldon attended the press conference announcing the petition drive and has promised to contribute at least $250,000.

ARKANSAS

In Little Rock, Lt. Governor Mike Huckabee took advantage of the Governor's absence to proclaim February 27th - March 5th as "Christian Heritage Week," after the Governor had refused. Huckabee had been asked to sign the proclamation by members of the group, *Arkansas Christians for America,* which ran ads during the last presidential campaign under the banner, "Christian Beware."

CALIFORNIA

In Vista, on-going controversy on the Religious Right-dominated school board prompted threats of a recall effort by citizens groups who cited the board's efforts to push creationism into the curriculum, on-going attempts to introduce *Sex Respect,* an abstinence-based curriculum, and the rejection of a grant aimed at low-income minority students. Rev. Billy Falling, head of the *Christian Voter's League,* threatened a lawsuit saying that the three targeted board members were discriminated against because they are Christian.

COLORADO

The Coalition on Revival has firmed up plans to move to Colorado Springs and expects to move by June. Their *Kingdom College,* expected to serve as a "Green Beret boot camp" and eventually train as many as 200 political activists a year, will open in August.

CONNECTICUT

A group called the *Committee to Save Our Schools* (SOS) has formed to fight Connecticut's statewide school reform plan, which they describe as *Outcome Based Education*.

DISTRICT OF COLUMBIA

Martin Mawyer's *Christian Action Network* announced plans to hold *The Rally to Restore America* conference in March in Washington, D.C. Mawyer called the conference a "rally for decency and religious freedom." Along with a fundraising letter to fund the conference, Mawyer sent petitions to his followers to demand that the Republican leadership elect someone to replace retiring House Minority Leader Bob Michel who will "oppose President Clinton and the Democrats on crucial issues...like gay rights, the National Endowment for the Arts, abortion, and the appointment of radical feminists to serve in the government."

FLORIDA

In Jacksonville, a group called *Liberty and Justice for All* attempted to ban *The Autobiography of Malcolm X* from all school libraries claiming that the book teaches children to be drug dealers and contains anti-white racism. Though ultimately unsuccessful, the group did convince a review committee to require parental permission before the book can be read by middle school students. Susan Lamb, the former president of the group says, "it has a biased presentation of one religion – Islam – against another – Christianity."

GEORGIA

In early March, the Georgia House passed HB 1950, which would require that library materials be reviewed by a local media committee if 1%t or 500 community residents objected to the material.

HAWAII

The legislature has approved a measure that defines marriage and asserts its role in changing any future policy. The law is aimed at nullifying a Hawaii Supreme Court ruling last year that said that denying marriage licenses to homosexual couples appeared to violate the Hawaii Constitution. Following that ruling, Religious Right and "profamily" groups threatened boycotts of the state, and a local group, Common Sense Now, formed to oppose changes in the law.

IDAHO

Promise Keepers, a Christian men's organization, will hold one of its 1994 regional conferences in Boise. Regional conferences are scheduled in four other cities.

ILLINOIS

In Chicago, a new group formed by Randall Terry and Patrick Mahoney of *Operation Rescue* called *Loyal Opposition* held a rally as part of an eight-cities tour to call for President Clinton's impeachment. The group says Clinton is "flagrantly promoting rebellion against God's word" and calls the Clinton Administration "the single most unChristian administration in the history of this country."

INDIANA

In the 9th Congressional District, Michael Bailey, who created the graphic anti-abortion ads used in several campaigns across the country in 1992, has said that he plans to run again in 1994.

IOWA

Anti-abortion rights electoral gains have made it likely that the Iowa legislature will pass laws mandating parental notification for minors and requiring clinics to report how many abortions they perform.

KANSAS

In Prairie Village, James Dobson's *Focus on the Family* ran a full page ad in the Kansas City Star to refute a local minister's sermon objecting to religious groups' political activities. The sermon, which was later reprinted in the *New York Times* and other papers, was entitled, *Government Is Not God's Work*.

KENTUCKY

The Kentucky Education Reform Act, in operation since 1991, has recently come under fire from conservative and Religious Right activists. One opponent told the *Lexington Herald-Leader* that the plan was designed to promote "humanism" and "witchcraft." Led by local activists and groups, including *The Family Foundation*, a state-wide group affiliated with James Dobson's *Focus on the Family*, opponents are trying to overturn the education reform program by legislative action.

LOUISIANA

The *Christian Coalition* of Caddo Parish opened a new Shreveport office. State Representative Melissa Flournoy commented that she and the *Christian Coalition* "share many of the same Christian philosophies, such as the importance of traditional family values."

MAINE

Jasper Wyman, former head of the Christian Civic League and leader of the state's antigay ballot initiative campaign, is running for governor on the 1994 ballot.

MARYLAND

In Salisbury, residents led by local pastors demanded that the *Wicomico County Free Library* ban two books dealing with homosexuality. The books, *Heather Has Two Mommies* and *Daddy's Roommate* drew the ire of Pastor Phillip Alan Lee who registered the first complaint. Lee said the books are "geared to change the attitudes and behavior of young children." After the library board of trustees voted 14-2 in favor of the books, Lee said he planned to take the matter to the county council.

MASSACHUSETTS

The president of the Massachusetts Senate has joined with the Catholic Church in calls for an amendment to the Massachusetts Constitution to remove the state's ban on financial aid to private schools. If successful, a referendum would go before the voters on the next ballot.

MICHIGAN

Following the Michigan Legislature's vote to rework funding for the state's school system, a coalition called the *Michigan Coalition for Parent's Choice* has formed to push for vouchers. The coalition includes *Michigan Family Forum, Citizens for Traditional Values, Concerned Women for America, Eagle Forum* and *Friends of Michigan Schools.*

MINNESOTA

Conservatives at the *University of Minnesota* have requested more than $12,000 in student fees to open the "J. Danforth Quayle *Traditional Family Values Cultural Center.* If funded, the center will run a referral service for single pregnant women, publish a newsletter, organize events and "provide a forum for the traditional American family values as espoused by our former vice president."

MISSISSIPPI

In Jackson, Bishop Knox, the principal suspended for allowing prayers on the high school intercom over the objections of his superiors was back in school and then out again. Knox was ordered reinstated by Hinds County chancery Court judge with back pay. The judge also ruled that Jackson School Board members must write guidelines to allow school prayer. Knox is being represented by the *American Family Association*.

MISSOURI

Pro-family forces led by the *Missouri Family Network* were successful in defeating a statewide ballot initiative to allow riverboat gambling. MFN organized in churches to get out the vote to defeat the measure.

MONTANA

A group called the *Helena Parents Commission* held a series of meetings at various schools throughout the district to organize opposition to school reform proposals in Helena. Peg Luksik's anti-OBE film has been circulating in the community and opponents have been using materials produced by the *Eagle Forum*.

NEBRASKA

Traditional Values Coalition of Nebraska has established a strong state presence, regularly testifying at hearings for state and local school boards on "traditional values." Cindi Lamm, the new state director of TVC-Nebraska, most recently testified against comprehensive sex education in schools and is putting together a State of Nebraska Voter's Guide.

NEW HAMPSHIRE

The state Senate Judiciary committee heard testimony on a bill that would prohibit discrimination based on sexual orientation. Those testifying against the bill included representatives from several churches as well as *Concerned Women for America*.

NEW JERSEY

Several attempts to initiate a voucher system are expected in the state this year. Governor Christine Todd Whitman made vouchers an issue in her campaign against incumbent Jim Florio, promising to set up an experimental voucher system. In Jersey City, Mayor Bret Schundler has been pushing voucher.

NEW YORK

The Institute for Justice has filed suit against the Mamaroneck school system arguing that requirements for community service violate constitutional prohibitions against involuntary servitude. A similar suit was filed in Chapel Hill, NC. The Institute for Justice has also sued school systems over vouchers.

NORTH CAROLINA

In Matthews, 25 families have initiated a lawsuit to prevent a church that ministers to gays from holding worship services in a building owned by the congregation. The *New Life Metropolitan Community Church* had requested a variance from the zoning board after purchasing a garage building that it intended to renovate. Residents of the town say they object to homosexuals worshipping in their community.

NORTH DAKOTA

The *Christian Coalition* organized meetings in Bismarck and Fargo in an effort to establish statewide chapters. North Dakota was one of only three states that did not have a statewide group.

OHIO

In Cincinnati, two new members of the City Council have asked the City Solicitor to draft legislation repealing Cincinnati's entire human rights ordinance. The two council members say that last November's successful campaign to repeal the sexual orientation section of the ordinance shows that Cincinnati residents are opposed to granting "special protection" for particular groups.

OKLAHOMA

The *American Family Association<D has renewed the campaign against the Corporation for Public Broadcasting*, citing the PBS broadcast of Annistead Maupin's *Tales of the City* "propaganda" designed to

"promote the homosexual lifestyle and agenda." The state legislature considered legislation to slash funding.

OREGON

A new PAC called Help America has formed to place a *Life Begins at Conception* measure on the ballot.

PENNSYLVANIA

In Philadelphia, *Focus on the Family* has set out after a Philadelphia multcultural curriculum. A Family News in Focus radio broadcast called the program a "Rainbow-like curriculum," a reference to the much-maligned and much-distorted *Children of the Rainbow* curriculum that was torpedoed in New York City by Religious Right organizing.

SOUTH CAROLINA

In Columbia, the *Christian Coalition* held a rally to launch a $1.4 million national campaign to defeat President Clinton's health care plan. The Coalition distributed packets containing congressional phone numbers and anti-Clinton plan postcards to mail to Congress. Rallies were scheduled for six other cities as well.

TENNESSEE

In Chattanooga, anti-choice activists opened the *National Memorial for the Unborn* in what was formerly the city's only clinic that performed abortions. The clinic was purchased by the *Pro-Life Majority Coalition* of Chattanooga last year. A feature of the memorial is the *Memorial Plaque Display* modeled after the Wailing Wall in Israel, which will include 35,000 plaques commemorating abortions performed at the center. Plans also call for a pool of tears, a chapel, and educational displays.

TEXAS

In Dallas, *Life Dynamics*, an anti-choice group, invited attorneys to its first abortion malpractice conference. The March 4th conference offered an "inside look at the abortion industry" and provided resources for attorneys who want to file suits.

VIRGINIA

Since Inauguration Day, Governor George Allen has shown that the Religious Right support for his candidacy was well placed. Allen has appointed a number of radical right figures including Kay Cole James of the *Family Research Council,* anti-choice activist Michael E. Thomas and Jesse Helms associate Becky Norton Dunlop. For his Inauguration Prayer Breakfast, he invited David Barton, of *Wall-Builders,* whose anti-church state separation views are popular in Religious Right circles.

WASHINGTON

In Lynden, a challenge to the book *A Thousand Acres* by Jane Smiley in the Lynden High School has led to the defeat of a tax levy for the school district. Though the school's curriculum advisory committee voted to keep the book, the principal dropped the book from the curriculum because the controversy refused to die down. The *Washington Alliance of Families* led the protests against the book.

WYOMING

A 1994 ballot measure, sponsored by the *Unseen Hands Prayer Circle,* would prohibit abortions in Wyoming except in cases of life endangerment In addition the measure would criminalize the use of certain contraceptives like the pill, Norplant, and the IUD. A district judge has rejected a challenge to the ballot proposal by pro-choice forces and the issue appears headed to the state Supreme Court.

In January, Vice-President Dan Quayle spoke at a training conference of religious-right activists in Fort Lauderdale, whose theme was *Reclaiming America*, and before the event began he stood at attention as the crowd of more than two thousand rose, faced a flag with a cross on it; and with hands on hearts, recited in unison, "I pledge allegiance to the Christian flag, and to the Saviour, for whose Kingdom it stands, one Saviour, crucified, risen, and coming again, with life and liberty for all who believe."

— Sidney Blumenthal, *New Yorker*, July 18, 1994

Born-Again Student Meets Secular Professor

Delos McKown

A while ago I chanced upon an instructor of English composition at Auburn University. She looked a little perplexed as she hailed me from a hallway. Knowing that I had something to do with secular humanism, she wanted to put a question to me. It seems that she had a female student who was polite and pleasant but would do none of her assignments and would turn in no written work.

When the instructor asked why the student was handing in no assigned work, the student said that her pastor, back home, had told her that when she got to college she should not do anything that a humanist told her to do. "It's all very simple," I said, "the poor girl cannot tell the difference between the kind of humanists who teach in the *humanities* and the kind of humanists who have a particular world view, one that profoundly aggrieves her pastor." To this I added, "Her pastor may not be able to tell the difference either." This absurd, funny, sad situation prompted me to write what follows.

After a liberal era of relative tranquility, from about 1935 to 1965, the ancient enmity between Athens (reason) and Jerusalem (religion) has flared up again. As our century winds down, taking our millennium with it, this battle is almost certain to spread and intensify throughout America. Arrayed on the one side are the forces of healthy skepticism, respect for logic, objective history, and the scientific method. On the other side are intense faith in special revelation, trust in biblical inerrancy, and the fear of the Bible-god that masquerades as wisdom. In human terms, the battle pits the urbane, tolerant, humanistically oriented citizen against people whom I like to call Fundagelicals, i.e., Fundamentalists, Evangelicals, and assorted religious rightists.

The front lines in the conflict between Athens and Jerusalem have been for some time (and remain) in public school classrooms. Trench warfare already characterizes many a local school board. Occasionally a significant skirmish occurs in a state board of education. Legislators at various levels are often conscripted (or volunteer), and not even the highest federal officials are exempt. Moreover, the theater of operations is now widening to include higher education.

The setting for the following analysis is the state institution of higher learning wherein the fundagelical student (who is most likely born-again) encounters methods of inquiry, critical standards, and course content that are profoundly unsettling to his/her faith. Our student also encounters people who are equally anathema, namely, instructors who are secularists (on principle or out of indifference) and liberal theists of various stripes. We need not force our student to meet what inferior newspapers call an "avowed atheist." Nor does it matter whether the secularist or liberal theist is a scientist by training or a "humanitist" (my newly coined word for anyone having to do professionally with the humanities).

The institutional setting in which our combatants vie with each other nestles in a cultural cocoon which must never be overlooked. Any society that can:

- accept a Savior-King as its deity and still be democratic politically,
- subscribe to the other-worldly virtues of Christianity and simultaneously be pragmatic, capitalistic, and fun-loving,
- adopt a theistic deontology in theoretical ethics and at the same time be Utilitarian in practice,
- wait expectantly (even eagerly) for the imminent return of King Jesus while pouring billions of dollars into education, research, and development (thus planning for a more distant future)

. . . is a society that can entertain a jumble of exceedingly diverse ideas and not perceive these to be incongruous when juxtaposed.

In liberal, tolerant times, the juxtaposition of incongruous, discordant notions can be more or less overlooked. As long as each person is sincere in belief and everyone is perceived as trying to get to the same place anyway, well, what difference does it make that some people (in this most scientific of centuries) still believe that the universe is not more than 10,000 years old, that Adam was created as an animated mud ball (thanks to Gerald Larue for this one!) whereas Eve was contrived from one of the mud ball's ribs, and that snakes are condemned to a diet of dirt? Besides, for Americans at least, to argue about religion is not only perceived to be futile but also impolite. Finally, one can always hope that, given time and a chance to reflect, the benighted will come to their senses and forsake their mistaken views. Thus, a live-and-let-live attitude respecting religion is generally adopted, especially in liberal, tolerant (and, perhaps, naive) times.

But our time – more conservative and less tolerant, religiously at least – is characterized by the recrudescence of scriptural literalism and the long-discredited belief, still espoused by legions, that the Bible is without error – in its "original autographs" at any rate. Of course nobody today has seen these primary materials from the Bible-god's pen, but (to the faithful) they can be depended on to resemble very closely the King James translation. Instead of being embarrassed or reticent over holding these and similar views, today's Fundagelicals have become exceedingly assertive in promulgating their religious views, in fighting the hated enemy (secular humanism), and in foisting their faith on others.

If they fail to re-make the public school system as an adjunct of their brand of religion, they will at least try strenuously to muzzle it so that nothing inimical to their faith is taught therein, or even heard. Failing that, they will create their own schools with their own tailor-made texts and curricula. The living products of these two kinds of schools are now entering our colleges and universities.

Replete with discredited beliefs, inhaling deeply the religious atmosphere of the time, and ever on the lookout for the hated secular humanist, our fundagelical student meets the secularized professor head-on in any one of a vast array of courses. Conspicuous among these are courses in critical thinking, general science, biology, genetics, astronomy, biochemistry, archaeology, anthropology, psychology, pre-history, ancient history, biblical literature, linguistics (particularly concerning the origins of language), philosophy (especially ethics, metaphysics, epistemology, and the philosophy of science), and physics (especially cosmology). Courses in world literature may also aggrieve our student.

Convinced that the Bible-god is the genuine article and that the fear of this deity is the beginning of all true wisdom, our student is prepared to follow the logic of these premises relentlessly. Not knowing that there is no fact per se or constellation of facts that can guarantee the objective existence of the Bible-god, the student will point fancifully to facts ranging all the way from continuing high church attendance in America to the mean distance between the sun and the earth (which happy fact prevents our planetary home from becoming either a gigantic cinder or an equally gigantic icicle).

Blissfully unaware that no system of natural theology has proved to be valid, the student will try to restate the tired old cosmological and teleological arguments and, when foiled, will lapse into analogical reasoning, weak and decrepit though it is. It is as though Hume and Kant had never lived!

If the secularized professor demurs, our student will resort to the Bible itself as the guarantee that the deity of its pages is the real one. When challenged to show that this deity not only exists but is also the author of those pages, the Fundagelical asserts that the Bible can be trusted absolutely, because it is inerrant, something no man or men, acting as author(s) could achieve. Inquiry will soon reveal that the person who makes this astonishing claim need not have read the Bible much nor to have understood what little was read. The assertion of its inerrancy is quite simply an article of faith (or based on circular reasoning, if reasoning at all) and as such passes beyond all question, for the believer at least.

Once the foregoing is accepted (as it is by millions upon millions), the fearful (and therefore wise) believer has but to look into the inerrant text to gain the safe kinds of information, belief in which pleases the Bible-god. Looking into this text, one finds, for example, St. Paul in the act of denigrating literacy, logic, and learning (I Cor. 1:20), or finds his recipe for self-stultification as the only way to wisdom (I Cor. 3:18), or discovers his general warning against the deceits of vain philosophy (Col. 2:8). To continue with examples, one can also find a four-cornered, flat earth floating on water (Is. 11:12, Ps. 24:2, 136:6), with heaven above and the earth below (I Thess. 4:16-17), the very rapid creation of everything in just one week (Gen. 1:1-2:2), the instantaneous gift of language to the one-day old Adam (Gen. 2:19), death as the punishment for sin rather than as the natural end of all organisms (Gen. 2:17), the notion of demonic infestation as causative of sin and sickness (Mk. 1:21-34, 2:6-9), the idea that seeds must die in the ground before new life can appear from them (Jn.12:24, I Cor. 15:36), the expectation that the moon will turn to blood at the end of history (Acts 2:20), and countless other oddities, not to say absurdities.

When asked why any sane person in the 20th century should believe any of the foregoing falsehoods about nature and humanity, our student has a ready answer . . . Miracles!

By now the professor who had hoped that none of this would come up (or that if it did it could be evaded) and whose superior may have decreed, "Avoid all discussion of religion with students," has had enough. So our exasperated professor unloads some or all of the following points on the student:

- Any fact, of course, can be interpreted theistically, but no fact requires it. So the question of deity remains just that – a question. This question cannot be answered by faith, except to the psychological satisfaction of the believer. Psychological satisfactions, it should be noted, are often illusory.

- Both science and history, as modes of inquiry, can proceed successfully without any assumption of or reliance on notions of divine purpose in nature or in human affairs. In short, cosmic and historical teleology are optional.

- The universe is not clearly and obviously an artifact or like one. To assume without adequate evidence that it is and that it must, therefore, have had an artificer is to beg the question – to commit a fundamental fallacy in reasoning. To associate the result of this fallacy with the Bible-god is to make a serious blunder worse.

- If an intelligent, rational artificer (of the universe) existed (or still exists) and at some time provided for rational self-disclosure to human beings, then that revelation has yet to be identified as such. Certainly it cannot be the book called the Holy Bible, for that collection of writings is full of contradictions, misstatements of fact, and conflicting interpretations.

- Though often reported, miracles, so-called, are suspect, because human beings lack the criteria for discriminating between any divinely engineered event and any rare (even unprecedented), unexplained (at the moment), but perfectly natural phenomenon. So, until distinguishing criteria are apprehended and explicated, nothing that has happened can legitimately be called a miracle. To do so is to beg the question again.

- Modern science has provided humankind with the best techniques for testing, confirming, or disconfirming ideas yet discovered. Its explanatory power, predictive ability, and technological fruitfulness provide the best "taste-test" for the "puddings of human experience." Science does not operate on the revelation (i.e., self-disclosure) of anything, on prayer, meditation, or the pious reading of "inerrant" texts but rather on technical training, human insight, hunches, free and open inquiry, the rigorous use of logic, and the willingness to specify what it would take to falsify any particular hypothesis tentatively offered as explanatory of whatever is at issue.

- Modern historiography, though not capable of experimentation per se (and therefore not scientific in the same sense as is chemistry, for example) proceeds, nevertheless, as far as its subject matter permits, along lines compatible with the hard sciences. It is noteworthy that modern historiography and textual criticism approach "inerrant" texts as they approach any other, but more modest, text, the "divine variable" being unapprehended and unusable – and thus dispensable.

Our fundagelical student, unfazed, now plays his/her ace with aplomb. Everything the professor has just said is based on the professor's faith and on that alone. The student admits readily enough to living within a circle of beliefs based on faith, but on faith in the one true deity. The professor's faith, though perhaps not consciously or deliberately based on faith in Satan, is nevertheless inspired by Satan, as our student sees it, making the professor into a malign tool of secular humanism with its "godless" reliance on evolution, moral relativism, and mere human rationality.

Our student is aided and abetted in this extraordinary line of reasoning not only by his/her theological preparation (rich in how to beg the question without ever knowing it – another name for faith) but also by a pernicious misunderstanding of democracy that is rife in America. Many, perhaps most, Americans seem to think that since we are all equal as citizens, there must also exist a democracy among ideas, each person's beliefs being on all fours with everybody else's beliefs, despite the strongest evidence to the contrary. Thus, nothing more is needed than the credentials of sincere belief for the ignorant to correct the learned or for the simple-minded believer to contradict the wise of this world and thereby to set the latter straight.

The bottom line in all of this is that (for the Fundagelical) the experiences of guilt and of subsequent grace (i.e., the certitude of forgiveness, the assurance of eternal weal, and the avoidance of everlasting woe) are as real, and self-certifyingly true as are sensory experiences of the everyday world and more to be trusted by far than the deliverances of reason. It does not, of course, ever occur to our Fundagelical that our common human experiences of guilt and grace are predicated squarely on our nature, i.e., on our sociobiology and on nothing else. The Fundagelical dismisses this out of hand as utterly trivial and hastens to embrace the *metaphysical* as the one true dimension of reality. The result of this is that the subjective contents of religious experience are rendered objective and concrete by the uncritical mind. The experience of being born-again, for example, is not to be treated as just a welcome psychological fact but is taken as the objective result of "divine" agency operating to create good in the believer's life. Thus does Jerusalem reply to Athens.

The chasm between fundagelical faith and secular science that could still be papered over in recent, liberal times cannot be papered over now when Fundagelicals, supported by powerful political forces, go on the offensive against secular humanism. The secular humanism which they mistakenly hold to be responsible for America's alleged apostasy (and resulting decline) and which they attack zestfully and dishonestly just happens to incorporate the epistemological bases of modern scientific knowledge.

Is it any wonder that the American Academy of Sciences and numerous other scientific organizations have finally and ever so reluctantly had to bestir themselves to refute that fundagelical farce known as "Scientific Creationism," all the while pretending that there is no conflict between science and religion? Warren Burger, former Chief Justice of the Supreme Court, might as well have whistled a hymn as to have ruled (in Lynch v. Donnelly, 1984) that the Constitution mandates the accommodation (rather than the mere toleration) of all religions, with hostility toward none. Those who labor in the leading research universities and those who end up teaching, at whatever level, whether in the nation's primary and secondary schools (public or private) or in higher education cannot accommodate all of their subject matter to the religious sensibilities of all of their students, nor should they.

This is impossible when fact and fiction, validity and invalidity, strong probability and equally strong improbability are at issue. To give equal time to the stork in obstetrics is neither to teach medical science nor the methods that undergird it. To teach critical thinking but simultaneously to exempt religion from its scrutiny is not to teach critical thinking. To attempt to reconcile Copernicus with Ptolemy for the sake of those fundagelical children whose religion requires geocentricity is both monstrous and impossible. Moreover, for the teachers of the nation to have to accommodate what they know to figments of imagination (such as "Scientific Creationism") in which their students have faith, is to create a generation alien to science and the scientific method and thereby to stultify the entire nation, crippling its competitiveness with other advanced societies.

The only religions worth observing, preserving, and celebrating, are those whose theologies and teleologies are permanently compatible with advancing knowledge. Academics, humanitists (sic), scientists, and members of the professions (including teachers at every level) should now rise up to challenge, to inhibit, to frustrate, and eventually to defeat (ideally through education) all who would hold knowledge and its dissemination hostage to any kind of ancient faith or modern irrationality.

Delos B. McKown, PhD, professor of philosophy, Auburn University. He is the author of With Faith and Fury, *Prometheus Books, 1985, a tragicomic novel of religion in America that satirizes the "Scientific Creationists."*

Jesus has now been reduced to a mantra . . . chanted mindlessly by followers, who have no idea of the relationship of doctrine to history and mythology . . .

— A. A. Snow

An "avowed atheist" is somebody who swears by Almighty God that there is no God. Have you ever met such a person?

— Bill Lindley

Jesus loves me, this I know . . . For the Bible tells me so.

— Popular children's Sunday school song

If fifty million people say a foolish thing, it is still a foolish thing.

— Anatole France

The fish in Christian symbolism represents Jesus Christ, and in the old Roman catacombs, the fish symbol appears frequently. The Greek word for fish is *ichthus* and the early Christians saw in the letters of this word a monogram summarizing their faith: "Iesous CHristos, THeou Uios Soter" (Jesus Christ, Son of God, Savior).

Fish: . . . But the Christian fish-sign was the same as that of the Goddess's yoni or Pearly Gate: two crescent moons forming a *vesica piscis.* Sometimes the Christ child was portrayed inside the *vesica,* which was superimposed on Mary's belly and obviously represented her womb, just as in the ancient symbolism of the Goddess.

A medieval hymn called Jesus "the Little Fish which the Virgin caught in the Fountain." Mary was equated with the virgin Aphrodite-Mari, Marina, who brought forth all the fish in the sea . . .

— *Mythology Dictionary*

Perhaps the saddest part of the story is that, according to our demographic research, all of the television evangelists are vying for a limited donor pool of approximately five million people. The great majority of these people are women, age 49 and older, many of whom are widows living on their husbands' pensions.

These evangelists are not fishers of men, but are in truth keepers of a very small aquarium filled with dying fish.

— Ole Anthony, of the Trinity Foundation,
testifying before a 1987 Congressional subcommittee
(as quoted in *The Wichita Eagle,* January 4, 1992)

Satan knows Jesus Christ is about to return to take over the governments of the world. So he masses his armies at Megiddo to block the Lord's return at Jerusalem.

The great armies of the Beast move from Megiddo into Jerusalem. This is called the battle of Armageddon.

— Rev. 16:16

Armageddon

Grace Halsell

I first went to Jerusalem in 1979 to research a book dealing with Christians, Muslims and Jews. While there I met many third-generation Americans, such as Bobby and Linda Brown of Brooklyn who together with 25 other couples – half of them from the United States – moved onto land of the Palestinians and took the land at gunpoint. They staked off 750 acres and put a strong iron fence around it. Israeli soldiers guard this settlement night and day. That is illegal under every international law.

One evening, we sat under the stars looking at the flickering lights of Palestinian villages. Bobby Brown, with a wave of his arm, said, "All the Palestinians have to leave this land. God gave this land to us, the Jews." This incident made a deep impression on me. I knew Bobby Brown could not use an Uzi – and confiscate land at gunpoint in Brooklyn. What made it all right for him to use a gun to take land from Palestinians? And moreover, why did we as American taxpayers give Israel the money to pay for the weapons – to confiscate Palestinian land? Had God deeded the land to Bobby Brown? Had the Palestinians been living there for 2,000 years, just holding it until Bobby Brown could claim it? I had to ask myself: Did I believe God had a Chosen Land and a Chosen People?

I returned home, and the questions remained. To research these questions, and how I and others felt about them, I signed to go on a conducted tour of the Holy Land with Jerry Falwell. On arrival in Jerusalem, our group went to the Old City and we approached the large Muslim grounds where the Dome of the Rock and Al-Aqsa Mosque are located. "There," said our Israeli guide, pointing to the mosque, "we will build our third temple."

As we left the site, I remarked to Clyde, a retired Minneapolis business executive, that the guide said a temple would be built there. But, I asked, what about the mosque? It is one of the three most sacred shrines in all of Islam – and holy to a billion Muslims around the world. "Oh," said Clyde, "The mosque will be destroyed. One way or another, it has to be removed. You know it's in the Bible that the temple must be built. And there's no other place for it." Clyde was convinced that Jews, aided by Christians, should destroy the mosque, build a temple and reinstate the killing of animals in the temple – all in order to please God.

Many Christians throughout this land feel the same as Clyde. They organized a Temple Mount Foundation to raise money to help Jewish terrorists destroy the Muslim mosque. I talked with several, including Terry Reisenhoover of Oklahoma and the Reverend James deLoach of Houston's Second Baptist Church.

The Rev. DeLoach visited in my apartment in Washington, and was proud to tell me he had raised and spent tens of thousands of dollars to defend Jewish terrorists charged with assaults on the mosque. He was also pleased to relate that he had entertained in his Houston home Jewish *yeshiva* students who were studying how to slaughter animals, to be used as sacrifice inside the temple they hope to build.

The Christians who want the mosque destroyed – and a Jewish temple built – follow a belief system called dispensationalism. In all of the world, in all of history, they place Israel on center stage. They contend that we must all go through seven time periods. The countdown on history began, they tell us, in 1948 – with the gathering of Jews into Palestine and the creation of the modern state of Israel. The dispensationalists believe in a God not of love, but of war: they believe in what is termed Armageddon theology.

Our group also traveled to Megiddo, located about an hour's drive north of Tel Aviv.

As we left the bus, I walked alongside Clyde, the retired business executive. As we looked out over the valley, Clyde exclaimed, "At last! I am viewing the site of Armageddon." We continued to gaze at fields – that in size would be lost in any Texas ranch – and Clyde talked of a 200-million-man army that would invade Israel –"right here," he said, and that a great decisive battle would ensue that would involve all the armies of the earth, and that this battle, involving nuclear weapons, would kill most of the inhabitants of this earth. I remarked that for such a big battle – the valley looked very small. "Oh, no!" Clyde says. "You can get a lot of tanks in there!" Clyde's eyes were shining. "When this battle begins, we – who are Born Again – will be lifted up, raptured –" He assured me he was not worried about the destruction of the earth, because he would not be here. But Up There. Watching. With his escape hatch, he seemed actually to look forward to the destruction of Planet Earth.

A couple of years passed, and I received a colored brochure of a Falwell-sponsored trip. Like the first brochure, it was printed in Israel. In this brochure, Falwell did not once mention that we would be traveling to the Land of Christ. Nor, for that matter, did he once mention the name of Christ. Once we arrived, we had no Christian guide – to any site where Christ was born, died or had his ministry. There was not a single planned visit to a Christian church – or a plan to meet any of the Christians living there, whose forebears have lived in Palestine since the days of Christ.

We had only Israeli guides, and the focus clearly was on military aspects. The Israeli guides gave us endless explanations of why the Israelis should keep all the land of historic Palestine, leaving nothing for the Palestinians.

Once we were on a bus tour, and I thought surely we would stop in Nazareth. "No," said the Israeli guide. The bus would not stop in Nazareth. No one contested the guide's decision. On the outskirts of Nazareth, however, our Israeli guide changed his mind. "We will stop in Nazareth for 20 minutes," he announced – "to use the toilet facilities." And thus we stopped. We left Nazareth without having seen it.

We proceeded to Jerusalem, where Falwell chose to honor Ariel Sharon, the burly general who masterminded the invasion of Lebanon, which injured and killed 200,000 Palestinians and Lebanese, most of them civilians. In introducing Sharon, Falwell said that in the annals of history, only a few great men came along. He named George Washington, Abraham Lincoln – and Ariel Sharon!

On another night, Falwell gave a big banquet – to honor the defense minister, Moshe Arens. Before introducing the defense minister, Falwell, in an aside to Arens, said, "Mr. Minister, I want to thank you for that jet airplane you gave me."

Falwell – and other dispensationalists – have a working alliance with militant Jewish Zionists. My latest book, *Prophecy and Politics*, deals with this marriage of convenience between militant Christians and militant Jewish Zionists. Each group uses the other, gains from the other. Christian Zionists, or dispensationalists, give Israel total support because they think there has to be an Israel there in place, not for the Jews, but for the battle of Armageddon, which they actually believe must occur. It's part of the required steps, they believe, that will lead to their Rapture and the Second Coming of Christ. Because of their scenario, they make a cult of the land of Israel.

The seedbed for this dispensationalism is over in Dallas, at the Dallas Theological Seminary. I met with John Walvoord, the president, an elderly gentleman who said God had given all of Palestine to the Jews. In talking with Walvoord, I kept referring to the suffering of the Palestinians. What about them? I asked. "I am referring to land," he said at one point. And he added, "You keep talking about spirit aspects."

It actually happens: those who make a cult of the land of Israel put this cult of land above the teachings of Christ. Jewish Zionists such as Begin and Shamir and Sharon support the Christian dispensationalists because the dispensationalists give them total support. In dealing with the criticism of this alliance between militant Christians and militant Jews, I think it is important to know the difference between religion and politics.

True faith, whether one is Christian, Muslim or Jewish, is religion. Zionism, whether one is Christian, Muslim or Jewish, is politics. And it is politics because it deals with land, not spiritual values.

In closing, I want to mention a trip I made to Basel, Switzerland. I attended the first Christian Zionist Congress. I was one of 589 persons from 27 countries attending this Congress. It was held in the same hall where Theodor Herzl had called the first Jewish Zionist Congress, about 100 years ago. Herzl had stressed that Jews were different and should live exclusively among Jews. Christian Zionists say the same. This conference was supported by the Israelis.

I listened to speakers who were Jewish Zionists as well as Christian Zionists. Rather than provide hope by suggesting steps whereby Jews and Arabs might reach reconciliation, and live together, in peace, each speaker seemed to reinforce the fears of the other. Rather than stress how much in common Arabs and Jews, and indeed all human beings, have in common, speakers told us: Jews are different. They must live exclusively among Jews.

Christian Zionists believe that God has ordained that the Jews control the land of Palestine, and that they control Jerusalem, and build a temple, and that they reinstate animal sacrifice.

The Christian Zionists approve every military action taken by the Jewish Zionists. If Israel bombs Iraq, as it has done, or invades Lebanon, as it has done, or shoots and kills Palestinian children, as it does, then Christian Zionists will say, "Well, that is a Chosen Land and a Chosen People. All of that is orchestrated by God."

Although our aid to Israel is more than we give to many countries, including all of India, Africa and South America, Christian Zionists will support these billions of your taxpayer dollars going to Israel, because of their interpretation that God wants that land as the landing base for the Second Coming of Christ. It is the *land* for which they care. They want it there, in place, so that the rest of their scenario, including their Rapture, can come to pass.

Somehow in all the sermons of Jerry Falwell and other Christian Zionists, I miss their telling us about the Sermon on the Mount. And I miss these militant Christians reminding us that Christ possessed a way that was *not* based on military strength.

His way was not to steal property and kill people for the sake of a temporary political kingdom on earth. Rather, as we know, Christ came to advance and enhance life. He came not to speak and support a cult of land. But he came to speak for the suffering, the destitute, the oppressed.

Indeed, He has a Chosen People. We are all chosen to do good, not evil. Chosen to seek and to work for peace, in the Middle East and in the world.

Grace Halsell has covered both the Korean and Vietnam wars as a journalist, was a White House speech writer for President Lyndon Johnson, and has written many books, among them Prophecy and Politics, *Lawrence Hill & Company, Westport, Connecticut.*

In the early centuries, the Christians had a word for greeting and departing; it was the word "maranatha," which means "The Lord is coming soon." We can think of no better way with which to say good-by — MARANATHA!

— Hal Lindsey

Dr. John Lightfoot, one of the most learned seventeenth-century scholars, concluded that creation was performed by the Trinity on 23 October 4004 B.C. at 9:00 A.M., 45th meridian time.

Three Cheers For The Creationists!

A. J. Mattill, Jr.

Lest Creationists think that rationalists are being hypercritical of creationism, let us give three cheers to the creationists for the services they are rendering to the cause of rational religion.

Cheer Number One goes to the creationists for serving rational religion by demonstrating beautifully that we must take the creation stories of Genesis at face value. Accordingly, there is only one way to understand the "days" of Genesis 1:1-2:4, and that is as literal twenty-four-hour days, not as geological eras. Creationists list twenty or more contradictions that arise between science and Scripture if the days are taken as geological eras instead of ordinary days.

This "veritable morass of contradictions" includes such ones as:

- Genesis says that plant life, even in such advanced form as the fruit tree, was made one 'day' before the sun and stars, but this would have been impossible if the day were really an aeon, as plants must have sunlight
- The Bible says that there was no rain on the earth up at least to the time of man's appearance (Gen. 2:5); geology says rains have existed since the earth first cooled
- The Bible says plants appeared on the third day and insects not until the sixth; this would be impossible if the days were aeons, since plants require insect pollination for their continued survival through reproduction.

Many Christians have taken the dishonest way of lengthening the days into millions of years, but the creationists make it clear that such an approach is nothing but a makeshift that is unacceptable biblically and scientifically. Creationists thus present us with a clear-cut "either-or." The creationist says: "The Genesis record is stubbornly intransigent and will not accommodate the standard system of geological ages. A decision must be made for one or the other – one cannot logically accept both."

The creationists have also shown irrefutably that those liberal and neo-orthodox Christians who regard the creation stories as myths or allegories are undermining the rest of Scripture, for if there was no Adam, there was no fall; and if there was no fall there was no hell; and if there was no hell, there was no need of Jesus as Second Adam and Incarnate Savior, crucified and risen. As a result, the whole biblical system of *salvation* collapses.

The creationists likewise correctly maintain that, if the biblical stories of the beginning of the world are myths, then the stories of the virginal conception and of the end of the world may be myths, too. Once we get on this mythological slide, we cannot logically stop sliding until we hit the bottom at agnosticism or atheism.

Evolution thus becomes the most potent weapon for undermining and destroying the Christian faith. The creationist says: "One cannot believe the Bible and be an evolutionist, or be an evolutionist and believe the Bible."

Creationists deserve **Cheer Number Two** for serving rational religion by effectively eliminating the idea of "theistic evolution," or the liberal Christian view that evolution is God's way of creation. Creationists rightly insist that evolution is inconsistent with a God of love. God is too benevolent and too kind to use billions of years of untold cruelty and wastefulness as his method of creation. He is too intelligent to plan it that way, and he is powerful enough to accomplish it in a better way.

Creationists insist that liberal Christians face the problem of why God chose to use five billion years of chance variations, natural selection, geologic upheavals, storm, disease, extinctions, struggle, suffering and death as an inscrutable prelude to His creation of man right at the very tail-end of geologic time. The creationist says: "God is not the author of confusion. Yet He is said to have surveyed the whole monstrous spectacle and pronounced it all 'very good' (Genesis 1:31). Away with your silly drivel about theistic evolution!"

Unfortunately, the creationists are blind to the fact that they also serve a cruel God who created this cold-blooded system where life feeds on life, where the strong destroy the weak, and where it is either kill or be killed, eat or be eaten. If the creationists trace such a harsh system to the fall rather than the original creation, as they do, then they must admit that it was hardly just for God to curse all people and all animals for all time for what two human beings did at the beginning of time.

Moreover, the creationists worship a God who is not only cruel but dishonest. He created Adam to look as if he had an umbilical cord. He created light waves to look as if they were coming from the sun or from old galaxies. He created organisms to look as if they were missing links. And he created everything to look as if it were old, even though it was brand new.

The creationists' God is also an uninformed God, who, according to Genesis, knows only about our sun and moon and the stars but knows nothing about other suns or moons or galaxies or quasars or black holes familiar to modern astronomers.

And the creationists' God is a bit too human, for he changed his mind and became sorry that he created people and beasts and decided to destroy all but a sample of them in a worldwide flood, only to start the whole bloody process once more (Gen. 6:5-7). Thus the creationists intentionally show the unacceptability of the liberal Christians' God of evolution and in so doing they unintentionally reveal the brutality of their own God of creation.

The creationists get **Cheer Number Three** for serving rational religion by proving that the Bible has errors. Yet the desire to vindicate the Bible as God's inerrant Word is the major reason for all of their studies and writings. Creationists says that if the Bible "contains scientific fallacies, it could not have been given by inspiration."

The creationists admit that the problem of relating biblical chronology to geological chronology is their most serious problem. According to Genesis 5 and 11, the period from Adam to Abraham is about two thousand years. Since Abraham lived about 2000 B.C., Adam was created about 4000 B.C. Archbishop Ussher of the seventeenth century calculated that creation took place in 4004 B.C. Then Dr. John Lightfoot, one of the most learned seventeenth-century scholars, studied the matter more profoundly and concluded that creation was performed by the Trinity on 23 October 4004 B.C. at 9:00 A.M., 45th meridian time.

Although modern creationists, following Ussher and Lightfoot, rely solely upon the biblical data as the only proper method of determining the date of creation, they are rather imprecise about the exact time of creation, generally claiming only that it took place less than ten thousand years ago. But even such a "young universe" is several thousand years older than the universe of Genesis. Hence the creationists do not uphold the accuracy of the Bible after all, for if God wrote the Bible, as creationists claim, then God should have been exact and not a few thousand years off.

To stretch the chronology of Genesis a bit, creationists are willing to admit that there are mini-gaps in the genealogies of Genesis that total several thousand years, but there are no maxi-gaps to extend the age of the earth to millions of years. But why, if God directly dictated genealogical lists to Moses, should there be any gaps at all?

Three cheers, then, for the creationists, for they have cleared the air of all dodges, escapes, and evasions made by Christians who adopt nonliteral interpretations of Genesis and who hold that evolution is God's method of creation. By thus showing that no compromise is possible between the Bible and evolution, the creationists have reduced all of the complexities of the creation-evolution problem to one simple question: Is Genesis correct in saying that God created the world in six twenty-four-hour days? Not many thinking people will have difficulty answering that question.

Three cheers for the creationists, for they have refuted their own case by demonstrating that the Bible is not inerrant in its chronology of the cosmos, which means, on their own admission, that the Bible is not inspired at all.

A. J. Mattill, Jr. is an author, lecturer, and professor of biblical studies at several southern colleges.

Creation: All was chaos . . . and out of that bulk a mass formed – just as cheese is made out of milk – and worms appeared in it, and these were the angels . . . and among that number of angels, there was also God, he too having been created out of that mass at the same time. Menocchio, a miller living in the 16th century, was regarded as a heretic and a threat to the Church. He was burned at the stake for the above notion concerning creation.

— Florence Grippe

I remember hearing a marvelous talk by Daisetz Suzuki in Ascona, Switzerland. It was, I think, his first talk there at the Eranos Foundation, and here was this group of Europeans in the audience and there was a Japanese man (he was about ninety-one years old at the time), a Zen philosopher. He stood with his hands on his side, and he looked at the audience and said: "Nature against God. God against nature. Nature against man. Man against nature. Man against God. God against man. Very funny religion."

— Joseph Campbell,
as quoted in *The Hero's Journey*

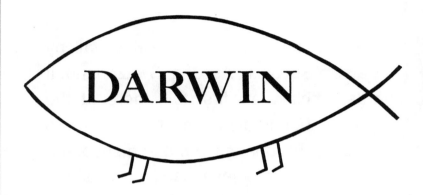

Piscis

The Fish (Ichthys, Piscis) has its origins in stellar and pagan religions, but has been claimed in many Christian circles as an original creation of Christianity. The fish joins a long list that includes the virgin birth, the Crucifixion, the Resurrection, the Triad (Trinity) and the final days – all adding to the argument that Christianity didn't replace pagan religion, but is the latest in a series of pagan religions.

Killing Darwin for Christ

Lawrence S. Lerner

Most persons' daily lives are not materially affected by what they believe or disbelieve concerning the history of the universe, the earth, and life on earth. Much less are their lives affected by what other people believe on these subjects. And, unless they happen to have children in public school, why should they care what is being taught there concerning cosmological matters such as creation?

Before I address this question, let me define exactly what creationism means in the present context. What I mean by creationism is almost exclusively the Protestant American fundamentalist movement that seeks to impose on the general public, by political means, a religion that revolves around the creation stories in the Bible. These fundamental creationists are divided into two bitterly opposed camps – the Young-Earthers and the Old-Earthers.

I will consider mostly the Young-Earthers, who believe that the first eleven chapters of Genesis (through Noah's flood and the Tower of Babel) constitute an infallible and complete account of the history of the universe and everything in it. They therefore hold that the purpose of modern scientific investigation is only to corroborate and flesh out the few hundred words of relevant text.

The more sophisticated Old-Earthers are willing as a minimum to admit that the universe is very old. Most Old-Earthers go further and accept the findings of modern geology. Some go still further and accept biological evolution as fact – except that they deny humans are part of the evolutionary process, and insist that the human race is a special supernatural creation of about 6000 years ago.

Indeed, the main stock in trade of Old-Earth propaganda is using the Young-Earthers as a foil against genuine scientists as extremists on the other side. Having created this fraudulent context, the Old-Earthers locate themselves in the sweet-reasonable center. The soft-core fundamentalist group called the American Scientific Affiliation circulated this insidious nonsense a few years ago in an expensive, slick booklet they sent to every junior-high science teacher and high-school biology teacher in the United States.

The most important thing to bear in mind about creationism – both Young- and Old-Earth – is that it is not really about science – it is about religion and politics. Creationists deliberately obscure this point for tactical and legal reasons, and because the trappings of science confer prestige in modern society.

What creationists peddle as their "scientific method" has two components. The first is to begin with unchallengeable statements – Bible stories – and to try to find, in carefully selected natural phenomena, purported confirmations of those statements. The second is to look for any inconsistency or controversy, no matter how small or evanescent, in real science (especially evolution theory) and to present that inconsistency or controversy as proof of the validity of the Bible stories. That is, creationists take the fallacious position that anything any scientist says that turns out to be wrong – or even controversial – is an automatic confirmation of the creationist point of view. This fallacy they call the "Two-Model Approach."

For example, the Institute for Creation Research's Gerald Aardsma told me in 1989 that he was building the world's most sensitive radiocarbon dating apparatus. He intended to use it to show that there is measurable carbon-14 in coal, thus proving that the coal is much less than millions of years old. But having visited his "laboratory," I would advise you not to hold your breath till he publishes this revolutionary result – or even until he gets his apparatus up and working. In any case, Aardsma now seems to be off on another tangent, judging from reports in the Institute's monthly "scientific" newsletter, Acts and Facts.

Another, more familiar example of creationist research is the annual and lucrative search for Noah's Ark. This is the specialty of John Morris, the son of the founder of the Institute for Creation Research. You probably know the plot. Every summer, an expedition is sent to a dusty Turkish town in the vicinity of Mt. Ararat. Turkish red tape keeps the expedition away from the mountain until the summer is almost over. Then the expedition hires a light plane or helicopter. They fly over Mt. Ararat, and there's the Ark! Finally obtaining official permission, they struggle up the mountain on foot and see the ice-sheathed Ark in the distance – just as the first winter storm closes in and drives them back. Then it's time to raise funds for next year's expedition.

These desultory efforts aside, the main effort of the creationists is not research but polemics – to quote or (more often) misquote real scientific findings out of context in such a way as to make them look damaging to real science. The scientific illiteracy of their intended audience assures creationist speakers that they can peddle any nonsense they like – even nonsense that they have been forced to publicly acknowledge as such in earlier appearances.

Real science proceeds, of course, in the opposite direction. Scientists use the results of observations to construct theories that suggest further observations. Implicit in the scientific process is the idea that no part of the structure is sacrosanct. Paradoxically, the great stability of the foundations of the major sciences arises directly from their complete openness to attack. As ex-preacher Dan Barker put it:

> Truth does not demand belief. Scientists do not join hands every Sunday, singing, "yes, gravity is real! I will have faith! I will be strong! I believe in my heart that what goes up, up, up must come down, down, down. Amen!" If they did, we would think they were pretty insecure about it.

Creationists deliberately foreclose the scientific method to themselves in advance. For example, the creationist flagship, the Institute for Creation Research, has an unamendable corporate By-Law requiring that every person associated with the organization – student, faculty, administration, or staff – annually sign a detailed declaration that describes in advance all of the conclusions his studies and research are going to produce. Refusal or failure to comply will lead to immediate dismissal – a point verified with pride by several ICR people at the time of my visit in 1989.

Just what do the creationists expect to accomplish? Quite clearly, they do not expect and do not try to influence scientists or to do real science. This omission would be puzzling only if one took seriously their oft-stated claim that the entire structure of evolution is collapsing under the weight of adverse evidence, and that it is only a matter of a few years before all biologists abandon evolution and become creationists. The main focus of the creationist movement is rather on the primary and secondary education system, and their facade of research and graduate institutions is intended only for prestige and licensure. Creationists, like other fundamentalists and orthodox religionists generally, reject the view that the aim of education is to learn how to think independently. Rather, they see education as inculcation and indoctrination.

An account of modern creationist efforts to subvert public-school science teaching is conveniently begun with the famous Scopes trial of 1925. According to a widely held myth, reflected in the movie

Inherit The Wind, the trial was a legal victory but a public humiliation for the creationists. There is some truth in this myth as in all myths. At the time, nearly all creationists were country folk of modest educational attainments, fearful of the mainstream currents in an America that had newly become more than half urban. But a view of the Scopes trial as a victory for science ignores the main practical result. As Grabiner and Miller pointed out in a 1974 article in *Science*, the Scopes trial obtained for the creationists exactly what they wanted – the disappearance of any useful treatment of evolution from nearly all of the high-school biology textbooks used in America from the mid-1920's through the late 1950's.

Thanks to the Russians and Sputnik, things changed after 1957. Sputnik led, among other things, to textbook reform and thus to the publication of the excellent evolution-centered biology textbook series, *Biological Sciences Curriculum Study*, about 1960. Parallel changes took place in the physical sciences. In California, distinguished scientists such as Jacob Bronowski served on science framework committees – the committees that determine the content of California textbooks. These events, taken together with Epperson vs. Arkansas, the 1968 Supreme Court decision that struck down anti-evolution laws, spurred creationists to much-increased activity.

The creationist community had itself changed significantly since 1925. Like most Americans, creationists were now mostly urban, though still with a disproportionate concentration in the South. Many of them were members of the urban middle class, and many had spent substantial time in school. However, the feeling that their community was threatened by social change was if anything amplified from what it had been in the 1920's. The creationist community had become a proportionately smaller but much more affluent and noisier group.

Since they had found it impossible to forbid the teaching of evolution, the creationists adopted a back-up strategy. They pushed creationism, but still as an admittedly religious concept. In Tennessee, for example, a law required that any textbook discussing evolution had to contain a statement that evolution was *theory*, and was not represented as scientific fact. Moreover, all such texts had to give equal space to other "theories" of origins, including, but not limited to, the Genesis account in the Bible. A similar approach was used in California, Texas, and some other states.

This approach was struck down in Federal District Court (Daniel vs. Waters, 1975), on the ground that the teaching of specific religious belief was prohibited by the First Amendment. Nevertheless, the practice still pops up frequently in one form or another around the country – at present, notably, in Morton, Illinois, a suburb of Peoria.

Present-day *scientific creationism* is rooted in the events I have just sketched. Unable to ban evolution, or to teach Bible stories in science classes, creationists began to claim that creationism was a scientific theory just like evolution. Flying in the face of logic, they simultaneously made the contradictory claim that evolution was a religious belief just like creationism.

A leading exponent of this dual approach was Henry Morris, a hydraulic engineer whose first book on the subject, *Biblical Cosmology and Modern Science,* was published in 1970. This new approach was bolstered by the birth in 1978 of the legal theory that creationist lawyer Wendell Bird christened "Balanced Treatment." If evolution or any subject implying a very old universe was taught, it had to be "balanced" by giving equal time to the cosmology and natural history expounded in Genesis.

Politically, a golden era was dawning for creationism. When Reagan became governor in 1967 and turned to rewarding his supporters with political posts, he appointed a number of creationists to the California State Board of Education. Owing to a last-minute flurry of activity on the part of the scientific community, the creationists failed by a whisker to require the teaching of creationism in California schools. Nevertheless, they did great damage to the 1969 California Science Framework – the document that details what science texts used in California public schools must contain.

Publishers got the word loud and clear. Evolution and cosmology disappeared from science texts, geology degenerated into a mere description of rocks, scientists disappeared from framework committees, and science curricula substituted a hodgepodge of disjointed factoids for the tight structure that characterizes real science. This was the period, too, when significant scientific findings were presented in such fatuous phrases as, "Many scientists believe that animals called dinosaurs may have lived perhaps a hundred million years ago." Because California buys 12% of the textbooks published in America, the effects were felt all over the country.

A period of stagnation followed, and anti-intellectualism flourished – not so much because the Religious Right was strong but because public interest in education was weak. Science textbooks degenerated in all areas because publishers adopted a broad interpretation of the conflict over evolution. Definitions and isolated facts were unlikely to arouse opposition, but discussions of the theoretical context of science – the context that makes science what it is – could cause real trouble. In any case, it takes effort and expertise to present scientific theory; vocabulary lists and catalogs of misconstrued facts were easy to devise and consistent with the then-popular practice of "dumbing down."

Reagan's installation as President in 1981 was followed immediately by a great flurry of creationist activity at the Federal level. Attempts were made to close a very successful Emergence of Man exhibit at the Smithsonian and to substitute a creationist display. Orange County Congressman William Dannemeyer tried to amend the 1982 Smithsonian appropriation to forbid expenditures on evolution displays.

Indeed, in 1981 Dannemeyer submitted a bill aimed at requiring that all Federal money be divided evenly between evolution and creationism – including but not limited to research, NSF and NIH grants, curriculum development, museum exhibits, and National Park Service naturalist programs and research. The early Reagan years were probably the closest the creationists ever got to realizing their aims on the national scale, but in general they failed. This failure is consistent with historical creationist experience.

In California, the current educational reform movement led to the selection of a 1988-89 Science Framework Committee that had several practicing scientists among its members. Superintendent of Public Instruction Bill Honig and his excellent staff provided support, and the 1990 Framework is a document I am proud to have worked on. The Framework presents science as scientists see it, as an inquiry into the natural world, not as a list of inscrutable facts.

Needless to say, the creationists lobbied hard against the Science Framework. They showed their usual disdain for science, raising their cry that evolution is "only a theory, not a fact," and demanding that the draft be revised to include a dictionary definition of theory. They obviously expected a definition reflecting the everyday, rather than the scientific, usage. (Webster's Third has five definitions of theory, and the fifth is the one the creationists wanted: "an unproved assumption.") The creationists were doubtless disappointed by the way their demand was finally met. When the new policy was adopted, it included a footnote with a definition taken from a scientific dictionary:

> **Theory:** an explanation or model based on observation, exper-
> imentation, and reasoning, especially one that has been tested
> and confirmed as a general principle helping to explain and
> predict natural phenomena: [e.g.,] the theory of evolution . . .

Ironically, this is the only occurrence of the word evolution in the
Policy, and the event provided the hard-working Framework Committee with some much-needed comic relief.

As I have already noted, California constitutes 12% of the textbook
market. Texas represents another 10%. So it was heartening to learn
that parallel events were taking place in Texas. In the late '80's, the
rapidly growing high-tech industrial sector was finding difficulty
attracting educated engineers and managers with children, owing to
the dismal reputation of the public education system. Under pressure from a group of business leaders led by H. Ross Perot, the
Governor had appointed knowledgeable people to the Texas Board
of Education, and the Board was emerging from the reign of terror
of the Gablers. Mel Gabler and his wife had for almost two decades
been the self-appointed guardians of right and good in Texas education, and they had vehemently opposed (among many other things)
any materials suggesting that the universe was more than 6000 years
old or so.

But in 1990, the Texas Board directed that all biology texts present
evolution as the central organizing principle of the life sciences. It
looked for a while that creationists would have their way anyhow,
because they got the Board to modify these words, substituting for
the word "evolution" the phrase "evolution, or any other valid
theory." At the last moment, however, the Board of Education
acknowledged that there was no other valid theory. With 22% of the
market to aim at, textbook publishers will have an incentive to write
about real science.

I have already mentioned that the powerhouse of creationist
activities is the Institute for Creation Research, located near San
Diego. ICR began as the graduate division of Christian Heritage
College, a bible school founded by fundamentalist preacher Tim
LaHaye, whose better-known wife Beverly is the head of Concerned
Women for America, a pro-censorship, anti-abortion, anti-con-
traception, anti-feminist organization. LaHaye and his friend Henry
Morris had no use for what most people would consider extremely
conservative, fundamentalist church colleges such as Wheaton, Cal-
vin, or Grove City, which LaHaye and Morris regard as soft on
Old-Earthism.

In 1980, ICR was spun off in order to protect the accreditation of Christian Heritage College by the Western Association of Schools and Colleges (WASC). While its major activities involve writing religious books and tracts and barnstorming at fundamentalist churches, ICR maintains the ICR Graduate School (ICRGS), which grants M.S. degrees in Biology, Geology, Physics, and Science Education. As ICRGS could not hope to obtain accreditation from WASC, it was obliged under California law to obtain a license from the State Board of Education if it was to grant Master's degrees in science. In 1980 the law was very loose and the license was easily obtained.

About that time, the proliferation of diploma mills in California became a scandal, and the postsecondary licensing law was tightened in 1984. ICRGS came up for license renewal under the new law in 1987, and a Visiting Committee was sent to evaluate the institution in 1988. The committee consisted of three real academic scientists and two professors from local bible schools, who were nominated by ICR itself. The end result of the brief visit was a 3-2 vote against relicensure.

Much tangled legal and administrative argument followed. It was eventually agreed to send a new committee in the summer of 1989, and I was appointed to that committee. Some of the other members of the committee were persons of the greatest distinction: one is Director of the UCLA Molecular Biology Lab and a member of the National Academy of Sciences; another is a renowned geologist and paleontologist, also an NAS member; and a third is a distinguished geneticist. The ICRGS nominee on the committee was a professor of physics and math at a small bible school in Ohio.

The committee spent four days in San Diego, having previously digested mountains of reports. The vote to deny extension of the license was unanimous, including even the ICRGS nominee (though he later qualified his view). The situation was crystal clear. Creationism and pseudoscience aside, ICRGS was simply not offering even the semblance of graduate-level study in any of the four areas in which it granted master's degrees.

Space does not permit a thorough review of the academic travesties the committee found; indeed, the committee report is a fat one.

Let me give just a couple of examples:
- A so-called graduate biology course used freshman texts intended for physical-education majors.

- A master's thesis purported to justify the picture of electromagnetic radiation (radio and light waves) abandoned by the scientific community in 1905, when Einstein published the special theory of relativity. It was accepted on the strength of only two signatures instead of the usual three – that of Dr. Thomas Barnes, who rejects all the physics done since 1895 as ungodly and atheistic, and that of the dean, whose doctorate is in fish culture.

With this and much more evidence in hand, the Committee recommended that the State Board of Education not renew ICR's license to grant master's degrees in science. ICR had been offered the alternatives of giving degrees in theology or religion, or even in creation science, but they refused these options. The legal wheels ground until, last November, it remained only for the Attorney General's office to file a petition in court. This they declined to do. While it is not clear why they declined, one educated guess is that budget cuts required them to cut their caseload, and ICRGS was a low priority. One might say that ICRGS owes its continued degree-granting powers to the popularity of the death penalty and the tenacity of drug lords.

The creationists have not given up the ghost on the national level, either. About thirteen years ago, despairing of getting accreditation for Young-Earth schools at all levels from the regional school-and-college accrediting associations, Henry Morris and some of his friends formed the Trans-National Association of Christian Schools, known by its acronym TRACS. Needless to say, TRACS requires of schools applying for its blessing strict adherence to Young-Earth doctrine, together with some other predictable religious tenets.

Accrediting associations are themselves certified by the U.S. Department of Education, and accreditation by a certified association entitles schools and colleges to such goodies as Federal scholarship and loan funds, among other things. TRACS failed Federal certification on three occasions during the Reagan administration because it did not meet the minimum standards. In late 1991, however, the Bush administration certified TRACS – presumably as part of its overall campaign to divert public funds to private (read church) schools.

Congress has raised questions about improper maintenance of standards in this certification, and there may be an investigation of the Department of Education in the future. However, such matters are not likely to raise much excitement among constituents in an election year, and I don't expect much action.

Creationism continues as an anti-intellectual, anti-scientific force in schools all over the nation. I have already mentioned Morton, Illinois. For years, the principal of the Weed, California middle school invited his pastor in to teach creationism to sixth- and seventh graders. The preacher finally went too far for the most callous sensitivities when he told a Catholic child she would go to hell if she didn't believe his way. Only recently has the principal agreed, in the face of local protest and strong advice from Sacramento, to review his activities.

In the much more sophisticated town of Livermore, California, home of Star Wars, a biology teacher teaches creationism in spite of student and parent protests. And for the past seven years in Mission Viejo, an upper-middle-class suburb south of Los Angeles, a high-school biology teacher has been teaching creationism, telling Jewish students that they are bound for hell, and fighting disciplinary action aimed at making him do his job and teach science. As part of his fight, he sued the school district and threatened to sue a girl who wrote a critical article for the school newspaper. His suit was based on the peculiar claim that he was being forced to violate the freedom-of-religion clause of the First Amendment because evolution is a religion.

The Rutherford Institute, which supports Religious Right lawsuits, at first provided help, but ultimately withdrew. The suit was thrown out of court by a judge who called the teacher a "loose cannon." He has now been reassigned to his primary specialty, physical education – certainly to the benefit of the biology curriculum! These are just a few examples of the persistence of bible stories in science classes.

So we return to the question with which I began. Why should anyone care about creationism? Because the intrusion of anti-scientific, anti-intellectual movements into the public school system is enormously damaging to society and – more immediately – to the possibility of teaching science properly in universities. Far too many students come to college loaded with prejudices, and with the possibility already foreclosed that they might become scientists, or even that they might come to a decent understanding of how science works. Each such student is a liability to the university and to society as a whole. Each such student is likely to become one of that already too-large group of citizens who, having spent many years in school, are not educated.

So it is important that everybody who believes that an educated citizenry is an essential asset to a modern nation pay attention to creationism and other anti-intellectual movements that aim at substituting nonsense for science in the public realm.

Lawrence S. Lerner, PhD, is a professor of physics and has written books on the history of science.

Which is more dangerous: fanaticism or atheism? Fanaticism is certainly a thousand times more deadly; for atheism inspires no bloody passion whereas fanaticism does; atheism is opposed to crime and fanaticism causes crimes to be committed.

— Voltaire

Just think of the tragedy of teaching children not to doubt.

— Clarence Darrow

The idea that God is an oversized white male with a flowing beard who sits in the sky and tallies the fall of every sparrow is ludicrous. But if by "God" one means the set of physical laws that govern the universe, then clearly there is such a God. This God is emotionally unsatisfying . . . It does not make much sense to pray to the law of gravity.

— Carl Sagan

Election Wrap-Up

Radical Right scored success rate of over 40 Percent in state and local battles

The *People For the American Way* today reported that the Radical Right racked up victories in more than 40 percent of the state and local races where they were involved.

Key wins for the movement include:

- Defeat of the Equal Rights Amendment in Iowa,
- Overturning gay civil rights laws in Tampa and Colorado,
- Control over at least three district school boards in San Diego County, California,
- Victories in dozens of state and local races.

People For president, Arthur J. Kropp, stated that there are many key lessons to take away from this election:

- The Radical Right was able to 'shop' their issues in 1992,
- They learned that anti-gay campaigns worked, even in a political year of high voter involvement which made their "stealth" strategy of running low-profile efforts more difficult to pull off,
- The Radical Right scored many state and local wins,
- The Radical Right is now uniquely positioned to fill the leadership vacuum in the Republican Party,
- With Clinton in the White House as their new enemy, they will have no trouble filling their fund-raising coffers,
- The Radical Right used the 1992 election to test the political viability of such key goals as increased control of education and opposition to equal treatment for gay citizens.

"We can't afford to write off the Radical Right's significant victories in 1992," said Kropp. "We've seen that the less exposure they receive, the more likely they are to succeed. We will continue to monitor their activity as they build toward 1994 and 1996."

To obtain a full copy of the *People For Action Fund* report on the Radical Right involvement in the 1992 election, contact the Communications Department at *People for* (202) 467-4999.

Church & Society

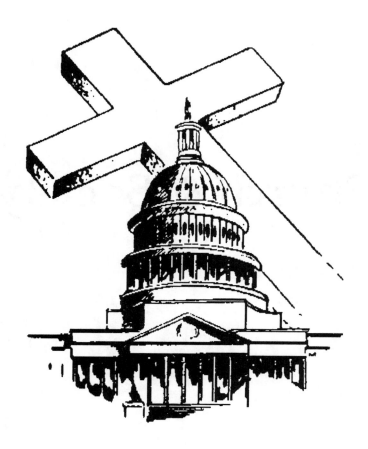

The "wall of separation between church and state" is a metaphor based on bad history, a metaphor which has proved useless as a guide to judging. It should be frankly and explicitly abandoned.

— Chief Justisce William Rehnquist

Church-State Separation: Endangered Species

Edd Doerr

On the lawn of the Massachusetts state capitol in Boston stand two statues. One is of Anne Hutchinson, tried and convicted in 1638 by both the church and the state and sentenced to exile in the wilderness for the crime of holding unauthorized discussions about religion with friends and neighbors in her own home. The other statue is of Mary Dyer, convicted of the crime of merely being a Quaker and executed by hanging on Boston Common in 1660.

These two statues symbolize the historically almost universal pattern of relations between religion and government, a pattern typically involving a union or close alliance between the civil power and one or several preferred or "established" organized religions.

The many and varied forms of church-state union have generally produced concentration of political, and often economic, power so great as to be inimical to democracy. Church-state unions usually work to the disadvantage of dissenters, freethinkers, and religious or lifestyle minorities. As we have seen, the church-state union in colonial Massachusetts led to exile for one woman and execution for another. Baptists were jailed in Virginia for not having the approval of the state church (Episcopal) to preach. Most of the colonies compelled people to pay taxes for the support of religion and made second-class citizens of members of disfavored religions.

The deleterious effects of church-state unions can be seen around the world today. In some Muslim countries, conversion from Islam to another religion is a capital crime. In some Muslim countries, Islamic religious law is applied to Christians and other non-Muslims. German citizens pay heavy taxes to their churches, while Norwegian and Swedish citizens pay milder taxes to support state churches. British citizens are taxed to support religious private schools, and public schools must offer daily prayer exercises. Germans may be prosecuted for "blasphemy," a religious offense. Examples could be cited endlessly.

By the time of the American Revolution, enough people in our increasingly pluralistic land had become fed up with church-state unions that efforts to separate religion and government paralleled the military effort to expel British troops. Key landmarks in the struggle for church-state separation were James Madison's 1785 *Memorial and Remonstrance Against Religious Assessments* and Thomas Jefferson's *Bill for Establishing Religious Freedom,* which became law in Virginia in 1785 and subsequently became a model for legislation and constitutional provisions in other states.

Two years after passage of Jefferson's bill, the present U.S. Constitution was drafted in Philadelphia. This remarkable document was a historically secular document, one that left religious matters to the individual conscience and which granted to government no authority whatsoever to involve itself in religious matters. Further, it specifically prohibited religious tests for public office and mandatory oaths.

As the original Constitution was widely criticized for lacking a specific bill of rights, adding one became a major item of business for the first Congress in 1789. The First Amendment, Article I of the Bill of Rights, states, "Congress shall make no law respecting an establishment of religion, or prohibiting the free exercise thereof; . . ." A decade later, in a well-thought-out letter to the Danbury, Connecticut, Baptist Association, President Thomas Jefferson declared that the First Amendment erected "a wall of separation between church and state."

The First Amendment and the rest of the Bill of Rights applied at first only to the federal government, as it was generally assumed that state constitutions and governments would protect the liberties of citizens of the states. By the end of the Civil War, it was obvious that the states were not up to functioning as effective guarantors of basic rights. The Fourteenth Amendment was added to the Constitution in 1868 to remedy that deficiency. Unfortunately, the Supreme Court did not see fit to apply the Bill of Rights to state and local government, as the Fourteenth Amendment was intended to do, until after World War I, and then only slowly and in a piecemeal way.

The United States invented and pioneered the principle of separation of church and state. That principle was often violated in our history, but it became even more fully implemented as time rolled on and was clearly accepted by most Americans. Beginning during World War II, the Supreme Court began applying the principle with a fair degree of consistency, requiring public schools to be religiously neutral, holding unconstitutional all major forms of tax support for church schools, and expanding the free exercise of religion except in cases of "compelling" government interest.

Perhaps the clearest expression of the separation principle is found in the Supreme Court's 1947 ruling in *Everson v. Board of Education:*

> The "establishment of religion" clause of the First Amendment means at least this: Neither a state nor the Federal Government can set up a church. Neither can pass laws which aid one religion, aid all religions, or prefer one religion over another. Neither can force nor influence a person to go to or to remain away from church against his will or force him to profess a belief or disbelief in any religion. No person can be punished for entertaining or professing religious belief or disbeliefs, nor church attendance or non-attendance. No tax in any amount, large or small, can be levied to support any religious activities or institutions, whatever they may be called, or whatever form they may adopt to teach or practice religion. Neither a state nor the Federal Government can, openly or secretly, participate in the affairs of any religious organizations or groups and vice versa. In the words of Jefferson, the clause against establishment of religion by law was intended to erect "a wall of separation between church and state."

It would be fair to conclude that for most of our history as a nation, implementation of the separation principle has racheted steadily forward, giving the United States the greatest degree of separation and free exercise of religion of any country. But dark clouds began to appear during the 1970s as religious fundamentalism and political ultraconservatism became closely allied.

Beginning of the End?

Religio-political changes now threaten church-state separation as never before. Former antagonists, such as the Catholic bishops and Protestant fundamentalist leaders like Jerry Falwell and Pat Robertson, began making common cause, joined by ultraconservative political groups eager to tap fundamentalist voter strength for other purposes.

The new war on church-state separation is fought on two fronts, the ideological and the practical.

On the ideological front, church-state separation, religious freedom, and basic democratic values are being subjected to a massive propaganda assault. Fundamentalist televangelists, conservative elements in the Catholic church, and ultraconservative columnists have campaigned unceasingly to discredit the separation principle, to insist that "moral majorities" have the right to impose their values on everyone by law. Reagan-appointed Chief Justice William Rehnquist devoted a long dissent in *Wallace v. Jaffree (1985)* to an attack on the separation principle, thus departing from the fairly solid line of support for separation by fifty years of Supreme Court justices. Rehnquist concluded:

> The "wall of separation between church and state" is a metaphor based on bad history, a metaphor which has proved useless as a guide to judging. It should be frankly and explicitly abandoned.

The opponents of separation in conservative religious hierarchies, and their allies in government and the legal profession, hold to a position generally labelled "accommodationism." This position is that the establishment clause was intended only to prohibit the establishment of a single national religion but would permit nondiscriminatory government aid to all religions.

This position is untenable for several reasons. For one, the first Congress, which drafted the First Amendment, considered and rejected just such "accommodationist" language. For another, at the time the Constitution and Bill of Rights were drafted and ratified, there was no state which retained a European or colonial style single establishment. Every state had either disestablished all churches or moved to a sort of multiple establishment (all trinitarian or Protestant forms of Christianity aided equally).

We have grown accustomed during the past half century to having the Supreme Court sort out church-state and religious liberty disputes generally in favor of a civil libertarian, separationist point of view, one harmonizing with the views of Jefferson and Madison. But no more. Thanks to the packing of the Supreme Court by Presidents Reagan and Bush, the Court can no longer be relied upon to settle church-state controversies in a Jeffersonian-Madisonian manner. We the People, then, will need to fight the battles for religious freedom and church-state separation in Congress and state legislatures, at the voting booth, in state courts, and in the arena of public opinion.

Let us shift gears from the ideological campaign against church-state separation to the direct, real-world theater of events.

Public Funds for Church Schools

In addition to church-state separation, our country's other great contribution to civilization is the public school. From humble beginnings in mid-seventeenth century Massachusetts, our country has evolved a system of secular, democratic, community-run common schools which now serve nine out of ten American school children. These schools are run by more than 15,000 school boards elected by local taxpayers and parents, though a few are run by boards appointed by elected officials.

Although many supporters of private schools were and are content to support their institutions with tuition and private donations, the Catholic bishops have campaigned since the mid-nineteenth century for one or another form of tax support for their private schools. Vatican policy has always favored tax support for Catholic private schools and succeeded in getting it in Canada, France, Britain, Ireland, Belgium, and other countries.

It should be pointed out, however, that large numbers of U.S. Catholic parents have always preferred public schools, that Catholic schools have never enrolled more than half of the Catholic children of school age, and that, since the Supreme Court's 1962-63 rulings against the largely Protestant practices of school-sponsored daily prayer and Bible reading, Catholic school enrollment has dropped precipitously from a high of 5.5 million in 1965 to less than half that number in 1992.

Various forms of federal, state, and local tax aid for nonpublic schools add up to about $2 billion annually. Yet they are only minor and peripheral aids which have managed to survive court challenges because they are considered acceptable under a "child benefit" rationale (as with transportation and textbook loans) or are considered justifiable as remedial aids.

But the Catholic bishops, operators of fundamentalist Christian and Orthodox Jewish schools, and politicians seeking what they believe to be a bonanza of sectarian bloc votes are not satisfied with a mere $2 billion. They have made it clear that their ultimate goal is parity, or near parity, with public schools in tax support.

The three principal ways in which this support has been sought in recent years are tuition reimbursement tax credits, tuition reimbursement grants, and tuition vouchers. Voucher plans are now the hot item for the "parochiaid" special-interest groups. Though they come in an almost infinite variety – involving greater or lesser amounts of money, greater or lesser amounts and kinds of government regulation, etc. —they all have basic similarities. They involve government-issued vouchers or chits which may be used to pay all or part of tuition at any private or public schools, the vouchers to be redeemed for cash from tax sources.

Voucher promoters defend their various plans on several grounds: They would provide "distributive justice" for parents who pay taxes for public schools. They would promote pluralism and diversity in education. They would break the "government monopoly" in education. Parents would have more educational "choice." These arguments have a superficial appeal, but they will not stand close scrutiny.

As for "distributive justice," our public schools are religiously neutral, controlled by local school boards, and meant to serve all children. If parents who prefer private schools for their children get tax support for that choice, then all taxpayers will be forced to support nonpublic institutions not under meaningful public control: "taxation without representation."

Pluralism and diversity are certainly desirable in education, but the individual child has much more diversity in public schools than in nonpublic schools, which tend strongly toward religious, ideological, and ethnic homogeneity.

Educational "choice," as applied to nonpublic schools, is grossly misleading. Parents may try to choose a particular private school for their children, but the real choice is exercised by the private school. It is the school which, in the last analysis, chooses which children to admit, which teachers to hire, which religion or ideology to impose through its curriculum.

Going beyond merely answering the arguments of the voucher proponents, the case against any form of tax aid for nonpublic schools is both multifaceted and compelling.

- Over 90 percent of nonpublic schools are sectarian: Catholic, Jewish, Missouri Synod Lutheran, fundamentalist, Christian Reformed, etc.
- Because of the pervasively sectarian nature of the vast majority of nonpublic schools, voucher plans would tend to attract religiously homogeneous student bodies and faculties. Nonpublic schools often discriminate in admissions. Nonpublic schools are not bound by the same rules as public schools, and are not governed by boards elected by all taxpayers.

- A voucher scheme would greatly increase education costs.
- The vast majority of nonpublic schools are operated by religious bodies which refuse to ordain women, which generally oppose freedom of conscience on abortion and often even contraception, and which often (as in many fundamentalist schools) teach that women must be subordinate or "submissive" to men.
- Availability of tax support for nonpublic schools would likely cause the private sector to grow. This would absorb more affluent and "able" students into selective nonpublic schools, which in turn would tend to convert public schools into "wastebaskets" for the poor, the handicapped, the disadvantaged, the discipline problems.

Not only is the case against vouchers and other forms of "parochiaid" compelling, but the public in general has never really fallen for the sectarian private interest propaganda. Major opinion polls in 1991 showed that Americans oppose tax support for nonpublic schools by a margin of 68 percent to 28 percent.

Although public opinion has remained solidly opposed to vouchers (though not to choice among public schools, which is quite another matter), powerful sectarian and political special interests remain strongly committed to promoting the scheme. And a determined and well-heeled minority has certain advantages over large but unorganized majorities. The bottom line, of course, is that the voucher advocates would, if they could, wreck church-state separation and public education while setting the stage for a new feudalization of society. Voucher plans were defeated in the Pennsylvania legislature in 1991 and in the U.S. Congress in 1992, but their proponents will not give up.

Freedom of Conscience on Abortion

Overshadowing the struggle over tax support for sectarian private schools is the increasingly bitter contest over whether women will continue to enjoy freedom of conscience in dealing with problem pregnancies.

Unintended or unwanted pregnancies have always been with us. It is estimated that between 30 and 50 million pregnancies are intentionally terminated annually throughout the world, proportionately more often in underdeveloped than developed countries.

Abortion was legal and common in this country until the late nineteenth century, when state medical associations lobbied restrictive laws through state legislatures as part of efforts to reduce competition in the healing professions.

Interest in re-legalizing freedom of conscience on abortion grew rapidly with the revitalization of the women's rights movement in the 1960s. By the end of the decade, some progress had been made in getting some state legislatures to liberalize abortion laws. But the cause of reproductive rights made a quantum leap forward in 1973 when the Supreme Court held in *Roe v. Wade* that the fundamental constitutional right to privacy covered the right to choose to terminate a problem pregnancy. The Court also held that the term "person" in the Constitution has never applied in a full sense to other than those who are born.

While Americans hold a wide range of opinions about the propriety of abortion under specific circumstances, a solid majority, including many people who regard abortion as morally wrong, believe that abortion decisions should be made by individual women and not by the federal or state governments.

Leaving reproductive decisions to women is the policy most consistent with constitutional principles regarding privacy, freedom of conscience and church-state separation, but powerful conservative religious leaders and their political allies see it differently.

Their successful strategies have included cutting off federal Medicaid payment for nearly all abortions, cutting off abortions for military and Peace Corps personnel and dependents, gagging family planning clinic personnel by presidential order from discussing the abortion option with women with problem pregnancies, passing restrictive state laws, and trying to get the Supreme Court to reverse *Roe vs. Wade*. Since 1981 the Reagan and Bush administrations have packed the Supreme Court with justices unfriendly to reproductive rights, with the result that beginning with the Court's 1989 ruling in *Webster vs. Reproductive Health Services,* the Court has shown itself favorable to state restrictions on abortion rights.

How far the Court will go in this direction cannot be predicted, but pro-choice leaders are not optimistic. Then, too, more extreme elements of the anti-choice movement have resorted to the bombing and torching of clinics, harassment of clinic personnel, and direct mob actions to close clinics. These latter actions often result in large numbers of arrests for trespassing, but the harassers seem to want to use imprisonment as a propaganda tool for their cause. The case against choice is based almost solely on religious beliefs of a sectarian character. The "respect life" rhetoric needs to be seen largely as a smokescreen. Familiarity with the anti-choice movement leads many to conclude that their concern is less for saving fetuses than for maintaining male dominance over women.

The religious bodies most actively seeking to limit freedom of conscience on abortion tend to be those which refuse to ordain women to the clergy, which oppose an Equal Rights Amendment, and which generally take the position that women should be submissive to men. Outlawing abortion is simply one of the best ways to keep women in a subordinate position to men. Religious bodies which are prochoice tend to place women and men on the same level.

Other problem areas

The preceding material covers, however sketchily, the three main areas of church-state controversy in the U S. today. But the list of problems goes on and on.

In 1990 the Supreme Court opened a real can of worms when it held, in a case involving use by Native Americans in Oregon of the religious sacramental hallucinogenic drug peyote, that states may interfere with the free exercise of religion without showing a "compelling" state interest, as previous rulings had required. This ruling could put the free exercise rights of all religious or lifestance minorities at the mercy of legislative majorities, stripping these citizens of protection they once had. As this is being written, a broad coalition of religious and civil liberties groups is pressing Congress to pass the Religious Freedom Restoration Act to reinstate the "compelling state interest" test for state interference with free exercise.

Early in his presidency, Ronald Reagan extended formal diplomatic recognition to the Holy See, the headquarters of the Roman Catholic Church. This act of favoritism toward one religious body, and discrimination against all others, surely violates the First Amendment. But an attempt by taxpayers and religious leaders to challenge the diplomatic move was cut short when the Supreme Court ruled that none of the plaintiffs, and presumably no one else either, had "standing" to bring the lawsuit.

This diplomatic linkage of the U.S. government with one church was part of a larger cooperation between the Reagan administration and that church, spelled out in a *Time* magazine exposé in February

1992. As a result of the close church-state tie, *Time* concluded, "the Reagan administration agreed to alter its foreign-aid program to comply with the church's teaching on birth control." Further, according to Reagan's first ambassador to the Vatican, the U.S. "selected different programs and abandoned others as a result of [Vatican] intervention."

Conclusion

This all-too-brief survey of the major church-state and religious liberty problem areas might lead some people to a gloomy pessimism. That is not my intention. Armed with knowledge and a commitment to preserve fundamental liberties, individuals singly and organized in groups can successfully defend church-state separation and individual freedom of thought and conscience.

The plaintiffs in the important church-state lawsuits have been courageous individuals. They have been aided by private attorneys and by organizations dedicated to defending basic rights.

Individuals may bring church-state problems to the attention of elected officials, or courts, or organizations set up to act on complaints. All citizens can and should vote for candidates committed to civil liberties and church-state separation. They can write letters to editors and to lawmakers. They can provide financial support to the groups working full time to defend fundamental rights. Among the organizations active in the fields of church-state separation and freedom of conscience are the American Civil Liberties Union, Americans for Religious Liberty, The Religious Coalition for Abortion Rights, Catholics for a Free Choice, The National Abortion Rights Action League, and the Planned Parenthood Federation of America. In addition, a number of Protestant and Jewish agencies exist to defend civil liberties.

The history of the future is not yet written. We the People will write it.

Edd Doerr is an author of many articles and books on the separation of Church and State and is President of Americans For Religious Liberty, P.O. Box 6656, Silver Spring, Maryland, 20906.

"Leave the matter of religion to the family altar, the church, and the private schools, supported entirely by private contributions. Keep the church and the state forever separated.

— Ulysses S. Grant

"I believe in a wall between church and state so high that no one can climb over it.

When religion controls government, political liberty dies; and when government controls religion, religious liberty perishes.

Every American has the constitutional right not to be taxed or have his tax money expended for the establishment of religion.

For too long the issue of government aid to church related organizations has been a divisive force in our society and in the Congress. It has erected communication barriers among our religions and fostered intolerance."

— Sam Ervin

The Tax-Free Ride

Austin Miles

As a guide said to me in a richly furnished, gold-leafed monastery and library outside Vienna, "This monastery was built by other than 'Christian' means," indicating that "Christian" should stand for something good and honorable. It does not – the ghosts of Christianity's victims will forever haunt the universe.

Even though its methods of accumulating wealth and its consequent power are more sophisticated today, it is still plundering nevertheless with a continuous holy rape upon the pocketbook of every American. Because the churches are tax-exempt, the average citizen pays an additional $925 a year in taxes to support them.

The tax-free ride has granted the churches access to unlimited wealth. Growing in power and ownership, they now own 20-25 percent of all real estate in America. According to the IRS, church donations total over 19 *billion* dollars a year. This does not include profits from businesses, stock holdings, bond holdings, retirement centers, or lease-back arrangements.

The Mormon Church alone collects at least $4.3 billion a year from its members and another $400 million from its many business enterprises purchased with tax-exempt donated money.

The churches own 81 billion dollars' worth of tax-exempt real estate in Texas and $1.3 billion in Los Angeles County alone. Consider the prime real estate owned by them in New York City, Chicago, Boston, in every state – the amount involved is staggering.

The high-living religious leaders pay no taxes on any of that property or on the income that is generated on those properties. Now ask yourself: "how much in taxes do I have to pay for my home and business?" Every tax dollar that the church avoids paying, you as an individual taxpayer must make up. If taxes are necessary to run the United States, and the church takes a percentage out of those taxes, someone must make up for the slack, and that someone is you. At the expense of all of us, churches have enjoyed enormous privileged wealth.

We have been caught on the horns of a 'tradition' that has allowed the church to skirt around a well-defined law that positively prohibits state aid to any church organization. This sensitive issue has perplexed legal scholars since the constitution was written, only because of the reluctance of anyone to take a firm stand in the matter.

In Volume 12 of the *American Law and Procedure*, page 180, this assessment sums up the problem:

> 191. Tax Exemptions. It may be argued with much force that the exemption of certain property from taxation is equivalent to assisting it by public taxation to this extent, as other property must pay somewhat more in consequence. Where the property exempted is that of a class, rather than of an individual, the question really becomes one of proper classification of purposes of taxation, rather than one as to a public purpose. The two run into each other, however, as where a constitution forbids state aid to any church or religious sect. The payment of money derived from taxation to a church is certainly invalid under this provision, but tax exemptions of the property of churches and religious bodies are almost everywhere upheld, probably because historically these exemptions have generally been made.

So, expert legal opinion is that the tax-exempt status of churches is illegal. We have simply allowed tradition to replace valid law.

Good Works

Historically this has been allowed with the clear understanding that the church would relieve the state from social and welfare responsibilities by providing for the poor with whatever monies and property it accumulated. Any excess monies would be used for this purpose only, not to be accumulated.

Right from the beginning of this clearly understood agreement, there were certain (legally understood) prohibitions of activity and conduct for such tax benefits. And this is the exact statement of purpose as defined by the Federal Government, "by devoting itself exclusively to the public good."

Instead of using excess monies to help the poor as they are supposed to do, most of these churches use it to greedily invest for more profit in ventures totally unrelated to church activity. A classic example is the Catholic Church which preaches against birth control. One of the Vatican's biggest investments for profit is in the pharmaceutical firm that manufactures birth control pills.

Here are some examples of being "good stewards of God's money": In February of 1992, a group of Baptist ministers repeatedly offered beauty contestant Desiree Washington one million dollars in cash if she would withdraw her rape charges against boxer Mike Tyson. William Bright of Campus Crusade For Christ offered Universal Studios one million dollars cash for the negative of the film *The Last Temptation of Christ"* so he could burn it. In May of 1992, Pat Robertson offered United Press International six million dollars in cash (money he accumulated from tax-free donations to his tax-free religious organization) to buy the wire service, which would put him in a position of control in the secular media. What does all of this have to do with the public good, or of helping the poor?

An example of the public good (that we finance with additional taxes forced upon us) comes out of The Church of Christ in Laporte, Colorado. The pastor, Rev. Pete Peters, with a national radio program, has published and distributed through the mail (with postage subsidized by us), some of the most vile hate literature this author has ever read. In his booklet *Death Penalty for Homosexuals is Prescribed in the Bible* (May 1992), he advocates that this biblical law be incorporated in our national law; "Even though our satanic courts will not uphold God's word, Christians, the true dedicated ones, will put into force God's law and judgment concerning this crime." In other words, it is our Christian duty to kill a homosexual for God.

In another paper on the subject, Pastor Peters says there will be a big rock party for all queers and faggots. Anti-semitic literature goes out regularly. His booklet *The Inadvertent Confessions of a Jew,* in which he wants all Jews run out of America, is a classic study of hate mongering. And it doesn't stop with these two groups the good reverend has targeted.

Tax-exempt churches urge their followers to disobey the law (such as in the abortion protests). They use their tax-free, donated-to-God money to drag into court any individual who does not agree with them, who does not want to be approached by Christian recruiters in public places, or who criticizes them publicly. This kind of expensive litigation now goes on daily. Churches finance, out of donated dollars for god, legal groups such as The Rutherford Institute whose function is solely to enforce biblical law as the law of the land.

Political Activity

Christianity is determined to wipe out many of our freedoms. This is a serious threat. The well-funded right-wing Christians have combined their efforts and organized into a powerful voting bloc. They have tied up so many senators and representatives, having their own religious lobbying groups, that it has been next to impossible to enforce any kind of tax laws or tax violations against them, allowing them to continue to gain in power with unlimited funds.

One of the clearly defined laws applicable to tax-exempt religious organizations is that churches cannot engage in any political activity and cannot engage in more than an insignificant amount of lobbying activities. This is stated in IRS Manual sections 501(c)3 and 170(c)2. Thus, according to law, if a church intervenes in a political campaign or engages in substantial lobbying, then its tax-exempt status is jeopardized. So, simply put, section 501(c)3 church organizations are subject to a ban on political activities, *period.*

According to the *Overview of Tax Rules Applicable to Exempt Organizations* that was prepared for the House Committee on Ways and Means, it states:

> Prohibited political activity involves the participation or intervention, directly or indirectly, in any political campaign on behalf of or in opposition to any candidate for public office. The office involved can be national, state, or local; and it is not required that the election be contested or involve the participation of political parties.
>
> The critical issue in determining whether an activity constitutes intervention in a political campaign is whether it reflects or advances a preference between competing candidates.

A nasty, special Assembly election in California in 1991 provides us with a model case of typical gross violation of established law regarding tax-exempt organizations. B.T. Collins, running for the Fifth Assembly seat, faced the wrath of Rev. Glenn Cole of Capitol Christian Center in Sacramento, who used his tax-exempt church property and pulpit to endorse Barbara Alby, contrary to the law that prohibits such intervention in a political campaign by a church enjoying tax-free privileges.

Rev. Cole has freely admitted to the media that members of his flock are readily solicited to vote for the candidate of *his* choice. Furthermore, Rev. Cole, in violation of the tax-exempt laws, has a history of using his sermons to support like-minded Republican candidates. In 1990, Rev. Cole and his church helped Republican Assemblyman David Knowles, who was a member of his Capitol Christian Center, defeat veteran Assemblyman Norm Waters, a Democrat from Plymouth, California.

Rev. Cole also sets up voter registration tables outside his church sanctuary (but still on tax-exempt church property) to sign up new supporters for his candidates who have been motivated by his political sermons.

Rev. Cole, in his capacity as a Minister of the Gospel, wrote fund-raising letters which were sent to supporters on behalf of fellow Christian Barbara Alby. Soliciting campaign funds and contributions is another violation of 501(c)3 which also states: " . . . the publishing or distributing of statements that support or oppose a candidate is an example of political intervention." According to tax law 501(c)3: "The critical issue in determining whether an activity constitutes intervention in a political campaign is whether it reflects or advances a preference between competing parties."

Rev. Cole cleverly used the law to circumvent the solicitation of funds issue by declaring that his was an "independent action by an individual in his private capacity and not as a church organization." If he was working as an individual, a private citizen, then why did he continue to stick the title "Reverend" to his name as well as printing the name of his church on the letterhead of his fund-raising letter? (Hint: see Romans 3:7)

Lobbying

What is described as "substantial lobbying" is another prohibition of tax law 501(c)3. "Substantial" is defined by the Joint Committee on Taxation as over 5% of time, which means sermon time, either in church or on tax-exempt Christian radio and television broadcasts. According to the IRS tax code: "A section 501(c)3 organization is engaged in lobbying activity if it advocates the adoption or rejection of legislation. The term 'legislation' includes action by Congress, or any State or local legislative body, or by the public in a referendum, initiative, constitutional amendment, or similar procedure. Lobbying includes (1) directly contacting members of a legislative body or their staff to propose, support, or oppose legislation, (2) grassroots lobbying, urging the public to contact legislators or legislative staffs to propose, support or oppose legislation and (3) more generally, advocating the adoption or rejection of legislation."

IRS wants to tax churches but has been frustrated. As one official said to me during a personal meeting: "Congress makes us jump through a hoop seven different ways just to try and audit a church organization. They have tied our hands." The late Senator Heinz once told me: "Congress does not want to offend the religious right. They cave in to their demands to gain their votes. The rest of the population they are supposed to serve be damned."

We have been sold out. The churches are not even accountable for the enormous wealth they continue to accumulate. Congressman J.J. Pickle, Chairman of the House Committee on Ways and Means and of its Subcommittee on Oversight, has written two letters to the IRS Commissioner demanding to know what steps will be taken in order to ensure that the tax laws regarding churches are enforced. At this writing, the Commissioner still has not responded.

International

There is even a sinister side to this coddling of the churches by our government. Respected churches in every community, such as the Episcopal, Presbyterian, Lutheran, Methodist, Baptist, and others belong to the National and the World Council of Churches. To the public, this would appear to be a mark of responsibility and accountability, being under such a supervisory umbrella. A large portion of donations taken in by these mainline churches goes to the support of the World Council of Churches and its affiliates.

I once visited the offices of the World Council of Churches in New York, as a minister, to request permission to use the chapel at Kennedy Airport for interdenominational services. I was ill-prepared for what I found in those offices. I saw young militants in shirtsleeves scurrying about, telephones all going at once, revolutionary posters on the walls with the names of countries targeted. One poster that stood out had the word "GUATEMALA" with a large clenched fist in front of it. A chapel in the building, larger than most churches, with highly polished floors and pews, obviously never functioned as a place of worship. I had nightmares for the next several nights over those offices and the shocking truth that I learned about them and the organization.

The World Council of Churches and its affiliate, The National Council of Churches, supported by church-donated dollars, quietly help to finance selected covert operations and wars. Totally financed by the World Council of Churches, the bloody overthrow of Uganda President Milton Obote on Feb. 2, 1971 put madman Idi Amin in power. One of the sickest tyrants in history, Idi Amin, who cruelly tortured his opponents to death, burned hundreds alive, and executed countless others, is one product of church-donated dollars.

The CIA-spawned Contras, Ronald Reagan's pet project, were financed in large part by right-wing fundamentalist Christians. The leader of the Contras, Adolfo Calero, a professed born-again Christian, attracted the blind support of "fellow believers" who contributed millions of dollars to "help the cause." Bobby Yerkes, a central character in my book *Don't Call Me Brother*, donated so much money to the Contras "as his Christian duty," that Adolfo Calero called him personally to invite him to a banquet in Studio City. I was in Yerkes' house when that call came in.

In chilling testimony given at American University in Washington, D.C., and televised over C-Span on Dec. 12, 1989, ex-CIA officer John Stockwell told how the Christian Contras burst into the huts of innocent villagers. He saw them drag a man out of one house and castrate him in front of his wife and children. These savages next raped his wife, then cut off her breasts with their bayonets. Her terrified children were forced to watch.

Again, these atrocities were partially financed by the dollars put in the collection plates of the neighborhood churches that tell the faithful that these special collections go to the "world hunger fund." Compounding the tragedy, the Nicaraguans are wonderful people, love Americans and still cannot understand why America would do this to them.

Any individual with even a shred of decency and social responsibility would have no choice but to speak out against any church even remotely connected to that hoodlum organization and to confront these pastors and members of their flock. Clearly, the giving of money to any church only brings evil. Mainline churches support left-wing causes and killings, and fundamentalist churches support right-wing causes and killings. Killing should not be the function of the church. The blood is on the hands of every donor.

What To Do

The acceptable time is at hand to take stern, definitive action against this betrayal of humanity. First, an organized protest, without let-up, should be directed against the illegal tax-exempt status flaunted by the church, which violates the established constitutional rights of those who do not believe in the church or God. Why should the population at large be forced to support churches? Let the churches be supported by those who use them, not by the extra taxation of those who do not.

With the exception of the Tax Commissioner in Washington, D.C., IRS is unhappy with their inability to collect taxes from the churches. They, too, feel the sting of the recession of the '90's. IRS is cutting employment, re-shuffling and eliminating jobs, all because of a decline in tax collections while the churches get richer.

IRS needs and wants our help with the church problem. Everyone I've spoken with has told me the same thing: "There must be public awareness and public response on this issue." Publicity and more publicity; in other words, let our voices be heard to generate support from the public at large. This is needed. Send letters to the editors of newspapers and to congresspeople and representatives without let-up. These voices must be heard loud and clear. Call in local radio talk shows on this issue. Christians are doing all these things and that is how they have succeeded – so far – in walking all over us.

The churches must be required to obey the law like the rest of us. The entire church-tax issue must be changed. We must insist that Congress either enforce the tax laws regarding tax-free 501(c)(3) churches, or be forced to make a public statement that tax-exempt *restrictions* apply to every organization *except* religious ones. This would spotlight the issue and injustice of it.

Here is a possibility that I happened on by accident, that may be helpful in combating this tax issue – the Grand Jury! Every county has one. From their own manual they tell of their "watchdog responsibilities." One of those responsibilities is " . . . to examine certain nonprofit corporations to ensure that their duties are lawfully conducted. The grand jury reviews and evaluates procedures utilized by these entities to determine whether more efficient and economical policies may be employed."

Even though this concerns mainly nonprofit corporations receiving county or city funds, the church corporations do receive benefits from the higher taxes we pay to support them. It is certainly worth a try. Write the foreman of your local grand jury. You can find the information by calling the clerk of Superior Court. Then write him a letter, individually, one with several signatures or on behalf of a group and demand that an investigation of the abuses of their nonprofit status be instituted. Then, let the area media know of this request, with a copy of your letter sent to news directors.

Meanwhile, I will propose to the IRS that they have on their next tax forms the following: "If you approve of churches being tax-exempt, check this box and you will be charged the higher rate of tax in order to offset what the churches do not pay. If you disapprove churches being tax-exempt, check this box and you will be charged the lower rate of tax." Now this will get attention and put this entire issue in proper perspective.

There is no separation of Church and State when we are forced to pay a higher rate of tax in order to subsidize the church. The tax law is now discriminatory favoring Christians over non-Christians. This is unconstitutional and needs a solid test case. The concept of freedom of religion must be re-defined. Freedom of religion means that anyone in America has the right to worship privately in their homes or churches without interference. Religious freedom does not mean that Christians can use their tax-exempt status to interfere with the secular world and push their doctrines off on the public.

Austin Miles is a minster, author of many articles, and books. He is the Author of Don't Call Me Brother *and* Setting The Captives Free, *Prometheus Books, Buffalo, New York.*

The House Chaplain gets a salary of – and this is not a typo – $115,300. Not to be outdone, the Senate Chaplain spends much more per member-soul on his small body of 100 legislators. He receives about the same salary as his House colleague, but he has an overall budget of $300,000, including pay for secretaries and office space to help him shepherd his sometimes wayward flock.

If it worked, it might be worth the price. But thus far there are no signs of divine intervention in the chambers of the U.S. Congress.

— Martin L. Gross
The Government Racket: Washington Waste from A to Z

Circumcision was practiced in Egypt as long ago as 4000 B. C. According to the inscription on this bas-relief from the Ankh-Mahor tomb at Sakkara, the youth balks and must be held by the doctor's aide.

— Adopted from:
  Sixth Dynasty basrelief
  from the tomb of
  Ankh-ma-hor at Saqqara.

Honey, They Cut The Kid!

Religious Traditions and Circumcision

Gerald A. Larue

The practice of the painful mutilation of the foreskins of infant males in America rests upon biblical and religious traditions plus spurious medical fiction (prevention of penile infection, penile cancer, cervical cancer in partners of uncircumcised males). It is my intention to examine the biblical background for this practice.

Just when and why circumcision was first practiced in the ancient Near East is not known, but it was widely attested in antiquity. Bodies from 4000 Before the Common Era (B.C.E.) exhumed in Egypt disclose evidence of circumcision. Ancient Egyptian art, on those occasions when the genitals of Egyptian males were depicted, provides pictorial evidence of male circumcision.

However, not all Egyptians were circumcised. X-rays of the mummy of the Eighteenth Dynasty Pharaoh Ahomse (16th century B.C.E.) prove that he was not circumcised. It is possible that his successor, Amenhotep 1, also was uncircumcised. It has also been suggested that although circumcision was common among the upper classes and may be recognized as a puberty rite, it was not a requirement. The poorer, common folk did not have to undergo it.

Circumcision was practiced by some Semitic groups. Jeremiah, in the seventh century BCE, included Edomites, Ammonites and Moabites as among the circumcised. Assyrians and Babylonians were not circumcised. Nor were Philistines who are derivatively defined in the Bible as "the uncircumcised" (Judg. 14:3; 15:18; I Sam. 14:6).

The earliest reference to circumcision in the Bible is in a folk-tale (written prior to Genesis 17) associated with Moses:

> Then it happened, at a stopping place along the way, that
> Yahweh met him (Moses) and tried to kill him. Then Zipporah
> (Moses' Midianite wife) took a piece of flint and cut off her son's
> foreskin and touched Moses' feet (genitals) with it, saying, "You
> are my blood-bridegroom." So he let him alone. At that time she
> said "blood-bridegroom" in reference to circumcision. (Exod.
> 4:24-26).

This strange insertion into the tenth-century B.C.E. temple fiction about Moses suggests that circumcision became Hebrew custom through contact with the Midianites.

Anti-Judaism became a major issue under one of Alexander's successors named Antiochus IV, who ruled Judea from Syria. He forbade circumcision, and his agents killed those whose infants were circumcised, together with the circumcised baby. After a bitter struggle, the Jews experienced a brief time of freedom, before they came under Roman domination.

Interestingly enough, towards the close of the second century B.C.E., when the Jewish prince Hyrcanus invaded and conquered Idumia, he offered the Idumenas a choice: to be exiled or to become Jews. They chose the latter, were circumcised, and thus became instant Jews. They were not truly accepted by traditional Jews, and when Herod the Great – the strongest Jewish ruler – assumed the throne, his Idumean background earned him the label of "half-Jew." Circumcision was not enough.

Circumcision in the Christian Scriptures

The first Christians were Jews and were therefore circumcised. The Gospel of Luke reported that Jesus was circumcised on the eighth day (2:21). The apostle Paul was also circumcised on the eighth day (Phil. 3:5). As the Christian church began to move out into the Mediterranean world and attract non-Jews, circumcision became a problem for converts. The issue came to a head (no pun intended!) in the Galatian controversy.

Paul established new Christian groups in the Greek world. His pattern seems to have been as follows: he would speak in a Jewish synagogue concerning the end of the age and Jesus as the Christ and means of salvation. Some Jews would listen; others rejected him. Among those attending the synagogue were non-Jewish Greeks, attracted perhaps by the monotheistic faith and ethical ideals. Some were drawn to Christianity but, when they wished to join the new group, they were informed by the conservatives in the church that before they became Christians they had to become Jews and be circumcised. Paul saw this demand as a stumbling block inasmuch as adult male Greeks had no intention of being circumcised. Therefore he wrote to the Christian church he had founded in Galatia.

In this letter he challenged the validity of circumcision as a criterion for membership in a Christian church. He castigated the leaders in Jerusalem. He pointed out that Cephas (Peter) had been two-faced in the matter by swaying to the conservative side when confronted by the circumcision party after agreeing that Paul's mission was to the circumcised (Gal. 2). Paul argued that "in Christ Jesus neither circumcision nor uncircumcision count for anything" (5:6), and expresses the wish that for members of the circumcision party the circumcision blade might slip and more than the foreskin be removed so that they might "mutilate themselves" (5:12).

The same issue appears to have surfaced among the Christians in the city of Corinth. Paul wrote a letter to them stating:

> Was anyone already circumcised when he was called (to be a Christian)? Let him not seek to remove the marks of circumcision. Was anyone uncircumcised when he was called? Let him not seek circumcision. (I Cor. 7:18).

Obviously, there were some who sought to disavow their Jewish heritage by removing the mark of circumcision, just as their ancestors had done during the time of the Maccabees.

For Paul neither circumcision nor uncircumcision counted for anything. Ultimately the matter was referred to the Jerusalem council where, after serious debate, it was decided circumcision was not a requirement for membership in the Christian community (Acts: 15).

Conclusion

For present day Jews, circumcision is both a covenant rite and a naming ceremony. Orthodox Jews follow ancient practices. On the eighth day, the infant son is taken to the Mohel (the circumciser) for a rite performed according to a primitive ritual. The blood flow is stopped by wine, held in the Mohel's mouth – a custom which some Jews find revolting. These believers are fulfilling Torah requirements. Non-orthodox Jews may have their sons "done" in a hospital setting. Even Jews who have moved away from Judaism toward a secular or humanistic way of life continue to have their sons circumcised. Christians, too, have their male offspring circumcised in some cases because Jesus was circumcised, but far more often in an un-thinking, uncritical way as something that is done to newborn males. As better information regarding circumcision is circulated, out-moded beliefs concerning medical or health benefits will be dis-carded. Only ancient beliefs will remain as a stimulus for the continuation of this barbaric custom.

Dr. Gerald Larue is professor emeritus of biblical history and archeology at the University of Southern California and chairman of the Committee for the Scientific Examination of Religion.

Dr. Spock On Circumcision

I used to lean toward routine circumcision at birth. Now that circumcision is not recommended to stop masturbation and now that the theory about cervical cancer has been disproved, there is no excuse for the operation – except as a religious rite. So, I strongly recommend leaving the foreskin alone.

— Dr. Benjamin Spock,
Baby and Child Care (1985)

Female Genital Mutilation

Fran P. Hosken

Reprint from *Truth Seeker*, July / August 1989

According to a conservative estimate, at least 84 million women and girls are mutilated today in Continental Africa, and similar operations are practiced along the Persian Gulf and the southern part of the Arab Peninsula. With increasing mobility of African and Middle Eastern immigrants to Europe, the U.S. and also to Australia, these mutilations are being exported all over the world. There is no doubt, and anecdotal evidence exists, that immigrants from Somalia, Sudan, Ethiopia, or certain ethnic groups of Kenya, Nigeria, etc., are having their small daughters mutilated in the U.S.

The objective of infibulation is to make sexual intercourse impossible. At present, infibulation is practiced mostly by Moslems, according to all available sources, because of the importance and value they attach to virginity. Women who are infibulated have to be cut open to allow sexual intercourse, and more cuts are needed for delivery of a child. All girls, without exception, must undergo this mutilation, as it is a requirement for marriage.

All the operations are performed on the ground, under septic conditions, with the same knife or tool used on all the girls of a group operation, which is still the custom among many ethnic groups in rural areas. In cases of fatalities, neither the operator nor the operation are ever blamed Rather, an evil spirit is held responsible, or the ritual was not performed properly according to the wishes of the ancestors, or the girl herself is at fault because she had sex before she was operated on.

Infibulation or pharaonic circumcision is practiced in the Sudan and adjoining areas throughout Somalia, parts of Ethiopia, Southern Egypt and Northern Kenya and in some areas of West Africa. Infibulation or pharaonic circumcision is the most drastic and damaging operation. It is called "Pharaonic," as the operation according to historic documents was already recorded in ancient Egypt more than 2000 years ago in pharaonic times. The term infibulation is derived from "fibilla" which means clasp or pin in Latin and goes back to the old Romans: a fibula was used to hold together the folds of the toga, the loose garment all Roman men wore. The Romans also fastened together the large lips of slave girls to prevent them from having sexual intercourse, as becoming pregnant would hamper their work.

The followers of the Ethiopian Christian Church and the Copts in Egypt (more than 7 million adherents) have always mutilated the genitals of their female children. Indeed, all religions (with the exception of the Scottish Protestant Church in Kenya in the 1920s) have actively supported or tolerated the mutilation of girls to make them pliable subjects of the dominant patriarchal community that vests all rights in the males.

There is no doubt that genital mutilation does permanent life-long physical and psychological damage to women. The full impact of the often terrible psychological consequences has never been systematically investigated, though it is known that numerous young women commit suicide, as for instance reported in Burkina Faso.

Fran P. Hosken is editor of Women's International Network News, *has published major reports on female genital mutilation, and has served as advisor to the World Health Organization.*

African women have now started to organize to fight against these terrible genital mutilations in a systematic way.

— Fran P. Hosken

Female Sexual Castration In Cairo, Egypt

Mohamed Badawi

Reprint from *Truth Seeker*, July / August 1989

Female genital mutilation is a common and popular practice throughout Egypt, where every day thousands of young girls are subjected to this torture and mutilation. Religious institutions and ancient social customs are primarily responsible for the genital mutilation of female children. The full social and psychological consequences of mutilating the genitals of female children have yet to be evaluated. Preliminary evidence, however, suggests that the psychological consequence of female genital mutilation is very similar to that of rape victims.

What can be done to bring an end to female genital mutilation in Egypt and other countries? The use of force would only drive it underground and increase the resistance to cultural change. Educational programs that are directed to Egyptian families, the agents who perform the genital mutilations (midwives, doctors, barbers), and the political and religious leaders on the harmful and devastating effects that these procedures have upon women will contribute significantly to the elimination of female genital mutilations.

Specific attention must be given to the effects of genital mutilations upon reproductive processes and the marital sexual relationships. Men need to understand that their marital sexual relationships and happiness will be significantly enhanced when the female genitals are not mutilated. Finally, the education of women must be accelerated if these objectives are to be realized.

Mohamed Badawi, M.D., M.P.H., is a graduate of Cairo University School of Medicine, the University of Michigan School of Public Health, and Al-Azhar University School of Medicine, Cairo. He is currently completing a doctoral program at the Johns Hopkins Univ. School of Public Health.

Religion and its practices have consistently been one of women's fiercest enemies . . . The fact that many women do not realize this shows how thorough the brainwashing and intimidation have been.

— Arnold Toynbee, historian

Margaret Sanger

Leaving Court of Special Sessions after arraignment, October 1916
— Sophia Smith Collection

Woman's Right

Steve Allen

It is fascinating that the purest form of the respect-for-life philosophy that motivates at least some anti-abortionists is consistent with the general thrust of Humanist thinking over the last couple of centuries, but it relates scarcely at all to much Christian behavior of the past 2,000 years.

Two basic questions are: (1) What is life? (2) When, in the human context, does it begin? While at first the answers appear obvious, the relevant realities are complex. For some time it has been possible to keep human tissues, separated from bodies, alive. They need only be placed in an aqueous environment and provided with such nutrients and methods of waste-disposal as their individual cells require. We can, then, point to a brain, a heart, a lung, or other portions of a once-conscious body and state, quite accurately, that it is alive.

Yet if someone were to destroy such an organ, would it be reasonable to accuse him of murder? There is no question that he was destroying living human tissue. But it is equally as clear that the individual organ was nevertheless not a human being. Why? Because it did not have a mind. If then, it is only the existence of brain-function and/or mind that establishes the existence of a human, it follows that the termination of a fetus that is just a few days old can hardly be equated with arbitrarily ending the life of a six-month-old child or of an adult.

On this point, incidentally, there is invaluable relevant information in Exodus 21:22, which refers to two men who engage in physical combat and who, in thrashing about, bump into a pregnant woman who suffers a miscarriage as a result. In both rabbinical and early Christian commentary there is a clear distinction between punishments thought suitable for two outwardly similar crimes. If the fetus that dies is unformed, the common opinion was that the guilty individual need not receive the death penalty. But if the fetus is formed – which is to say in the late stage of development – then that is a much more serious matter and the death penalty is considered appropriate punishment. This makes clear that, quite aside from the question as to whether it is ever appropriate to refer to the medical disruption of a developing fetus as *murder*, it was not correct at one time to use such a term if the unborn individual was in a very early state of development.

For an excellent analysis of this question, see "Two Traditions: The Law of Exodus 21:22-23 Revisited" by Stanley Isser in the *Catholic Biblical Quarterly* (Jan. 1990).

As noted above, a growing segment of the Christian Right openly advocates that the proper solution to present-day social problems is to make the United States formally and legally a Christian nation with a government entirely under Christian domination and guided by the laws and principles of both the Old and New Testaments. This would require repeal of the First Amendment.

Needless to say, such Christians are members of the pro-death-penalty camp. If (1) they succeed in their ambitions, (2) abortion is outlawed because it is considered murder, and (3) all murderers must be executed by the state, then it logically follows that the many millions of American women who would beyond question continue to have illegal, secret abortions would have to be put to death if detected.

Concerning certain aspects of the abortion controversy, there is surprisingly little disagreement or debate. Statistically speaking, few people think it is permissible to end the life of a fetus in the last several weeks of its development. This is so simply because a baby in the eighth or ninth month is clearly a human being and is therefore entitled to all the rights that society is prepared to accord a newborn or any adult citizen. (An interesting sidelight on this point is that in Nationalist China, America's ally against the Communists, the practice of infanticide was widespread among poor families, particularly if the children were female. When the Communists assumed control of that country in 1949, they legislated against the practice.)

Fundamentalists have, of course, attempted to justify their stand against abortion by citing the Bible, just as an earlier generation of fundamentalists used scriptural texts to try to justify their opposition to new birth-control devices or their acceptance of slavery. Among the passages used to oppose abortion are Ephesians 1:4, 2 Thessalonians 2:13, and Jeremiah 1:5. These and similar texts emphasize divine foreknowledge and election by stressing that God knew his prophets and apostles when they were in the womb.

Fundamentalists have pressed these texts further in the service of their metaphysical conjecture that the entity in the womb, from the moment of conception, is a person. What they failed to note was that their premises lead them into the heretical doctrine of reincarnation.

According to the book of Jeremiah, the Lord said to his prophet, "*Before* I formed you in the womb I knew you." (italics added)

According to Hebrews 7:9-10, Levi the priest was within the loins of his great-grandfather, Abraham. If one used Jerry Falwell's exegetical methods in interpreting Scripture, one might conclude that Levi existed as a 100 percent person in Abraham's loins. This suggests that Abraham would have been guilty of manslaughter or negligent homicide if by fortuitous nocturnal emission he had allowed the innocent Levi to escape from his loins. (See Joe E. Barnhart, *The Southern Baptist Holy War*, Austin, Texas Monthly Press, 1986, pp. 159-160.)

According to Luke 1:42, another antiabortion passage employed by fundamentalists, when pregnant "Elizabeth heard the greeting of Mary the babe leaped in her womb." Elizabeth herself is then quoted as saying "the babe leaped in my womb for joy" (1:44). But this does not prove anything, because a pregnant woman, feeling the fetus moving, can attribute any emotion she wants to the baby she is carrying. Most women simply speak of the baby's "kicking."

Barnhart also notes:

> For many years, a number of [fundamentalist] preachers like Jerry Falwell and W. A. Criswell raised no prophetic voice against the known brutalities of racism or unjust treatment of women. Now suddenly they have turned into bleeding hearts over almost microscopic zygotes. With little sustained concern for the civil-rights movement when it had to do with conspicuous persons of minority status, some of the antiabortion preachers have recently begun to deliver impassioned and eloquent speeches about the civil rights of the fertilized egg.

There is the general perception that the new organism, which in its early stages is a small blob of matter, can hardly be referred to as a human being, consisting, as it may, of only a few dozen cells. Nature itself daily aborts millions of such creatures and, in fact, not only at early stages. The majority of those who take a clear-cut, no-abortions-under-any-circumstances position naturally wish to make it impossible to terminate the life of even these forms.

Most opponents of abortion seem unaware of the fact that the European and American successes in legalizing the practice during the last half-century grew largely out of public concern about the thriving market in criminal abortions. Few of these were performed by licensed medical practitioners. Not surprisingly, the results were often horrendous, so far as the life and health of the unfortunate mothers were concerned. Informed citizens eventually said, in effect,

"It makes no sense to continue to permit so much death and suffering. If abortions are going to take place, as they obviously will continue to do, then the procedure ought to be performed under controlled circumstances by qualified medical professionals." This is certainly not the only rationale for legalized abortion, but since it is part of the larger argument, it must be taken into account.

To the great number of those who have not yet taken a formal position concerning the difficult question of abortion but who have at least been exposed to arguments from both sides, it may seem that at one end of the field are those who think that abortion is, generally speaking, a positive and justified act, and those on the opposite side who believe that it is a simple act of murder.

If there is a single person on earth who views abortion as favorably as he views playing tennis or reading a good book, he would be in urgent need of psychiatric attention. Abortion, like many medical procedures, is a sad business.

As for my own position – with which I would not trouble the reader except that I have frequently been asked to state it for the record – I am opposed to abortion in the sense that I can envision an ideal state in which no such medical procedure would ever be necessary.

And it is not difficult, after all, to at least imagine, if not bring about, a utopian situation in which almost no further abortions would be desired or performed. Such a situation, of course, would involve far more widespread use of methods of birth control than is practiced at present. The debate as to whether there is an over-population problem has never, in the present century, been worth the attention of any serious or informed person because everyone sensible agrees that there is. Even the Catholic church acknowledges that there are too many people in certain places for the available food supplies to sustain.

Many sincere and intelligent Catholics are so disturbed that their church only acknowledges the population problem and resists serious efforts to alleviate it, that they simply ignore Catholic doctrine on birth control and make their own moral decisions. Nor do they have much difficulty in finding priestly confessors to tell them that they are entitled to let their conscience be their guide on such difficult questions.

Among the many prominent Catholic thinkers who are at odds with their church on the question of contraception is James T. Burtchaell, C.S.C. The details of his argument on the question may be found in *The Giving and the Taking of Life: Essays Ethical* (1989).

Father Burtchaell is professor of biblical theology and ethics at the University of Notre Dame, and his collection of essays was published by the University of Notre Dame Press. Moreover, the book is referred to in respectful tones by the Jesuit magazine *America* (Oct. 14, 1989). None of this would happen if Burtchaell's was simply the voice of a lonely heretic. It is my assumption that, on this question, the majority of Catholic intellectuals are on the side of common sense and therefore in opposition to their church.

One of the reasons that millions of abortions will continue to take place, regardless of the views of American conservatives, is that, though great numbers of eggs are being fertilized, not all the potential children are *wanted by either or both of their parents*. In a large percentage of the cases, this is because the parents are not married. In some instances, they are married, but to other individuals. And in cases where a married mother and father are the parents-to-be, they too, by the millions, are deciding, for whatever good or poor reasons, that they do not want the particular birth that will result if nothing is done to interrupt the cellular development in the womb.

Life is difficult enough for even the more fortunate among us in the present day. For those new arrivals who are not welcomed by loving parents, the eventual results are almost invariably horrifying. This relates, in a very direct way, to the problem of child abuse in American society. In one city alone, New York, over a hundred children are killed by their own parents each year. Nor is such a death a sudden, swift release. It usually results from a long series of savage beatings, sometimes – the very soul shudders – accompanied by sexual abuse.

The future society that was serious about trying to diminish the need for abortion would incorporate a vigorous program of instruction on sex, starting at the appropriate early grade-level. There is a tendency to assume that because modern America is inundated by sexual themes on a morning, noon, and nightly basis, high school freshmen have absorbed so much information about the subject that they do not require further formal instruction. However, research has shown that the same old historic ignorance of sex prevails and is one of the factors contributing to the present unhappy picture.

Should instruction about sex restrict itself to a description of the plumbing, so to speak? Absolutely not. Should it incorporate moral and ethical considerations? Certainly. The only sort of moral component that is automatically ruled out in American public schools is that which represents a strictly sectarian religious viewpoint. In other words, the Catholic church, which still feels that masturbation and birth control are grave sins, clearly ought not to be permitted to impose that view on the American process of public education.

The sort of moral considerations that could quite properly be incorporated into a program of instruction are those indicated by common sense, social custom, and practicality. Young boys, to give a specific instance, must be taught that they have no right to force their sexual attentions on anyone else, that to persist in doing so is called rape, and that it is a grave crime, punishable by imprisonment, in our society. Furthermore, it should be explained to immature boys that rape is wrong not simply because it is illegal but also because it is a cruel violation of the Golden Rule.

Young men and women should also be taught that until they are absolutely certain they want children, they shouldn't even think of having them. The present situation would be an outrage if only one unwanted child was born, but we are talking about millions.

It must be stressed that for those teenagers, especially the older among them, who would, despite moral advice, continue to lose emotional control in certain instances, largely because of the dictates of nature itself, there would have to be a great deal of information provided concerning methods of birth control and, for the unmarried, birth prevention. This returns us to a key and dramatic factor in the ongoing public dialogue on the ancient problem of irresponsible sexual activity.

Nature itself has always provided one means by which intercourse may be avoided. That is masturbation. But the largely Christian participants in the antiabortion camp belong to churches which are very clear in their condemnation of the practice of self-stimulation. Many of them are also, though with less unity, opposed to all practical methods of birth control. As a result of these two views, those who would do away with abortion in fact contribute to an increase in unwanted pregnancies and therefore a demand, on the part of millions of young women, that those pregnancies be terminated. We see, therefore, that among those elements of society that worsen the problem are the forces that want to make abortion unavailable for everybody.

Another feature of the better society in which abortions would be unnecessary would be a humane and civilized adoption program in which every child that was either unwanted by its natural parents or which became suddenly orphaned would be taken into a new and loving home. But such visions are, of course, fantasy. We are unfortunately forced to address the problem in the context of present reality, which is deeply depressing. Millions of children are presently being born to parents who either have little or no interest in them or who, if they do feel some rudimentary form of love for their newborns, are themselves so socially handicapped that they are simply incapable of responsibly assuming the role of parents. There are few orphanages either and a tremendous shortage of foster-care homes.

Another crucial requirement in any society prepared to outlaw abortion would be a massive and well-funded program of health care for the poor, day-care centers for infants whose mothers must work, family-counseling services, and other such agencies. Unfortunately these are in painfully short supply at present, largely for the reason that the conservative elements of society refuse to underwrite such compassionate programs with their tax dollars. Moreover, when, despite their wishes, a certain amount of tax revenue is allocated to such benign programs, conservative spokesmen complain vociferously about these expenditures. They cannot have it both ways. If they are serious about bringing about a sharp revision of the long-standing legality of abortion, it follows that the number of births will rise by the millions. It would rise even more, of course, were it not for the inescapable fact that armies of women will continue to insist on abortions, and will get them, if new laws are passed, generally from the same type of back-alley practitioners who have provided such services for centuries.

There is evidence that at least a minority of anti-abortionists realize this, and we find, in the field of Catholic social services, for example, admirable instances of willingness to lend additional support to orphanages, adoption agencies, and day-care centers. One hopes that if the wishes of the conservative minority prevail in law and abortions are, in fact, outlawed or sharply curtailed, then the victors will not simply turn their backs on the millions of unwanted infants. This will, of course, require anti-abortionist forces to stop complaining about taxes and start making clear that they care about the poor in America in ways actually detectable to the poor.

Steve Allen is one of America's most creative minds, author, lecturer, and entertainer. This article , originally titled Abortion, *is from his book,* Steve Allen on the Bible, Religion, & Morality, *available from Prometheus Books, Buffalo, New York.*

Tempest Over Arizona Republic Cartoon On Child-Molesting Priests

News-maker Steve Benson, a Mormon cartoonist employed by the *Arizona Republic,* learned the power of the Catholic Church when he penned the cartoon above, first appearing on July 28, 1992. His cartoon is still making news in the Southwest. Columns of angry and supportive letters have been printed since by "Benson Backers and Bashers." Arizona has been rocked by several sexual scandals in recent years, with priests convicted for molesting children and cover-ups and collusions by powerful church officials revealed. *Reprinted by permission: Tribune Media Service.*

To begin to solve a problem; the first step is to admit you have one.

— Henry Ford

Sexual Child Abuse In The Church

Annie Laurie Gaylor

The general consensus in the United States of the 1990's is that if it is religious, it must be good. Criticism of religion is discouraged and stifled. It remains socially unacceptable to point out the main objections which skeptics and freethinkers have to religion: that it is both untrue and harmful. Ironically, while criticism of religion rarely makes the mainstream, the slandering and scapegoating of atheists is so acceptable that polls have shown that most Americans would not consider voting for an atheist for President.

The public harbors illusions straight out of the stuff that made William Jennings Bryan such a successful religious demagogue. One of his typical statements was, "Outside of the church are to be found the worthless; the criminal, and the degenerate, those who are a burden to society rather than an aid."

Christian religious indoctrination has taught believers that what makes you a good person is what you believe, not what you do. "Get right with God" and everything else falls into place, is the fundamentalist view. In this black-and-white world, the good are the Christians who will go to heaven; the bad are the hell-bound unbelievers.

While the more liberal branches of Christianity usually reject this simplistic bifurcation of the world and this narrow understanding of morality, they too believe that being a Christian is what makes one "good." Their benevolent view of Jesus and the parts of the bible they deign to acknowledge as relevant to today's world, does not permit exploration of the darker side of Christianity. History is replete with the recorded abuses and savageries of organized religion when it comes to power. Human sacrifices to appease the gods: the Crusades, the Inquisition, the execution of millions of women under the direction of the bible, pogroms against Jews, the Holocaust, Jonestown, Guyana, etc.

Believers in our society are indoctrinated to ignore the bloody history of religion, and to pay effusive lip service to belief in God, Jesus, the bible, and God's holy representatives on earth. Ordained ministers and priests are "men of God," "God's holy instruments," a race apart, anointed. It is then no wonder that clergymen who wish to misuse power and betray trust are in a unique position to do so. Newspapers are full of reports of financial exploitation, sexual transgressions during pastoral counseling, and what has surfaced since the mid-1980's as one of the most persistent public relations problems facing both Catholic and Protestant churches today: the criminal sexual abuse of children by ordained clergymen.

Professionals agree that pedophiles, sexual abusers of children, often seek out professions or activities which bring them into contact with children. Largely unexplored is the role Christianity may play in possibly molding criminal abusers. Researchers know that a typical child molester is a "good Christian" and often a church-goer active in church activities. Why should this be so? Havelock Ellis wrote, "In all countries religion, or superstition, is closely related with crime." It should not be surprising that crime is connected to the religious mentality and its ideology: such beliefs as original sin, the sacredness of gruesome bible teachings and inflexibility of moral codes, the absolution of sin through confession, a lack of personal responsibility for one's actions, and terrifying specters of a jealous god and evil devils.

Religious doctrine encourages power toward women and children, and such inequities invariably lead to abuse. Christian doctrine emphasizes submission and teaches the exemplary Christian to follow like sheep, and "become as little children" (Matthew 18:3). The classic Christian concept that human nature is innately "depraved" and sinful may also be a self-fulfilling prophecy.

Does the Christian ministry attract sexual deviants, or mold them? It may be an unanswerable riddle. When one looks at fallen televangelist Jimmy Swaggart, one may surmise that the more he ranted against the temptations of pornography and illicit sexual relations, the more he was trying to overcome his own impulses, and fighting his own nature. Or one may speculate that the deep sexual repressions of the fundamentalist religion, coupled with the unhealthy adulation he received as one of God's chosen, corrupted what was once an innocent nature.

In either case, the mixture of ministerial power with religion's social inequities and repressive doctrines is demonstrably explosive.

Extent Of The Problem

The social myth persists that a child molester is most apt to be of low-class breed lurking in dark hallways, interested in abduction of children he does not know. In fact, most sexual abusers of children are respectable, otherwise law-abiding people who cultivate friendly relationships with their chosen prey, and may escape detection for precisely those reasons. Research agrees that the typical child molester is able to harm large numbers of children without being caught, in part, because he has already established a trusting relationship, playing on children's sense of loyalty, vulnerability, shame, and naivete, and fortifying his power to silence them through bribery, coercion and violent threats. In case of a molesting man of the cloth, add to these threats the supernatural ones of God's wrath or hellfire.

One study released by Rev. Ronald Barton and Rev. Karen Lebaczq (March, 1990) for the Center for Ethics and Social Policy of the Graduate Theological Union at Berkeley, found that a quarter of all clergy have engaged in sexual misconduct.

The largest study of pedophiles was directed by researcher, physician and psychiatrist Gene G. Abel, M.D., of Emory University School of Medicine, for the Antisocial and Violent Behavior Branch of the National Institute of Mental Health. The landmark eight-year study revealed that, "Molesters often become youth ministers, day-care workers, Boy Scout leaders, teachers, Big Brothers and pediatricians" (Dr. Abel and Nora Harlow, "The child Abuser," Redbook Magazine, August 1987). They add, "He is often an active Christian who is involved in his church."

Abel's study discovered that 403 pedophiles had molested more than 67,000 children! Pedophiles who targeted male victims averaged 282 victims, while pedophiles who targeted girls averaged 23 victims. Other studies have uncovered more traditional findings of higher incidences of abuse of girls.

Roman Catholic canon attorney Father Thomas Doyle has estimated that about 3,000 Roman Catholic priests are pedophiliac abusers (an average of 16 priestly sex abusers per diocese).

The offices of the national monthly *Freethought Today* of Madison, Wisconsin receive three to four newspaper clippings per week from readers detailing a new criminal or civil court accusation against a priest or Protestant minister. It has surveyed reported cases in North America during the years of 1988 and 1989 and found 250 reported cases of criminal charges involving child-molesting priests, ministers or ministerial staff in the United States and Canada. The study revealed that Catholic priests were acquitted or dismissed of child molestation charges at a higher rate than Protestant ministers. Similarly, Catholic priests received a higher rate of suspended sentences when convicted, and when sentenced, spent considerably less time in jail or prison.

In these cases, involving 190 ordained clergy and 60 non-ordained clergy staff, such as Sunday school teachers, crimes mainly occurred at church locations. One convicted priest molested victims just before giving Mass. Sexual abuse occurred at the sacristy, in the rectory or church van. About half of the clergymen were officially involved in youth functions. About a third were accused of molesting youths during camping trips, youth group activities, retreats and crusades. About 20% were accused of molesting children at religious schools, 21% at church homes for children or through foster care. Eleven percent were accused of abusing children only during counseling sessions, although other cases also involved counseling.

A briefer study confirmed the earlier findings of a Catholic versus Protestant double standard, with priests receiving lighter sentences that Protestant ministers, and non-ordained clerical staff receiving by far the heaviest sentences. Catholic priests accused in 1990 were prosecuted mainly for molesting boys, while about half of the Protestant clergy were charged for crimes involving female victims. Cover-ups were specifically noted in newspaper reports in 38% of the cases, including many Protestant cases. The most blatant cover-up that year involved a Salvation Army minister who was permitted to keep his job and was given continuing access to children after back-to-back arrests for sexually abusing children during bible classes.

Shockingly, 11 out of the 46 Protestant ministers charged in 1990 with criminal sexual abuse had prior convictions – nearly a quarter of the cases, all dating since 1985. Most of the men had received light sentences, enabling them to return to the pulpit, and resume sexual abuse of children, quickly. Churches are not only failing to check ministers' records, but in some instances are knowingly hiring convicted child molesters. Defendants often unabashedly used their piety and positions to ask for (and sometimes receive) court leniency.

The first nationally breaking news story about church cover-ups of sex crimes broke in 1984, when well-known attorney Gloria Allred of Los Angeles brought the country's first "clergy malpractice" lawsuit that year on behalf of Rita Milla, a devout Catholic teenager. One day Father Santiago Tamayo reached through the broken screen in the confessional to fondle her breast. By January 1980, he was engaging in sexual intercourse with her. He introduced her to Father Cruces, who also used her sexually. In all, five other priests encouraged her compliance, flaunting their religious authority over the sheltered teenager. Rita later told news media that the priests had told her sex was natural, and that "priests get lonely, too." She was aiding them in their religious work.

When she became pregnant in January 1982, she was packed off to the Philippines. She told her family she would be "studying medicine." The priests intended for her to have her baby in secrecy and leave it there, giving her only $450 to last seven months. She lived with cockroaches and ate only one meal a day, nearly dying during childbirth of eclampsia. Her family rescued her, and Rita and her baby daughter returned to the states, after Bishop Abaya of the Philippines promised to help her.

When that aid failed to materialize, Rita went to Bishop Ward of Los Angeles for help. He said there was nothing he could do. After that final betrayal of trust, Rita and her mother filed the landmark clergy malpractice suit, seeking to establish paternity, set up child support, and sue the priests and the church for civil conspiracy for breach of fiduciary duty, fraud, deceit and clergy malpractice — and "to protect other young women from the pain and suffering caused by priests who abuse their position of trust," said Attorney Allred. The courts dismissed the case, citing a one-year time limit.

When Allred called the press conference to expose the scandal and announce the suit, all seven priests mysteriously vanished without trace, according to the archdiocese of Los Angeles. In 1991, Tamayo finally resurfaced, documenting to media that the diocese had warned him and his cohorts to flee the country. Tamayo offered proof that the church had known his whereabouts for years, including during the time when Allred tried unsuccessfully to serve him and the other priests with legal papers. The archdiocese had sent him monthly payments for years while he hid out in the Philippines.

In 1988, the church had finally set up a $20,000 trust fund for Milla's daughter, after she agreed to drop a slander suit against a bishop. The church lawyer maintained it was not an admission of liability, but an act of benevolence for the child. A paternity suit remains to be resolved.

A second nationally renowned case was filed in 1985, focusing more public attention on Catholic cover-ups. Father Gilbert Gauthe, of Louisiana, admitted to molesting 37 boys and one girl. He pleaded guilty on various charges in October 1985 and was given a 20-year prison sentence which cannot be paroled. The families of many of his victims went to court when they learned that a bishop and monsignor were aware of child molestation reports against Gauthe for more than ten years before his abuse was halted. Gauthe had molested some of the children as many as 200 times, including anal and oral rape, during church outings, when alone with children, in the rectory, sacristy, confessional and the priest's camper.

Small-town Catholics turned against the families as trouble-makers. All but one family agreed to settle their civil lawsuits out of court. But Faye and Glenn Gastal had their day in court. After their son, eleven, testified in court, he received a one-million-dollar award for damages from the Catholic Church on February 7, 1986. His parents received $250,000 as compensation for their pain, ostracism and harassment.

The Gastal boy testified that he was led to believe that being molested by priests was part of his job as altar boy. He thought his parents knew what was happening: "I thought he was doing the right thing because he was a priest." Later, the priest guaranteed his silence by threatening that "he would hurt my daddy, he'd kill him."

In what is the classic Catholic "musical chairs" mode of dealing with accusations against priests, it was revealed that the church had simply transferred Gauthe to new, unsuspecting communities. Parents had confronted the priest as early as 1972. In 1974, Gauthe admitted to a bishop that he had made "imprudent touches" in "one isolated case." The following year, the bishop appointed him chaplain of the diocesan Boy Scouts. In 1977, more parents complained. Gauthe was directed to seek psychiatric treatment by church officials, but in 1978 was transferred to another family parish. The sworn statement of one church official was, "I am trained as a priest to forget sins." The enormity of the scandal prompted even the National Catholic Reporter to condemn the cover-up. The church has paid at least $14 million to the victims of Gauthe alone.

The willingness of congregants to support an accused clergyman has numerous illustrations. One 1986 criminal case revealed the extent to which fundamentalist backers of a convicted molesting preacher would go. Christian supporters from three states filled the courtroom during hearings against Rev. James Britton Myers, of Kenosha, Wisconsin. Although he was convicted of the heinous crime of raping a little girl at his Christian school over a five-year period, starting when she was five, one member of his congregation called the crime "one drop of ink in a crystal-clear water."

A judge in California was inundated with letters of support asking him to pardon Father Andrew Christian Andersen, who was found guilty in 1986 of 26 counts of child molestation. Following the guilty verdict, Andersen was hugged by a church pastor and dozens of supporters. The judge sentenced him only to five years' probation, with the condition that he serve it at a church-owned treatment facility in New Mexico. Although the Diocese of Orange had received a report by a mother that her son had been abused by him, Andersen had been permitted to continue regular contact with altar boys for the following three years.

The church never reported anything. He had been sent for some counseling, but quickly resumed molesting, and was not removed from positions involving the supervision of boys. He was finally reported to authorities by a psychiatrist counseling a 13-year-old altar boy. The postscript of this cover-up is that Andersen's probation was revoked in 1990 and he was sentenced to six years in state prison, following his arrest in New Mexico for forcing a teenaged boy into a car, assaulting him and trying to sodomize him.

The extent to which a minster-molester is held above suspicion, despite blatant criminal acts, is exemplified by a 1987 criminal suit in Nashville. The arrest of Rev. Jack Law, a Baptist minister, was heralded by a headline, "Girl, 5, Raped Under Pew." He was accused not only of that, but of molesting and raping her two sisters. These crimes took place at the family home as well during an outing arranged by him so the girls could help him distribute religious tracts. The girls had tried to tell their parents, but were not believed. "Being a preacher," the father said of him to local media, "we thought he was a good man." Law killed himself that year rather than face trial.

The devout often find it unthinkable that a respected member of the clergy could molest children, especially boys, who are often considered invulnerable to exploitation. A case in point occurred in Tampa, Florida, when a mother walked in on Rev. Fonville Gandy when he was placing his hands on her son's genitals. He told her he was giving her son an "anatomy lesson," and she believed him!

Obviously she could not permit herself to believe the evidence before her very eyes that a minister could betray her trust, sexually abuse her child, then lie and cover up. The mother realized the truth when Rev. Gandy was later arrested for other molestations, and she testified against him during his trial. Gandy was sentenced in 1986 to five years in prison.

Why are churches often a safe harbor for criminal child molesters? There are many answers to that question. It is, in part, because children are taught to give "men of God" special deference and obedience. Sherryll Kerns Kraizer, author of Safe Child Book and a pioneer in developing sexual abuse prevention, writes: "Many children tell me that their body belongs to God." A young child who assumes his or her body is not their own, but is "owned by God," will be vulnerable to abuse by an esteemed "man of God."

Clergy, whose role includes "pastoral counseling," are trusted and sought after for confidences and guidance. Clergy are often in contact with depressed or hurting parishioners, who are expected to confess and confide deeply personal feelings. The Catholic Church's traditional ritualistic confession of "sins" sets up an opportunity for children to be inappropriately questioned by priests on intimate or embarrassing topics.

Finally, churches are used to operating as though they were above the law. Unlike other nonprofit groups, churches are not required even to file information on financial arrangements, and are accustomed to special favors and community approval. While many do not come to the rescue of the battered principle of state/church separation when it is under assault, they wave the First Amendment banner vigorously when it comes to investigations by public authorities of wrong-doing within church doors. They treat these cases as a crisis of faith, rather than as criminal actions.

Churches are not policing themselves, and are often unpoliced by the state. Even under fire, churches are dragging their feet to institute reforms. Since 1986, the Church Mutual Insurance Company has formally advised church clients to fingerprint all applicants for church positions, to carefully check out resumes and gaps in resumes, to call references and demand them for work with children, to institute careful monitoring of church day cares, to make sure two adults act as chaperons of field trips, to take, in short, the kinds of precautions that public schools and better child care facilities have been taking for years.

Are the churches doing it? No. Several denominations have passed position papers or policies for dealing with internal investigations once a complaint has been lodged privately. None has announced steps in keeping with all the recommendations of the Church Mutual Insurance Company. The hierarchy of the Catholic Church insists that each diocese must make its own policies and determinations. In 1990, Auxiliary Bishop A. James Quinn of Cleveland told a conference of canon attorneys to consider hiding the crimes, by sending files on priests accused of child molestation to the Vatican Embassy in the District of Columbia, which he maintains is outside the reach of the U.S. Courts. "If there's something there you really don't want people to see, you might send it off to the Apostolic Delegate," said Quinn.

In addition, church officials are either exempt by law from the mandatory child abuse reporting laws, or prosecutors are interpreting those laws as if they were exempt. Any action taken by churches largely has been in reaction to civil suits against them, when their pocketbooks are threatened, and, to a lesser extent, due to unfavorable publicity.

The Catholic hierarchy in particular has been outspoken in trying to minimize or defend abusers within its ranks. Typical of public statements was the opinion of Archbishop James Hayes, quoted in the Toronto Star (July 2, 1989): "The church exists to pardon and heal . . . There may be cases where the child was chasing after the man, looking for affection, and whatever happened, happened only once." Milwaukee Archbishop Rembert Weakland editorialized in the May 1988 Catholic Herald: "We must not imply that the abuser is not guilty of serious crime, but we could easily give a false impression that any adolescent who becomes sexually involved with an older person does so without any degree of personal responsibility. Not all adolescent victims are so innocent; some can be sexually very active and aggressive and often quite streetwise."

With such attitudes, was it surprising that Cardinal John O'Connor of New York City wanted to offer Father Bruce Ritter a job, even after a probe of his Covenant House network for runaways found him guilty of sexual and financial misconduct in 1990? Ritter was never prosecuted for a 20-year pattern of sexual misconduct.

If religion or any institution depends on the sexual subordination or exploitation of children or women, then it is better that such institutions should cease to exist. If it is a question of the survival of the churches versus the safety of children, then our allegiance clearly must be with the children.

In 1988, I appeared on a *People Are Talking* television show in San Francisco, to speak about my book, *Betrayal of Trust: Clergy Abuse of Children,* along with a Catholic mother whose son had been molested by a priest, and opposite a local priest and fundamentalist minister in San Francisco. The audience remained stoic as the Catholic mother and I regaled them with horror stories of betrayal and sexual abuse of children by clergymen. But when one of the clergymen on the show "exposed" the fact that I am an atheist, a loud collective gasp was sounded from the good Christians in the audience.

It was a telling demonstration of that narrow bigotry, inculcated in so many Christians, that goodness has far more to do with one's professions of faith than with conduct and actions.

This corrupted idea of morality not only produces an audience that is more shocked at atheism than it is concerned about victims of abusive ministers, but has produced a malignancy of collusion and cover-up in the churches. The religious scandal of clergy abusing children should rightfully close many church doors.

Annie Laurie Gaylor is an author, lecturer, editor of Freethought Today, *co-founder, along with her mother, Anne Nicol Gaylor, of the Freedom From Religion Foundation, Madison, Wisconsin.*

Instead of weeding out the offenders, the Catholic Church's policy has been "geographic cure" – or moving offenders out of the area. Very few times has the Church lived up to its responsibility of punishment, removal or counselling for the Church and God's representatives . . .

— Jason Berry

The Secret Sins Of The Sanctuary

Arthur Melville

The expression "secrets breed sickness" is relevant to us today – most obviously in the structures of government, religion and family. That dysfunctions rest on a foundation of secrets – that is, lies – is nothing new; the structures of society simply can no longer bear the cumulative weight of the lies. The resulting symptom of the secrets is addictive behavior, be it substance addiction, such as cocaine or alcohol, or process addiction, such as gambling or incest – the addictive symptom will actively persist as long as the secrecy of the behavior is preserved. A process addiction that today demands much attention is that of clerical pedophilia – specifically that of Catholic priests sexually abusing children.

The celibate male hierarchy of the Catholic Church, in which I participated as a missionary priest, has historically needed to cover its dysfunctions with secrets in order to maintain its strict control over large segments of the populace. Principal among the tools employed by the Catholic Church for such control are: the manipulation of beliefs and the establishing of the hierarchy as the determinant of appropriate sexual behavior.

From that perspective it follows that the Church would prohibit the questioning of authority and that it would preoccupy itself and its members with what it considers to be, and what it condemns as, sins of sexuality. However, the hierarchy seems to have forgotten that "He who casts the first stone . . . . " is always relevant for those who consider themselves the designers of social morality.

Having long disregarded the fact that suppression of healthy sexuality leads to pathology, and having established itself as the standard-bearer of sexual mores by vowing to lives of carnal and reproductive abstinence, the hierarchy is now experiencing a long-overdue backlash. Its own priests are being identified as frequent violators of society's basic morality and as perpetrators of child sexual abuse. The same hierarchy that has long condemned the laity is now confronted with humiliation, embarrassment and shame as a growing number of its members are being caught and exposed, not simply in the common sins of sex on which the church has commonly judged the laity, but in sins of deviant sexuality that are illegal as well as immoral.

I view with compassion unfortunate souls whose troubled lives revolve around addicted behavior, and I particularly empathize with the many sexually addicted priests. For fifteen years I lived in the environment that attracted these men, harbored them and kept their illnesses secret. However, I have difficulty feeling compassion for the distraught bishops, who, trained and skilled in the art of control, have lied and conspired to keep the clerical pedophiles and their behavior hidden, and thus have abetted and perpetuated the sexual transgressions against innocent children.

Child molestation by clerics has long been a secret part of the Church's history, with the well-connected and powerful hierarchy able to hide the truth by using tactics of pressure, politics and deceit. Only when the American judicial system finally became involved were the secret sins of the sanctuary forced into the open. A bishop can no longer save face by simply transferring the sick priest to another parish as a potential predator to a new batch of innocents.

Strengthened by recent revelations, victims and their families are finding the courage and legal support to confront the hierarchy for past and present abuses. The cases seem endless and financially overwhelming. An already questioning laity is angry and confused.

The Church, like any other monolithic structure, is reluctant to change, moved to do so only by failing finances or a threatening restiveness of its subjects. But even with the costly legal damages being awarded to the victims of the priests and growing distrust of a large segment of the laity, the American bishops refuse to take effective action. They remain stymied by the possibility of further loss of trust and subservience on the part of the faithful and the effect on financial contributions. Also knowing that any broadening of the clerical scandal could diminish their traditionally prestigious position among governing structures, the bishops are caught between revealing the whole truth and loss of control. The result is that they only choose to establish remedial steps for dealing with identified violators and their victims, thus hoping to somehow curtail continued fallout.

The bishops, like parents in a dysfunctional family who are committed to keeping secrets, lack the integrity and motivation to heal. I sincerely doubt that they possess the necessary strength of character and the indispensable humility needed to deal with the essence of the problem – to reach into the soul of the structure of the Church and bring forth and confess before the laity the underlying truth – that the very nature of the institution cultivates and fosters the sexual deviancy of its celibate members.

We will know if and when the Church is sincere in wanting a healing when the bishops choose to go to the source of the problem, acknowledging that the sin lies not simply with the perpetrators, but also with the hierarchy itself, and even more so with the very institution that gives the hierarchy its position of power. Can we expect any less from the "successors of Jesus" than that they confess their own inadequacies and hypocrisy, and evaluate publicly and reveal fully the humanly developed historical context of the problem found in the institutional traditions, attitudes, beliefs and teachings?

They might begin by evaluating some aspects of the religious structure through which dysfunction, control and secrets lead to sexual abuse:

- The rewarding priestly life of prestige and power that prohibits intimate relationships draws like a magnet those who harbor sexual inhibitions, inadequacies and fears, men not capable of the prohibited relationships who in turn are not expected to recognize their symptoms or deal with their psychological problems. Prolonged isolation, such as all-male seminary, becomes a fruitful breeding ground for unhealthy social behavior that seeks dysfunctional and deviant relationships.

- A priesthood that holds as divine mandate the exclusive participation of men and thus the implicit superiority of men will attract men who feel inferior to women. Such an environment becomes a hotbed for socio-sexually maladapted personalities and their accompanying problems. Adults who feel incapable of relating to their peers are attracted to a life in which they are free to and expected to relate to children.

- That only men can be called to the highest service of the Church obviously creates general but subtle arrogance among "the chosen." Presumed supremacy lends to permissiveness in acting out hidden or unacceptable behavior.

- Celibacy is accepted as a necessary means to the goal of the priesthood. But when the thrill of the goal withers and frustration has no acceptable outlet, latent pathology easily unfolds.
- Alcoholism is endemic among the clergy, the bottle frequently being the only legally and ecclesiastically acceptable answer to the pain and loneliness of even the committed celibate. And, as is well known, it lowers social inhibitions.
- A hierarchy trained to distance itself from the people and distrust its followers with the truth, keeps secret the deviant behavior of its members, encouraging further deviancy.
- A hierarchy with its focus on eternal salvation tends to overlook common worldly knowledge, such as the fact that abused children become abusing adults. With a longstanding and high incidence of abuse among the clergy, it is unacceptable that clerical applicants have never been examined or evaluated for incest or other forms of childhood abuse.

Catholic nuns, however, are conducting surveys to identify the number of incest survivors among their ranks. Though many predict that the survey results may be shockingly high, these studies are not being done at the request of a secretive hierarchy. Instead, to avoid being controlled, blocked and possibly punished by the hierarchy, the nuns are keeping their surveys away from the bishops until they are completed.

After having spent nine years in the seminary, six years in the priesthood, and the past fifteen years as a psychotherapist working with addicts, I am familiar with what sexually addicted priests have to go through in their recovery process, and wonder if the bishops will provide the supportive and loving environment, and environment committed to integrity, that is needed for recovery. That the bishops send the offenders into isolation, therapy or rehabilitation does not mean healing, nor does it end the bishops' responsibility, or even begin to identify the source of the problem. One of the keys to recovery from any addiction is full disclosure of the behaviors and the making of amends, none of which is possible in an atmosphere which insists on secrecy and the hiding of the problem.

Addictions do not go away. They must be managed every day for the rest of one's life. Controlling or dysfunctional systems that generate and support addictive behavior must be exposed and those addicted must be able to separate from such an environment in a healthy manner. If the secrets or lies of the system are encouraged or permitted, regression and the continuance of the problem are guaranteed. By its very nature, Catholicism, with its extreme position on sexuality, fosters a dysfunctional environment.

Perhaps the healing must begin with the laity. A healthy laity would do well to distinguish between a religious system and spiritual development, and to commit to personal growth rather than to a religious leadership in denial. And the Catholic bishops must see that the recovery process is important not only to the perpetrators, but to themselves and especially to their disheartened laity. The same rules and principles of recovery apply to all: rigorous truth and loving support are basic and essential. Nothing less can be expected from those who would follow in the footsteps of Him who said, "Suffer the children to come unto me," Nothing less can be accepted for the children abused by clergymen, already cast in the role of sexual abusers of the future.

If the steps taken by the bishops today regarding clerical pedophilia are only meant to maintain control and contain the existing problem, we are then witnessing a serious step in the weakening and possible demise of one of the West's most ancient and revered institutions.

Arthur Melville holds a B.A. in philosophy, a Master's in Religious Education, and a Ph.D. in Clinical Psychology. A former Maryknoll missionary priest, he worked six years in the mountains of Guatemala. His recent book, With Eyes to See, A Journey from Religion to Spirituality, *was published by Stillpoint Publishing. He is married and a psychotherapist, maintaining a private practice in Long Beach, California.*

Since 1985, the Catholic Church has paid out over $350 million in damages related to sexual abuse.

— Jason Berry

Boxer & Feinstein

Barbara Boxer (right) with Diane Feinstein (left) in Los Angeles. California is the first state to be represented by two women in the U.S. Senate.

— Associated Press Photo

Woman

Robert Green Ingersoll

In the olden times when religions were manufactured – when priestcraft and lunacy governed the world – the women were not consulted. They were regarded and treated as serfs and menials – looked upon as a species of property to be bought and sold like other domestic animals.

Women have through many generations acquired the habit of submission, of acquiescence. They have practiced what may be called the slave virtues – obedience, humility – so that some time will be required for them to become accustomed to the new order of things, to the exercise of greater freedom. So, I say, equal rights, equal education, equal advantages.

In every field where woman has become a competitor of man she has either become or given evidence that she is to become his equal. My own opinion is that woman is naturally the equal of man and that in time, that is to say, when she has had the opportunity and the training, she will produce in the world of art as great pictures, as great statues, and in the world of literature as great books, dramas, and poetry as man has produced or will produce.

I think the influence of women is always good, in politics, as in everything else. I think it is the duty of every woman to ascertain what she can in regard to her country, including its history, its laws and customs. Woman above all others is a teacher. She, above all, determines the character of children, that is to say, of men and women. There is not the slightest danger of women becoming too intellectual or knowing too much. Neither is there any danger of men knowing too much. At least, I know of no men who are in immediate peril from that source.

I am a firm believer in the equal rights of human beings, and no matter what I think as to what woman should or should not do, she has the same right to decide for herself that I have to decide for myself. If women wish to vote, if they wish to take part in political matters, if they wish to run for office, I shall do nothing to interfere with their rights. I most cheerfully admit that my political rights are only equal to theirs.

Think of making your wife a beggar! Think of her having to ask you every day for a dollar, or for two dollars, or fifty cents! "What did you do with that dollar I gave you last week?" Think of having a wife that is afraid of you! What kind of children do you expect to have with a beggar and a coward for their mother?

Editor's Note: In this regard the reader should know that Ingersoll himself simply put money in a cashbox in his house and every member of the family helped herself.

In my judgment, the woman is the equal of the man. She has all the rights I have and one more, and that is the right to be protected. If there is any man I detest, it is the man who thinks he is the head of a family – the man who thinks he is "boss".

Women are not willing to suffer here, with the hope of being happy beyond the clouds. They want their happiness now. They are beginning to think for themselves.

I regard the rights of men and women equal. In Love's fair realm, husband and wife are king and queen, sceptered and crowned alike, and seated on the selfsame throne. The gentlemen of today show more affection for their dogs than most of the kings of England exhibited toward their wives.

Most women are driven at last to the sewing needle, and this does not allow them to live. It simply keeps them from dying. No girl is safe in the streets of any city after the sun has gone down. After all, the sun is the only god that has ever protected woman. In the darkness she has been the prey of the wild beast in man.

I think the women who have been engaged in the struggle for equal rights have done good for women in the direction of obtaining equal wages for equal work. There has also been a tendency among women in our country to become independent – a desire to make their own living – to win their own bread.

The men who declare that woman is the intellectual inferior of man, do not and cannot, by offering themselves in evidence, substantiate the declaration. Husbands as a rule do not know a great deal, and it will not do for every wife to depend on the ignorance of her worst half. The women of today are the great readers, and no book is a great success unless it pleases the women.

No woman should be forced to live with a man whom she abhors. There never will be a free generation of great men until there has been a generation of free women – of free mothers.

Nothing gives me more pleasure, nothing gives greater promise for the future than the fact that woman is achieving intellectual and physical liberty. It is refreshing to know that here, in our country, there are thousands of women who think and express their own thoughts – who are thoroughly free and thoroughly conscientious. Woman is not the intellectual inferior of man.

Science must make woman the owner, the mistress of herself. Science, the only possible savior of mankind, must put it in the power of woman to decide for herself whether she will or will not become a mother. This is the solution of the whole question. This frees woman. The babes that are born will be welcome. They will be clasped with glad hands to happy breasts. They will fill homes with light and joy.

As long as woman regards the Bible as the charter of her rights, she will be the slave of man. The Bible was not written by a woman. Within its lids there is nothing but humiliation and shame. She is regarded as the property of man.

Man having been the physical superior of woman always accounts for the fact that most of the high gods have been males. Had woman been the physically superior, the powers supposed to be the rulers of Nature would have been women. Instead of being represented in the apparel of man, they would be luxuriated in trains, low-necked dresses, laces and black hair.

If we wish to find what the Bible thinks of woman, all that is necessary to do is read it. We will find everywhere she is spoken of simply as property – as belonging absolutely to the man. We will find that whenever a man got tired of his wife, all he had to do was give her a writing of divorcement, and then the mother of his children became a houseless and homeless wanderer. We will find that men were allowed to have as many wives as they could get, either by courtship, purchase, or conquest.

Nearly every religion has accounted for all the devilment of this world by the crime of a woman. What a gallant thing that is. And if it be true, I had rather live with the woman I love in a world full of trouble, than to live in heaven with nobody but men.

Robert Ingersoll was America's finest orator and foremost leader of Freethinkers. Mark Twain, Thomas Edison, Eugene V. Debs, and Elizabeth Cady Stanton used to gather to hear the speeches of "the great agnostic." From the writings and speeches of Robert Green Ingersoll, edited by Roger E. Greeley in his book The Best of Robert Ingersoll, *available from Prometheus Books, New York.*

All women have been sexually abused by the Bible teachings, and institutions set on its fundamentalist interpretations. There would be no need for the women's movement if the church and Bible hadn't abused them.

— Father Leo Booth

The bible and the church have been the greatest stumbling blocks in the way of women's emancipation.

— Elizabeth Cady Stanton

The memory of my own suffering has prevented me from ever shadowing one young soul with the superstitions of the Christian religion.

— Elizabeth Cady Stanton

The most violent element in our society is ignorance.

— Emma Goldman

The clergy never discovered any injustice to woman; and only one in a thousand could see it when it was pointed out.

— Joseph McCabe, *The Religion of Woman,* 1905

Los Angeles, California

Know all men by these presents that

Alan Albert Snow

having satisfactorily completed the requirements of
this university and upon the recommendation of
the faculty hereby award the degree of

Doctor of Divinity

with all rights, privileges, honors, appertaining thereto in testimony, whereof the seal of the university
together with the signatures of the officers have been duly affixed
this Second Day of May, Nineteen-Hundred and Ninety-Four.

Paul L. Moffat Ph.D
President

Mary D. Lewis M.B.A.
Registrar

Available to anyone for $30.00

Profits from the Prophet

The Associated Press reported that in 1990, Americans gave, donated, or were coerced into giving over 48 billion dollars to churches, religious cults and T.V. evangelists – most of it non-taxable! The vast majority of church money goes to real estate, T.V. transmissions, propaganda, radio, book publications, etc.

Jimmy Swaggert was candidly quoted by the Associated Press as saying, "I'm on T.V. raising money so I can afford to be on T.V. to raise money."

— "Doctor" Alan Snow, D.D. (Hon.), M.A.

Dr. Jesus and His Degreed Disciples

Alan Albert Snow

One form of religious fraud that has become a growing industry in the United States is the proliferation of bogus religious schools, colleges, universities, and seminaries. These bogus schools are operated by uneducated and uncredentialed frauds who use America's liberal religious tax-exemption and tax-free laws to create more uncredentialed practitioners of mail-order religious degree mills and divinity schools that require very little if any theological knowledge to be awarded an honorary or similar kind of "doctorate" in metaphysics, astrology, New Age thinking, Wicca, or parapsychology. These mail-order or storefront colleges are often accredited by equally bogus "international" accrediting organizations that were founded by the same founders of the degree mills.

Many of these mail-order churches or ministries run ads in tabloid and New Age newspapers and magazines. They often read "FREE MINISTERIAL LICENSE!" or "DEGREES! PH.D. AND DOCTORAL DEGREES! RUSH NAME AND ADDRESS TO: . . ." Almost all of these mail-order religions operate out of a post office box. Even world-famous outspoken atheist Madalyn Murray O'Hair made use of the infamous Universal Life Church's free credentials to found her own atheist *Poor Richard's Universal Life Church* which was operating out of her American Atheist Center in Austin, Texas. Her own story of her church was covered in her 1986 book *An Atheist Speaks* (published by her American Atheist Press, Austin, Texas).

Many little Bible and Christian fundamentalist ministries and churches have their own church-run ministry schools, often run and operated by only the church pastor. Many of these little Bible schools award endless honorary degrees of Doctor of Divinity to the most illiterate and uneducated preachers of their little sects, cults, and churches. All of this nonsense is legal and supported by our freedom of religion laws.

It has always been fascinating that the hillbilly televangelists on the radio and T.V. have such authoritative titles like "the Reverend Doctor" or "Doctor Minister." The style, message, and bad grammar just did not match the kind of education that a real "doctorate" should have.

Investigation has shown that the great majority of "reverend doctors" in our most conservative and fundamentalist churches and religious programs are either very badly educated by the most loose and non-accredited Bible schools or they have no formal education at all. The credentials and degrees that are used by so many of our nation's preachers are obtained by mail-order diploma mills or are awarded by fundamentalist Bible schools and colleges by the thousands each year to preachers who are already successful in their public ministries.

Investigating the educational backgrounds of many of the high-profile ministers from the Rev. "Dr." Billy Graham to the Rev. "Dr." Jimmy Swaggart finds that most of them have either the minimal Bachelor's degree or no academic education at all. The doctorates that they all have are almost always "honorary" and were given to them by either a church board of directors or a little Bible school. After writing to several of these churches and schools, I have also received by return mail the same credentials and degrees that are used to legitimize and legalize many of the public ministries that are running and ruining the lives of millions of uninformed and unquestioning religious devotees.

Research has shown me that most theological degrees that appear behind the names of ministers, priests, and rabbis are honorary, NOT EARNED. Almost all churches, temples, and religious organizations are in the totally legal habit of handing out honorary degrees in order to give the appearance of importance, knowledge, and authority. In the United States, the D.D. degree (the Doctor of Divinity degree) is always honorary.

Even the Rev. Dr. Billy Graham, whose real education was a Bible course at the unaccredited Bob Jones University in Florida, and the Florida Bible Institute (now Trinity College), has many honorary D.D.s awarded to him simply because he became a prominent fundamentalist evangelist and was successful because of his own natural gifts.

He was, for all practical purposes, self-educated. Most, and in my opinion, possibly 99% of the fundamentalist preachers on radio and

T.V. have no formal education or are badly educated. Their "doctorates" are almost always as non-academic as I have described in this report.

Dr. Alan Albert Snow, D.D. (Hon.) is a member of the Board of Directors of the Institute for Judeo-Christian Origins Studies, California State University, Long Beach. He is also a charter member of the Institute for Dead Sea Scrolls Studies, Biblical Archaeology Society, and earned his M.A. at the School of Theology, Claremont, California.

Honorary degrees

The honorary degree is the stepchild of the academic world, and a most curious one at that. It has no more relationship or connection with academia than bandleader Doc Severinsen has with the world of medicine. It is purely and simply a title that some institutions (and some scoundrels) have chosen to bestow from time to time, and for a wide variety of reasons, upon certain people. These reasons often have to do with the donation of money, or with attracting celebrities to a commencement ceremony.

The honorary Doctorate has no academic standing whatsoever, and yet, because it carries with it the same title, "Doctor," that is used for the earned degree, it has become an extremely desirable commodity for those who covet titles and the prestige they bring. For respectable universities to award the title of "Doctor" via an honorary Doctorate is as peculiar as if the Army were to award civilians the honorary title of "General" – a title the civilians could then use in their everyday life.

More than one thousand traditional colleges and universities award honorary Doctorates (anywhere from one to fifty per year, each), and a great many Bible schools, spurious schools, and degree mills hand them out with wild abandon to almost anyone willing to pay the price. And that is why we have Doctor Michael Jackson, Doctor Ed McMahon, Doctor Frank Sinatra, Doctor Ella Fitzgerald, Doctor Mr. Rogers, Doctor Captain Kangaroo, Doctor Doctor Seuss, Doctor Jane Pauley, Doctor Bob Hope, Doctor Robert Redford, Doctor Stevie Wonder, Doctor Dan Rather, and thousands of other doctors.

— John Beam, Ph.D., *College Degree by Mail*

The "Mind Control" Controversy

What is Coercive Persuasion?

Is there such a thing as *brainwashing?* Is the way in which cults recruit and indoctrinate their members an example of such mind control?

In his book on mind control and ego destruction, Robert J. Lifton lists eight elements that he found to be intrinsic to the complete involuntary conversion of a person to a new and absolute philosophy, a process he calls *totalism.* They are:

- **Milieu Control:** The purposeful limitation of all forms of communication with the outside world, sleep deprivation, a change in diet, control over who one can see and talk to.

- **Mystical manipulation:** Teaching that the control group has a special *(divine)* purpose and that the subject has been chosen to play a special role in fulfilling this purpose.

- **Need for purity:** Convincing the subject of his former impurity *(before joining the control group)* and the necessity of becoming pure or perfect as defined by the group.

- **Confession:** Getting the subject to let down barriers and openly discuss innermost fears and anxieties.

- **Sacred science:** Convincing the subject that the control group's beliefs are the only logical system of belief and therefore must be accepted and obeyed.

- **Loading the language:** Creating a new vocabulary, by creating new words with special meanings understood only by members of the group, or by giving new and special meanings to familiar words and phrases.

- **Doctrine over persons:** Convincing the subject that the group and its doctrine take precedence over any individual in the group or any other teaching from outside it.

- **Dispensing of existence:** Teaching the subject that all those who disagree with the philosophy of the control group are doomed.

"You deplore the demonstrations that are presently taking place in Birmingham," wrote Southern Baptist Martin Luther King in April 1963. "But I am sorry that [you] did not express a similar concern for the conditions that brought the demonstrations into being." In a public meeting in Savannah, Georgia, that summer, youthful Ku Klux Klan members wore the Christian cross on their robes, while Protestant and Catholic churches joined together in the great "March on Washington" for civil rights and equal opportunities for jobs.

Religious "Love" Yields Holy Wars

It is a historical fact that behind all of the wars and violence of human history, and behind every gun, has been a religious scripture. Christianity spread, not by 'love,' but on the bloody sword of Constantine. So, to help you keep it straight as to the religious slaughter in the name of 'love,' here is an update.

Iran . . . . Muzzling mulish mullahs that may object to a 'holy war' (**What about Yugoslavia?**)

India . . . . Hindus vs. Muslims

Punjab . . . . Indian Sikhs vs. Indian Hindus

Kashmir . . . . Kashmiri Muslims vs. Indian Hindus

Sri Lanka . . . . . Tamil Hindus vs. Sinhalese Buddhists

Azerbaijan . . . . . Azerbaijan Muslims vs. Armenian Christians

Cyprus . . . . Turkish Muslims vs. Greek Orthodox

Holy Land . . . . . . Palestinian Muslims vs. Israeli Jews

Northern Ireland . . . . Christian Roman Catholics vs. Christian Protestants

United States . . . (WHICH UNITED STATES?) Christian Fundamentalists (still in 1994 _ WHAT ABOUT 1996?) trying to read archaic biblical mythology as literal historical fact. . . vs. scholarship. . . abortion counseling . . . the U.S. Bill of Rights and the Constitution . . . classic literature . . . classical humanism . . . women's rights . . . what about gay rights?

And yet, at the heart of all of the religious traditions is scripture that counsels a human being to act in a way in which he would have others act toward him.

Christianity . . . . "All things whatsoever you would that men should do to you, do even so for them." (Matt. 7:12)

Islam . . . . "No one of you is a believer until he desires for his brother that which he desires for himself." (Sunnah)

Judaism . . . . "What is hateful to you, do not to your fellow-man. That is the entire Law; all the rest is commentary." (Talmud, Shabbat 31a)

Buddhism . . . . . . "Hurt not others in ways that you yourself would find hurtful." (Udana-Varga 5:18)

Brahmanism . . . . "This is the sum of duty: Do naught unto others which would cause you pain done unto you." (Mahabharata 5,1517)

What irony! What a religious quagmire of hypocrisy and contradictions. Even Pope John Paul II, with words from Vatican City, recently addressed this issue. He called "freedom of conscience our inalienable right." He said, "Religious fundamentalism (everywhere) is our greatest threat to world peace. Fundamentalism breeds totalitarianism and intolerance."

The Pope highlighted the sickness of the world's religions with these words: "People must not attempt to impose their own 'truth' on others."

These words coming from Vatican City would give some hope that a spiritual evolution is possible, even in dogmatic traditions. Thomas Jefferson said it before the Pope. From Jefferson's Notes on Virginia:

"Millions of innocent men, women and children, since the introduction of Christianity, have been burnt, tortured, fined, imprisoned; yet we have not advanced one inch toward uniformity. What has been the effect of this coercion? To make one half of the world fools and the other half hypocrites. To support roguery and error all over the earth. Let us reflect that it is inhabited by a thousand millions of people. That these profess probably a thousand different systems of religion. That ours is but one of that thousand."

The enormous damage that has been done to our fragile planet and the human species by religious ignorance and superstitions is just beyond the comprehension of any sensitive mind. Dogmatic and doctrinal religions have been historically, and are today, intolerably alien to human intelligence. We are surrounded by savagery, by zealots and fanatics acting in "the name of God."

Our most ardent hope can be that out of the ashes of religious hatred and superstitions can rise the phoenix of a refined spirituality, creating a revolution in the sphere of human consciousness.

William Edelen is a writer, lecturer and author of The Edelen Letter, *P.O. Box 916, Kenwood, CA 95452.*

Holy Wars of the 1990's

The tragedies of Croatia, Bosnia, Herzegovina, Serbia, Northern Ireland, Palestine, Israel, Iraq, etc. can be ended with one of three actions.

1. Acknowledge that there is no supernatural source for our existence, purpose for being, or cause of action, and that we are beings that behave as one would expect form an animal with our evolutionary heritage.

2. Eliminate religious bigotry.

3. Separate Church from State – Whenever one religion dominates a government, it invariably exercises the force of government to physically, economically or spiritually convert, dominate, expel or exterminate those who do not share their mythology.

Action 1 is most unlikely, because discomfort with the unknown leads to the invention of myth, or the acceptance of myth by those seeking to control the uncomfortable. Few are ever fully secure with the unknown.

Action 2 is more likely. Ignorance and fear die with knowledge, but the inferiority that is the source of bigotry inhibits the education. Inferiority is difficult to unlearn.

Action 3 is the most likely achievable. By limiting government to the protection of person and property, which necessarily includes the freedoms to contract and associate, among others, no one group can dominate another. Where this is the case, peace and prosperity prevail.

I urge you to support the National League fort the Separation of Church and State and Americans United the Separation of Church and State in this endeavor.

Jim Lorenz, President, The National League for the Separation of Church and State, P.O. Box 1257, Escondido, California 92033.

Battlelines Being Drawn . . .

Peace demonstrators were labeled subversive, unpatriotic and undesirable.

The Peace Symbol

This is the anti-nuclear emblem or peace symbol. It is composed of a Tyr rune, ⊗, lengthened up-ward, or by the rune ⊗ turned upside down. In Germanic countries ⊗ is interpreted as a Todesrune, the rune of death, or an inverted life rune.

According to some sources ⊗ was conceived by placing the signs "N" and "D" (for Nuclear Disarmament) from the international marine flag signalling system on top of each other and circumscribing the combination with a circle.

Some state that ⊗ was invented by Lord Bertrand Russell. S.T. Achen, however, claims that it was designed by G. Holtom at the request of Russell. In any case it was initially used as a rallying sign in 1958 at the first demonstration against Aldermaston (a British research center for the development of nuclear weapons).

The power of this symbol is emphasized by the fact that the South African government, during the 1970s, seriously considered forbidding it. They found it "anti-Christian" and "pro-Communist."

Achen, the late Danish semiotician, wrote that ⊗, ironically, was forbidden at times in some of the communist countries.

Much to do was made when U.S. war protesters displayed the "Peace: symbol when the Christian U.S. government launched its nuclear sub *Corpus Christi* (body of Christ).

— Carl G. Livngman, *Dictionary of Symbols*

"I believe there are more instances of the abridgment of the freedom of the people by gradual and silent encroachments of those in power than by violent and sudden usurpations."

James Madison

400

Think For Yourself

Celebrating the World Day of Prayer in 1986

Pope John Paul II and Professor Elio Toaff, Chief Rabbi of Rome — the two current "authorities" have attempted to unite two long-time religious rival dogmas. — *AP-Wirephoto*

Independence From Authority

Anne Nicol Gaylor

A Freethinker Speaks Out

If you are an independent person, even reading the definition of the word *authority* can generate sparks and make the feathers fly! Listen to some of these definitions. Authority: the right to command and to enforce obedience. Authority: superiority derived from a status that carries with it the right to give orders and to expect obedience. Authority: the power to require and receive submission. I am sure some of you are feeling mutinous just reading these definitions! And I applaud that.

Whether the authority is government, the army, religion, a teacher or parents, blind obedience is not palatable to the independent personality. Reason is palatable. Even a young child appreciates reasoning. Poor teachers will tell you, "Do this because I say so." Good teachers will explain *why*.

What has freethought to do with authority? Why do freethinkers so often reject authority? A freethinker is someone who forms opinions, especially opinions about religion, on the basis of reason, and forms those opinions independent of authority, tradition and established belief. Therefore freethinkers reject authority if that authority is not based on reason.

In matters of religion, freethinkers may label themselves in other ways. An atheist is a freethinker. An agnostic is a freethinker. A rationalist is a freethinker. So is a humanist. All of these come under the umbrella of freethought because they are people forming their opinions about religion on the basis of reason.

You know, these are lovely words: Freethought, Freethinker, Reason, Humanist, Agnostic, Atheist. They may get bad press and raise the hackles of the Religious Right, but they are words rich in thought and filled with meaning.

In my home state of Wisconsin, we have a wonderful history of freethought. It has been written out of the history books, but at the turn of the century in Wisconsin, there were 30 freethought congregations around the state. These were groups of people, primarily German immigrants, who rejected conventional religion and its deities. Their German name was "Freie Gemeinde," which literally translates as free community or free congregation.

Most of these congregations had freethought halls where they met, and they ranged from the modest to the imposing. One of them, the century-old Freethought Hall in Sauk City, Wisconsin still stands. It dominated the life of Sauk City for decades; it is the center of the social, intellectual and cultural life of this city on the Wisconsin River. It was the scene of many local theatricals as well as visiting professional productions and lectures. Even the public high school graduation exercises were held in it, since it offered the largest auditorium in town. Annual celebrations were a spring festival and a celebration in honor of Thomas Paine on his birthday. The Frei Gemeinde of Sauk City and their Freethought Hall enjoyed prestige and acceptance. There was no social stigma about being a freethinker – just the opposite was true.

Make no mistake about that. These congregations did not establish churches; they established freethought halls. These German immigrants were strongly anti-clerical. In many instances they had been forced to leave Germany where, in the words of one descendant still connected to the present-day Sauk City Freethought Hall, "They had to ask permission even to publish a pamphlet."

The Sauk City Freethought Hall, built in 1884, is still in remarkably good condition and stands in a whole city block with pretty trees. The auditorium or lecture room is the same today as it was 100 years ago, with beautiful birch flooring and the original benches lining the walls. It is used sparingly these days, but an occasional wedding or memorial service is held there. After all, where are freethinkers to go for these ceremonies? If you want to be free from the supernatural aura of a church, what's left to choose for a wedding is the bleakness of a judge's chambers. A church setting is anathema for those who believe in freethought.

Now why should a church setting be repugnant to a freethinker? Why are there people like me who have vowed never to participate in or attend a religious service of any kind? It is because we know what great harm religion has done and continues to do – not just long ago in the Dark Ages, or today in countries like Ireland or Iran, but ongoing harm, all the time, right now in this country. We do not want to support the institution responsible for that harm, however token that support might appear to be.

Every woman in the world would have a special reason never to support a religion – Christian, Jewish, Muslim, Hindu, Buddhist, Shinto, whatever – because almost every religion throughout history has been a patriarchal institution that devotes a great deal of its time and treasure to keeping women in their place.

Even those few Christian denominations that recognize women's rights to some extent still promote the Bible, that textbook of sexism, racism, meanness, murder and mayhem. And how does anyone trust or respect a religion that is based on that book? What good are so-called protestations or disclaimers of "But our church is different, our church is liberal" when that manual of misogyny is the basis of all Christian and Jewish belief?

Let me quote just one Bible verse. If every other verse in the Bible were pure and pleasant, I would still be speaking out against the Bible because of this verse. It is a verse that historically may be the most influential verse in all the Bible, because it was employed as the direct justification for the murder and torture of countless women. That verse, Exodus 22:18, is: *"Thou shalt not suffer a witch to live."* That single verse, that single sentence with its divine sanction of belief in witches and its divine sanction of their death, gave Christians justification for the murder of thousands, some say millions, of women. This commandment was acted on by church and state, by clergy and king. It was the god-given rationale for the unspeakable torture and murder of women.

Although it has been almost three centuries since the last so-called witch was put to death by Christians, that verse is still there in Exodus, *unchanged.* When clergy, Sunday school teachers and the media tell everyone that Bible is a good book, they never say: "Watch out for verses like Exodus 22:18. That's not so good." Or, "Don't do *everything* that God tells you to do." Or, "Careful, kids, the Bible is not a dependable behavior guide." You will never hear admonishments such as these from the pulpit or read them in your daily paper or hear it on the radio. Only freethinkers are saying these things.

Perhaps the Bible could be forgiven if it had only one terrible god-given verse. But it overflows with them. In fact, in the words of Ruth Hurmence Green, looking for something good in the Bible is like wading through a sewer to find a gem. "They told me the Bible was a book about love," she wrote, "but I studied every page of that Bible, and I couldn't find enough love to fill a salt shaker."

Some critics of freethought will say, "But no one really believes in all of that Bible stuff any more." But the fact is that people do believe in the inerrancy of the Bible. The poll taker Gallup tells us that 38 percent of the people in this country say that they believe that everything in the Bible, *everything,* is literally true, word for word. I would remind you that includes rising from the dead, walking on water, rivers parting, talking snakes, voices from burning bushes, magic wands and rods, demons, giants, angels, devils, ghosts, disembodied voices, unclean spirits and curing blindness with spit, to name just a few of the Bible's wonders.

Now Gallup tells us that another 43 percent of the U.S. population say that the Bible is the word of a god, although everything in it may not be literally true. This 43 percent probably do not believe in disembodied voices and curing blindness with spit, but they still pay homage and respect to a book filled with myth and superstition, absurdities and gross teachings.

So today it is a fact that a substantial number of citizens in this country are Bible literalists; they are fundamentalists. And we are told, again by pollsters, that fundamentalism is that part of the religious community that is on the increase. What that says to me is that there is an urgent need for education about what exactly is in the Bible. Aside from the fundamentalists, I think it is fair to say that we are a nation of Bible illiterates. The fundamentalists have read the Bible and to their discredit are still promoting it. They are the ones to watch.

Let us go back to the Bible; let us check some of the things it says – some of the commandments to do this and not to do that. If you were to follow the god of the Bible's teachings, here are some, just a very few, of the things you would do, the actions you would take:

- You would kill a woman who was not a virgin when she married, even if she happened to be your own daughter. You would kill her in a terrible way, by stoning her to death. You are instructed to do this in Deuteronomy 22:21. It is part of the Mosaic Law, just as the Ten Commandments are part of it. And this commandment still is being carried out in parts of the Near East today.

- If your child hits you or swears at you, you are to put that child to death. (Leviticus 20:9)

- If you attend church and know of a child born out of wedlock who attends your church, you would see that the child was publicly exposed and could no longer be a member of the church. You would find the commandment for that in Deuteronomy, Chapter 23:2. "A bastard shall not enter the congregation of the Lord even unto the tenth generation."

- You would advocate death for homosexuals. It's very, very clear in the Bible. "If a man also lie with mankind as he lieth with a woman, both of them have committed an abomination; they shall surely be put to death; their blood shall be upon them" (Leviticus 20:13). There is further rationale for killing homosexuals in the New Testament where Paul tells us in Romans, Chapter 1:27,32, that homosexuals are "worthy of death."

- Do you have a stubborn or rebellious son? Hearken to Deuteronomy; "If a man have a stubborn and rebellious son which will not obey the voice of his father, or the voice of his mother, and that, when they have chastened him, will not hearken unto them: then shall his father and his mother lay hold of him . . . and all the men of his city shall stone him with stones that he die." (21:18-21)

- You would support slavery. It is entirely possible that the Civil War with all its devastation and death might have been avoided had the Bible not taught that slavery was god-ordained. If you research slavery and Christianity and read the sermons that were given in the 1850's, both North and South, you will find that a majority are most erudite, well-written and eloquent in their *defense* of slavery.

God and the Bible enter all the arguments, all the sermons, all the editorials of the time in support of slavery. The Bible tells us how to buy and sell people, and that slaves are to obey their masters. Abolitionist Theodore Parker once said that if "the whole American church had dropped through the continent and disappeared altogether, the anti-slavery cause would have been further on . . ."

According to Genesis 9, the biblical deity first ordained slavery because of the behavior of Noah's son Ham who committed the apparently unpardonable sin of observing his drunken father's nakedness. God punished Ham, with typical biblical justice, by condemning Ham's son Canaan to be "a servant of servants." In some complex rules for slavery in Exodus, a father is allowed to sell his children, and a slave is referred to as his owner's "money." No wonder the slaveholders brandished their Bibles. In Timothy (6:1), Paul tells slaves to honor their owners: "Let as many servants as are under the yoke count their own masters worthy of all honor, that the name of God and his doctrine be not blasphemed."

In Ephesians (6:5) servants are to be obedient "with fear and trembling." Titus (2:9) says they must please their owners "in all things." Peter (2:18) orders "Servants, be subject to your masters in all fear." In the Epistle of Paul to Philemon, Paul sends the slave Onesimus back to a servitude from which he had fled. As for Jesus, he left the laws of slavery exactly as he found them, and his terrible parables (as author Ruth Green calls them) are filled with references to slaves and masters, none of which denigrates slavery in any way. Blacks who say they "love" the Bible truly revere the chains that used to bind them.

• Has your hand ever offended you? Has your eye offended you? If you apply the teachings of the New Testament you would chop off that hand and gouge out that eye. A few people still do this in the United States today. Some deluded person "gets religion," which means being overcome with guilt and fear, studies the Bible and then cuts off a hand or foot or gouges out an eye, following the teachings of Jesus in Matthew.

• Following the teachings of both the Old and New Testaments, you must believe in and practice sexism. The gods of the Bible are sexist gods. In the United States today the Equal Rights Amendment would be the law of the land were it not for the Bible believers. They made the difference in keeping those last states from ratification. "Let the women learn in silence with all subjection. But I suffer not a woman to teach, nor to usurp authority over the man, but to be in silence. For Adam was first formed, then Eve. And Adam was not deceived, but the woman being deceived was in the transgression." (Timothy 2:11-14)

Elizabeth Cady Stanton, who worked all of her adult life for women's right to vote, said most succinctly: "the Bible teaches that woman brought sin and death into the world, that she precipitated the fall of the race, that she was arraigned before the judgment seat of Heaven, tried, condemned and sentenced. Marriage for her was to be a condition of bondage, maternity a period of suffering and anguish, and in silence and subjection she was to play the role of a dependent on man's bounty for all her material wants, and for all the information she might desire . . . Here is the Bible's position of woman briefly summed up."

The common assumption that the Bible is a book filled with beauty and wisdom dies hard. But open your Bible at random. Your eye may light on something respectable or some dull, obtuse passage, but it is just as apt to encounter a verse like this, straight from "the Lord:" "Take all the heads of the people and hang them up before the Lord against the sun." (Numbers 25:8) Or, "And this is the thing that ye shall do, ye shall utterly destroy every male, and every woman that hath lain by man." (Judges, 5:30) Or, "Behold, I will corrupt your seed, and spread dung upon your faces." (Malachi 2:3) and here is Jesus: "Think not that I am come to send peace on earth. I come not to send peace but a sword. For I am come to set a man at variance against his father, and the daughter against her mother, and a man's foes shall be they of his own household."

Some Bible apologists will say, "But try Psalms. That's beautiful."

Do try Psalms. On the very first page you will find this:

Ask of me
And I shall give thee the heathen
For thine inheritance
And the uttermost parts of the earth
For thy possession.
Thou shalt break them with a rod of iron;
Thou shalt dash them in pieces like a potter's vessel.

Think about that. In one portion of one psalm the Bible and its god are mandating slavery, imperialism, the occupation of others' lands and mass murder and mayhem!

There is a one-liner that is a Psalm they never teach in Sunday school for obvious reasons: "Happy shall be he who taketh and dasheth thy little ones against the stones" (Psalms 137:9). If teachings such as these are good, what possibly could be represented as bad?

Other apologists, loath to let go their "good book," will point to the Song of Solomon. "This is beautiful, they say, such wonderful imagery. In the first place, the Song of Solomon is about four pages in length. Could those four pages, even if they were pure, make up for the grossness of the rest of the book? And the Song of Solomon is not pure; it is sexist. And what of its verses:

"My beloved put in his hand by the hole of the door and my bowels were moved for him (6:4), and "We have a little sister, and she hath no breasts: what shall we do for our sister in the day when she shall be spoken for?" Poor little sister – biblically doomed because she has a flat chest.

Reflect on the past and religion's role in it. Reflect on what religion has wrought, from the bloody Crusades to spread Christianity by the sword, the Dark Ages when religion ruled the world, the Inquisition with all its horrors, the persecution of women under the Bible's mandate about witches, religion's support of slavery, and the war after war after war based on religious differences, with "God" somehow on both sides.

Reflect on what religion has wrought in modern times. Religious wars still rage, in Ireland, in the Near East, in Yugoslavia. Not so long ago, Reverend Jim Jones, ordained minister in a mainstream church, who started his religious career with phony cancer cures, finally took 900 people to their deaths. Reflect on this needless tragedy, had only his church somewhere along the line held him accountable. Reflect on religion's indifference today where women struggle for equality, and where churches use their strength and power to keep women oppressed. Religion is the heavy; it is the reason a woman's right to control her own reproductive life constantly is in jeopardy.

Robert Green Ingersoll, the agnostic orator of the last century whose views on such topics as racism, sexism, peace and equality would do credit to speakers today, once summed up authority and religion. "There is no authority in churches or priests," he said, "no authority in number of majorities. The only authority is Nature, the facts we know . . . I stand by the religion of reason."

Anne Nicol Gaylor is a founder and president since 1978 of the Freedom From Religion Foundation, whose headquarters are in Madison, Wisconsin. She has been a long-time activist for women's rights.

For who is to tell you the truth? . . . No one. You must search it out yourself! The Department of War will not tell you. Certainly the Church isn't going to tell you the truth . . . Search in all the obscure places . . . not the established high towers and cathedrals for the answers.

— William Allen White, Editor, *Emporia Gazette*

The Day America Told The Truth

Americans are making up their own rules and laws

Only 13 percent believe in all of the Ten Commandments. We choose which laws of God we believe. There is absolutely no moral consensus in this country — as there was in the 1950s and 1960s. There is very little respect for the law or for any law.

Ninety percent of all Americans believe in God. It is "Who" that God is that contains the surprises.

An afterlife in hell is not something very many Americans honestly fear. Most Americans (82 percent) profess to believe in an afterlife that includes both heaven and hell (55 percent of us believe in the existence of Satan).

We are confident, however, that our future prospects are bright. Almost half of us (46 percent) expect to spend eternity in heaven vs. only 4 percent who see their future in hell. In this respect, we have not lost the optimism for which we are famous.

The United States is far and away the most violent industrialized nation on the earth.

James Patterson and Peter Kim, authors of The Day America Told The Truth, *Penguin Books USA Inc., New York, NY, 1991*

Gallup Poll Update

It's been reported that over 85% of church goers get their understanding of god from their church (less than 40% attend on a regular basis), minister and the Bible; although less than 24% of all church goers have read the Bible completely. Ten percent said they had a "personal experience" – the remainder said they didn't know.

One of the obvious conclusions is that the followers have known only what others have told them, or what others want them to know. Are you one of these?

When you were young, did you question all the answers?

— Crosby, Stills, Nash & Young

I believe in the fireside. I believe in the democracy of home. I believe in the republicanism of the family. I believe in liberty, equality and love.

— Robert G. Ingersoll
1833 – 1899

Wisdom From Ingersoll

- A believer is a bird in a cage. A freethinker is an eagle parting the clouds with tireless wing.

- I want no heaven for which I must give my reason; no happiness in exchange for my liberty; and no immortality that demands the surrender of my individuality.

- Banish me from Eden when you will; but first let me eat of the fruit of the tree of knowledge.

- The man who invented the telescope found out more about heaven than the closed eyes of prayer ever discovered.

- Fear paints pictures of ghosts and hangs them in the gallery of ignorance.

- Superstition is, always has been, and forever will be, the foe of progress, the enemy of education and the assassin of freedom.

- Liberty is my religion.

- No one pretends that Shakespeare was inspired, and yet all the writers of the books of the Old Testament put together could not have produced Hamlet.

- Religion can never reform mankind because religion is slavery.

- Theology is not what we know about God, but what we do not know about Nature.

- If a man would follow, today, the teachings of the Old Testament, he would be a criminal. If he would strictly follow the teachings of the New, he would be insane.

- When I speak of God, I mean that god who prevented man from putting forth his hand and taking also the fruit of the tree of life that he might live forever; of that god who multiplied the agonies of women, increased the weary toil of man, and in his anger drowned a world — of that god whose altars reeked with human blood, who butchered babes, violated maidens, enslaved men and filled the earth with cruelty and crime; of that god who made heaven for the few, hell for the many, and who will gloat forever and ever upon the writhings of the lost and damned.

Our appreciation to Steven Kropko from Atheists United, P.O. Box 5329, Sherman Oaks, CA 91413 for these quotations.

BANNED BOOK WEEK
1992

CENSORSHIP:
OLD SINS IN
NEW WORLDS

Truth Seeker In The Trenches

Gay Talese

An American nation that had audaciously rebelled against the mother country over economic and political issues remained none-theless subservient to English laws on sex, and no man was more successful at reinforcing America's puritanical roots than Anthony Comstock, who referred to himself as a "weeder in God's garden."

There was relatively little protest against Comstock's tactics during the 1870's in the major newspapers, most of whose publishers felt, as did the politicians, that opposing Comstock might be inter-preted as tolerating crime, as well as perhaps subjecting their own private lives to Comstock's scrutiny.

A few smaller publications, however, representing the under-ground press of that time, were vehement in their coverage of Comstock, particularly one paper with offices on lower Broadway called *The Truth Seeker*. This weekly was owned and edited by an unremitting skeptic and Bible-debunking agnostic named D. M. Bennett, whose inspiration was Thomas Paine and whose editorial policy favored birth control, the taxation of church property, and a respect for freedoms Comstock would deny.

In his writings, D. M. Bennett compared Comstock to Torque-mada, the inquisitor general of fifteenth-century Spain, and to seven-teenth-century witch finder Matthew Hopkins. "Hopkins," wrote Bennett, "was clothed with a species of legal authority to prowl over several of the shires of England, seizing his victims wherever he could find them, and Comstock had been clothed with a similar sort of legal authority to prowl over some of these American states, hunting down his unfortunate victims in the same kind of way."

Since sexual obscenity was now a federal offense in America – punishable by fines as high as $5,000 and imprisonment as lengthy as ten years – Bennett insisted that it should be so clearly defined by the government that every citizen would understand its meaning as well as citizens understood the meaning of such crimes as murder, homicide, rape, arson, burglary, and forgery. But regrettably the

crime of obscenity was imprecisely defined, and was therefore interpreted variously by different citizens, judges, juries, lawyers, and
prosecutors, thus remaining on the lawbooks to be exploited by
powerful people whenever they felt the need, for whatever reason,
to create criminals.

If the circulation of sexual material was to be excluded from the
mail primarily for the moral protection of the young, as Comstock
claimed, then Bennett suggested that all mail being sent to homes
and schools be inspected by parents, teachers, or guardians, and not
by government censors and religious fanatics. Bennett believed, as
did many prominent skeptics of his time, that organized religion was
oppressive, anti-intellectual, and contrived to control and deceive
people with its promises of posthumous paradise for those who
obeyed its doctrines, and threats of eternal hell for those who did
not; and its liturgy, based on myth, went unchallenged by the
government as it mollified great masses of people who might otherwise be rebelling in the streets against the injustices of life on earth.

Bennett saw the major churches and the government as partners
in the perpetuation of a compliant public, and they thus maintained
their privileged status. The churches, which were exempt from
taxation and therefore amassed enormous wealth and property,
refrained from condemning the sometimes barbarous acts of a
government at war; and the government often provided policemen
to support the church's invasion of people's privacy.

Religion's presumption that it had the right to regulate what
people did with their own bodies in bed, that it could pass judgment
on the manner and purpose of sex, could control how sex was
portrayed in words and pictures, could prevent through censorship
the sinful specter in a parishioner's mind of an impure thought
thereby justifying thought control – incensed the agnostic passions
of D. M. Bennett, who regarded it as a violation of antitheological
basis upon which the founding fathers had established the American
Constitution.

Being endlessly vituperative on this subject, and having the
temerity to express it in print, made inevitable Bennett's confronta-
tion with the law, which did occur on a wintry day in 1877 when
Anthony Comstock himself, accompanied by a deputy United States
marshal, appeared at Bennett's office with a warrant for his arrest.
Comstock, stern and solemn, charged Bennett with having sent
through the mail two indecent and blasphemous articles, both

having appeared in The Truth Seeker. One article was called "How Do Marsupials Propagate Their Kind," the second was "An Open Letter to Jesus Christ."

As Comstock stood before him, Bennett quickly defended his right to publish the articles, adding that neither was indecent nor blasphemous. The piece about marsupials, written by a contributor to the newspaper, was a scientific article that answered precisely and discreetly what the title asked. The letter to Christ, which Bennett had composed, did question the veracity of Mary's virginity, but Bennett believed that he was legally entitled to ponder this miracle.

If Comstock was looking for obscenity, Bennett said, there was much of it in the Bible, and he suggested the tale of Abraham and his concubine, the rape of Tamar, the adultery of Absalom, the lustful exploits of Solomon. Comstock, impatient, told Bennett to get his coat. Comstock wanted no more of this irreverence, and so Bennett did as ordered, and was taken as a prisoner to the office of the United States commissioner in the Post Office building, on Broadway and Park Row. There his bail was set at $1,500 and a pretrial hearing was scheduled for the following week. Comstock hoped to make Bennett the first victim of the federal law against defiling the mail.

After obtaining bail, Bennett immediately began to campaign for his defense, and he published new attacks on Comstock and the law. Many people were inspired to support Bennett, including his distinguished friend and fellow agnostic, the lawyer Robert G. Ingersoll. Ingersoll, who like Bennett had been reared in Illinois, had served valorously as a colonel in the Union cavalry, being greatly motivated not by the war itself, but by his opposition to slavery. His parents had both been outspoken abolitionists more than twenty years before the war, causing his father, a Presbyterian minister, to shift from one congregation to another, spending more time in debate with churchgoers than in communal worship, a situation that contributed to younger Ingersoll's early skepticism of Christian virtue.

After the war, Robert Ingersoll practiced law and frequently defended the radical causes of his day, and his abhorrence of censorship made him a natural enemy of Comstock. If the government intended to support Comstock by censoring such articles as had appeared in The Truth Seeker, then Ingersoll was anxious to defend Bennett's cause up to the Supreme Court, and he so informed the Postmaster General in Washington.

The evidence against Bennett, being neither lewd nor lascivious, and no doubt protected by the First Amendment, was not a case that Comstock was likely to win at the highest level of the law; and it was perhaps a belated recognition of this, following Ingersoll's intercession, that prompted the Postmaster General to quietly drop the case against Bennett.

Most citizens in this situation, having just thwarted the government and the formidable Comstock, and perhaps anticipating the censor's wish for revenge, might have thereafter pursued life more prudently; but not D. M. Bennett. He celebrated the occasion in his newspaper by accelerating his criticism of Comstock, urging the repeal of postal censorship, and calling for the legalization of contraceptive instruction and devices. He also wrote and published a lengthy diatribe on Christianity, describing its history as a holy massacre, bloody conquests in the name of Christ, while its popes indulged in acts of debauchery, incest, and murder.

Bennett portrayed the apostle Paul as an impious proselyte, a hypocrite, and a woman hater who initiated the antifeminist tradition in the Roman Church.

Bennett described Paul II as a "vile, vain, cruel, and licentious pontiff, whose chief delight consisted in torturing heretics with heated braziers and infernal instruments of torment." Bennett saw the Jesuits as henchmen of secret horrors, and called Martin Luther a man of "insane violence" and John Calvin a "calculating, cruel bigot." Pius IV "filled the papal palace with courtesans and beautiful boys for the purpose of satisfying his sensual passions and assuaging his lubricity"; Pius VI "was guilty of sodomy, adultery, incest and murder"; and Sixtus V "celebrated his coronation by hanging sixty heretics." After similarly describing dozens of other popes, saints, reformers, evangelists, and Puritans, Bennett concluded that Anthony Comstock "has proven himself equal to almost any of his Christian predecessors in the work of arresting, persecuting, prosecuting, and ruining his fellow beings."

Bennett published this in 1878. In that year he was again arrested by Comstock, but the religious critique was not mentioned in the warrant, for even a work as vitriolic as that might be considered defensible under the free speech amendment. Comstock had something better, a strictly sexual pamphlet called Cupid's Yokes that advocated free love, denigrated marriage, favorably described people living in an erotic commune devoid of restrictions, and boldly asked: "Why should priests and magistrates supervise the sexual organs of citizens any more than the brain and stomach?"

While Bennett had neither written nor published this pamphlet – it was the work of an already imprisoned Massachusetts freethinker named E. H. Heywood – Bennett had reportedly been selling it, in addition to other controversial literature, at a convention near Ithaca, New York; and Comstock was confident that responsible people would be less eager to openly support Bennett now than they had been after his first arrest.

But there was rising public sentiment against Comstock at this time, it being the fifth year of his antivice crusade, and Bennett was again able to arouse through his newspaper considerable support and financial aid for his defense. The case did go to trial, however, and a severe judge – introducing to American jurisprudence the illiberal English law of 1836 that declared an entire literary work obscene if any part of it was obscene and was inappropriate for youthful readers – achieved a guilty verdict against Bennett for selling the pamphlet. The judge then sentenced Bennett to thirteen months of hard labor at the penitentiary in Albany.

Thousands of citizens soon petitioned President Rutherford B. Hayes to pardon Bennett, and there was talk of appealing to the Supreme Court; but these efforts were diminished when Comstock, who had somehow obtained love letters written by the sixty-year-old Bennett to a young woman, publicly condemned Bennett as a lecherous adulterer. Bennett's admission from prison that he had written the letters did not help his cause with some people, including Mrs. Bennett and the wife of President Hayes; and it was reportedly Mrs. Hayes who urged her husband to ignore the Bennett petition.

Bennett served the full term at hard labor and was greatly debilitated by the experience. After his release he traveled in Europe, leaving the editorship of his paper to an associate who had run it during his imprisonment. In 1881 Bennett published a book called *An Infidel Abroad*, a collection of his own typically irreverent articles and comments that had established him in the free-thought movement of nineteenth century America.

D.M. Bennett died in 1882, a year after publishing *An Infidel Abroad*.

Gay Talese is the author of Thy Neighbor's Wife, *Dell Publishing Co., 1980. This is an extract from his book.*

Freethought on Trial

The Spanish Inquisition, first imposed in Spain in 1478 and extended by Holy Roman Emperor Charles V to the Netherlands in 1521, promoted the questions and burning of "heretics" under government auspices.

Freethinker On Trial

On April 13, 1992, a court case in Los Angeles could have set a precedent that would have drastically affected the lives of all freethinkers.

The trial was based on charges that my book, *Don't Call Me Brother*, was " . . . a vitriolic attack upon organized Christianity." The four-million-dollar-plus lawsuit filed in Superior Court also screamed 'libel' and 'slander'. After a lengthy and costly process, the court ruled that my book was not defamatory.

At the same time, Mr. & Mrs. Kenneth Hahn, a couple in their 70's, questioned their Assemblies of God Church in upstate New York regarding the conduct of its pastor. They were ordered to leave the meeting. Three days later they were arrested at their home by sheriffs, taken to jail, fingerprinted, subjected to mug shots and locked up. Kenneth Hahn suffered a stroke during the ordeal. This was the ultimate of church harassment.

Legal actions such as these now go on *daily*. A growing number of "Christian Coalition" legal groups, the most notable being The Rutherford Institute headed by John Whitehead and "Christian Advocates Serving Evangelism" headed by Jay Sekulow, have sprung up throughout the U.S. These well-funded pressure groups keep court calendars clogged.

A point is to be made in these cases. Anyone who dares to question or criticize the church, or those who object to Christian interference in their lives, will be punished severely. However these cases come out, the victims suffer severe financial loss, possible ruin and emotional assault. The church with unlimited tax-exempt wealth gloats over this fact. They have the funds to keep their dissenters tied up in court forever, and real justice is the loser.

Gospel gladiators accompanied by their lawyers are now marching through the lives of everyone. This is the new look of Christianity. Yet I do not recall reading where Jesus took a team of lawyers with him to enforce the *Sermon on the Mount*. On the contrary, he stated: "Woe unto you, lawyers!" (Luke 11:52). Here is another proof that today's Christianity is phoney. These misfits cannot be true followers of Jesus when their conduct is the antithesis of his teachings.

Perhaps the freethinkers who actually read the Bible should teach the Christians what Christianity is all about.

Austin Miles is an minster, author of many articles, and books. He is the Author of Don't Call Me Brother *and* Setting The Captives Free, *Prometheus Books, Buffalo, New York.lers*

In 1428, forty-four years after his death, John Wycliffe's bones were dug up and burned. His ashes were thrown into the River Swift in an attempt by the medieval church to stamp out his "unsavory" memory.

Life As A Freethinker

Dear Readers: We sent the following questions to Mr. Richard Bozarth and these are his replies:

How do you define Freethought?

Freethought is the repudiation of all coercion of authority or tradition in philosophy, theology, and ideology. It is the commitment to the theory that the power of cultural institutions can be morally exercised only when that power is limited by guaranteed and protected civil liberties possessed equally by all citizens.

I know this definition does not have much resemblance to the definition found in dictionaries. However, like any other authority, a dictionary is right only when it is right. I also know that other Freethinkers apparently accept the definition as right (for example, The Secular Humanist Press, published by the Humanists of Washington, routinely defines a Freethinker as "a person who rejects authority and dogma, forming opinions about religion on the basis of reason and rational inquiry independently of tradition, authority, or established belief").

If the dictionary definition is right, then Freethought is no more than an unruly genre of theology and its existence is dependent on the existence of religionism because religionism is the subject addressed by Freethought. I repudiate that, because Freethought is not about religionism. It did not begin as a genre of theology and it does not continue today as a genre of theology. If some day every single human being on Earth is a Natural Atheist and religionism has become an historical artifact like the Roman Empire, I say that Freethought will not lose any of its cultural relevance and necessity.

Freethought is not about religionism. The two subjects of Freethought are *intellectual liberation* and *civil liberties*. The theory of Freethought addresses the means for pursuing intellectual excellence and the means for establishing and maintaining a moral culture. Freethought does not ignore religionism. When it deals with religionism, it is analyzing how religionism influences the pursuit of intellectual excellence and how religionism in the form of cultural institutions influences the morality of a culture.

A person also cannot say that Freethought is dominated by thinking about religionism, which could be an interpretation of the dictionary definition, assuming some person would want to try to save this definition. Freethought is dominated by thinking about civil liberties, among which separation of state and church shares equal importance, and this means that government is the cultural institution that receives the overwhelming majority of attention in Freethought thinking. Religionism in the form of cultural institutions receives most of the attention Freethought gives to it in the context of determining what relationship between state and church will most likely produce a moral culture.

The origin of the dictionary definition is understandable. When Freethought emerged as a cultural force after the revival of secular civilization during the Renaissance, religionism and the government were essentially identical. Western culture was theocratic. The church either ruled countries directly or formed theocratic partnerships with secular governments. Then the first problem for Freethought was separating state and church, and the solution was to discredit the moral authority and dogmatic truth religionism has always claimed for itself. Freethinkers in the beginning had no choice about having religionism dominate their thinking.

All Freethinkers know that there is still work to be done, because *We The People* do not study history and because the church has never ceased striving to be reunited with the state. Today, the primary problem facing Freethought is how to establish and maintain a moral government – that is, one which guarantees and protects civil liberties for all the citizens it serves. To achieve a moral government would be to eliminate the threat of state and church becoming reunited, because civil liberties are impossible in a theocracy or a theocratic partnership between state and church.

How do you as a Freethinker determine your morals?

To determine if some behavior is moral, I ask three questions about it: Is this behavior harmful to me? Is it harmful to my co-citizens? Is it harmful to my culture?

The possible answers are three: "Yes," "No," and "Maybe, Depending On The Circumstances." "Yes" and "No" are easy to deal with. "Maybe, Depending On The Circumstances" is what makes life interesting.

Does Freethought affect your sense of purpose?

To be an organized Freethinker is to be part of the Freethought Movement, which has the purpose of creating a moral culture that guarantees and protects the civil liberties of all the citizens within it. This does give me a sense of purpose, but it does not outweigh other elements of my life that provide me a sense of purpose, such as my writing and my marriage.

How does Freethought affect your close relationships?

My close relationships have become restricted to Freethinkers, and this applies to my family as well. I cannot feel close to non-Freethinkers even if genetically related to them. I can get along amiably with them if they are willing to be amiable with me, but closeness is out of the question.

Do you try to change others to your point of view?

Of course. What is important is that I allow others to change my point of view if they can produce convincing evidence that demonstrates I am wrong or at least less right than I had thought I was. This is the only effective means of pursuing intellectual excellence, which, after all, is one of activities that flourishes best under the influence of Freethought.

Do you consider common sense as a close ally?

Common sense, if used prudently, pragmatically, and in conjunction with doubt, is certainly useful. However, before anything is considered common sense, there should be convincing evidence that it is worthy of being common sense. So much of what is called common sense is actually unthinking and lazy submission to tradition.

Do you have favorite Freethought writers?

Friedrich Nietzsche, Joseph McCabe, Bertrand Russell, George Smith, and Barbara Dority.

How do you know you're right?

Actually, what I strive for are degrees of probable certainty. How high the degree of probable certainty I assign to any of my conclusions is based on the mass of convincing evidence supporting the conclusion. The greater the mass of supporting evidence, the higher the degree of probable certainty. Evidence is acquired by the pursuit of intellectual excellence – which in turn should improve the ability to correctly interpret the evidence.

I know I have attained a high degree of probable certainty (confidence) when those who disagree with me cannot produce evidence that makes me skeptical about my degree of probable certainty. Examples of extremely high levels of confidence are Natural Atheism and evolution.

Is there a specific incident in your life where being a Freethinker was a major benefit?

If I had not been a Freethinker, I would not have met my wife. If I had not been a Freethinker, I would not now have Barbara Dority and Jim Rybock as friends. If I had not been a Freethinker, I would not have written *The Means and End of Freethought, A Case Against Madalyn Murray O'Hair, Interrelated Essays on an Experience*, and *No Time to Wallow in the Mire*.

How does a Freethinker handle death and dying?

That would depend on the foundation the Freethinker's philosophy is erected upon. My philosophical foundation is Natural Atheism, which means death doesn't mean anything to me. I want to live as long as I am capable of enjoying the living.

The only aspect about dying that falls under Freethought concerns whether or not voluntarily dying belongs within the realm of civil liberties. As a Freethinker, I cannot accept that it is moral to force a person to live. Suicide should be the very last option a person considers, and taken only when it is absolutely certain that there is no hope a person can ever enjoy living again. Suicide should also be dignified and the means humane, especially for the terminally ill. I am certain that, if our culture can learn to accept suicide as being in the realm of civil liberties, it could finally get beyond the hypocrisy of the "sanctity of human life" and begin to understand the importance of the quality of human life and to find ways to enhance the enjoyment of living.

✷ ———————————————————————— ✷

Reprint from Vol. 119 #1 Truth Seeker *magazine, oldest Freethought publication, founded in 1873.*

I was born a heretic. I always distrust people who know so much about what God wants them to do to their fellows.

— Susan B. Anthony

Finding that no religion is based on facts and cannot therefore be true, I began to reflect what must be the condition of mankind trained from infancy to believe in error.

— Robert Owen

I believe in honesty and truthfulness, not because I fear a god or a devil, but because I think it is the best way for people to live together. I believe in helping others because when we cooperate with our neighbors we make life easier for all. I believe in treating others as I want to be treated – but I certainly do not believe in turning the other cheek and the truth is that I never knew any Christians who did either.

— James Hervey Johnson

Un Autre Monde

Painting of the night sky by Grandville, 1844.

What Is To Be The New Mythology?

Joseph Campbell

We live today – thank God! – in a secular state, governed by human beings (with all their inevitable faults) according to principles of law that are still developing and have originated not from Jerusalem, but from Rome.

The concept of the state is yielding rapidly at this hour to the concept of the ecumene, i.e., the whole inhabited earth; and if nothing else unites us, the ecological crisis will. There is no need any more for those locally binding, sociopolitically bounded, differing forms of religion which have held men separate in the past, giving to God the things that are Caesar's and to Caesar the things that are God's.

"God is an intelligible sphere whose center is everywhere and circumference nowhere." So we are told in a little twelfth-century book known as *The Book of The Twenty-four Philosophers*. Each of us – whoever and wherever he may be – is then the center, and within him, whether he knows it or not, is that Mind at Large, the laws of which are the laws not only of all minds but of all space as well. For we are the children of this beautiful planet that we have lately seen photographed from the moon.

We were not delivered into this planet by some god, but have come forth from it. We are its eyes and mind, its seeing and its thinking. And the earth, together with its sun, this light around which it flies like a moth, came forth, we are told, from a nebula; and that nebula, in turn, from space. So that we are the mind, ultimately, of space. No wonder, then, if its laws and ours are the same! Likewise, our depths are the depths of space, whence all those gods sprang that men's minds in the past projected onto animals and plants, onto hills and streams, the planets in their courses, and their own peculiar social observances.

Our mythology now is to be of infinite space and its light, which is without as well as within. Like moths, we are caught in the spell of its allure, flying to it outward, to the moon and beyond, and flying to it inward. On our planet itself all dividing horizons have been shattered. We can no longer hold our loves at home and project our aggressions elsewhere; for on this spaceship Earth there is no "elsewhere" any more. And no mythology that continues to speak or teach of "elsewheres" and "outsiders" meets the requirement of this hour.

And so to return to our opening question: What is to be the new mythology?

It is – and will forever be, as long as our human race exists – the old, everlasting, perennial mythology, in its "subjective sense," addressed to the waking of individuals in the knowledge of themselves, not simply as egos fighting for place on the surface of this beautiful planet, but equally as centers of Mind at Large – each in his own way at one with all, and with no horizons.

Joseph Campbell, – educator, author, and editor. Excerpt from Myths To Live By, *Viking Press, 1972.*

The ancient Italian solar deity regarded by the Romans as presiding over doors and gates and beginnings and endings.

– Janus –

Appendix

Off With His Head!
An edited view of Mt. Rushmore
National Monument, minus
non-Freethinker "Teddy"
Roosevelt.

Appendix A

Partial List Of Freethinkers

John Adams — US President, promoter and signer of the Declaration of Independence

Samuel Adams — Moving spirit in the Boston Tea Party, signer of the Declaration of Independence

Ethan Allen — Hero in the Revolutionary War; wrote *Reason the Only Oracle of Man*

Steve Allen — Author, humorist, and entertainer

Isaac Asimov — Leading science fiction author and Humanist, past honary president American Humanist Association.

Sir Alfred Jules Ayer — English philosopher, author of *Language, Truth and Logic*

Dan Barker — Former preacher, now with Freedom From Religion Foundation

Bela Bartok — Hungarian composer and collector of folk music

Clara Barton — Founder of the American Red Cross Society

Frank L. Baum — Writer, author of Oz books

Pierre Bayle — Most important skeptic of the 17th century

Alexander Graham Bell — Inventor of the telephone

D.M. Bennett — Founder in 1873 and first editor of *Truth Seeker*, a freethought magazine

Mary Bennett — Second editor of *Truth Seeker*, a freethought magazine, wife of D.M. Bennett

Samuel Beckett — Irish author

Sir Isaiah Berlin — Professor of philosophy, Oxford University

Jonathan Boag — TV journalist and political activist

Charles Bradlaugh — British Parliamentarian, freethought activist

Marlon Brando — Movie actor; specializes in morally intense roles

Giordano Bruno — Philosopher, monk, burned at the stake in 1600

Luther Burbank — Horticulturist and plant breeder

John Burroughs — Nature lover and naturalist; biographer and close friend of Walt Whitman

George Gordon Byron — English poet and dramatist

Helen Caldicott	Environmentalist, opposes nuclear weapons
John C. Calhoun	American statesman of the early 19th century; favored states' rights
Albert Camus	Essayist, novelist, short-story writer, playwright, journalist
Rachel Carson	Environmentalist, author of *The Silent Spring*
Wang Chong	Essayist, *Discourses Weighed in the Balance*
Chapman Cohen	Author, editor of *London Freethinker*
Francis Crick	Nobel Laureate in physiology or medicine
Norman Cousins	Editor, Saturday Review
Voltairine DeCleyre	Early 20th-Century woman freethinker
Ralph DeSola	Past editor of *Truth Seeker*, a freethought magazine
Clarence Darrow	Lawyer
Charles Robert Darwin	English naturalist, author of *Origin of Species*
Erasmus Darwin	English botanist and physician, grandfather of Charles
Charles Dickens	Novelist
Dorothea Dix	Pioneer in the treatment of mental illness
Edd Doerr	Exec. Dir. of Americans for Religious Liberty
Feodor Dostoevski	Russian novelist
Frederick Douglass	Abolitionist
Thomas Alva Edison	Inventor
Paul Edwards	Editor of *Encyclopedia of Philosophy*
Charles W. Eliot	President of Harvard for 40 years
Albert Ellis	Founder of Rational-Emotive Therapy
Ralph Waldo Emerson	American philosopher and author
Epicurus	Greek philosopher
Epictetus	Roman philosopher, slave
Desiderius Erasmus	Writer, scholar, anticlerical cleric
Edward Everett	Politician, minister, Harvard president
Antony Flew	British philosopher, atheist
Joseph Fletcher	Visiting Prof. of Medical Ethics at U. of VA
George William Foote	English freethinker, co-editor of *The Bible Handbook*
Benjamin Franklin	American writer, statesman, and inventor
Sigmund Freud	Austrian neurologist
Betty Friedan	Author of *Feminine Mystique*

Erich Fromm	Psychoanalyst and author of *The Sane Society*
Robert Frost	American poet
Yuri Gagarin	USSR astronaut reported "I don't see any God up here."
Matilda Joslyn Gage	Suffrage leader
Galileo Galilei	Astronomer, physicist, "Eppur Si Muove!"
Mohandas Gandhi	Nationalist leader, Hindu, organizer of non-violent resistance
Martin Gardner	Science journalist, skeptic
William Lloyd Garrison	Abolitionist
Siddhartha Gautama	Indian philosopher
Marshall Gauvin	Author of major freethought literature
Anne Nicol Gaylor	American freethinker, founder with daughter, Annie Laurie Gaylor, of Freedom From Religion Foundation
Annie Laurie Gaylor	Editor of *Freethought Today*, author, lecturer, and speaker for women's rights
William Godwin	English philosopher
Emma Goldman	Early 20th-Century radical feminist
Horace Greeley	Founder *New York Tribune*
Roger E. Greeley	Unitarian Minister, compiler of Robert G. Ingersoll
Armand Hammer	American industrialist, secular philanthropist, past president of Occidental Petroleum
Robert Heinlein	Science fiction author
Katharine Hepburn	Movie actress; emphasizes feminine independence both in real life and in her movie roles
Thomas Hobbes	English philosopher
George Jacob Holyoake	English social reformer
Oliver Wendell Holmes	American physician and author
Julia Ward Howe	Abolitionist and suffragist
Hsun-tzu	Naturalistic Confucian philosopher
Elbert Hubbard	Author, editor
David Hume	British philosopher and man of letters; author of *Dialogues Concerning Natural Religion*
Mark J. Hurley	Former member of the Secretariat for Non-Believers
Ian Hutton	Past editor of *Truth Seeker*, a freethought magazine
Aldous Huxley	English critic and novelist
Julian Huxley	Humanist; biologist; first director of UNESCO

Thomas Henry Huxley	English natural scientist and essayist
Robert Green Ingersoll	American orator, "The Great Agnostic"
William James	American psychologist, philosopher
Thomas Jefferson	U.S. President, lawyer, statesman, diplomat, philosopher
B.C. Johnson	Author of *The Atheist Debater's Handbook*
James Hervey Johnson	Past editor of Truth Seeker, a freethought magazine, and major benefactor to freethought
Carl Gustav Jung	Swiss psychologist
Immanuel Kant	German philosopher, considered by some to be one of the greatest of modern thinkers
Rudyard Kipling	English author
Lester Kirkendall	Sexologist, humanist
J. Krishnamurti	Spiritual teacher
Stanley Kubrick	Movie maker, famed for *2001: A Space Odyssey*
Paul Kurtz	Prof. Philosophy at State U. of NY; editor, publisher
Corliss Lamont	Formed National Emergency Civil Liberties Commission; leading figure of American Humanist Association
Bolder Landry	Author, anthropologist, founder of Thomas Paine Foundation
D. H. Lawrence	English writer
Norman Lear	Television producer, produced *All In The Family,* etc. Founder of *People For the American Way*
John Locke	English philosopher
Henry Wadsworth Longfellow	American poet
James Madison	U.S. President and youngest of the Founding Fathers; helped bring about ratification of the Constitution and passage of the Bill of Rights
Horace Mann	American educator
George Mason	Prime mover in getting the Bill of Rights adopted
Edgar Lee Masters	American poet
Henry Louis Mencken	American journalist, editor and author
James Michener	American author
John Stuart Mill	Utilitarian philosopher and moralist, economist
Henry Miller	American writer
Maria Mitchell	American astronomer

Friedrich Nietzsche	Philosophical pioneer; anti-Christian
Ernest Nagel	Naturalist, philosopher
Florence Nightingale	English nurse, philanthropist
Madalyn Murray O'Hair	Founder of American Atheist
Thomas Paine	Writer and political theorist. The mind behind the American Revolution and the Declaration of Independence
Indumati Parikh	President of Radical Humanist Association of India
Linus Pauling	Nobel Peace Prize winner, chemist
Pablo Picasso	Spanish painter, sculptor
Benjamin Pierce	Mathematician, astronomer
Sir Karl Popper	British philosopher
James W. Prescott	Neuropsychologist, authority on violence, past editor of *Truth Seeker*, a freethought magazine, founder and director of The Institute of Humanistic Science
Joseph Priestley	English clergyman, chemist, author of *History of Electricity*
Protagoras	Greek philosopher, teacher, and first grammarian – "man is the measure of all things"
George Pullman	Invented railroad sleeping car
Ayn Rand	American writer, Objectivist philosopher
A. Philip Randolph	African-American labor leader
Goparaju Rao Gora	Indian companion of unbelief and social reform
Allen Walker Read	Lexicographer
Ernest Renan	Philosopher, Bible scholar, expert in Semitic languages
Fernando De Rojas	Spanish dramatist
Jean Jacques Rousseau	French publisher and author
Bertrand Russell	English philosopher, mathematician, writer
Carl Sagan	Astronomer, scientist, writer, TV host
Andrei Sakharov	Soviet physicist, humanist, peace activist
Margaret Sanger	Leader in birth-control movement
George Santayana	Spanish-born American philosopher
Jean-Paul Sartre	French philosopher and writer
Arthur Schopenhauer	Philosopher
Theodore Schroeder	American libertarian crusader and publicist

Michael Servetus	Spanish physician and theologian, burned at the stake
William Shakespeare	English playwright and poet
George Bernard Shaw	English-Irish playwright
Percy Bysshe Shelley	English romantic poet, wrote *The Necessity of Atheism*, husband of Mary Wollstonecraft
Upton Sinclair	American writer
B.F. Skinner	Behaviorist, psychologist, signed 1973 Humanist Manifesto
Warren Allen Smith	Writer, author of *Who's Who in Hell*
Charles Lee Smith	A leading American atheist of the 20th century, past editor of *Truth Seeker,* a freethought magazine
George H. Smith	Author of *Atheism: The Case Against God*
Socrates	Athenian philosopher
Alexander Solzhenitsyn	Russian novelist
Herbert Spencer	Philosopher, psychologist, sociologist
Baruch Spinoza	Philosopher
Gordon Stein	Atheist writer, philosopher, and editor of *The Encyclopedia of Unbelief* and the *Rationalist*
Emily Jennings Stowe	Founded Canada's first woman suffrage society
David Friedrich Strauss	German skeptical writer and biblical scholar
Mark Twain	American author, humorist
Giulio Cesare Vanini	Italian martyr
Gore Vidal	American author, movie and TV personality
Catherine Vogel	Burned in 1539 for being a Unitarian
Francois-Marie Voltaire	French poet, playwright, novelist, historian, essayist
Johann Wolfgang Von Goethe	German poet,
Gottfried Wilhelm Von Leibniz	German philosopher
Alfred Russel Wallace	Naturalist, devoted life to scientific entomology
Edward Alexander Westermarck	Finnish anthropologist
Walt Whitman	American poet, true inheritor of Emersonian principles
Oscar Wilde	Writer
Mary Wollstonecraft	Wrote *A Vindication of the Rights of Woman*, friend of Thomas Paine

Appendix B

Freethought Terms

Compiled by William B. Lindley
from dictionaries and other sources

Agnostic: One who believes that the proposition "There is a God" is undecidable. Ingersoll, the Great Agnostic: "The clergy know that I know that they know that they do not know."

Atheist: 1. One who is without belief in a God or gods. 2. One who denies that God exists. This is the more common usage, and receives the Psalmist's slur: "The fool hath said in his heart,'There is no God.'"

Belief: 1. Conviction or acceptance that certain things are true or real. 2. Faith, especially religious faith. (But some religious people insist that faith is not belief!) One may believe that a certain proposition is true. One believes *in* something in at least two different senses: (1) believe that it exists ("I believe in elephants but not in fairies."); (2) believe that something is good, where existence is not in question ("I believe wholeheartedly in jogging.") To believe *on* is to have or experience a trust relationship with an alleged supernatural entity. "Believe on the Lord Jesus Christ, and thou shalt be saved . . ." – Acts 31:16. To believe with no clause or phrase following is mindless, but the term is sometimes used that way.

Blasphemy: Mockery of or obscene reference to an entity that is worshipped. Distinct from libel, as said entity has no standing in court. All blasphemy laws violate the constitutional provisions for free speech and religious liberty. Thomas Paine claimed that the Bible "is a book of lies, wickedness and blasphemy; for what can be greater blasphemy than to ascribe the wickedness of man to the orders of the Almighty?"

Deism: Belief in the existence of a deity or source of life on the evidence of reason and nature only, with rejection of supernatural revelation. Thomas Paine was a Deist.

Dogma: A religious belief or set of beliefs as formally defined by a church authority. Skeptics use the term in a derogatory sense to refer to opinions not grounded on evidence but held stubbornly.

Faith: 1. Unquestioning belief that does not require proof or evidence. 2. Unquestioning belief in God, religious tenets, etc. 3. complete trust, confidence, or reliance.

Freethought: Thought unrestrained by deference to authority, especially in matters of religion and government. Its two subjects are intellectual liberation and civil liberties.

Fundamentalism: A movement in American Protestantism which stresses the inerrancy of the Bible not only in matters of faith and morals but also as literal historical record and prophecy, e.g., creation, the virgin birth of Christ, his second coming, etc. The term came into use with the publication of a series called The Fundamentals: A Testimony to the Truth (1909-1913). The World Christian Fundamentals Association was organized in 1919. The narrow sense of the term is thus confined to a part of conservative Protestantism in the U.S., but it has also been used more recently to label similar movements in other religions and other countries, e.g., Muslims in Iran and some Arab countries.

Heresy: Opinion or doctrine at variance with the orthodox or accepted doctrine, especially of a church or religious system. An example is the attempt to block the movie *The Last Temptation of Christ*, which portrayed Jesus Christ as both fully divine and fully human, the orthodox Christian belief. Shock and outrage at the explicit portrayal of Jesus' humanness nudged some self-styled Christians into the Apollinarian heresy, condemned in 451 C.E.

Humanism: Used with a lower-case "h", it refers to the Renaissance movement toward a more human-centered culture and to the disciplines of the humanities that came as a consequence into the colleges and universities. Used with an upper-case "H", it refers to the 20th-century movement in the U.S. and Europe toward a non-theistic and human-centered alternative to religion, notably with the 1933 Humanist Manifesto. A Humanist is one whose concern for humanity is primary, overriding considerations of religious or metaphysical doctrine. The world-level organization for the Humanist movement is the International Humanist and Ethical Union.

Ignostic: One who has no concern about the supernatural or the existence of a Supreme Being. The term "indifferentist" is also used.

Infidel: 1. One who does not believe in a particular religion, especially the religion that predominates in one's own culture. 2. One who holds no religious belief. The term is often used when people of different cultures are in the same place at the same time.

Justify: To show to be just, right, or in accord with reason. The religious sense ("we are justified by faith") is not that we are shown to be already just, but that we *become* just. The term is used especially in ethical argument: for example, an ethical relativist might deny a need to justify his position. Analogous terms in questions of fact are *validate, confirm, prove.*

Know: To have a clear perception or understanding of; be sure of or well informed about. There are at least three senses: (1) to know *that,* to be sure of a proposition or fact; (2) to know *how,* to possess a skill – the knowledge here is kinesthetic or nonverbal; and (3) to be acquainted with, as to know a person or town. Religious people often use the term as synonymous with *believe,* but with an overwhelming *feeling* of certainty. G. E. Moore, a British analytical philosopher, used the term that way, e.g., "I *know* that I have a book in my hand," and was criticized by Wittgenstein for this.

Minimifidian: Having the least possible faith. Person from Missouri. Criticized by Jesus in Matt. 6:30 and other verses.

Nontheist: One who is without belief in God. Equivalent to definition 1 of **atheist** (above), but used as a substitute by those who do not wish to wear the "atheist" label. Atheists (sense 2), agnostics and ignostics are all nontheists.

Rationalist: One who accepts reason as the only authority in determining one's opinions or course of action. Defined narrowly, and contrasted with empiricism, rationalism even omits sense evidence as a source of knowledge. Defined more broadly, rationalism uses logic and sense evidence together to make a coherent and testable model of the world, and is contrasted with religious faith or the acquisition of knowledge through unquestioning acceptance of authority.

Reason: The ability to think, form judgments, draw conclusions, etc. Reason is that human skill which makes sense of the world, and is thereby our means of surviving and prospering in the natural world. The term is often contrasted with *faith.*

Religion: 1. Belief in a supernatural entity that created and rules the universe; worship of and obedience to such an entity. 2. The binding together of a community in thought and action, or that thought and action of an individual which that person considers of supreme importance or "ultimate concern"; this latter sense need not involve the concept of the supernatural. Humanists quarrel over whether Humanism is a religion, because some insist on the first sense, while others insist on the second.

Secular: Pertaining to the world, or to things not religious, sacred, or spiritual: temporal, worldly. A Secular Humanist is thus a person of this world whose primary concern is humanity.

Skeptic: 1. One who doubts, questions, or suspends judgment upon matters generally accepted. 2. One who doubts religious doctrines. In the present freethought community, those who actively investigate claims of the paranormal are (admiringly) called skeptics. Universal skepticism is the claim that no genuine knowledge is possible. Adopting such a stance can lead one to despair and thence to blind faith.

Truth: That which is in accord with the facts of reality. Truth is the set of all true statements. The question "What is truth?", then, is properly shifted to the testing of specific claims of truth. Since there is no limit to the number of such claims, "The Truth" as an entity can never be possessed, but can only be asymptotically approached.

William B. Lindley is associate editor, Truth Seeker, *a Freethought magazine, founded in 1873.*

The true believer is an archenemy to three things, all for the same reason. He believes totally in what he totally believes in – thus he is an enemy of himself, of truth and all that cross his path.

— Eric Hoffer

Words are things, and a small drop of ink, falling like dew upon a thought, produces that which makes thousands, perhaps millions, think.

— Lord Byron

Appendix C

Illustrations And Photos

What do the following have in common?

Tooth Fairy

Adam & Eve

Easter Bunny

Archangel Gabriel

Santa Claus

Noah

Fairies

Gold Plates

Trolls

Jehovah

Ghosts

Evil Spirits

Devil

Thor

Sherlock Holmes

Job

Elves

Virgin Mary

Leprechauns

Virgin of
  Guadalupe

Krishna

Our Lady of Fatima

Count Dracula

The Black Madonna

Witches/Brujos

Warlocks

Fortune Tellers

Faith Healers

Demons

Flying Reindeer

Unicorns

Cherubs

Griffins

Mercury

Cain and Abel

Apollo

Jesus Christ

Tower of Babel

Isis

Big Foot

Loch Ness Monster

Flying Saucers

Flying Nuns

Zeus

Rudolph

Papal Infallibility

Robin Hood

Allah

Political Promises

Ark of the Covenant

Gold at End of
  Rainbow

Heaven

Three Wise Men

Purgatory

Hell

Utopia

Oz

Lost Dutchman
  Mine

Peter Pan

Ark

Tinker Bell

Two tablets with 10
  Commandments

Witch Doctors

Guardian Angel

Elvis Presley alive
  and living in L.A.

The Five Loaves

Pegasus

Dr. Frankenstein

Wicked Witch of
  the West

Holy Ghost

Hercules

The Good Thief

Paul Bunyon

Mermaids

Manna

E.T.

Angel of Death

Four Horsemen of
  the Apocalypse

Star of Bethlehem

Moses' Magic Rod

Sorcerer's Stone